NEGIMA!

29

Ken Akamatsu

TRANSLATED AND ADAPTED BY
Alethea Nibley and Athena Nibley

LETTERING AND RETOUCH BY
North Market Street Graphics

Negima! volume 29 is a work of fiction. Names, characters, places, and incidents are the products of the author's imagination or are used fictitiously. Any resemblance to actual events, locales, or persons, living or dead, is entirely coincidental.

A Kodansha Comics Trade Paperback Original.

Published in the United States by Kodansha Comics, an imprint of Kodansha USA Publishing, LLC., New York.

Publication rights for this English edition arranged through Kodansha Ltd., Tokyo.

First published in Japan in 2010 by Kodansha Ltd., Tokyo.

ISBN 978-1-935-42956-2

Printed in the United States of America.

www.kodanshacomics.com

9 8 7 6 5 4 3 2 1

Translator/Adapter: Alethea Nibley and Athena Nibley
Lettering: North Market Street Graphics

Honorifics Explained

Throughout the Kodansha Comics books, you will find Japanese honorifics left intact in the translations. For those not familiar with how the Japanese use honorifics and, more important, how they differ from American honorifics, we present this brief overview.

Politeness has always been a critical facet of Japanese culture. Ever since the feudal era, when Japan was a highly stratified society, use of honorifics—which can be defined as polite speech that indicates relationship or status—has played an essential role in the Japanese language. When addressing someone in Japanese, an honorific usually takes the form of a suffix attached to one's name (example: "Asuna-san"), is used as a title at the end of one's name, or appears in place of the name itself (example: "Negi-sensei," or simply "Sensei!").

Honorifics can be expressions of respect or endearment. In the context of manga and anime, honorifics give insight into the nature of the relationship between characters. Many English translations leave out these important honorifics and therefore distort the feel of the original Japanese. Because Japanese honorifics contain nuances that English honorifics lack, it is our policy at Kodansha Comics not to translate them. Here, instead, is a guide to some of the honorifics you may encounter in Kodansha Comics.

-san: This is the most common honorific and is equivalent to Mr., Miss, Ms., or Mrs. It is the all-purpose honorific and can be used in any situation where politeness is required.

-sama: This is one level higher than "-san" and is used to confer great respect.

-dono: This comes from the word "tono," which means "lord." It is an even higher level than "-sama" and confers utmost respect.

-kun: This suffix is used at the end of boys' names to express familiarity or endearment. It is also sometimes used by men

among friends, or when addressing someone younger or of a lower station.

chan: This is used to express endearment, mostly toward girls. It is also used for little boys, pets, and even among lovers. It gives a sense of childish cuteness.

Bōzu: This is an informal way to refer to a boy, similar to the English terms "kid" and "squirt."

Sempai/Senpai: This title suggests that the addressee is one's senior in a group or organization. It is most often used in a school setting, where underclassmen refer to their upperclassmen as "sempai." It can also be used in the workplace, such as when a newer employee addresses an employee who has seniority in the company.

Kohai: This is the opposite of "sempai" and is used toward underclassmen in school or newcomers in the workplace. It connotes that the addressee is of a lower station.

Sensei: Literally meaning "one who has come before," this title is used for teachers, doctors, or masters of any profession or art.

Anesan (or nesan): A generic term for a girl, usually older, that means "sister."

Ojōsama: A way of referring to the daughter or sister of someone with high political or social status.

-[blank]: This is usually forgotten in these lists, but it is perhaps the most significant difference between Japanese and English. The lack of honorific means that the speaker has permission to address the person in a very intimate way. Usually, only family, spouses, or very close friends have this kind of permission. Known as *yobisute*, it can be gratifying when someone who has earned the intimacy starts to call one by one's name without an honorific. But when that intimacy hasn't been earned, it can be very insulting.

A Word from the Author

Presenting *Negima!* volume 29! This volume finally gets back to the classmates. It has moé, serious battles, and a flashback to Nagi's day—it's stuffed to the gills with *Negima!*-ness.

The big mysteries of *Negima!* will be just about solved by the next volume, so don't miss it!

Thanks to all of you, there will be a long animated series starting in 2011! You've already come this far, so please stick with me until then. m(_ _)m

Ken Akamatsu's home page address
http://www.ailove.net/

NEGIMA!

MAGISTER NEGI MAGI

29

Ken Akamatsu

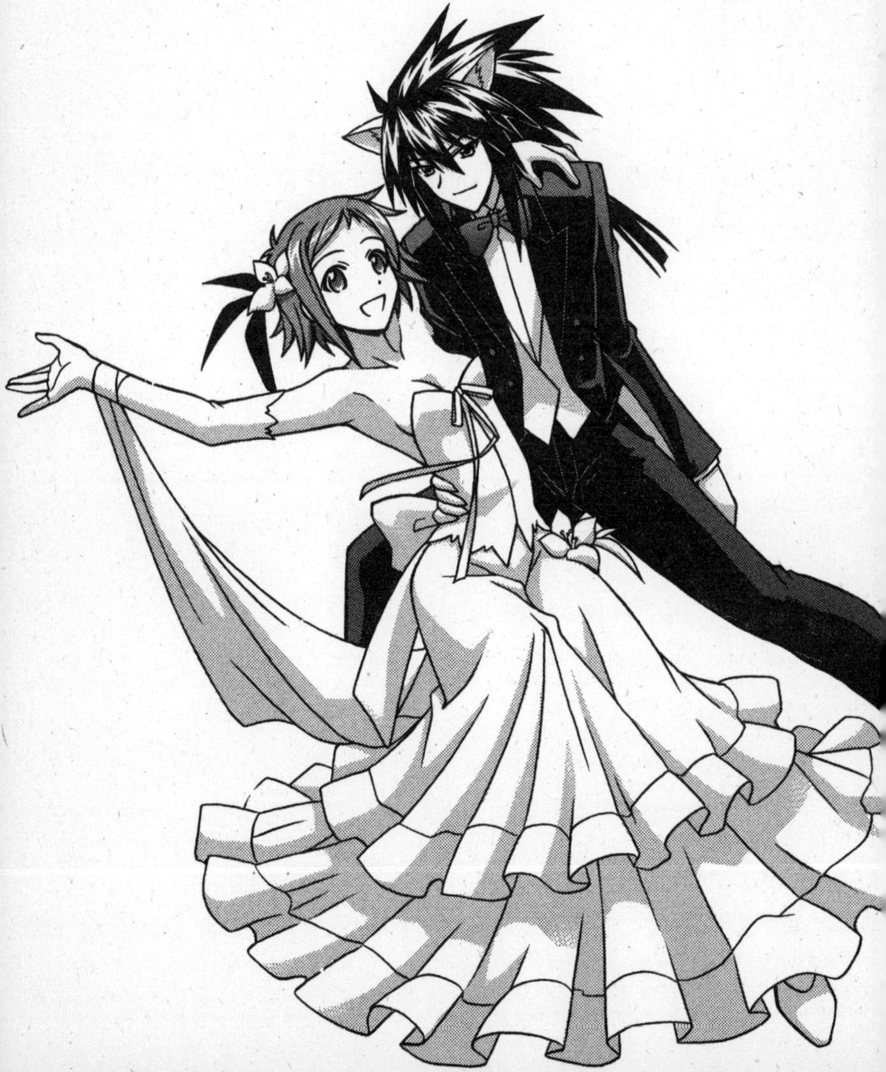

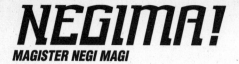

CONTENTS

259th Period: Outbreak!? Battle at the Peak of the Magical World!!.........3

260th Period: Battle at the Peak & Dance at the Peak of Class♡.........21

261st Period: Kissy Kissy Carnival♡.........39

262nd Period: Kissy Kissy Carnival♡ episode 2.........57

263rd Period: Kissy Kissy Carnival♡ episode 3.........75

264th Period: The Door to the Truth!!.........93

265th Period: Darkness Encroaches!.........111

266th Period: Confronting the Truth!.........129

267th Period: Father and Mother: The Tale of Their Destiny.........147

Fan Art Corner.........166

Fan Questions.........170

Mahora Academy Yearbook.........172

Cover Concept Sketches.........174

About the Creator.........176

Translation notes.........177

Preview of volume 30.........180

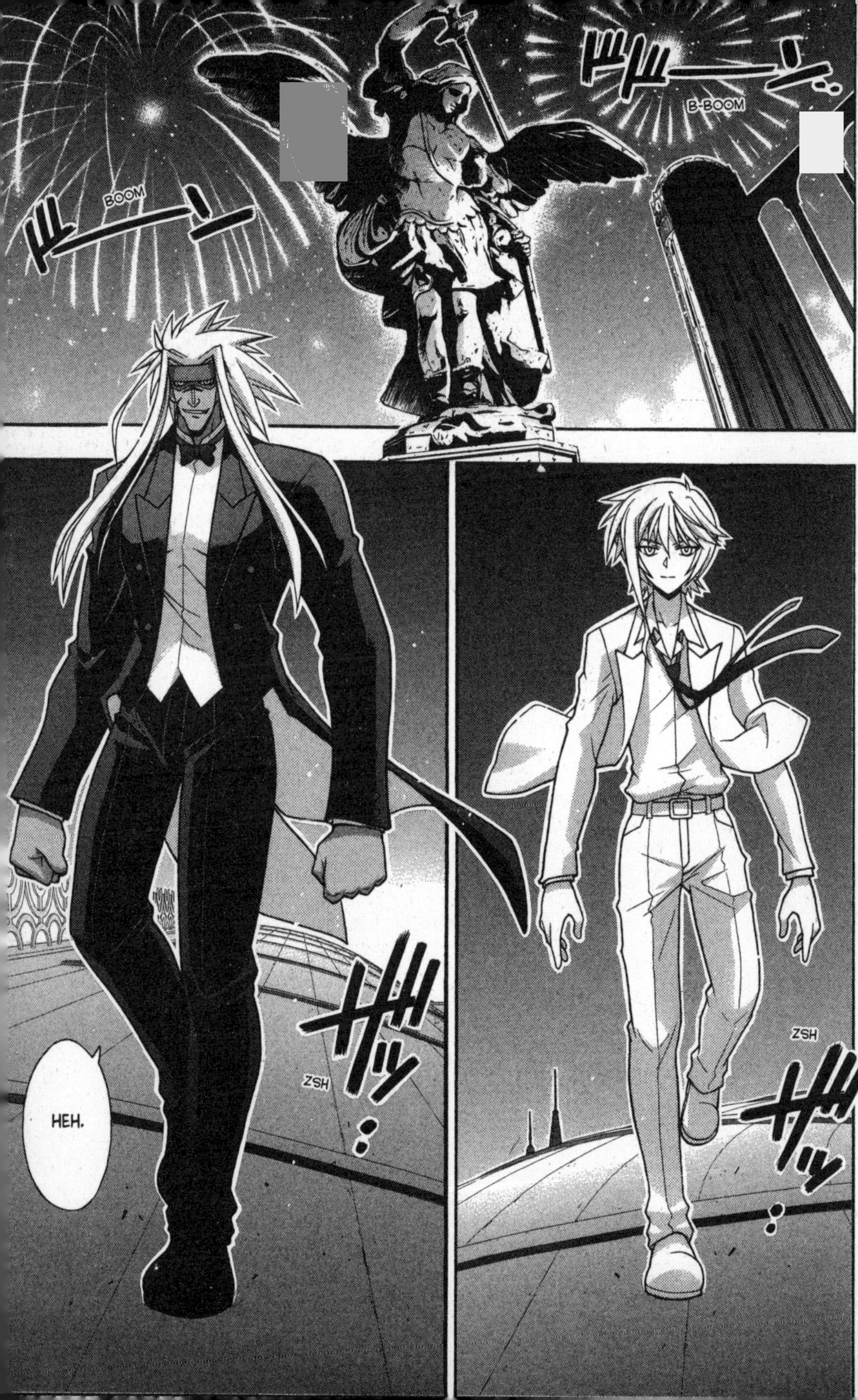
B-BOOM
BOOM
ZSH
ZSH
HEH.

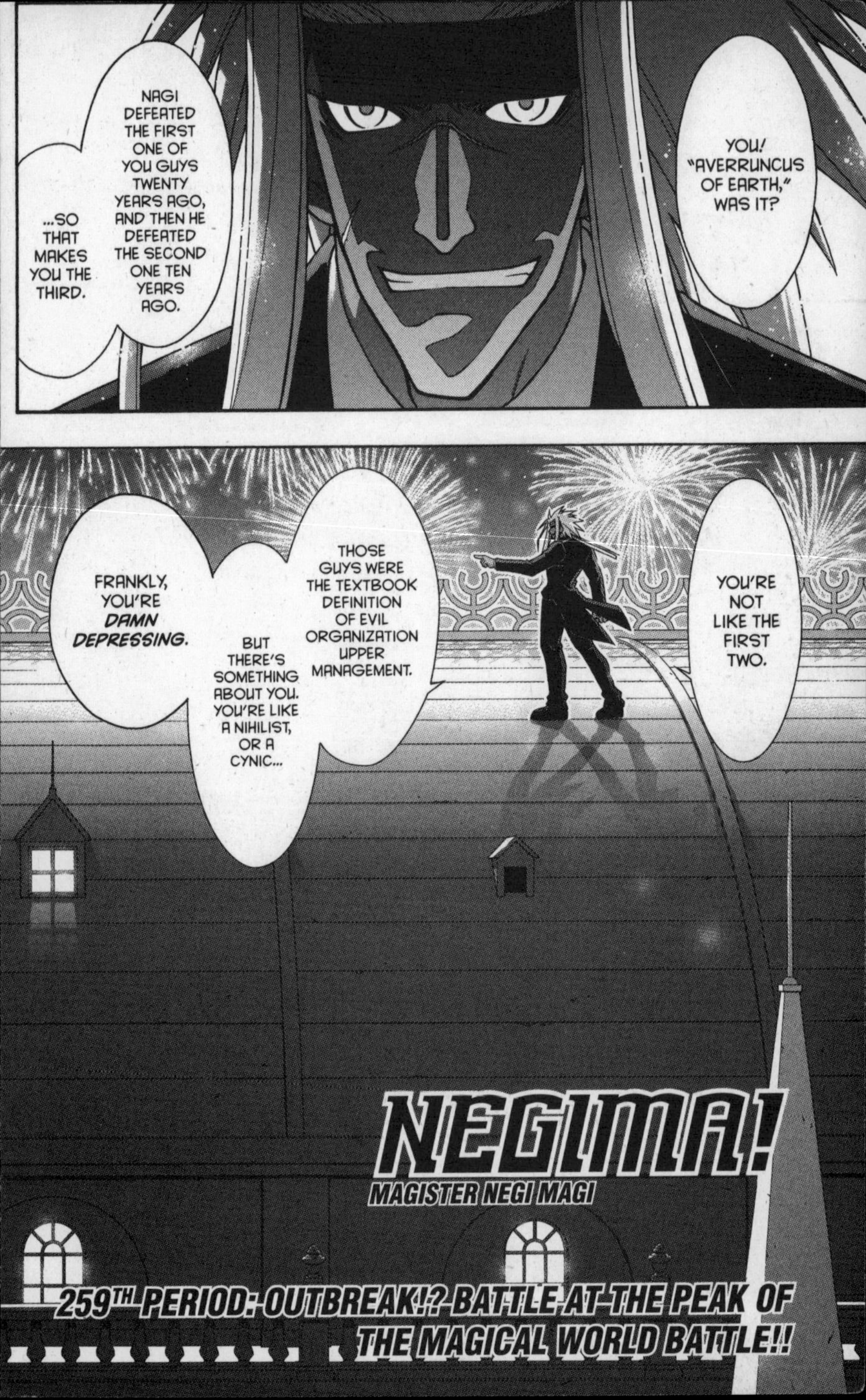
YOU! "AVERRUNCUS OF EARTH," WAS IT?
NAGI DEFEATED THE FIRST ONE OF YOU GUYS TWENTY YEARS AGO, AND THEN HE DEFEATED THE SECOND ONE TEN YEARS AGO.
...SO THAT MAKES YOU THE THIRD.
YOU'RE NOT LIKE THE FIRST TWO.
THOSE GUYS WERE THE TEXTBOOK DEFINITION OF EVIL ORGANIZATION UPPER MANAGEMENT.
BUT THERE'S SOMETHING ABOUT YOU. YOU'RE LIKE A NIHILIST, OR A CYNIC...
FRANKLY, YOU'RE *DAMN DEPRESSING.*
NEGIMA!
MAGISTER NEGI MAGI
259TH PERIOD: OUTBREAK!? BATTLE AT THE PEAK OF THE MAGICAL WORLD BATTLE!!

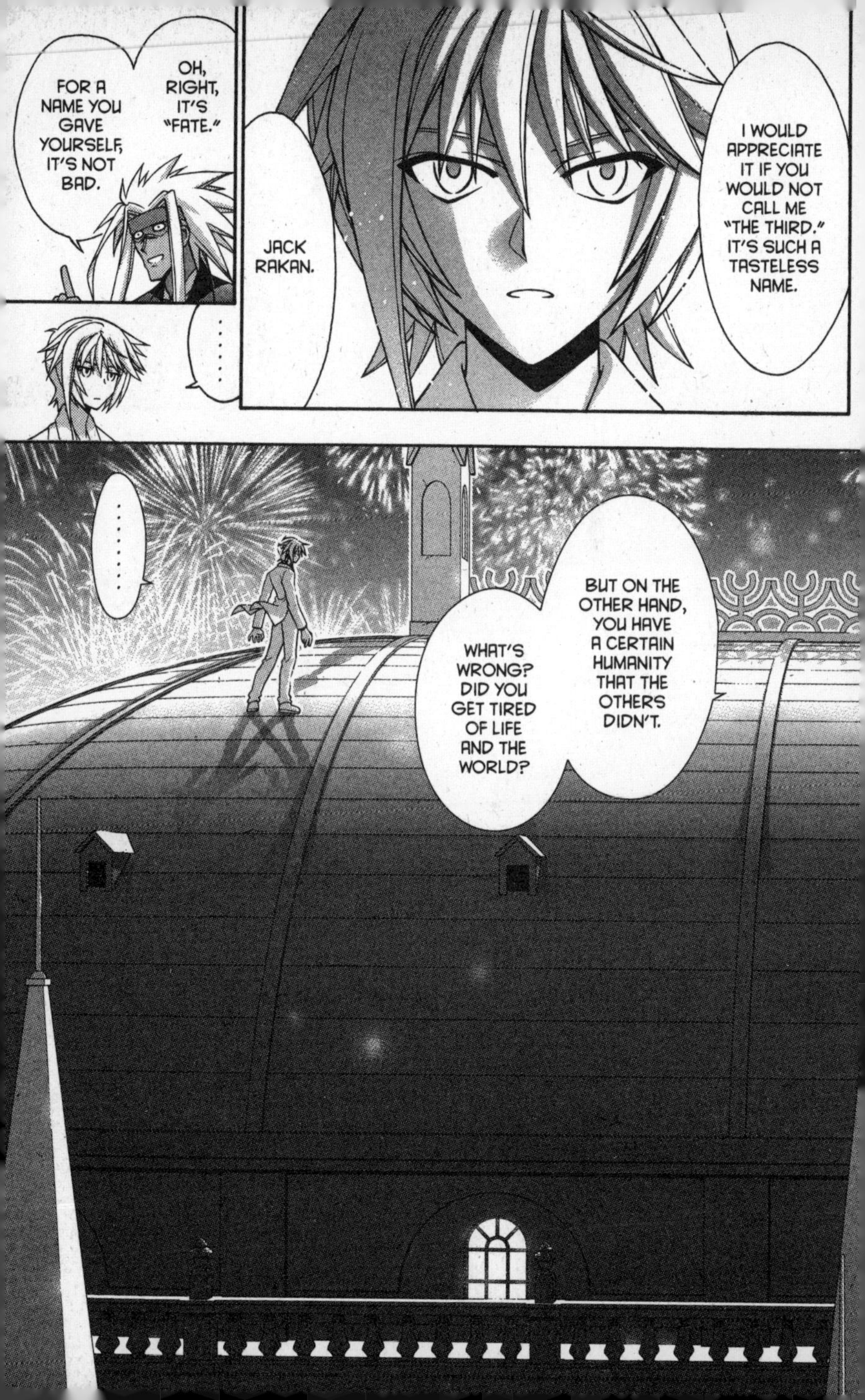
I WOULD APPRECIATE IT IF YOU WOULD NOT CALL ME "THE THIRD." IT'S SUCH A TASTELESS NAME.
JACK RAKAN.
OH, RIGHT, IT'S "FATE."
FOR A NAME YOU GAVE YOURSELF, IT'S NOT BAD.
......
BUT ON THE OTHER HAND, YOU HAVE A CERTAIN HUMANITY THAT THE OTHERS DIDN'T.
WHAT'S WRONG? DID YOU GET TIRED OF LIFE AND THE WORLD?
......

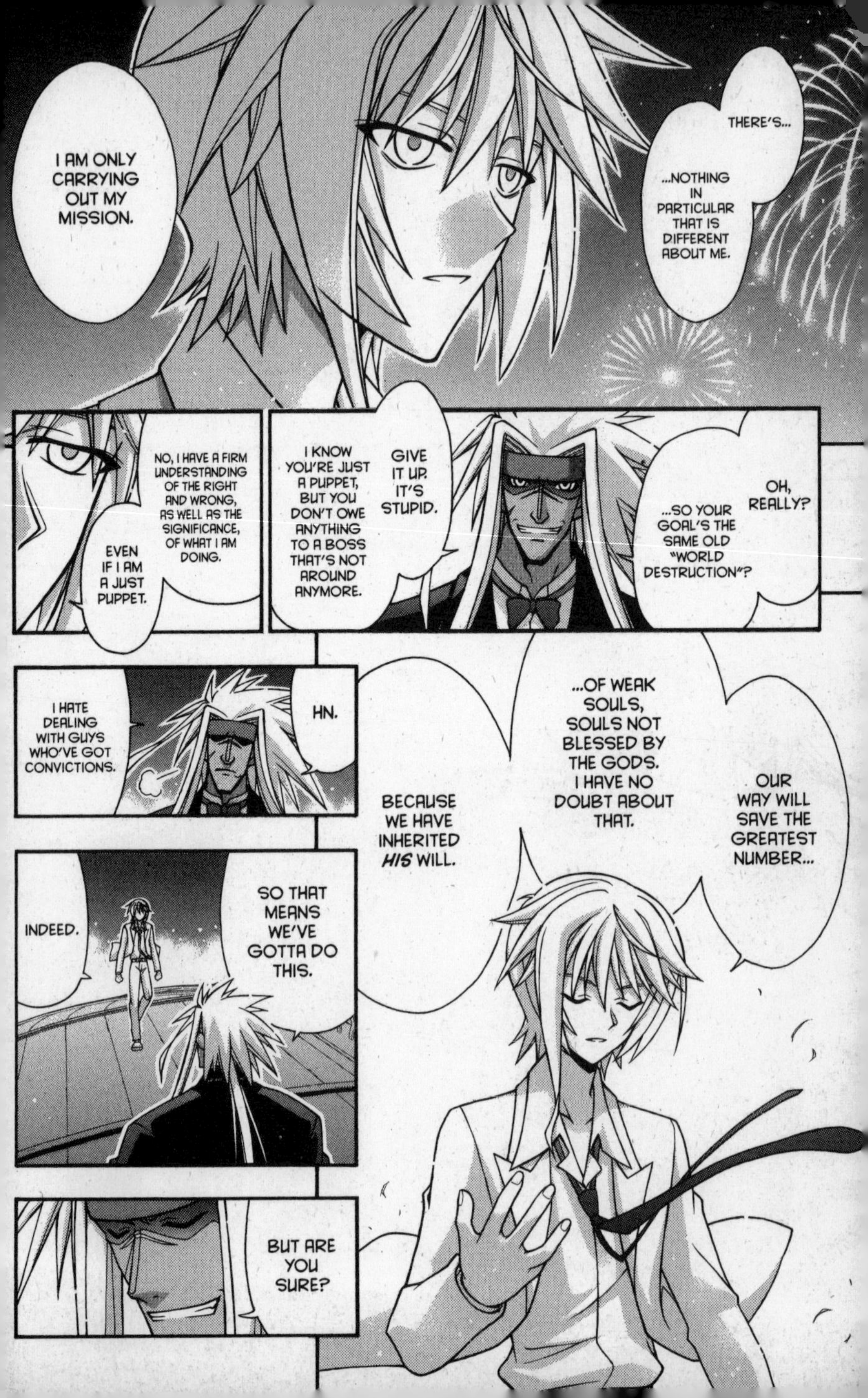
THERE'S...
...NOTHING IN PARTICULAR THAT IS DIFFERENT ABOUT ME.
I AM ONLY CARRYING OUT MY MISSION.
OH, REALLY?
...SO YOUR GOAL'S THE SAME OLD "WORLD DESTRUCTION"?
GIVE IT UP. IT'S STUPID.
I KNOW YOU'RE JUST A PUPPET, BUT YOU DON'T OWE ANYTHING TO A BOSS THAT'S NOT AROUND ANYMORE.
NO, I HAVE A FIRM UNDERSTANDING OF THE RIGHT AND WRONG, AS WELL AS THE SIGNIFICANCE, OF WHAT I AM DOING.
EVEN IF I AM A JUST PUPPET.
OUR WAY WILL SAVE THE GREATEST NUMBER...
...OF WEAK SOULS, SOULS NOT BLESSED BY THE GODS. I HAVE NO DOUBT ABOUT THAT.
BECAUSE WE HAVE INHERITED *HIS* WILL.
HN.
I HATE DEALING WITH GUYS WHO'VE GOT CONVICTIONS.
SO THAT MEANS WE'VE GOTTA DO THIS.
INDEED.
BUT ARE YOU SURE?

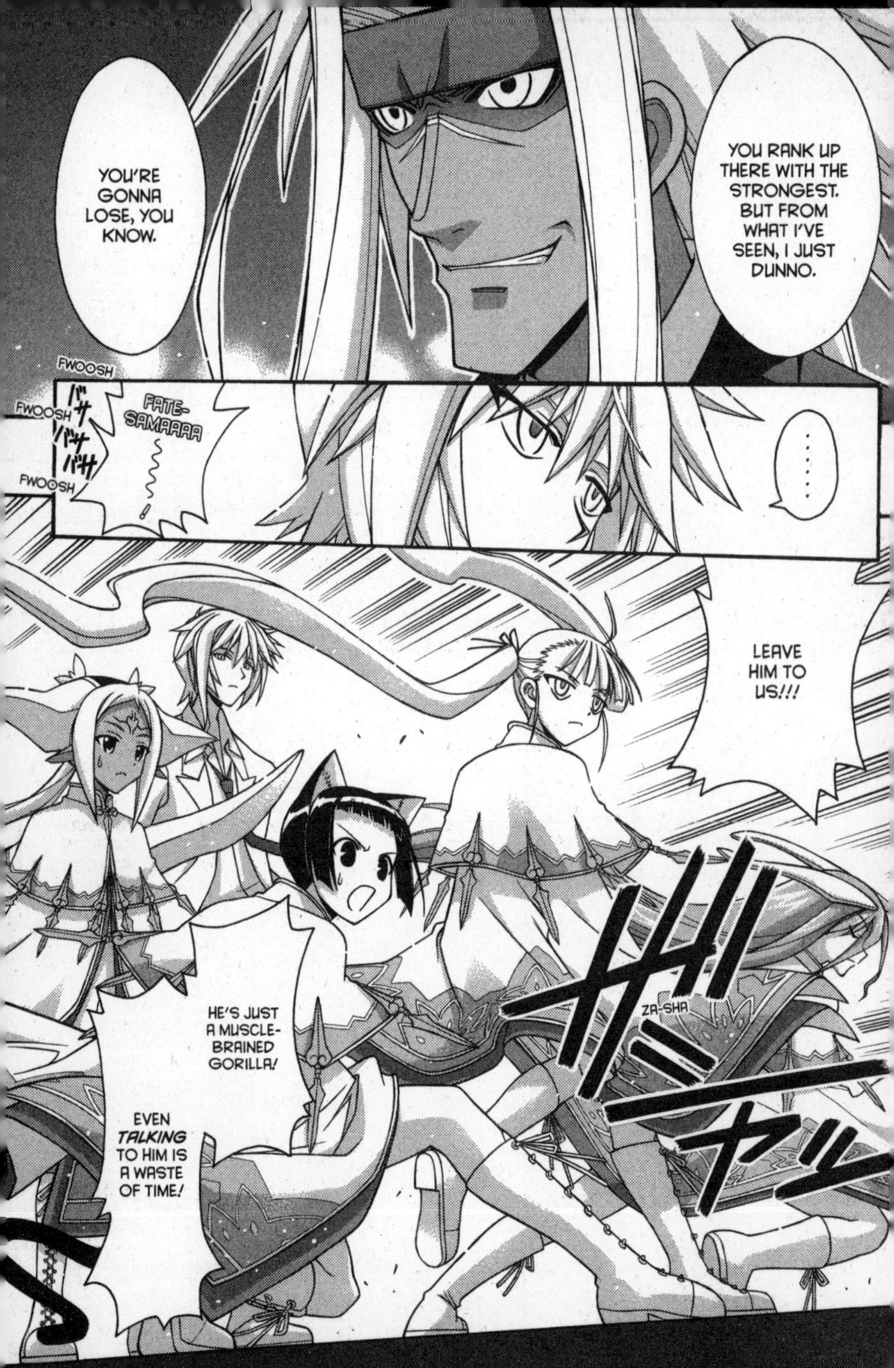
YOU RANK UP THERE WITH THE STRONGEST. BUT FROM WHAT I'VE SEEN, I JUST DUNNO.
YOU'RE GONNA LOSE, YOU KNOW.
......
FATE-SAMAAAA ~!
FWOOSH
FWOOSH
FWOOSH
LEAVE HIM TO US!!!
ZA-SHA
HE'S JUST A MUSCLE-BRAINED GORILLA!
EVEN *TALKING* TO HIM IS A WASTE OF TIME!

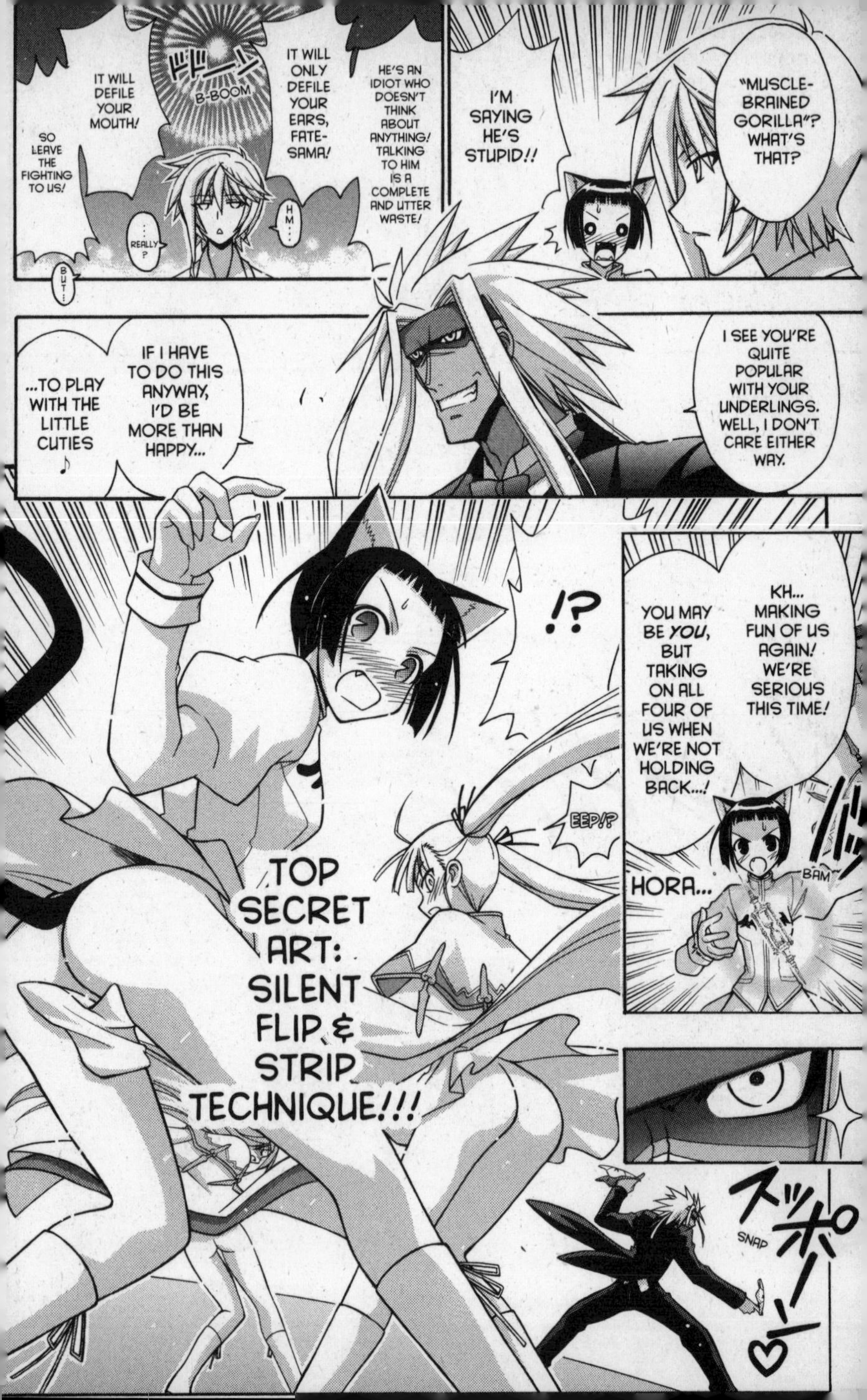
"MUSCLE-BRAINED GORILLA"? WHAT'S THAT?
I'M SAYING HE'S STUPID!!
HE'S AN IDIOT WHO DOESN'T THINK ABOUT ANYTHING! TALKING TO HIM IS A COMPLETE AND UTTER WASTE!
IT WILL ONLY DEFILE YOUR EARS, FATE-SAMA!
ドドーン
B-BOOM
IT WILL DEFILE YOUR MOUTH!
SO LEAVE THE FIGHTING TO US!
HM...
...REALLY?
BUT...
I SEE YOU'RE QUITE POPULAR WITH YOUR UNDERLINGS. WELL, I DON'T CARE EITHER WAY.
IF I HAVE TO DO THIS ANYWAY, I'D BE MORE THAN HAPPY...
...TO PLAY WITH THE LITTLE CUTIES ♪
KH... MAKING FUN OF US AGAIN! WE'RE SERIOUS THIS TIME!
YOU MAY BE *YOU*, BUT TAKING ON ALL FOUR OF US WHEN WE'RE NOT HOLDING BACK...!
BAM
HORA...
スッポーン
SNAP
♡
!?
EEP!?
TOP SECRET ART: SILENT FLIP & STRIP TECHNIQUE!!!

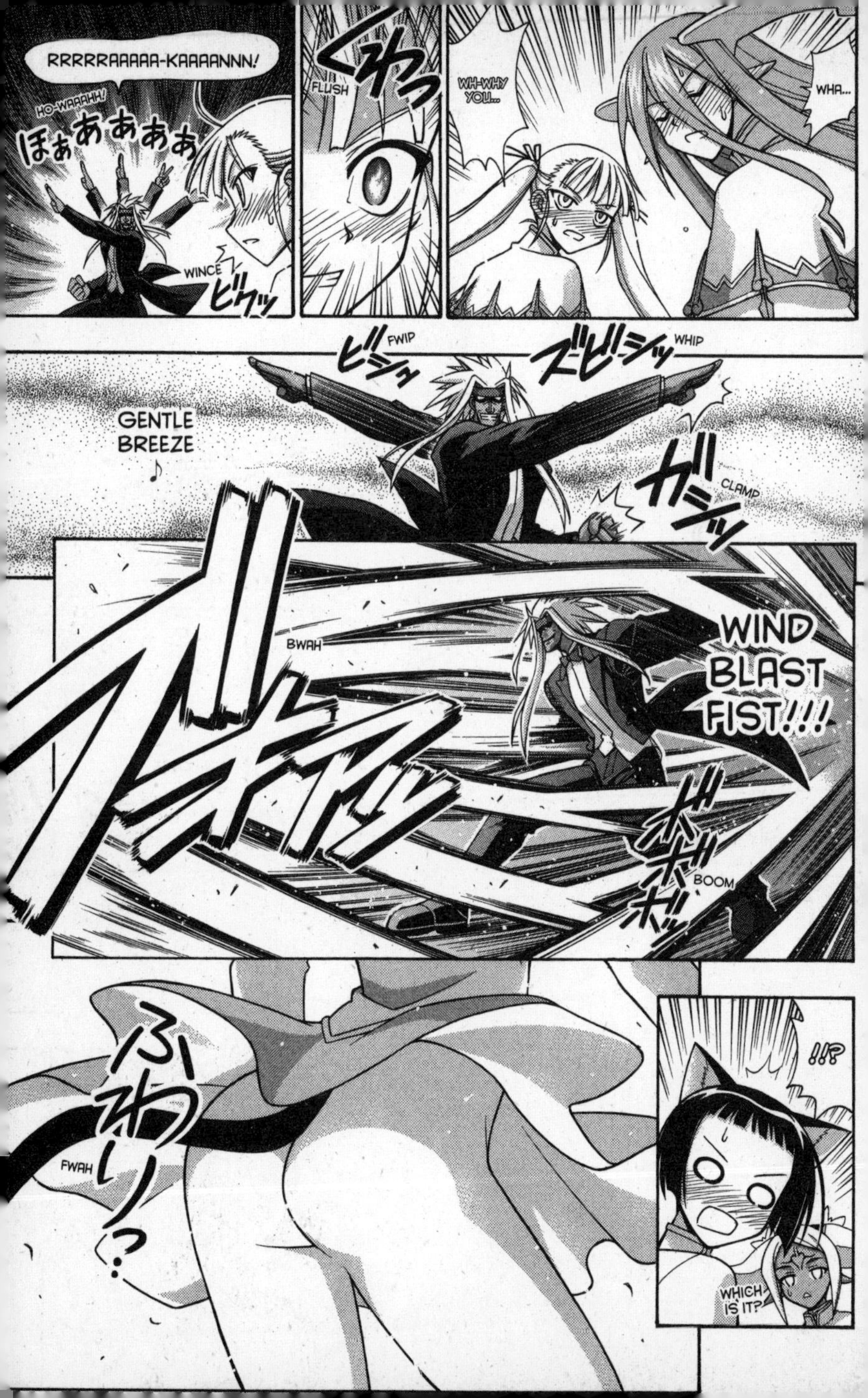

WHA...
WH-WHY YOU...
くわっ
FLUSH
RRRRRAAAAA-KAAAANNN!
HO-WAAAHH!
ほぁあああぁ
WINCE
ビクッ
ズビシッ
WHIP
ビシュ
FWIP
ガシッ
CLAMP
GENTLE BREEZE ♪
WIND BLAST FIST!!!
ボボボボッ
BOOM
BWAH
!!?
WHICH IS IT?
ふわりっ
FWAH

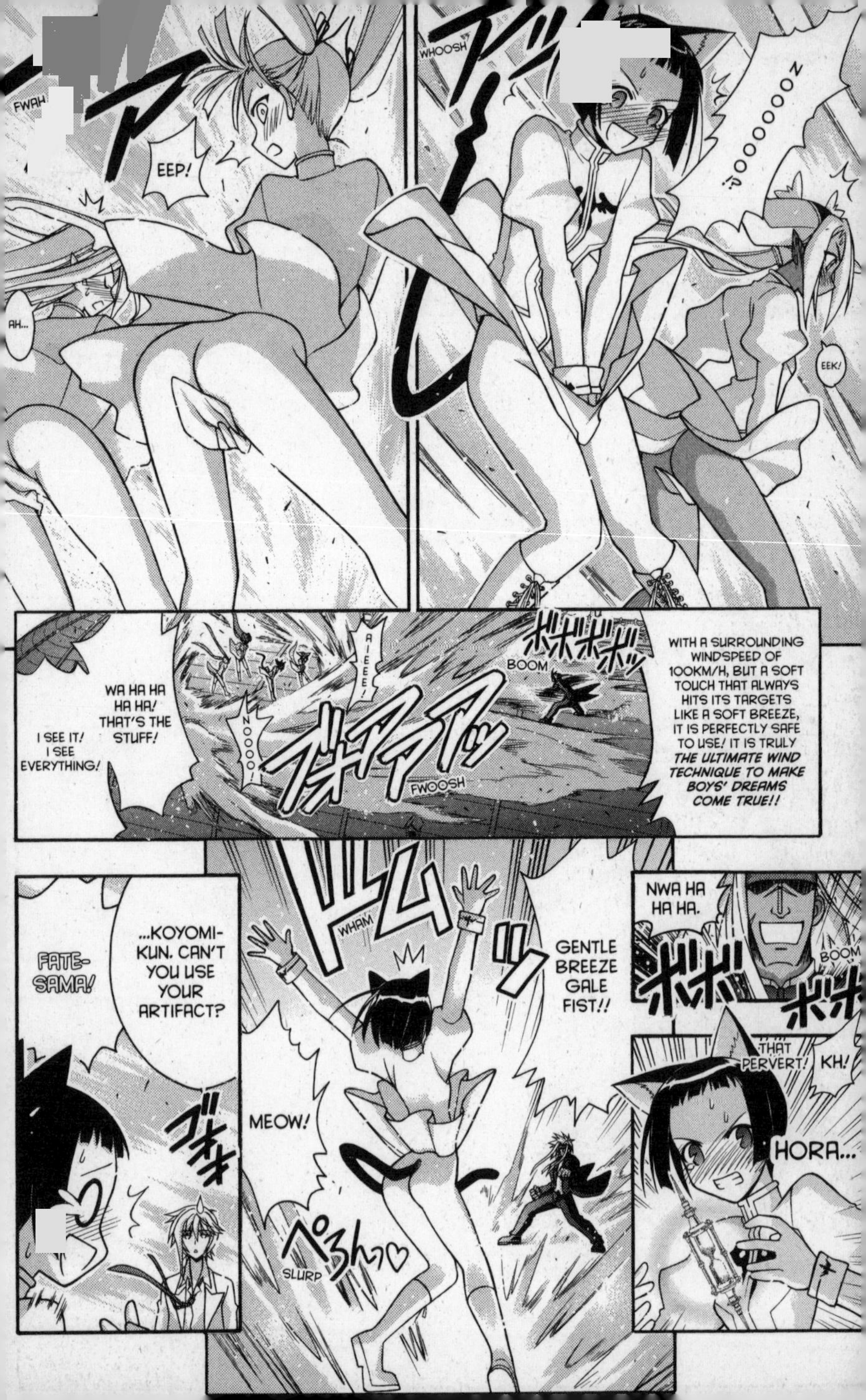
NOOOOOOO!?
WHOOSH
EEK!
FWAH
EEP!
AH...
WITH A SURROUNDING WINDSPEED OF 100KM/H, BUT A SOFT TOUCH THAT ALWAYS HITS ITS TARGETS LIKE A SOFT BREEZE, IT IS PERFECTLY SAFE TO USE! IT IS TRULY *THE ULTIMATE WIND TECHNIQUE TO MAKE BOYS' DREAMS COME TRUE!!*
BOOM
AIEEE!
FWOOSH
NOOOOO!
WA HA HA HA HA! THAT'S THE STUFF!
I SEE IT! I SEE EVERYTHING!
NWA HA HA HA.
BOOM
KH!
THAT PERVERT!
HORA...
GENTLE BREEZE GALE FIST!!
WHAM
MEOW!
SLURP
...KOYOMI-KUN. CAN'T YOU USE YOUR ARTIFACT?
FATE-SAMA!

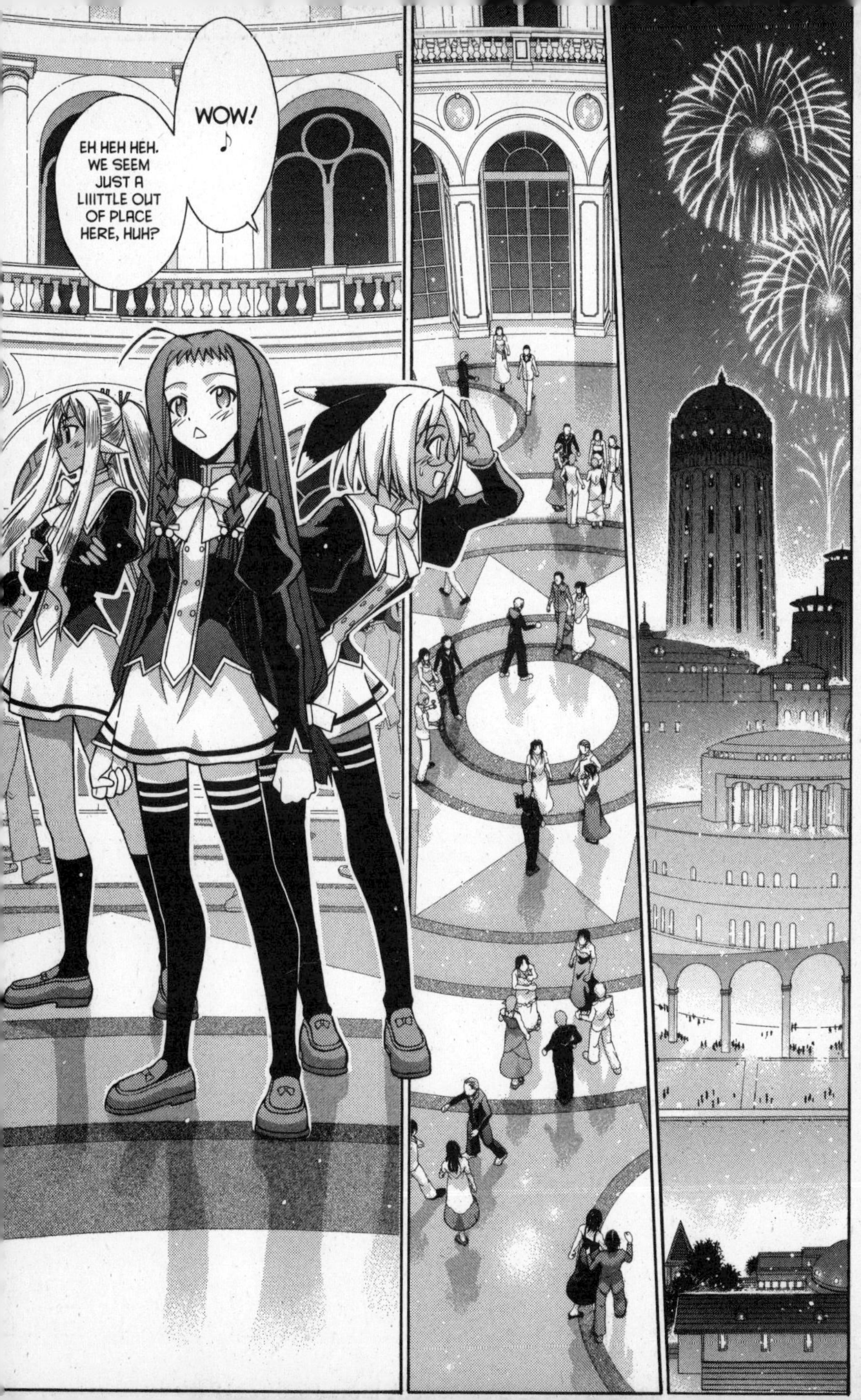
WOW! ♪
EH HEH HEH. WE SEEM JUST A LIIITTLE OUT OF PLACE HERE, HUH?

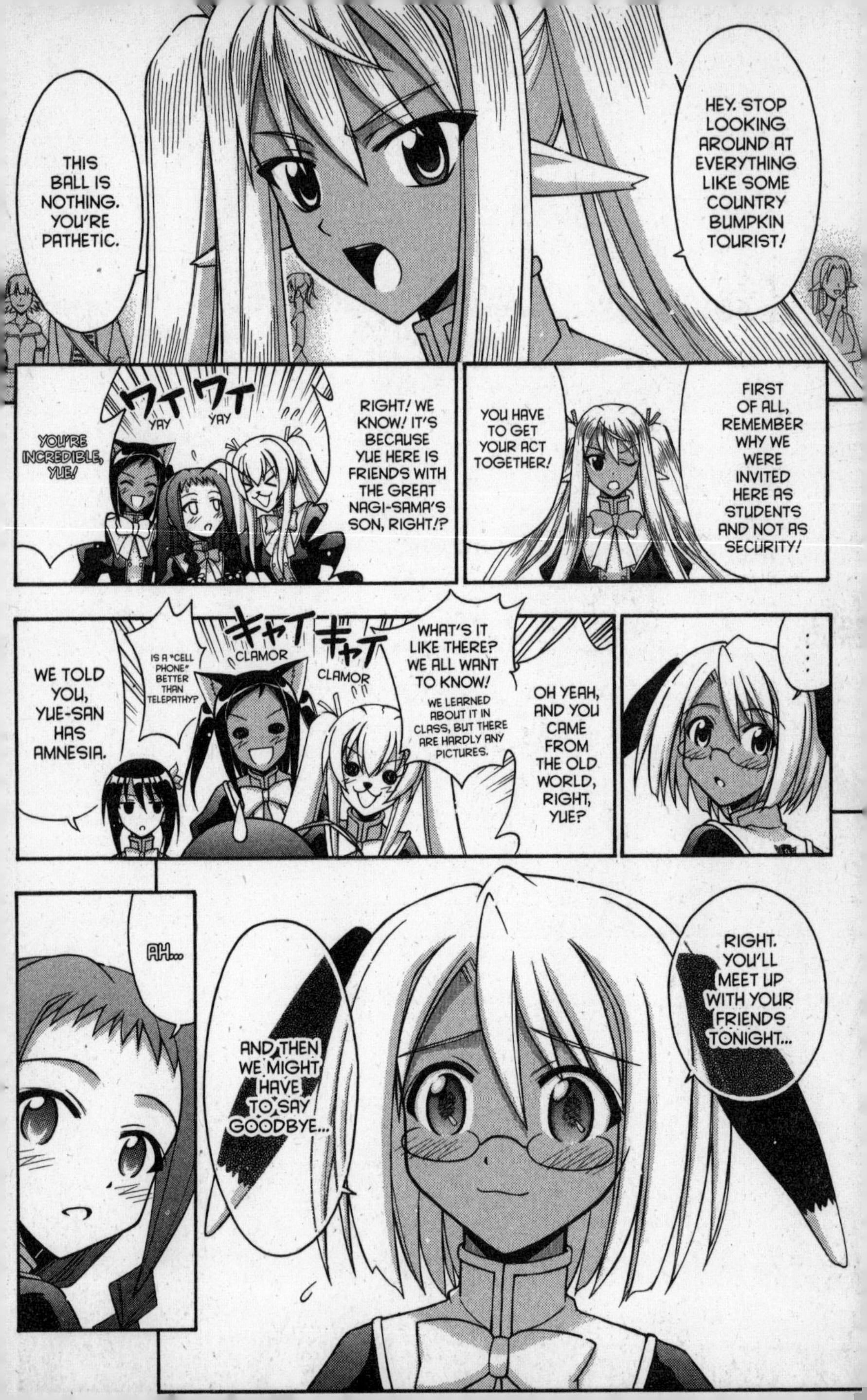
HEY. STOP LOOKING AROUND AT EVERYTHING LIKE SOME COUNTRY BUMPKIN TOURIST!
THIS BALL IS NOTHING. YOU'RE PATHETIC.
FIRST OF ALL, REMEMBER WHY WE WERE INVITED HERE AS STUDENTS AND NOT AS SECURITY!
YOU HAVE TO GET YOUR ACT TOGETHER!
RIGHT! WE KNOW! IT'S BECAUSE YUE HERE IS FRIENDS WITH THE GREAT NAGI-SAMA'S SON, RIGHT!?
ワイワイ
YAY YAY
YOU'RE INCREDIBLE, YUE!
...
OH YEAH, AND YOU CAME FROM THE OLD WORLD, RIGHT, YUE?
WHAT'S IT LIKE THERE? WE ALL WANT TO KNOW!
WE LEARNED ABOUT IT IN CLASS, BUT THERE ARE HARDLY ANY PICTURES.
キャイ ギャイ
CLAMOR CLAMOR
IS A "CELL PHONE" BETTER THAN TELEPATHY?
WE TOLD YOU, YUE-SAN HAS AMNESIA.
RIGHT. YOU'LL MEET UP WITH YOUR FRIENDS TONIGHT...
AND THEN WE MIGHT HAVE TO SAY GOODBYE...
AH...

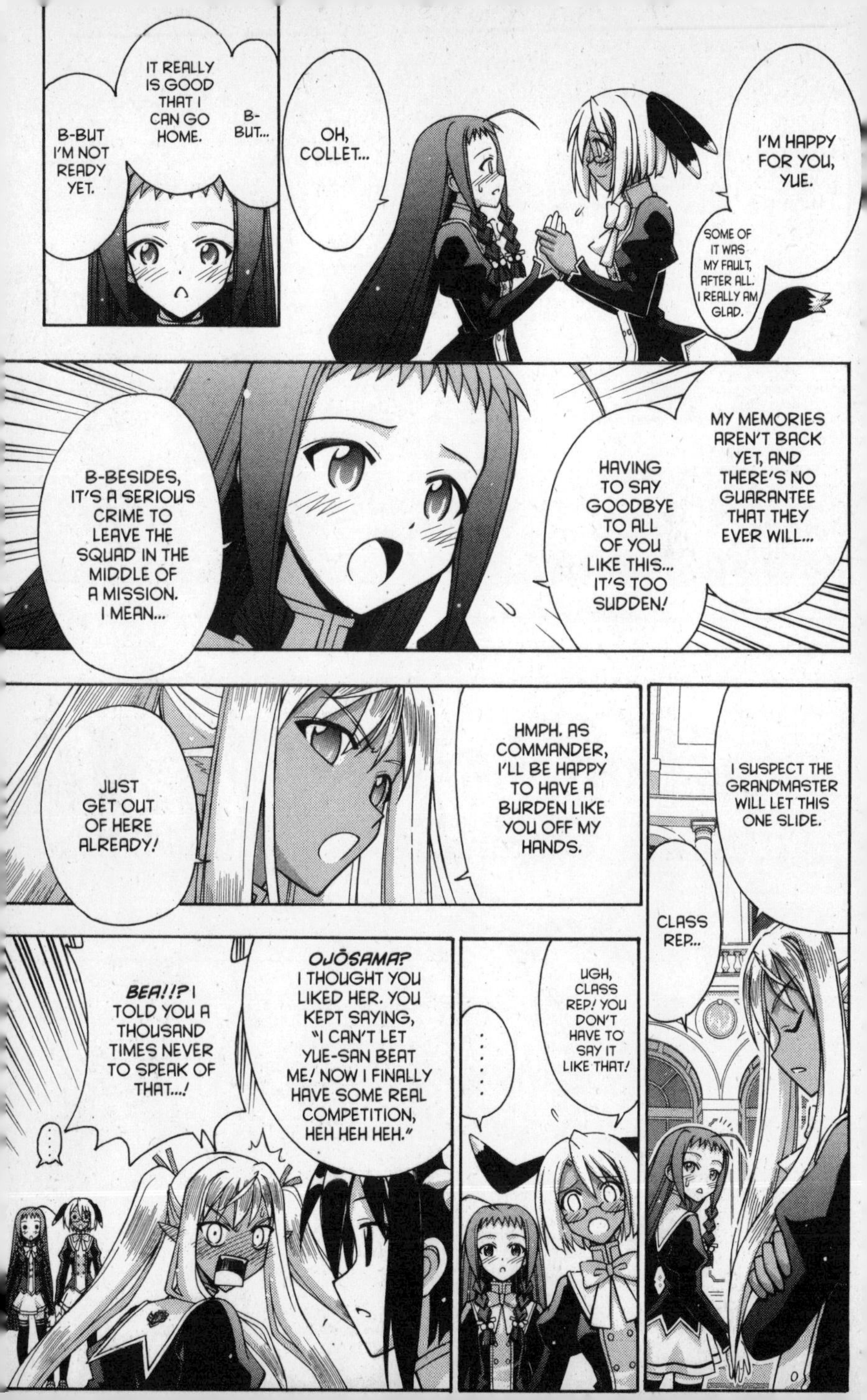
I'M HAPPY FOR YOU, YUE.
SOME OF IT WAS MY FAULT, AFTER ALL. I REALLY AM GLAD.
OH, COLLET...
B-BUT...
IT REALLY IS GOOD THAT I CAN GO HOME.
B-BUT I'M NOT READY YET.
MY MEMORIES AREN'T BACK YET, AND THERE'S NO GUARANTEE THAT THEY EVER WILL...
HAVING TO SAY GOODBYE TO ALL OF YOU LIKE THIS... IT'S TOO SUDDEN!
B-BESIDES, IT'S A SERIOUS CRIME TO LEAVE THE SQUAD IN THE MIDDLE OF A MISSION. I MEAN...
I SUSPECT THE GRANDMASTER WILL LET THIS ONE SLIDE.
CLASS REP...
HMPH. AS COMMANDER, I'LL BE HAPPY TO HAVE A BURDEN LIKE YOU OFF MY HANDS.
JUST GET OUT OF HERE ALREADY!
UGH, CLASS REP! YOU DON'T HAVE TO SAY IT LIKE THAT!
......
OJŌSAMA? I THOUGHT YOU LIKED HER. YOU KEPT SAYING, "I CAN'T LET YUE-SAN BEAT ME! NOW I FINALLY HAVE SOME REAL COMPETITION, HEH HEH HEH."
BEA!!? I TOLD YOU A THOUSAND TIMES NEVER TO SPEAK OF THAT...!
...

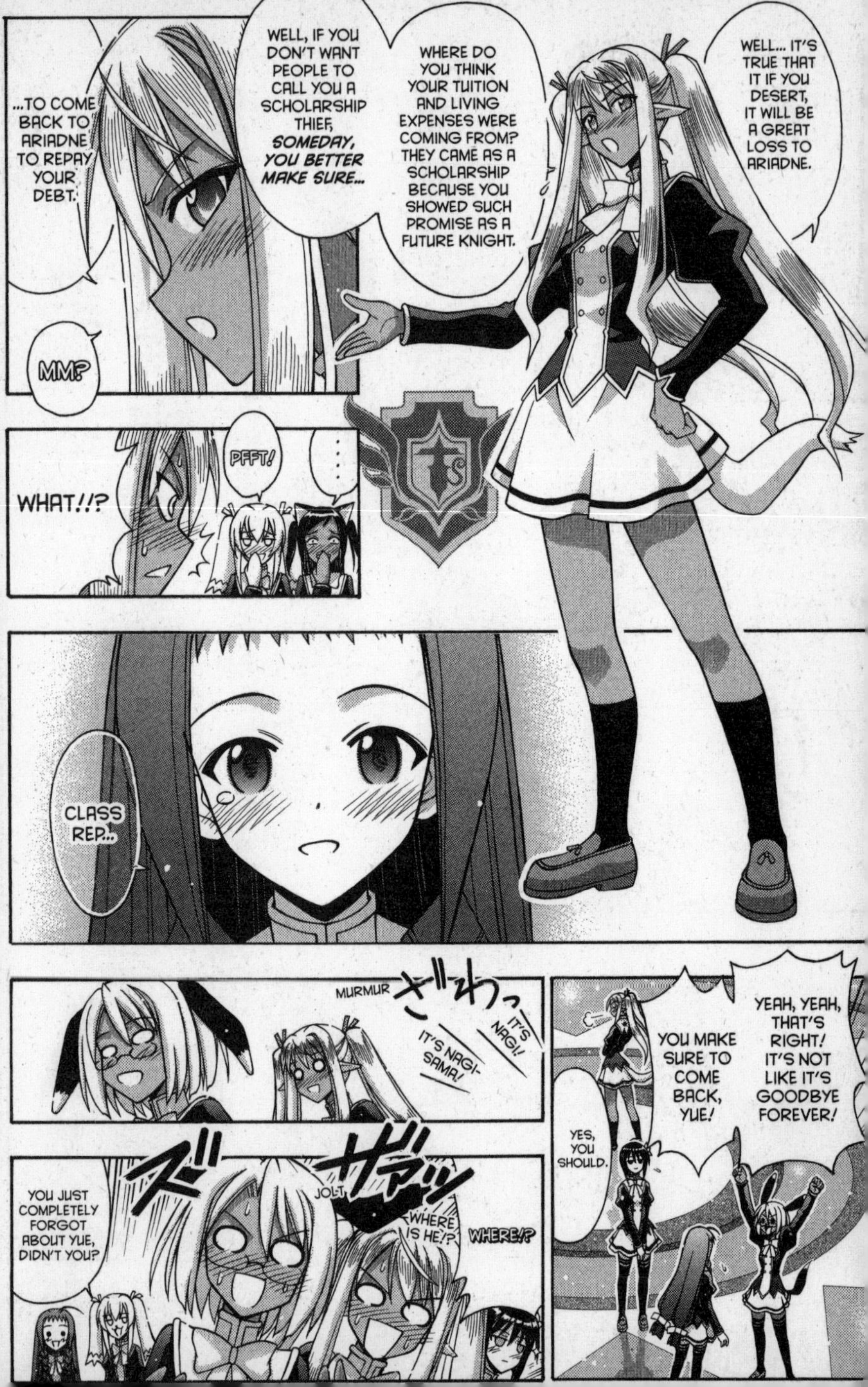
WELL... IT'S TRUE THAT IT IF YOU DESERT, IT WILL BE A GREAT LOSS TO ARIADNE.
WHERE DO YOU THINK YOUR TUITION AND LIVING EXPENSES WERE COMING FROM? THEY CAME AS A SCHOLARSHIP BECAUSE YOU SHOWED SUCH PROMISE AS A FUTURE KNIGHT.
WELL, IF YOU DON'T WANT PEOPLE TO CALL YOU A SCHOLARSHIP THIEF, *SOMEDAY, YOU BETTER MAKE SURE...*
...TO COME BACK TO ARIADNE TO REPAY YOUR DEBT.
MM?
...
PFFT!
WHAT!!?
CLASS REP...
YEAH, YEAH, THAT'S RIGHT! IT'S NOT LIKE IT'S GOODBYE FOREVER!
YOU MAKE SURE TO COME BACK, YUE!
YES, YOU SHOULD.
ざわっ
MURMUR
IT'S NAGI!
IT'S NAGI-SAMA!
ズザァッ
JOLT
WHERE!?
WHERE IS HE!?
YOU JUST COMPLETELY FORGOT ABOUT YUE, DIDN'T YOU?

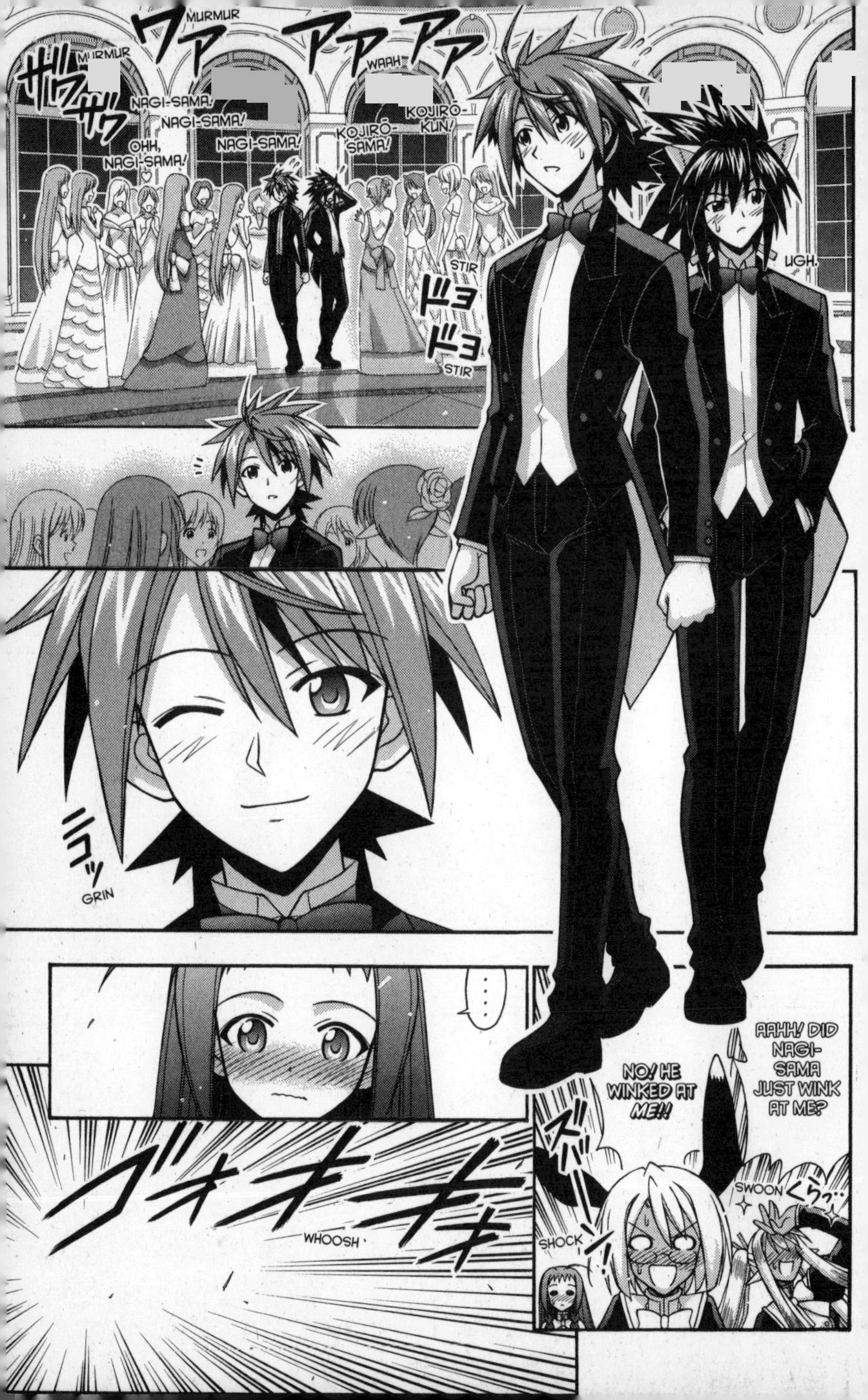

ワァ MURMUR
アァ アァ WAAH
ザワザワ MURMUR
KOJIRŌ-KUN!
KOJIRŌ-SAMA!
NAGI-SAMA!
NAGI-SAMA!
NAGI-SAMA!
OHH, NAGI-SAMA! ♡
STIR ドヨドヨ STIR
UGH.
ニコッ GRIN
...
ヴォオオオ WHOOSH
AAHH! DID NAGI-SAMA JUST WINK AT ME?
NO! HE WINKED AT ME!!
ズバーン SHOCK
くらっ SWOON

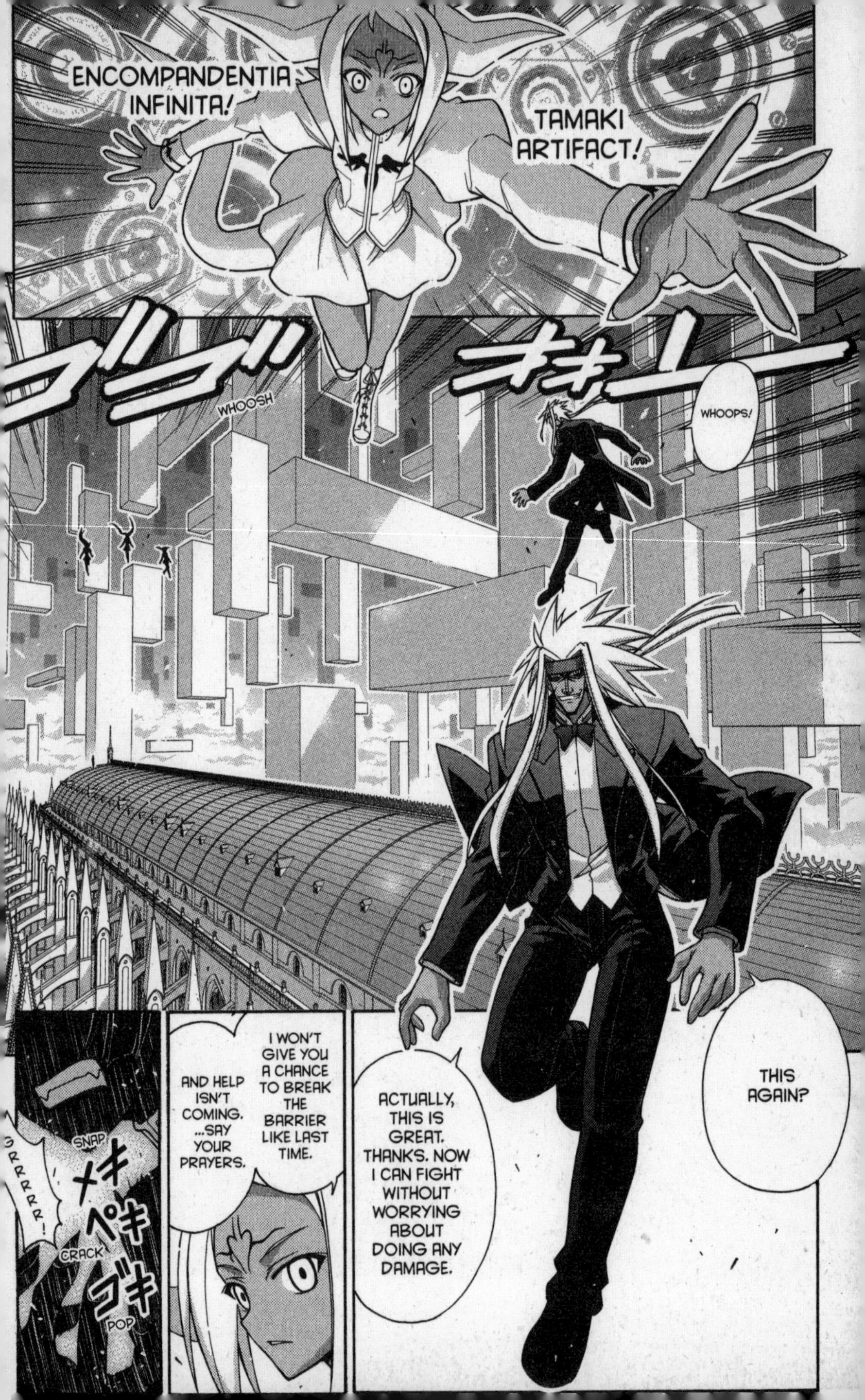
TAMAKI ARTIFACT!
ENCOMPANDENTIA INFINITA!
WHOOPS!
WHOOSH
THIS AGAIN?
ACTUALLY, THIS IS GREAT. THANKS. NOW I CAN FIGHT WITHOUT WORRYING ABOUT DOING ANY DAMAGE.
I WON'T GIVE YOU A CHANCE TO BREAK THE BARRIER LIKE LAST TIME.
AND HELP ISN'T COMING. ...SAY YOUR PRAYERS.
GRRRRR!
メキ
SNAP
ペキ
CRACK
ゴキ
POP

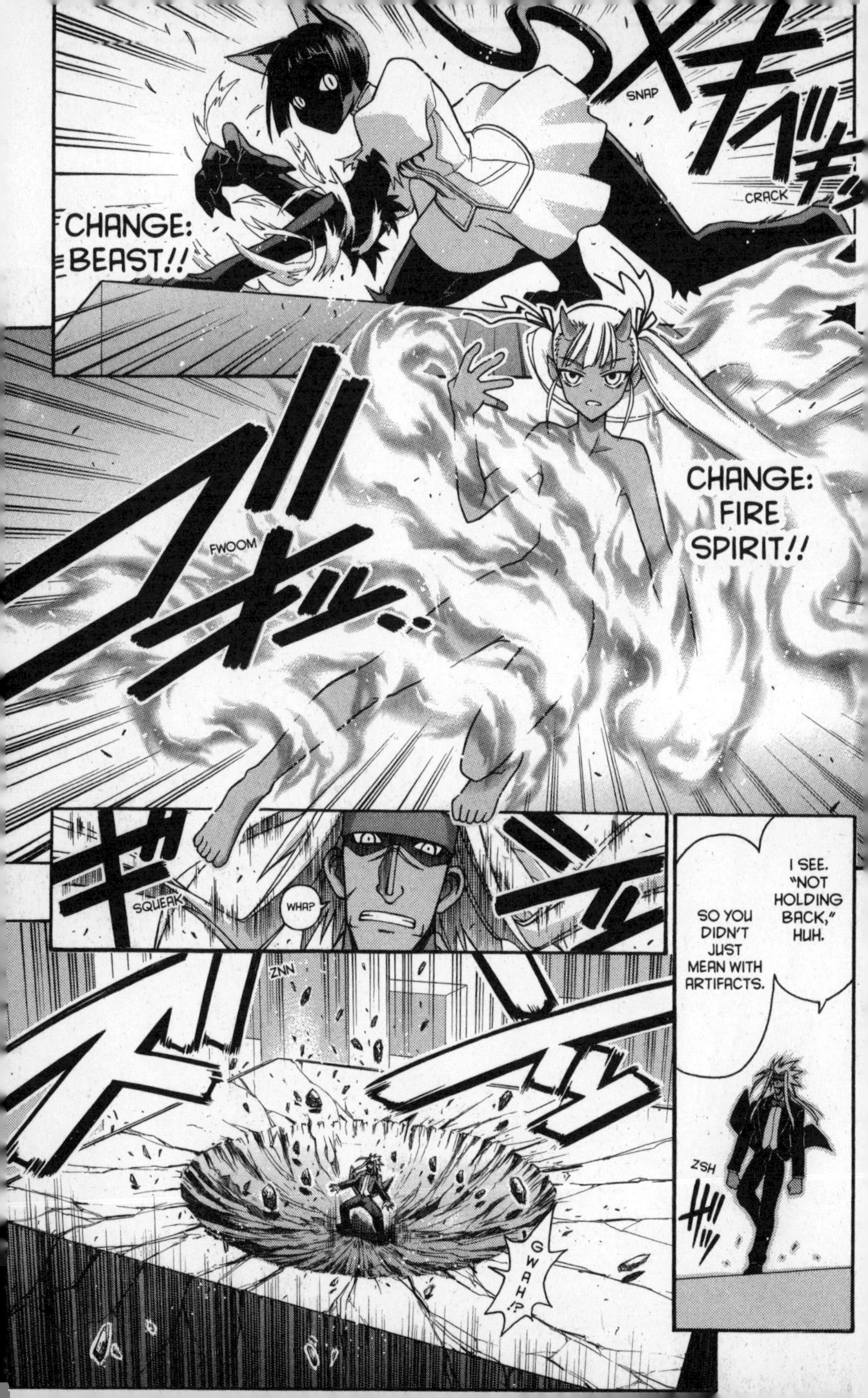
SNAP
CRACK
CHANGE: BEAST!!
CHANGE: FIRE SPIRIT!!
FWOOM
I SEE. "NOT HOLDING BACK," HUH.
SO YOU DIDN'T JUST MEAN WITH ARTIFACTS.
ZSH
WHA?
SQUEAK
ZNN
GWAH!?

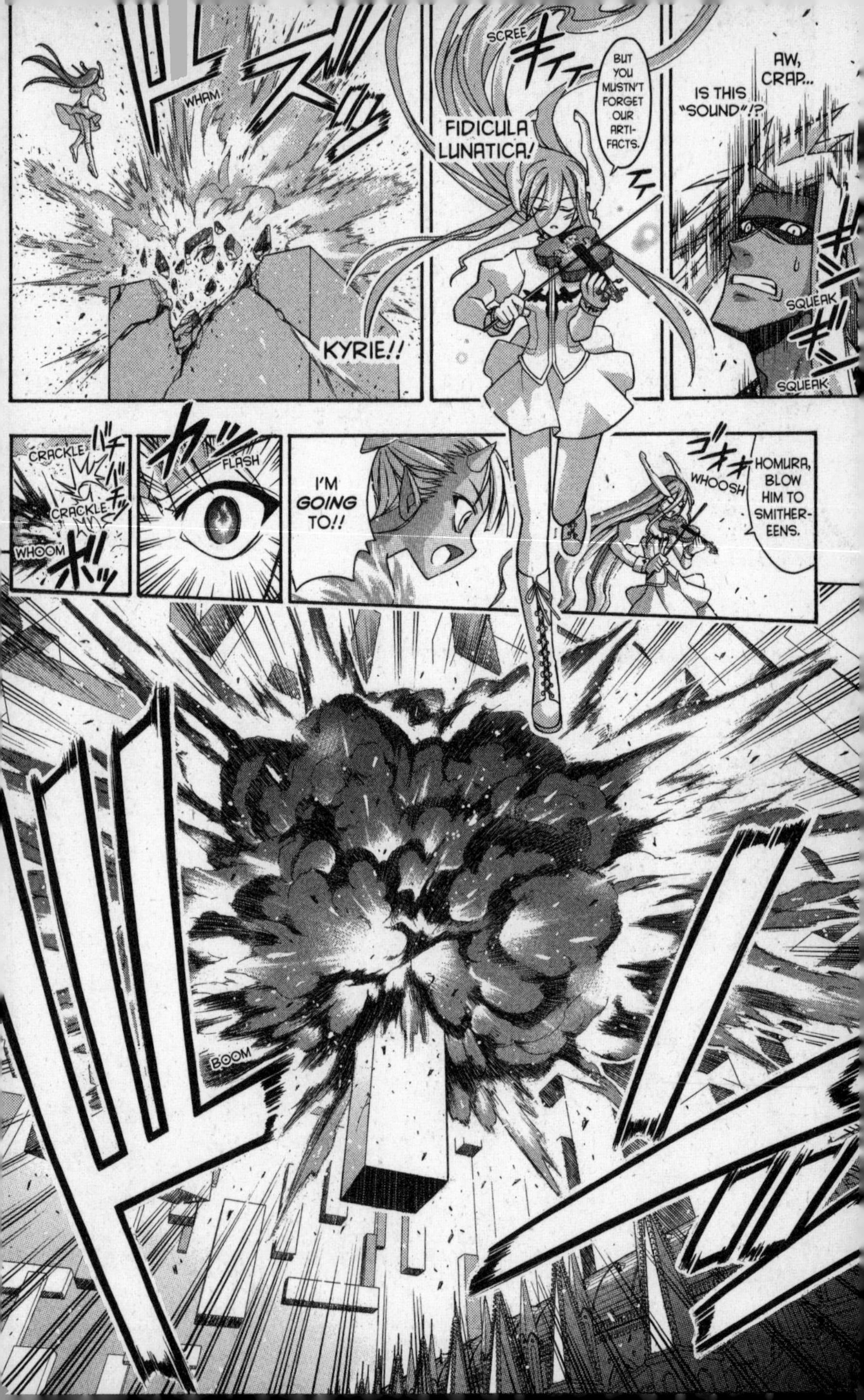
AW, CRAP...
IS THIS "SOUND"!?
SQUEAK
SQUEAK
SCREE
BUT YOU MUSTN'T FORGET OUR ARTI-FACTS.
FIDICULA LUNATICA!
WHAM
KYRIE!!
HOMURA, BLOW HIM TO SMITHER-EENS.
WHOOSH
I'M *GOING* TO!!
FLASH
CRACKLE
CRACKLE
WHOOM
BOOM

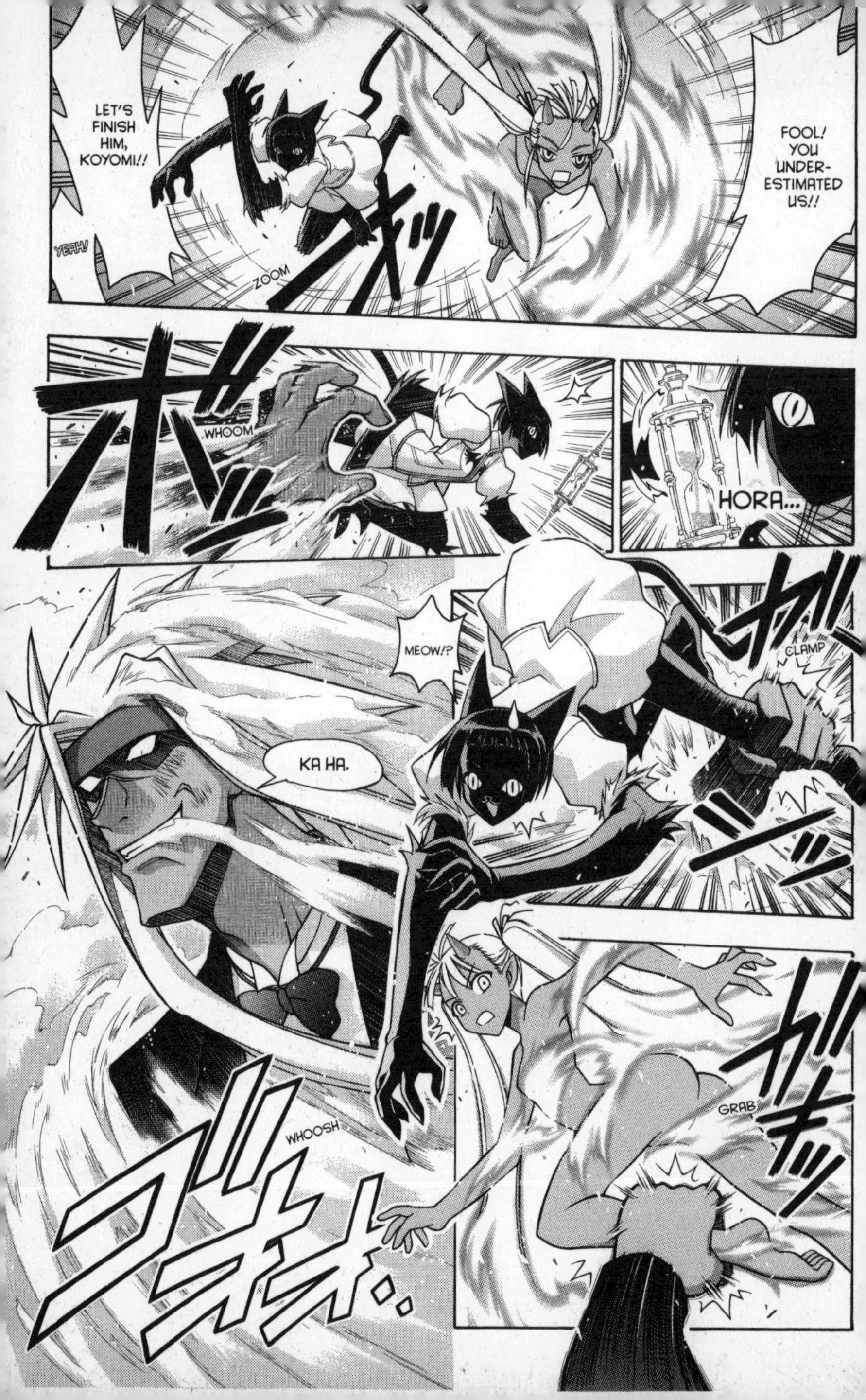
FOOL! YOU UNDER-ESTIMATED US!!
LET'S FINISH HIM, KOYOMI!!
YEAH!
ZOOM
HORA...
WHOOM
CLAMP
MEOW!?
KA HA.
GRAB
WHOOSH

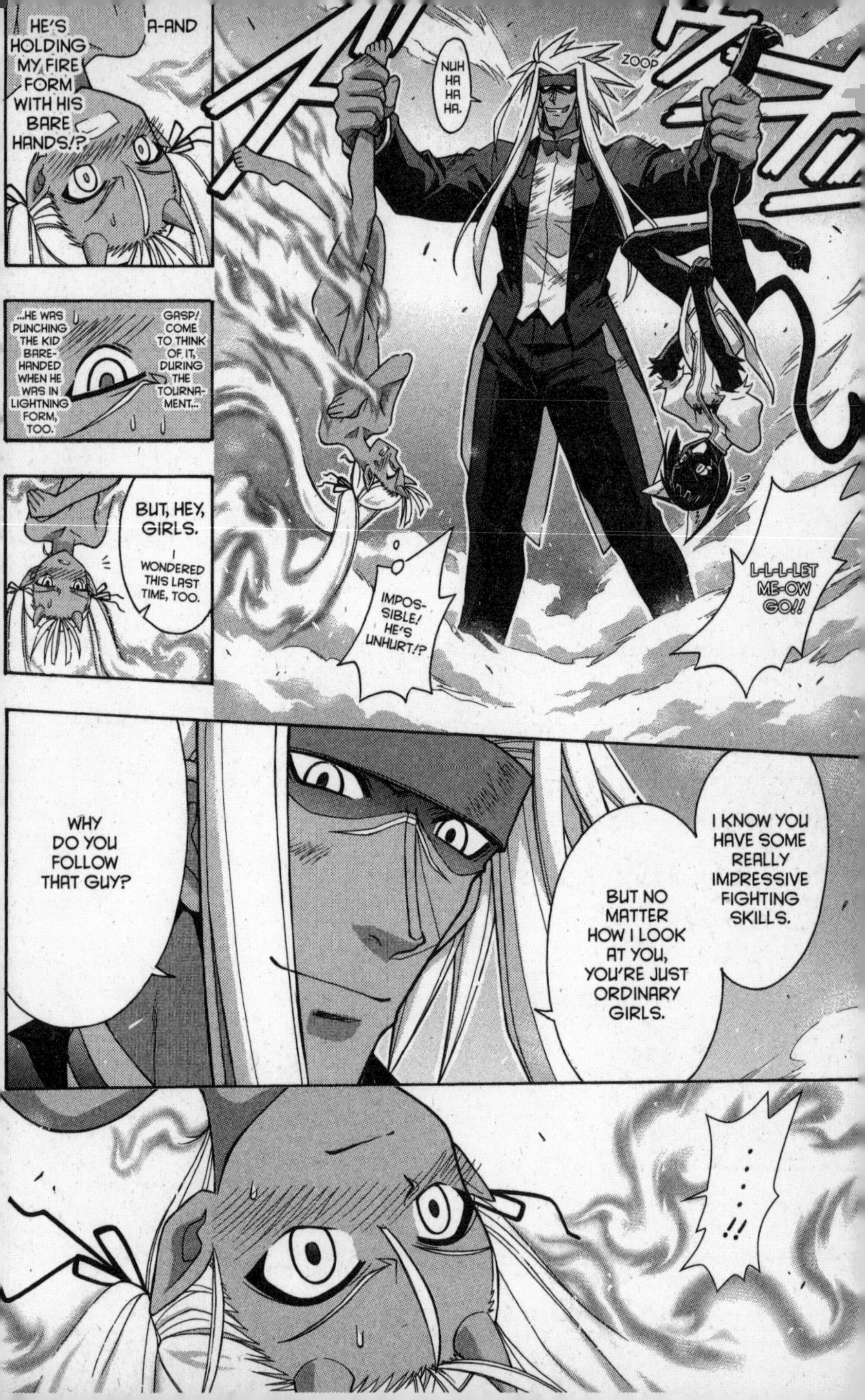
ZOOP
NUH HA HA HA.
L-L-L-LET ME-OW GO!!
IMPOSSIBLE! HE'S UNHURT!?
A-AND
HE'S HOLDING MY FIRE FORM WITH HIS BARE HANDS!?
GASP! COME TO THINK OF IT, DURING THE TOURNAMENT...
...HE WAS PUNCHING THE KID BAREHANDED WHEN HE WAS IN LIGHTNING FORM, TOO.
BUT, HEY, GIRLS.
I WONDERED THIS LAST TIME, TOO.
I KNOW YOU HAVE SOME REALLY IMPRESSIVE FIGHTING SKILLS.
BUT NO MATTER HOW I LOOK AT YOU, YOU'RE JUST ORDINARY GIRLS.
WHY DO YOU FOLLOW THAT GUY?
......!!

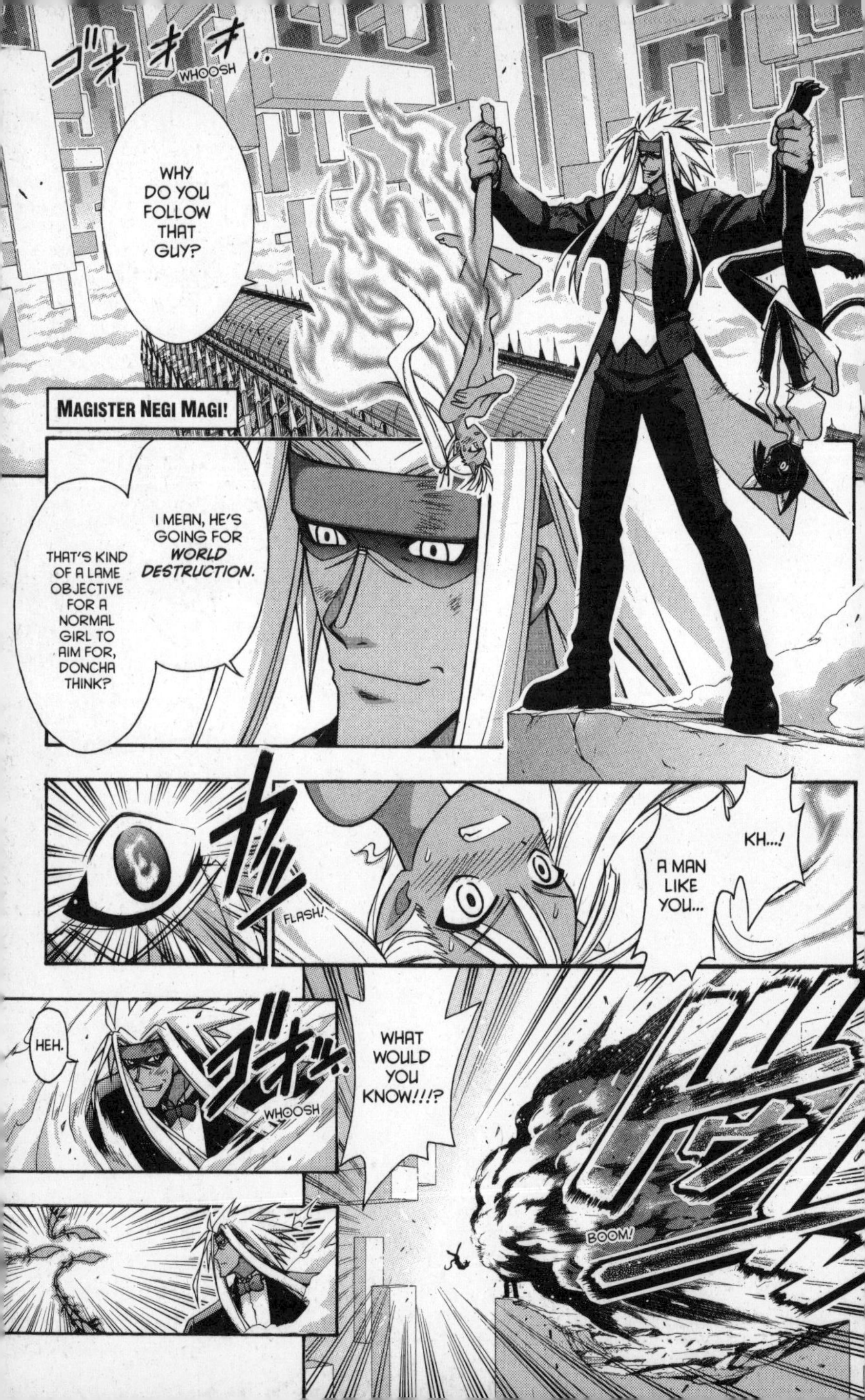
WHOOSH
WHY DO YOU FOLLOW THAT GUY?
MAGISTER NEGI MAGI!
I MEAN, HE'S GOING FOR WORLD DESTRUCTION.
THAT'S KIND OF A LAME OBJECTIVE FOR A NORMAL GIRL TO AIM FOR, DONCHA THINK?
KH...!
A MAN LIKE YOU...
FLASH!
WHAT WOULD YOU KNOW!!!?
BOOM!
HEH.
WHOOSH

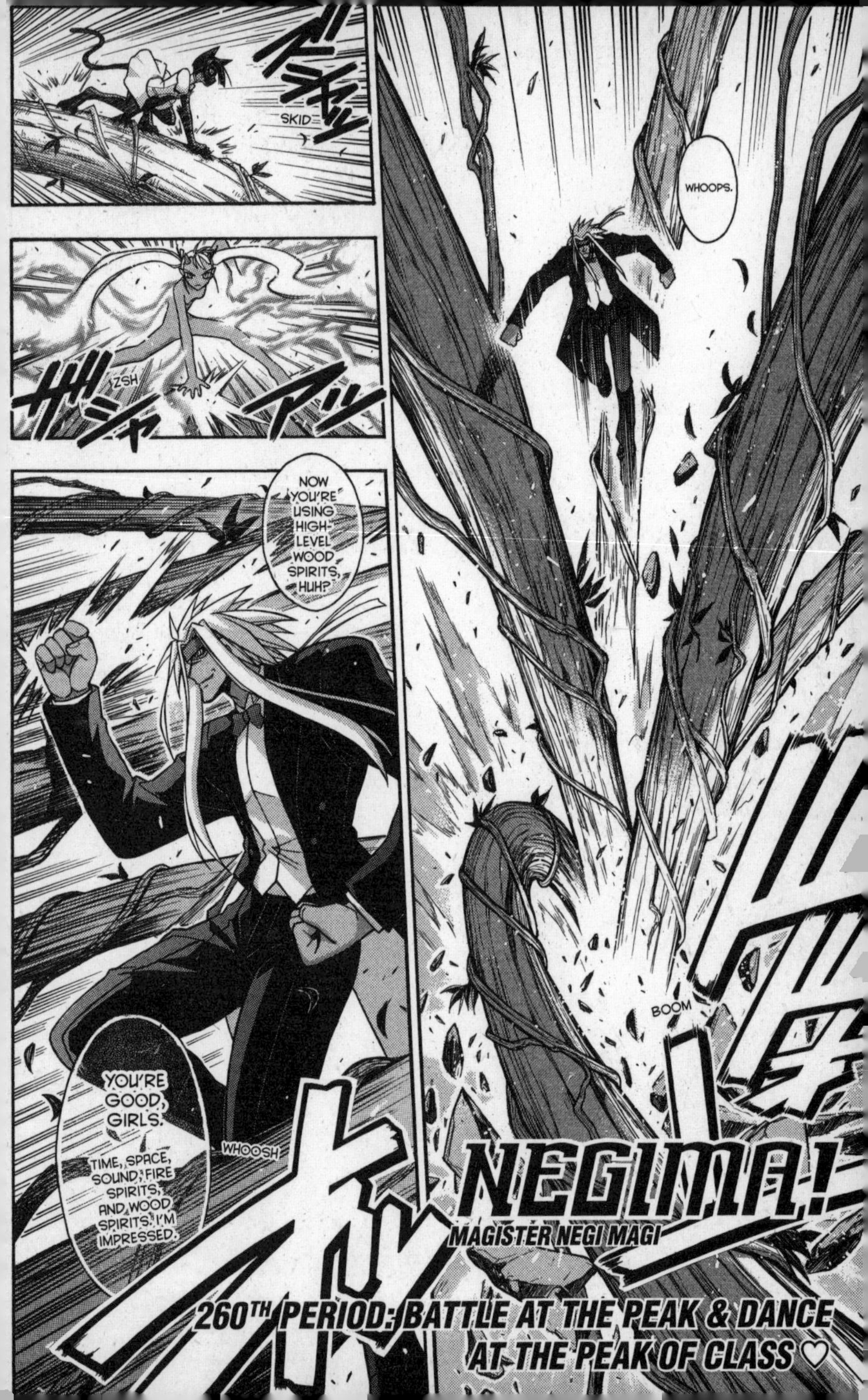
WHOOPS.
BOOM
SKID
ZSH
NOW YOU'RE USING HIGH-LEVEL WOOD SPIRITS, HUH?
YOU'RE GOOD, GIRLS.
TIME, SPACE, SOUND, FIRE SPIRITS, AND WOOD SPIRITS. I'M IMPRESSED.
WHOOSH
NEGIMA!
MAGISTER NEGI MAGI
260TH PERIOD: BATTLE AT THE PEAK & DANCE AT THE PEAK OF CLASS ♡

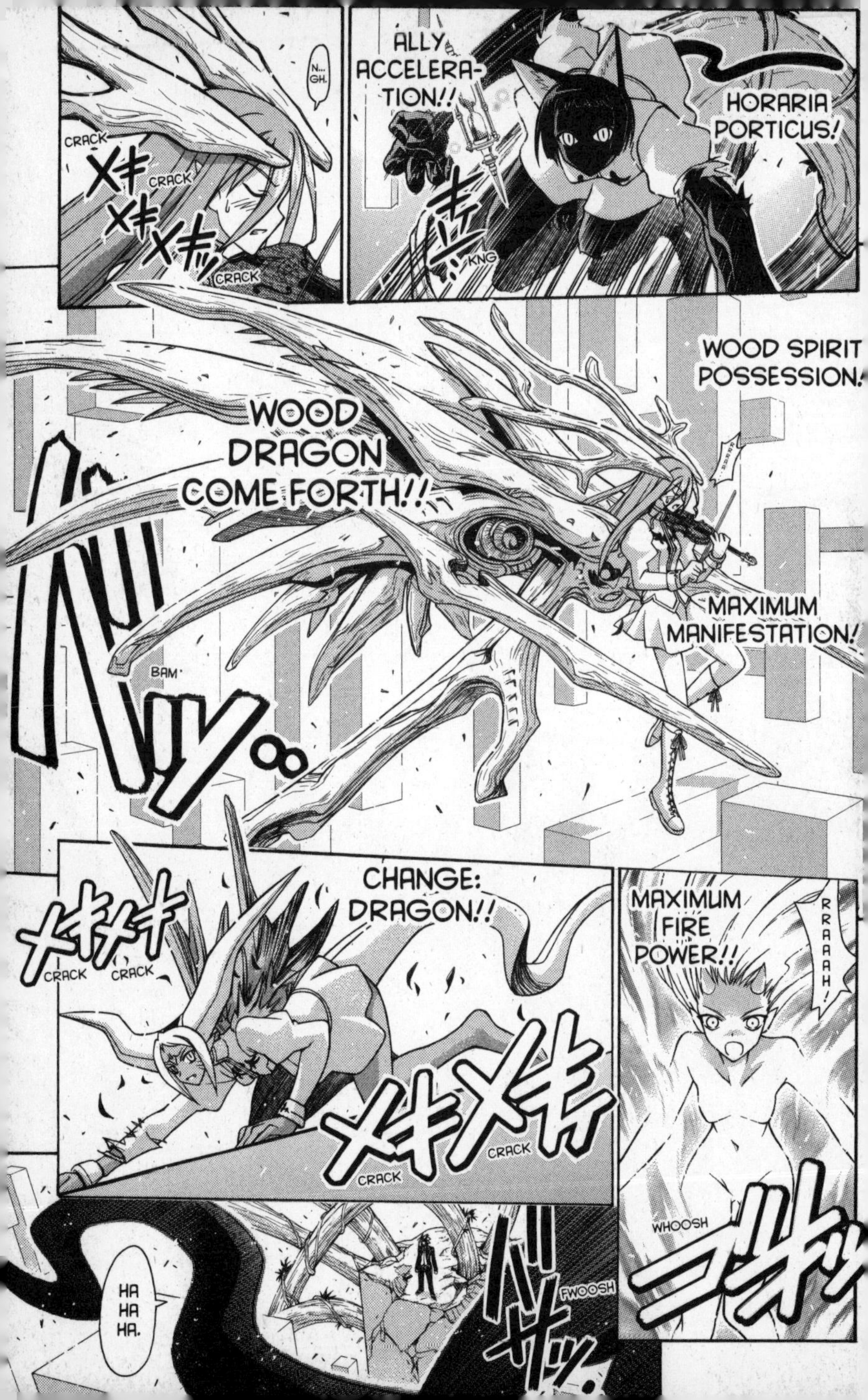
HORARIA PORTICUS!
ALLY ACCELERATION!!
KNG
N... GH.
CRACK
CRACK
CRACK
WOOD SPIRIT POSSESSION!
MAXIMUM MANIFESTATION!
WOOD DRAGON COME FORTH!!
BAM
RRAAAAH!
MAXIMUM FIRE POWER!!
WHOOSH
CHANGE: DRAGON!!
CRACK CRACK
CRACK
CRACK
FWOOSH
HA HA HA.

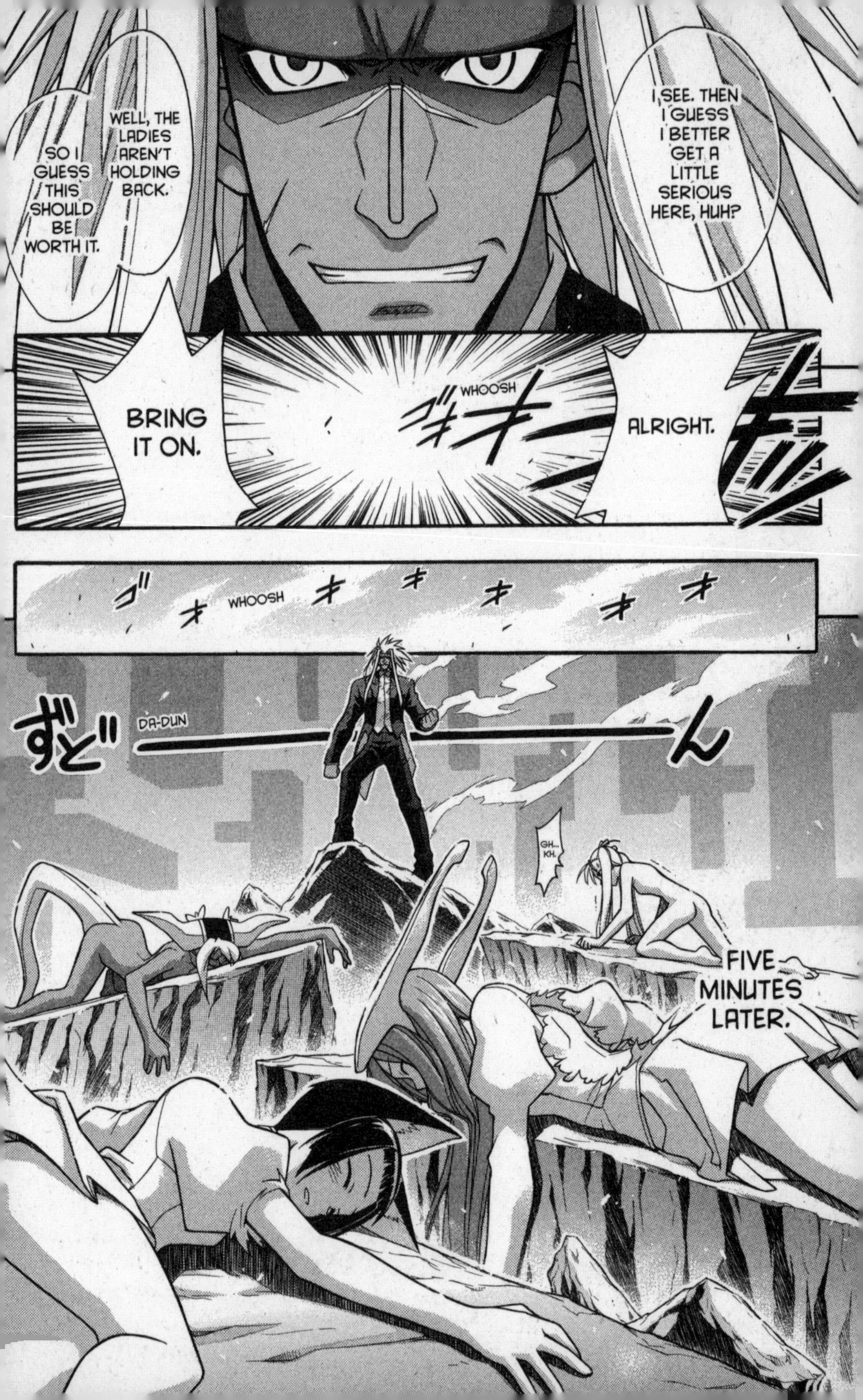

I SEE. THEN I GUESS I BETTER GET A LITTLE SERIOUS HERE, HUH?
WELL, THE LADIES AREN'T HOLDING BACK.
SO I GUESS THIS SHOULD BE WORTH IT.
ALRIGHT.
WHOOSH
BRING IT ON.
WHOOSH
DA-DUN
GH... KH.
FIVE MINUTES LATER.

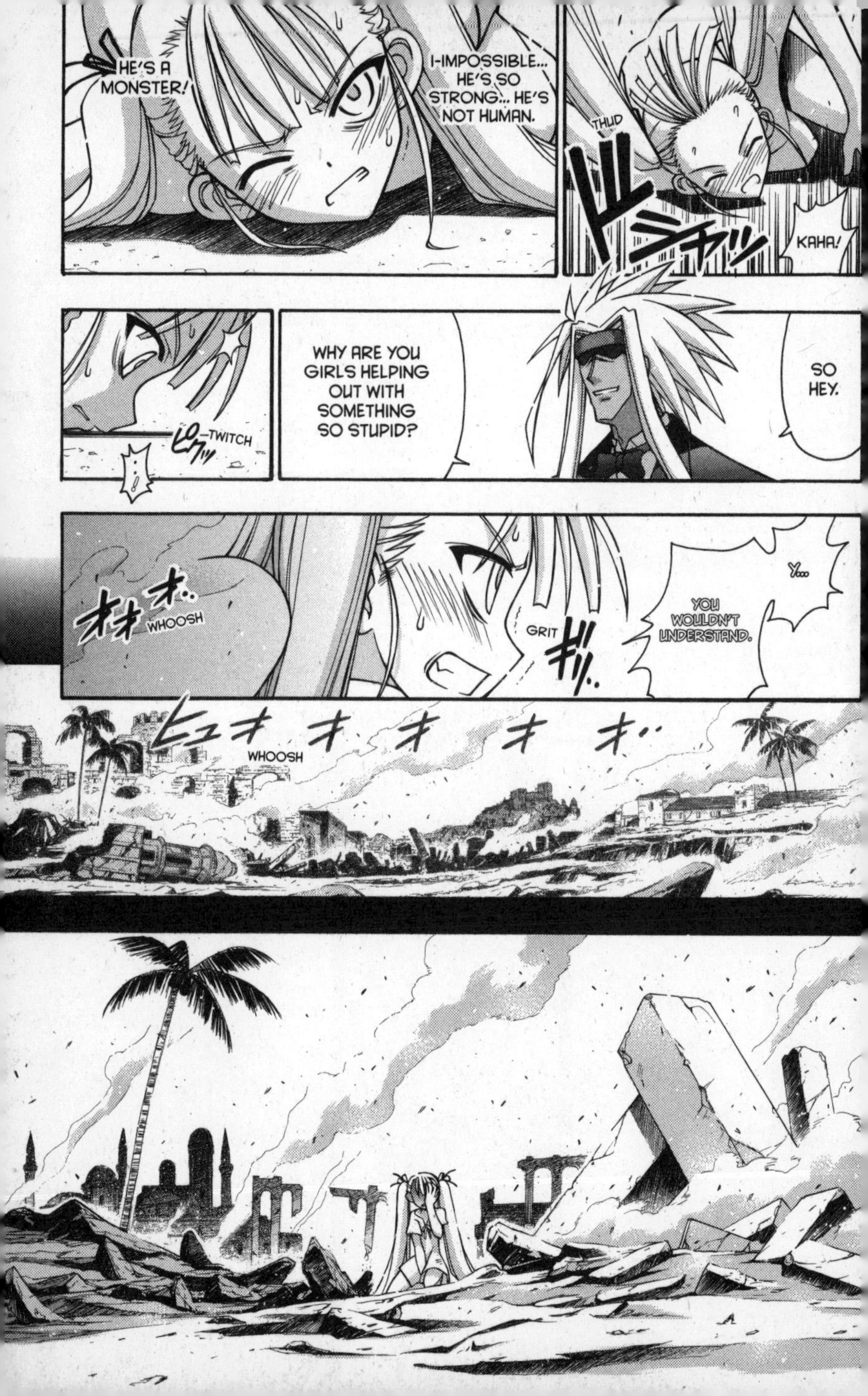

THUD
ドシャッ
KAHA!
I-IMPOSSIBLE... HE'S SO STRONG... HE'S NOT HUMAN.
HE'S A MONSTER!
SO HEY.
WHY ARE YOU GIRLS HELPING OUT WITH SOMETHING SO STUPID?
ピクッ TWITCH
!
Y...
YOU WOULDN'T UNDERSTAND.
ギリッ GRIT
オオオ.. WHOOSH
ヒュオオオオオ.. WHOOSH

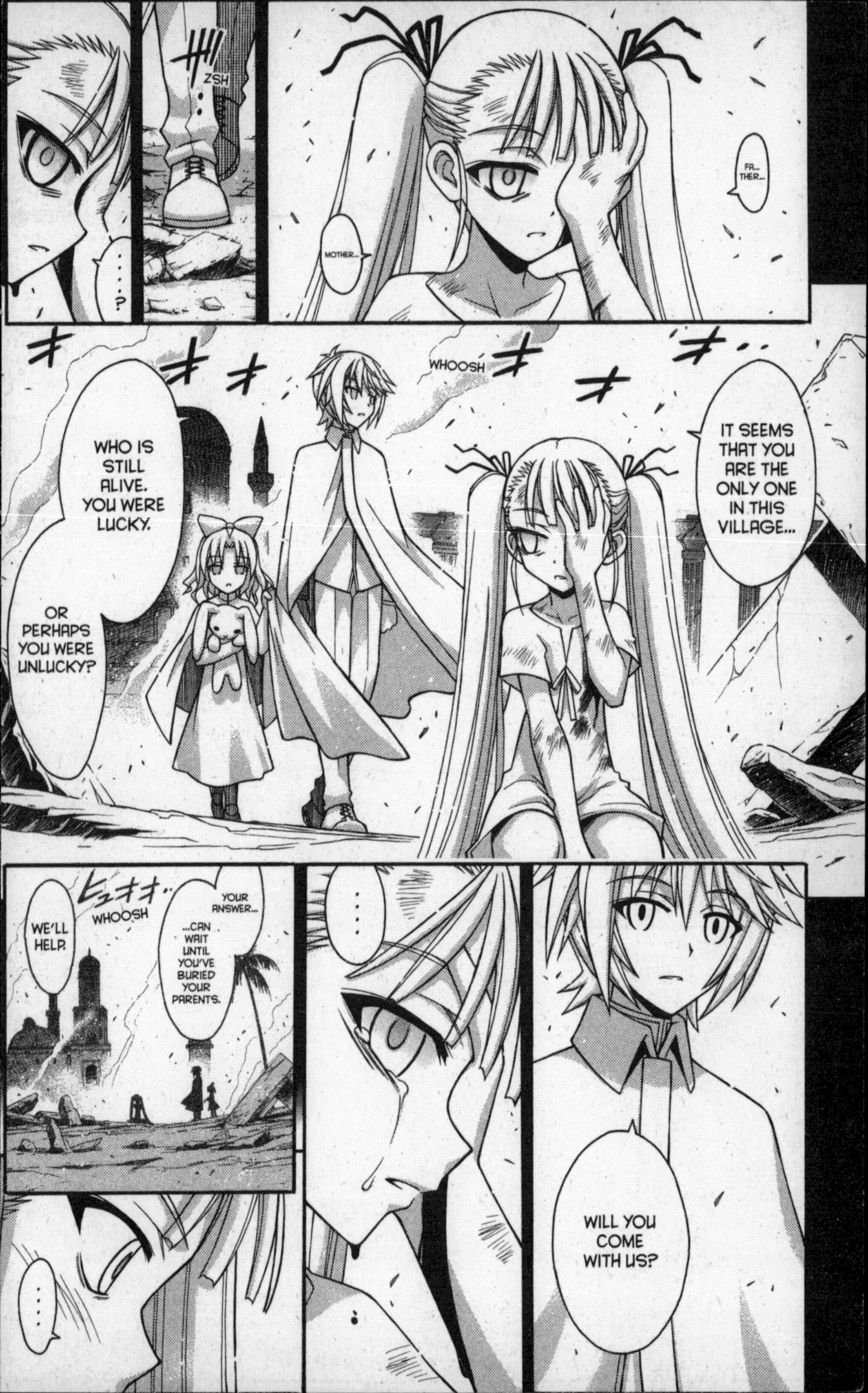
FA... THER...
MOTHER...
ZSH
....?
IT SEEMS THAT YOU ARE THE ONLY ONE IN THIS VILLAGE...
WHOOSH
WHO IS STILL ALIVE. YOU WERE LUCKY.
OR PERHAPS YOU WERE UNLUCKY?
WILL YOU COME WITH US?
....
YOUR ANSWER...
...CAN WAIT UNTIL YOU'VE BURIED YOUR PARENTS.
ヒュオオ
WHOOSH
WE'LL HELP.
....

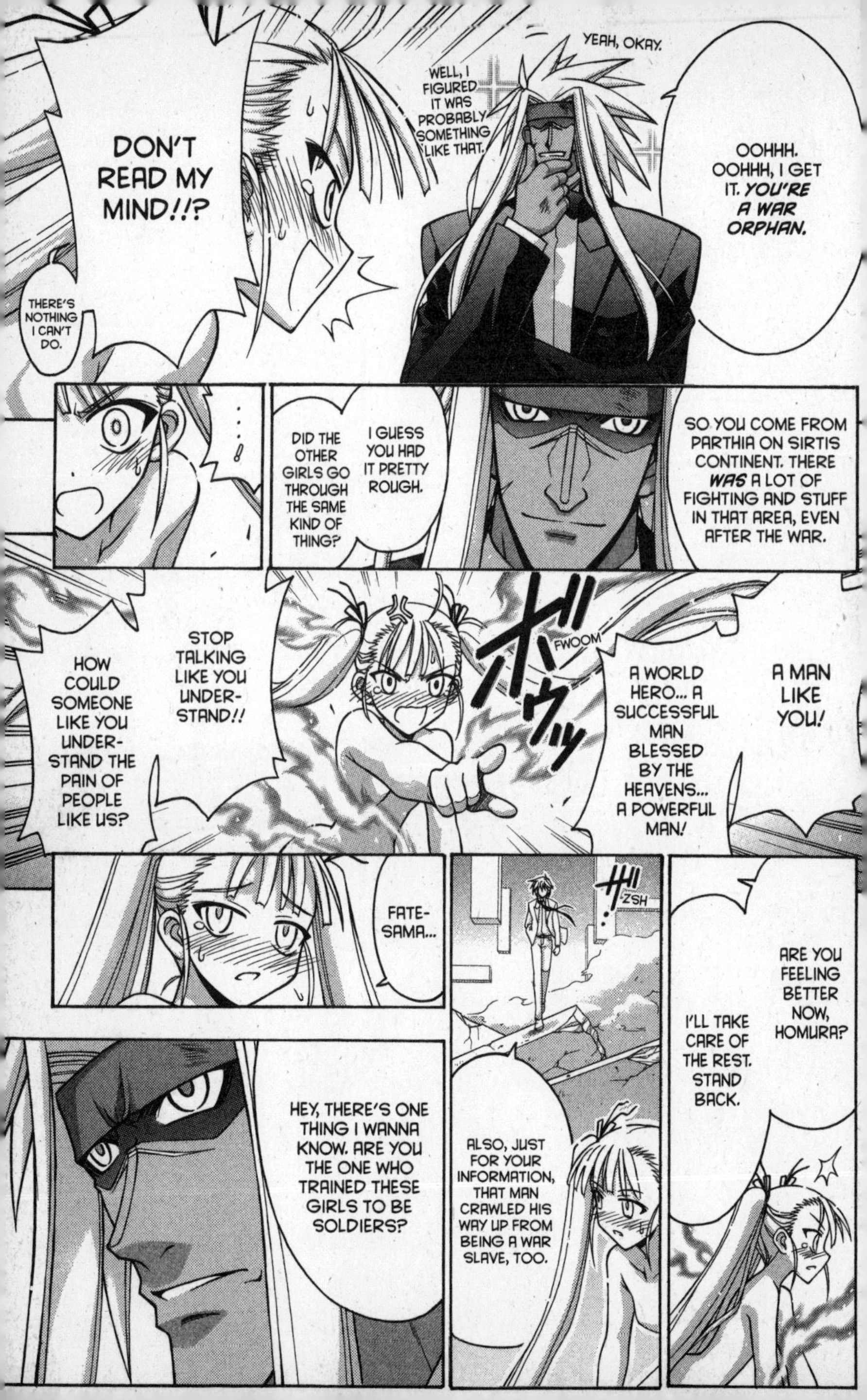
OOHHH. OOHHH, I GET IT. YOU'RE A WAR ORPHAN.
YEAH, OKAY.
WELL, I FIGURED IT WAS PROBABLY SOMETHING LIKE THAT.
DON'T READ MY MIND!!?
THERE'S NOTHING I CAN'T DO.
SO YOU COME FROM PARTHIA ON SIRTIS CONTINENT. THERE WAS A LOT OF FIGHTING AND STUFF IN THAT AREA, EVEN AFTER THE WAR.
I GUESS YOU HAD IT PRETTY ROUGH.
DID THE OTHER GIRLS GO THROUGH THE SAME KIND OF THING?
...!
A MAN LIKE YOU!
A WORLD HERO... A SUCCESSFUL MAN BLESSED BY THE HEAVENS... A POWERFUL MAN!
FWOOM
STOP TALKING LIKE YOU UNDER-STAND!!
HOW COULD SOMEONE LIKE YOU UNDER-STAND THE PAIN OF PEOPLE LIKE US?
ARE YOU FEELING BETTER NOW, HOMURA?
I'LL TAKE CARE OF THE REST. STAND BACK.
ZSH
ALSO, JUST FOR YOUR INFORMATION, THAT MAN CRAWLED HIS WAY UP FROM BEING A WAR SLAVE, TOO.
FATE-SAMA...
HEY, THERE'S ONE THING I WANNA KNOW. ARE YOU THE ONE WHO TRAINED THESE GIRLS TO BE SOLDIERS?

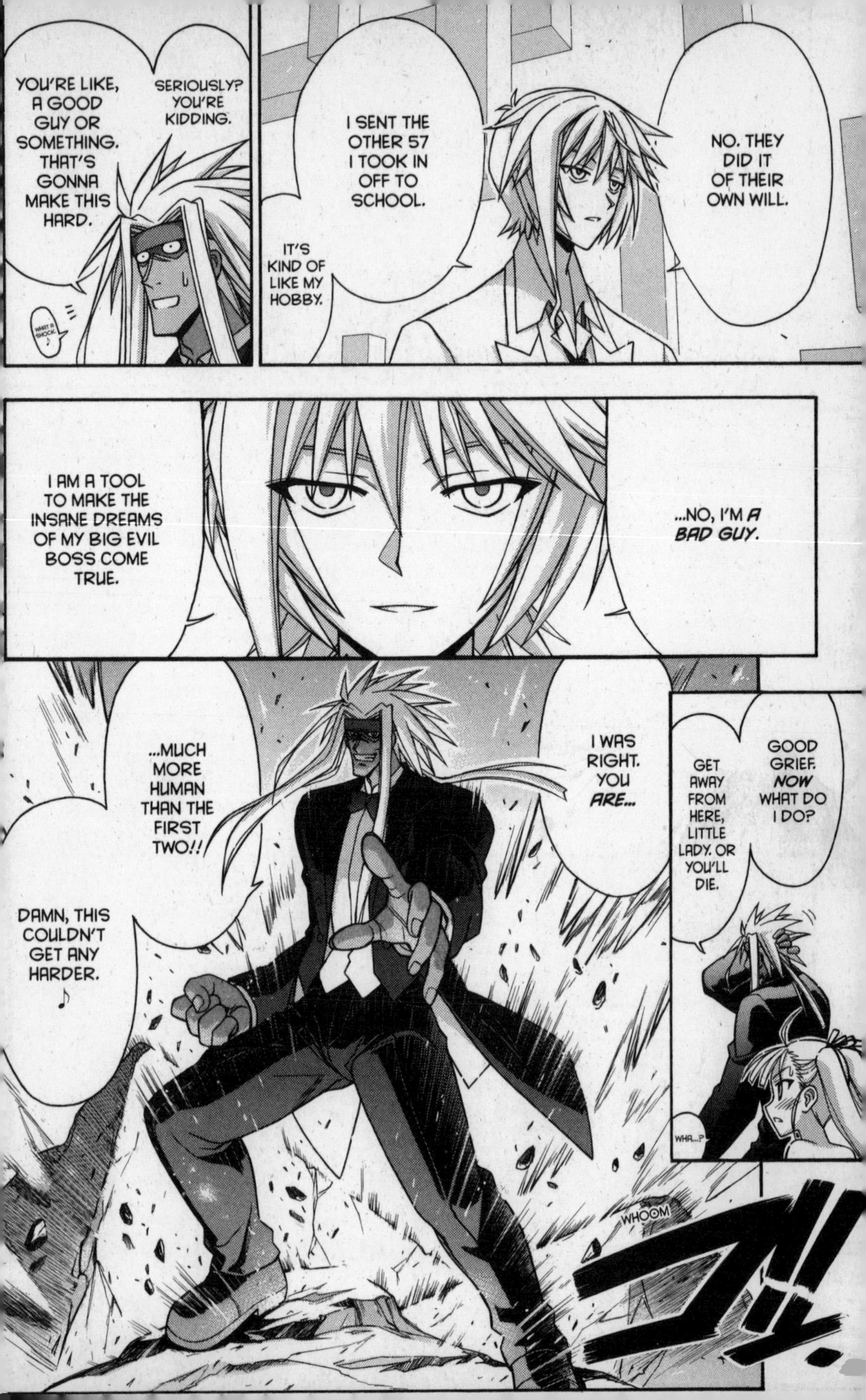
NO. THEY DID IT OF THEIR OWN WILL.
I SENT THE OTHER 57 I TOOK IN OFF TO SCHOOL.
IT'S KIND OF LIKE MY HOBBY.
SERIOUSLY? YOU'RE KIDDING.
YOU'RE LIKE, A GOOD GUY OR SOMETHING. THAT'S GONNA MAKE THIS HARD.
WHAT A SHOCK. ♪
...NO, I'M A *BAD GUY*.
I AM A TOOL TO MAKE THE INSANE DREAMS OF MY BIG EVIL BOSS COME TRUE.
GOOD GRIEF. *NOW* WHAT DO I DO?
GET AWAY FROM HERE, LITTLE LADY. OR YOU'LL DIE.
WHA...?
I WAS RIGHT. YOU *ARE*...
...MUCH MORE HUMAN THAN THE FIRST TWO!!
DAMN, THIS COULDN'T GET ANY HARDER. ♪
WHOOM

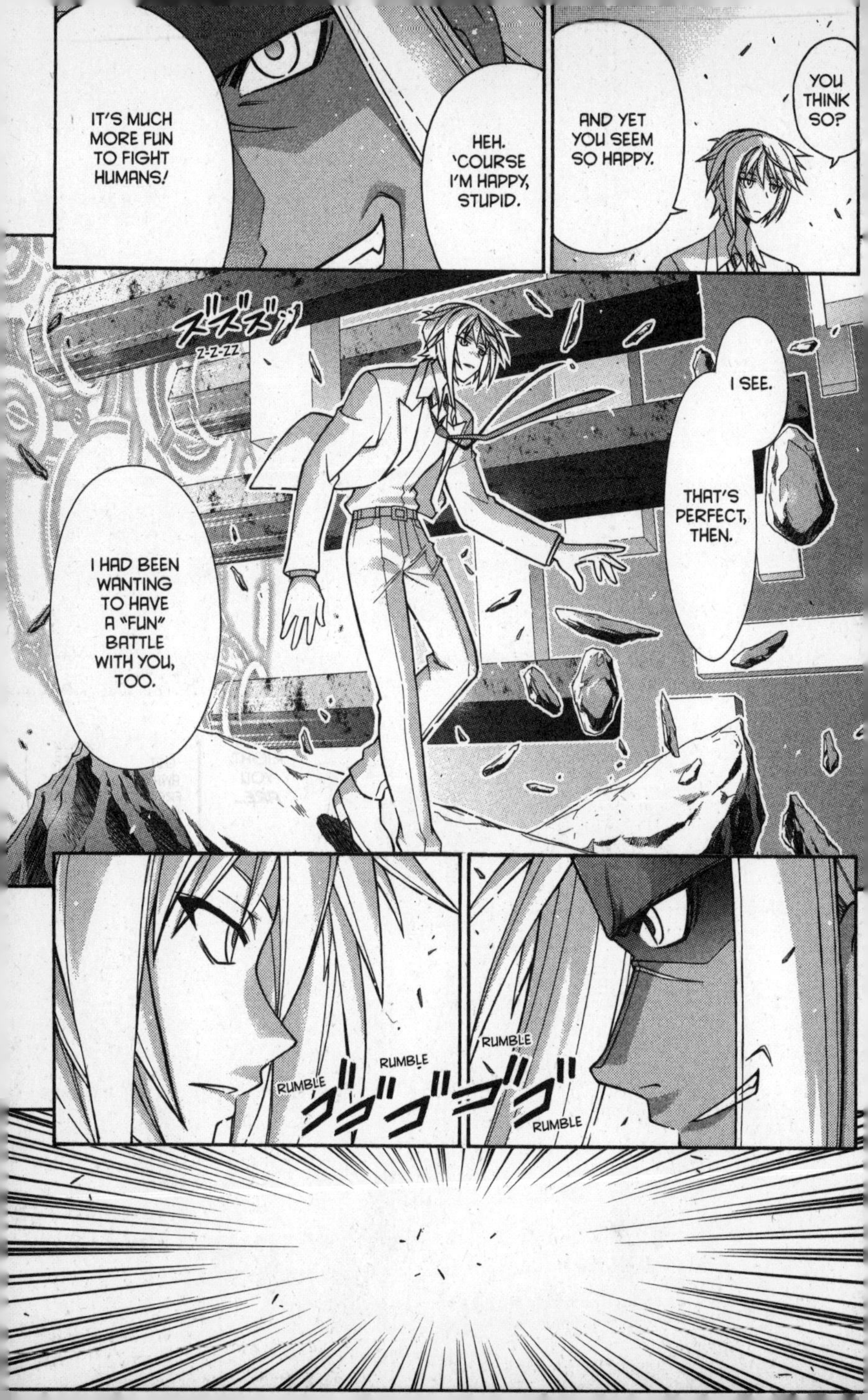
YOU THINK SO?
AND YET YOU SEEM SO HAPPY.
HEH. 'COURSE I'M HAPPY, STUPID.
IT'S MUCH MORE FUN TO FIGHT HUMANS!
I SEE.
THAT'S PERFECT, THEN.
ズズズッ
Z-Z-ZZ
I HAD BEEN WANTING TO HAVE A "FUN" BATTLE WITH YOU, TOO.
RUMBLE
RUMBLE
ゴゴゴゴ
RUMBLE
RUMBLE

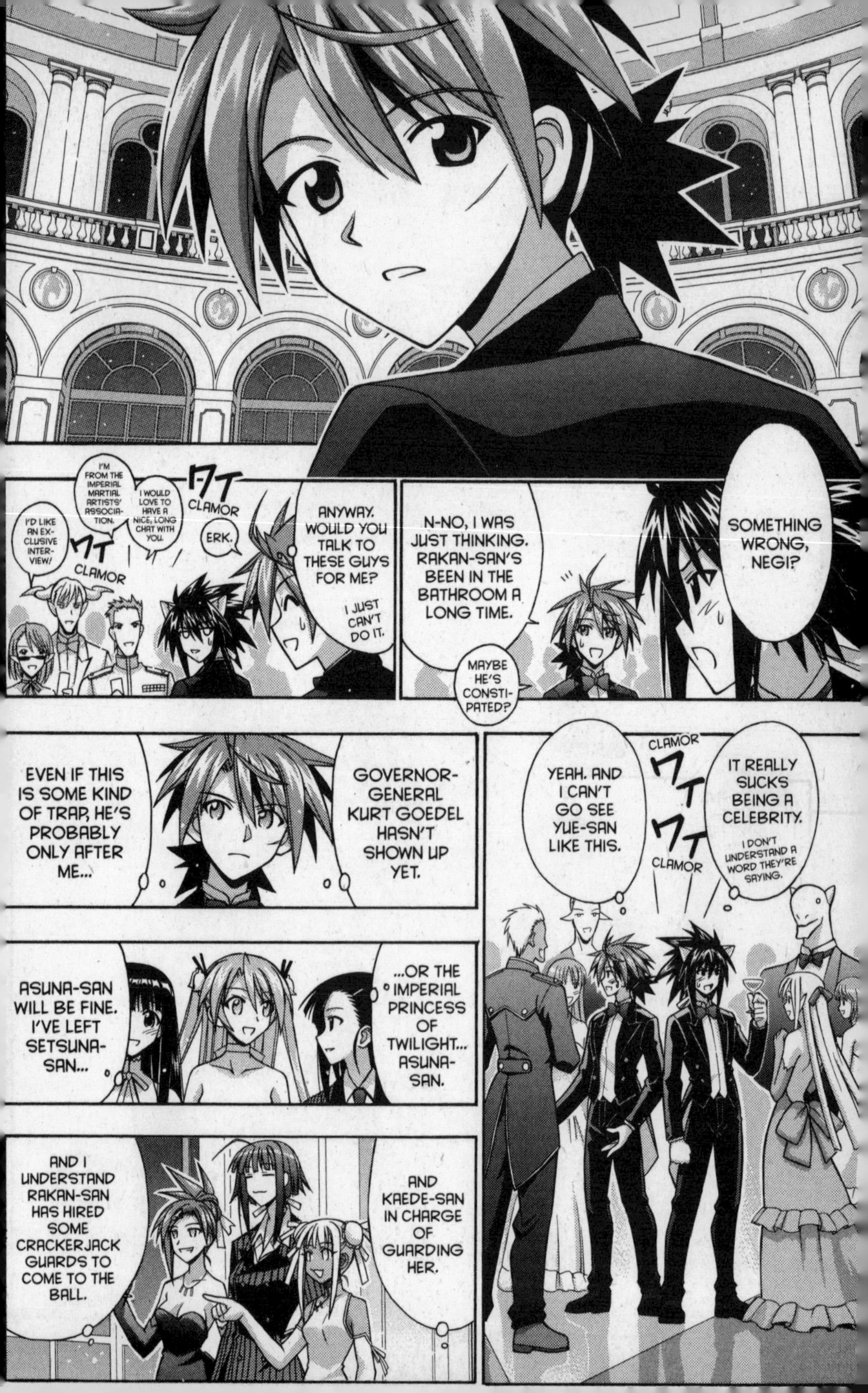
SOMETHING WRONG, NEGI?
N-NO, I WAS JUST THINKING. RAKAN-SAN'S BEEN IN THE BATHROOM A LONG TIME.
MAYBE HE'S CONSTIPATED?
ANYWAY. WOULD YOU TALK TO THESE GUYS FOR ME?
I JUST CAN'T DO IT.
CLAMOR
ERK.
I WOULD LOVE TO HAVE A NICE, LONG CHAT WITH YOU.
I'M FROM THE IMPERIAL MARTIAL ARTISTS' ASSOCIATION.
CLAMOR
I'D LIKE AN EXCLUSIVE INTERVIEW!
CLAMOR
IT REALLY SUCKS BEING A CELEBRITY.
I DON'T UNDERSTAND A WORD THEY'RE SAYING.
CLAMOR
YEAH. AND I CAN'T GO SEE YUE-SAN LIKE THIS.
GOVERNOR-GENERAL KURT GOEDEL HASN'T SHOWN UP YET.
EVEN IF THIS IS SOME KIND OF TRAP, HE'S PROBABLY ONLY AFTER ME...
...OR THE IMPERIAL PRINCESS OF TWILIGHT... ASUNA-SAN.
ASUNA-SAN WILL BE FINE. I'VE LEFT SETSUNA-SAN...
AND KAEDE-SAN IN CHARGE OF GUARDING HER.
AND I UNDERSTAND RAKAN-SAN HAS HIRED SOME CRACKERJACK GUARDS TO COME TO THE BALL.

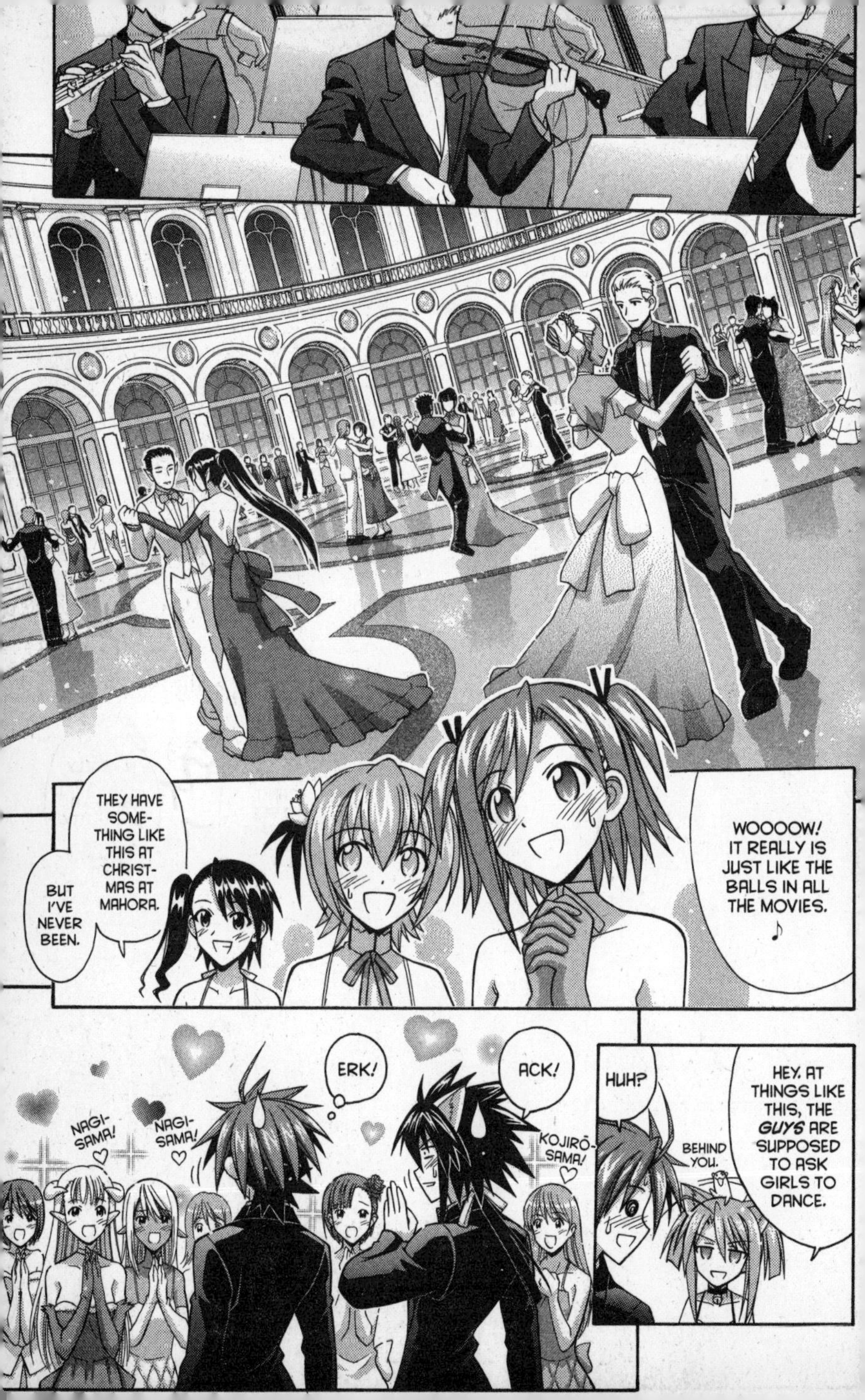
WOOOOW! IT REALLY IS JUST LIKE THE BALLS IN ALL THE MOVIES. ♪
THEY HAVE SOMETHING LIKE THIS AT CHRISTMAS AT MAHORA.
BUT I'VE NEVER BEEN.
HEY. AT THINGS LIKE THIS, THE *GUYS* ARE SUPPOSED TO ASK GIRLS TO DANCE.
HUH?
BEHIND YOU.
ACK!
KOJIRŌ-SAMA! ♡
ERK!
NAGI-SAMA! ♡
NAGI-SAMA! ♡

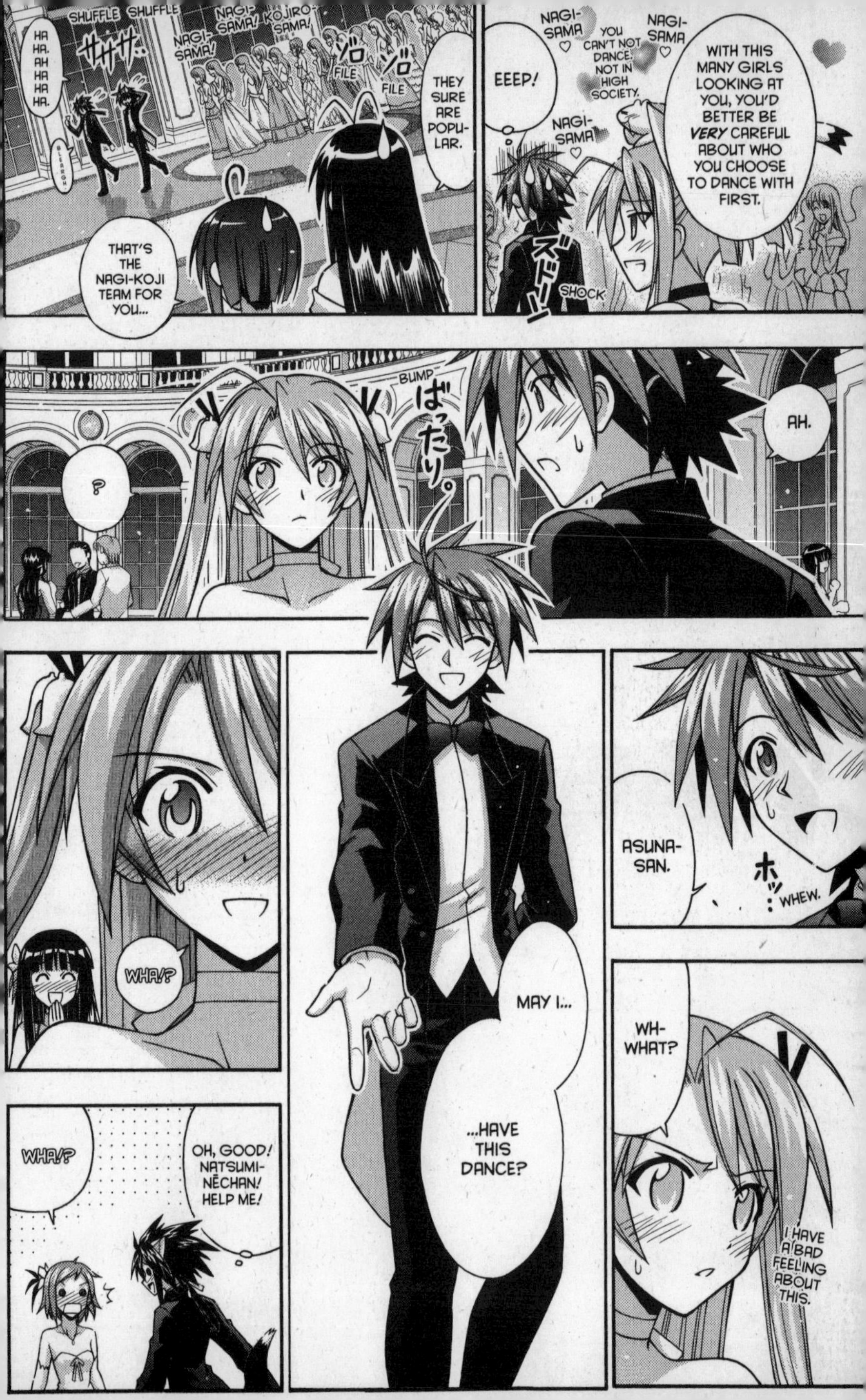

NAGI-SAMA ♡
YOU CAN'T NOT DANCE. NOT IN HIGH SOCIETY.
NAGI-SAMA ♡
WITH THIS MANY GIRLS LOOKING AT YOU, YOU'D BETTER BE *VERY* CAREFUL ABOUT WHO YOU CHOOSE TO DANCE WITH FIRST.
EEEP!
NAGI-SAMA ♡
SHOCK
KOJIRO-SAMA!
NAGI-SAMA!
NAGI-SAMA!
SHUFFLE SHUFFLE
HA HA. AH HA HA HA.
FILE
FILE
THEY SURE ARE POPU-LAR.
THAT'S THE NAGI-KOJI TEAM FOR YOU...
BUMP
AH.
?
ASUNA-SAN.
WHEW.
WH-WHAT?
I HAVE A BAD FEELING ABOUT THIS.
MAY I...
...HAVE THIS DANCE?
WHA!?
OH, GOOD! NATSUMI-NĒCHAN! HELP ME!
WHA!?

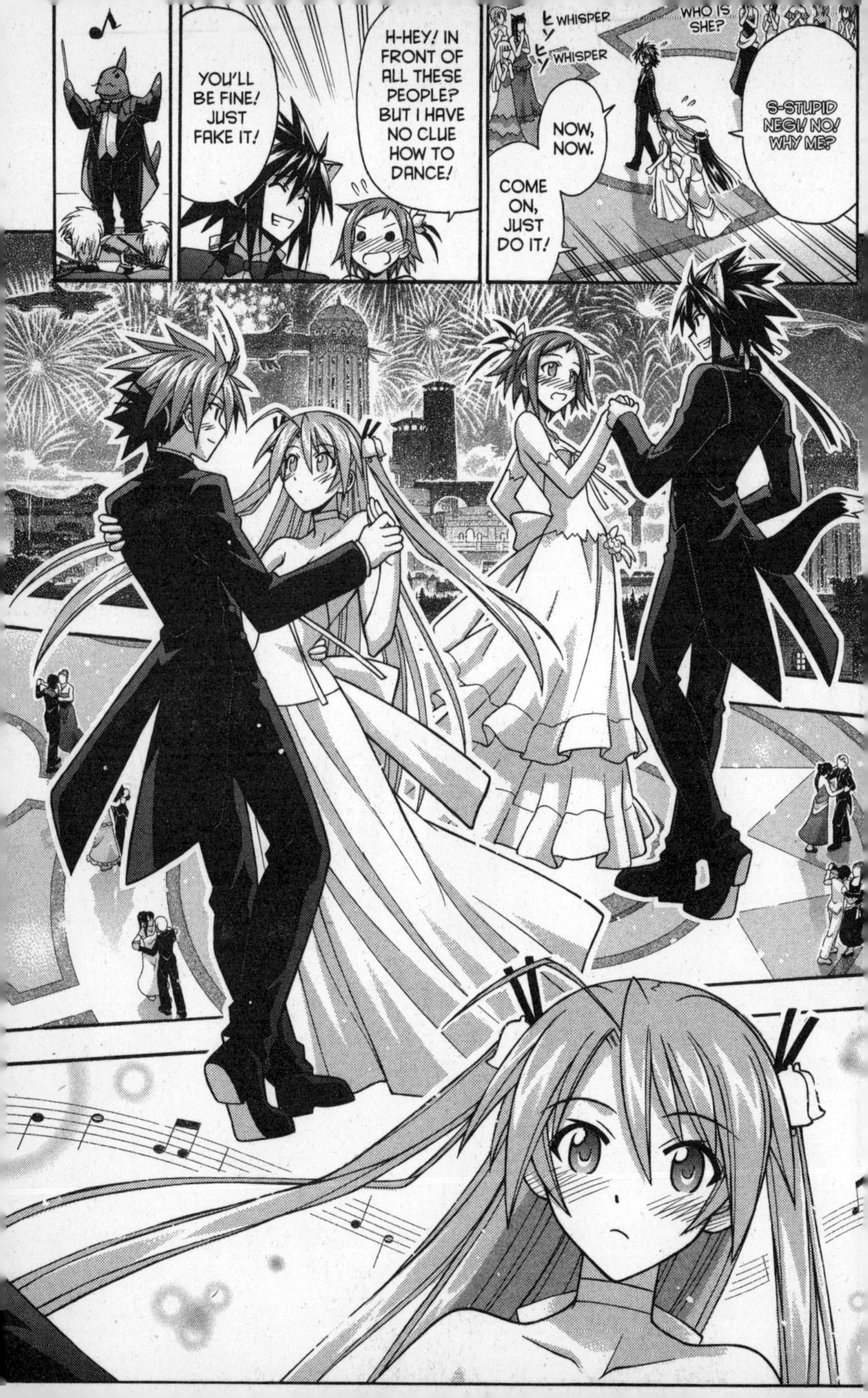
WHO IS SHE?
WHISPER
WHISPER
S-STUPID NEGI! NO! WHY ME?
NOW, NOW.
COME ON, JUST DO IT!
H-HEY! IN FRONT OF ALL THESE PEOPLE? BUT I HAVE NO CLUE HOW TO DANCE!
YOU'LL BE FINE! JUST FAKE IT!

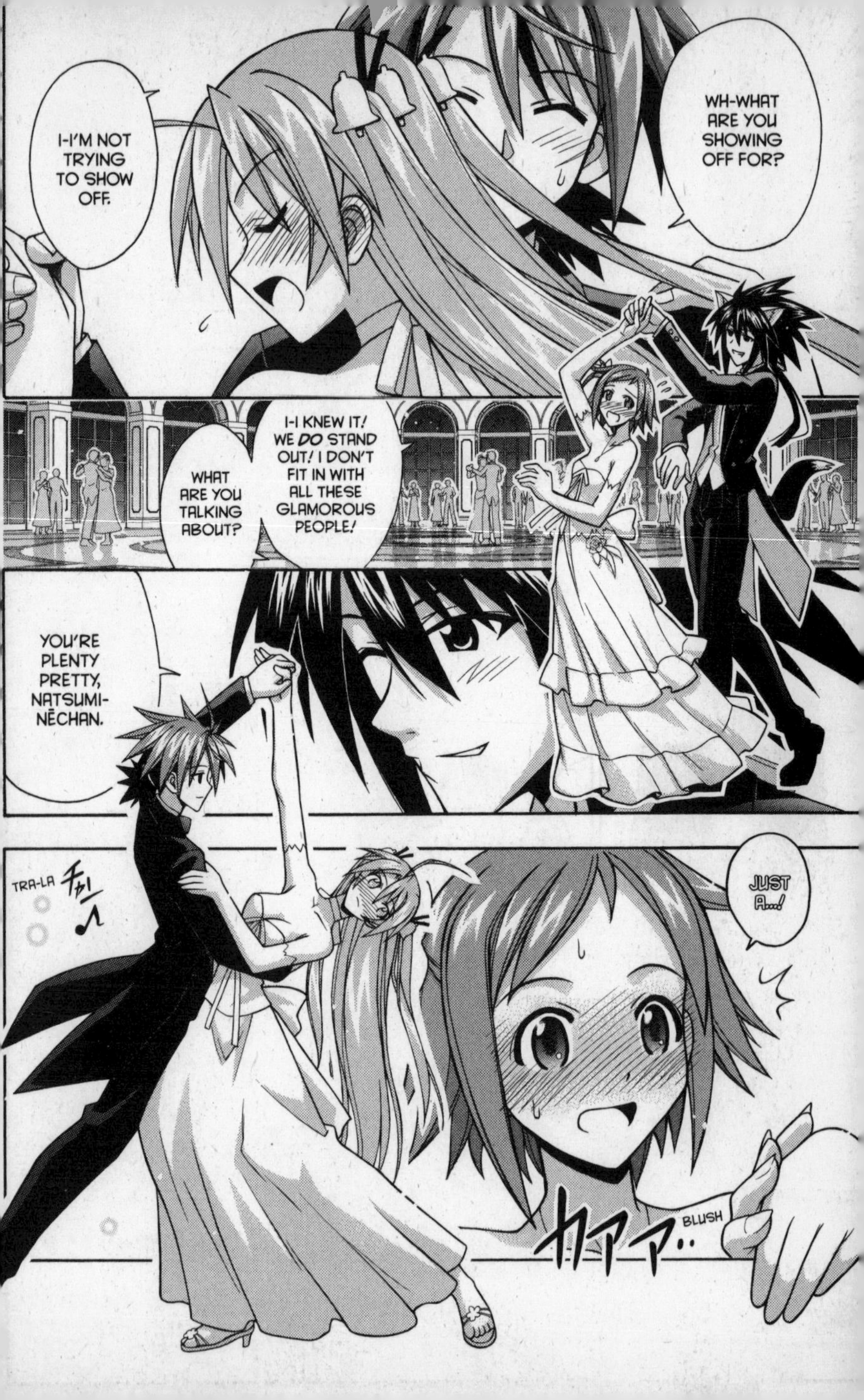
WH-WHAT ARE YOU SHOWING OFF FOR?
I-I'M NOT TRYING TO SHOW OFF.
I-I KNEW IT! WE DO STAND OUT! I DON'T FIT IN WITH ALL THESE GLAMOROUS PEOPLE!
WHAT ARE YOU TALKING ABOUT?
YOU'RE PLENTY PRETTY, NATSUMI-NĒCHAN.
JUST A...!
BLUSH
TRA-LA

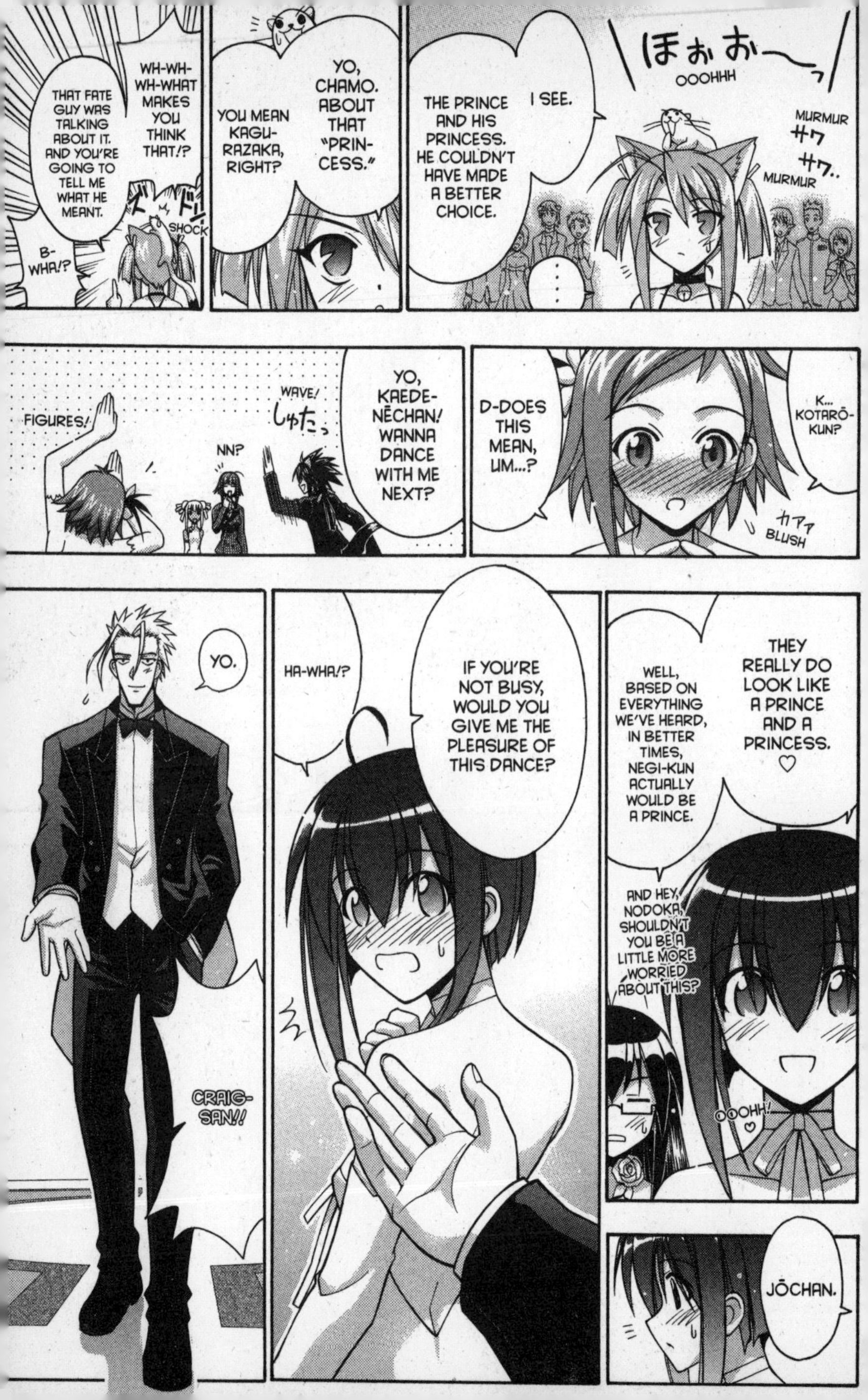
ほぉおー っ
OOOHHH
MURMUR サワ
サワ.. MURMUR
I SEE.
THE PRINCE AND HIS PRINCESS. HE COULDN'T HAVE MADE A BETTER CHOICE.
...
YO, CHAMO. ABOUT THAT "PRINCESS."
YOU MEAN KAGURAZAKA, RIGHT?
WH-WH-WH-WHAT MAKES YOU THINK THAT!?
THAT FATE GUY WAS TALKING ABOUT IT. AND YOU'RE GOING TO TELL ME WHAT HE MEANT.
ズドッ SHOCK
B-WHA!?
K... KOTARŌ-KUN?
D-DOES THIS MEAN, UM...?
カァァ BLUSH
YO, KAEDE-NĒCHAN! WANNA DANCE WITH ME NEXT?
WAVE! しゅたっ
NN?
FIGURES!
THEY REALLY DO LOOK LIKE A PRINCE AND A PRINCESS. ♡
WELL, BASED ON EVERYTHING WE'VE HEARD, IN BETTER TIMES, NEGI-KUN ACTUALLY WOULD BE A PRINCE.
AND HEY, NODOKA, SHOULDN'T YOU BE A LITTLE MORE WORRIED ABOUT THIS?
OOOHH! ♡
JŌCHAN.
IF YOU'RE NOT BUSY, WOULD YOU GIVE ME THE PLEASURE OF THIS DANCE?
HA-WHA!?
YO.
CRAIG-SAN!!

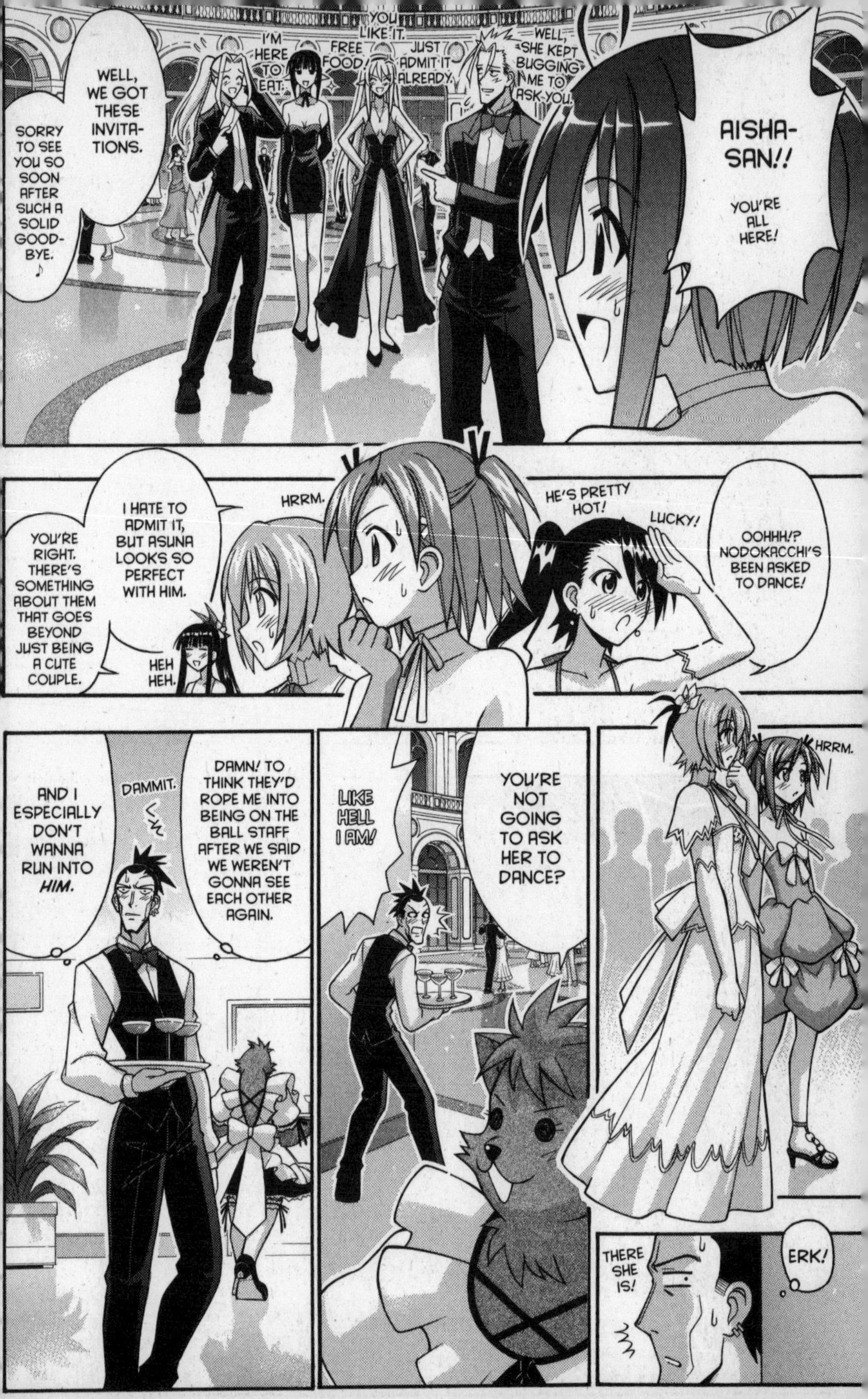
AISHA-SAN!!
YOU'RE ALL HERE!
WELL, SHE KEPT BUGGING ME TO ASK YOU.
JUST ADMIT IT ALREADY.
YOU LIKE IT.
FREE FOOD.
I'M HERE TO EAT.
WELL, WE GOT THESE INVITATIONS.
SORRY TO SEE YOU SO SOON AFTER SUCH A SOLID GOOD-BYE. ♪
OOHHH!? NODOKACCHI'S BEEN ASKED TO DANCE!
LUCKY!
HE'S PRETTY HOT!
HRRM.
I HATE TO ADMIT IT, BUT ASUNA LOOKS SO PERFECT WITH HIM.
YOU'RE RIGHT. THERE'S SOMETHING ABOUT THEM THAT GOES BEYOND JUST BEING A CUTE COUPLE.
HEH HEH.
HRRM.
ERK!
THERE SHE IS!
YOU'RE NOT GOING TO ASK HER TO DANCE?
LIKE HELL I AM!
DAMN! TO THINK THEY'D ROPE ME INTO BEING ON THE BALL STAFF AFTER WE SAID WE WEREN'T GONNA SEE EACH OTHER AGAIN.
DAMMIT.
AND I ESPECIALLY DON'T WANNA RUN INTO *HIM*.

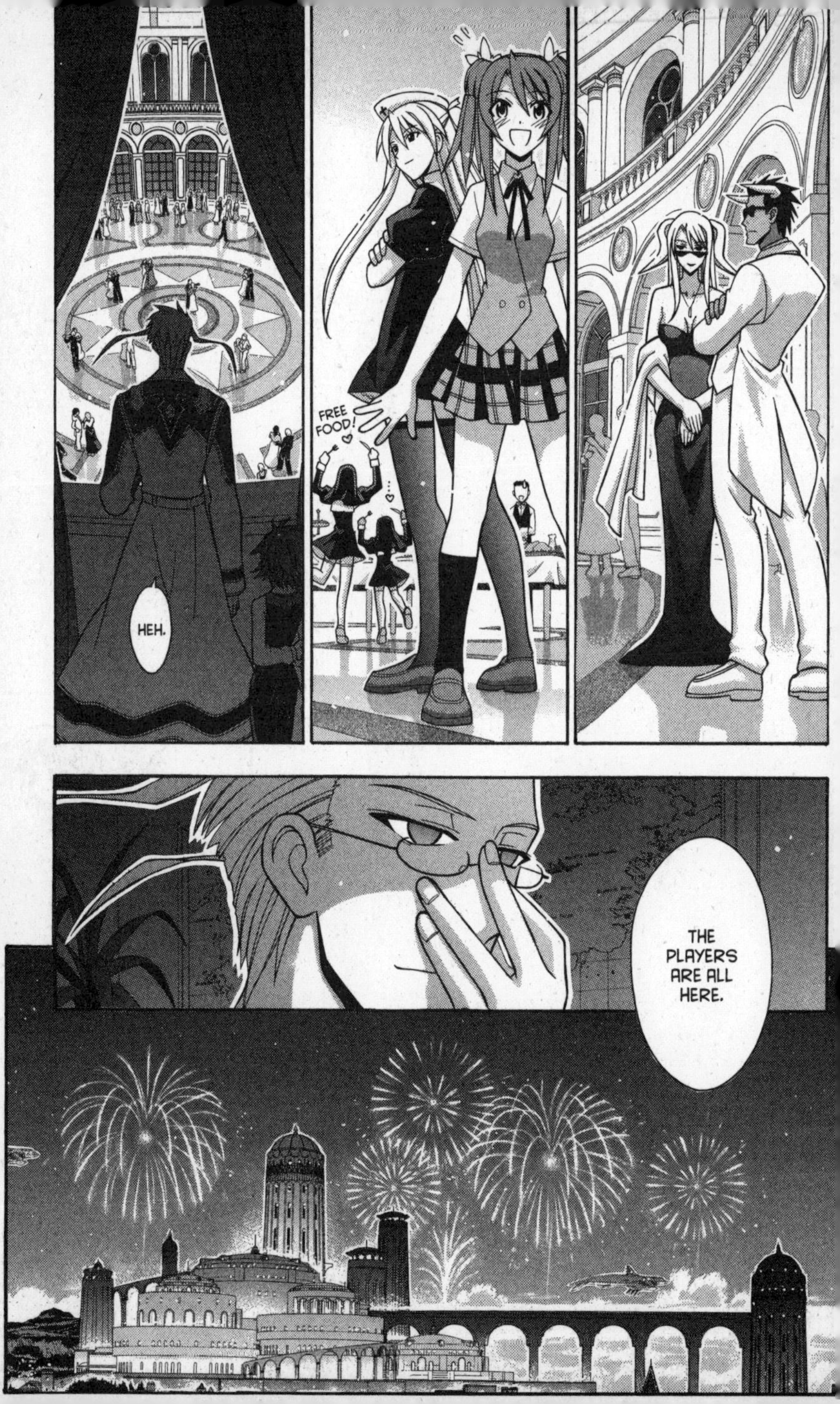
FREE FOOD!
HEH.
THE PLAYERS ARE ALL HERE.

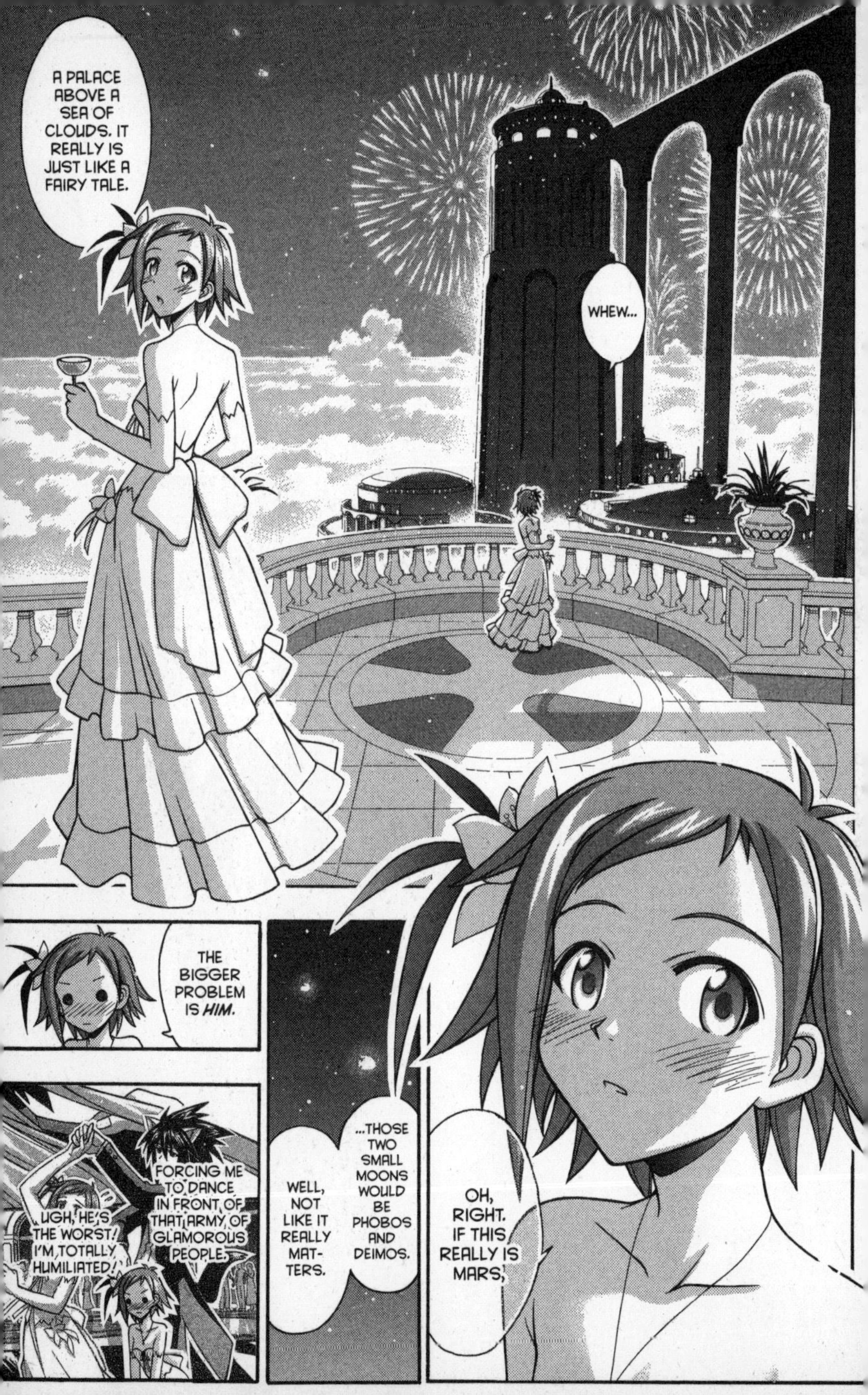
WHEW...
A PALACE ABOVE A SEA OF CLOUDS. IT REALLY IS JUST LIKE A FAIRY TALE.
OH, RIGHT. IF THIS REALLY IS MARS,
...THOSE TWO SMALL MOONS WOULD BE PHOBOS AND DEIMOS.
WELL, NOT LIKE IT REALLY MAT-TERS.
THE BIGGER PROBLEM IS *HIM*.
FORCING ME TO DANCE IN FRONT OF THAT ARMY OF GLAMOROUS PEOPLE.
UGH, HE'S THE WORST! I'M TOTALLY HUMILIATED!

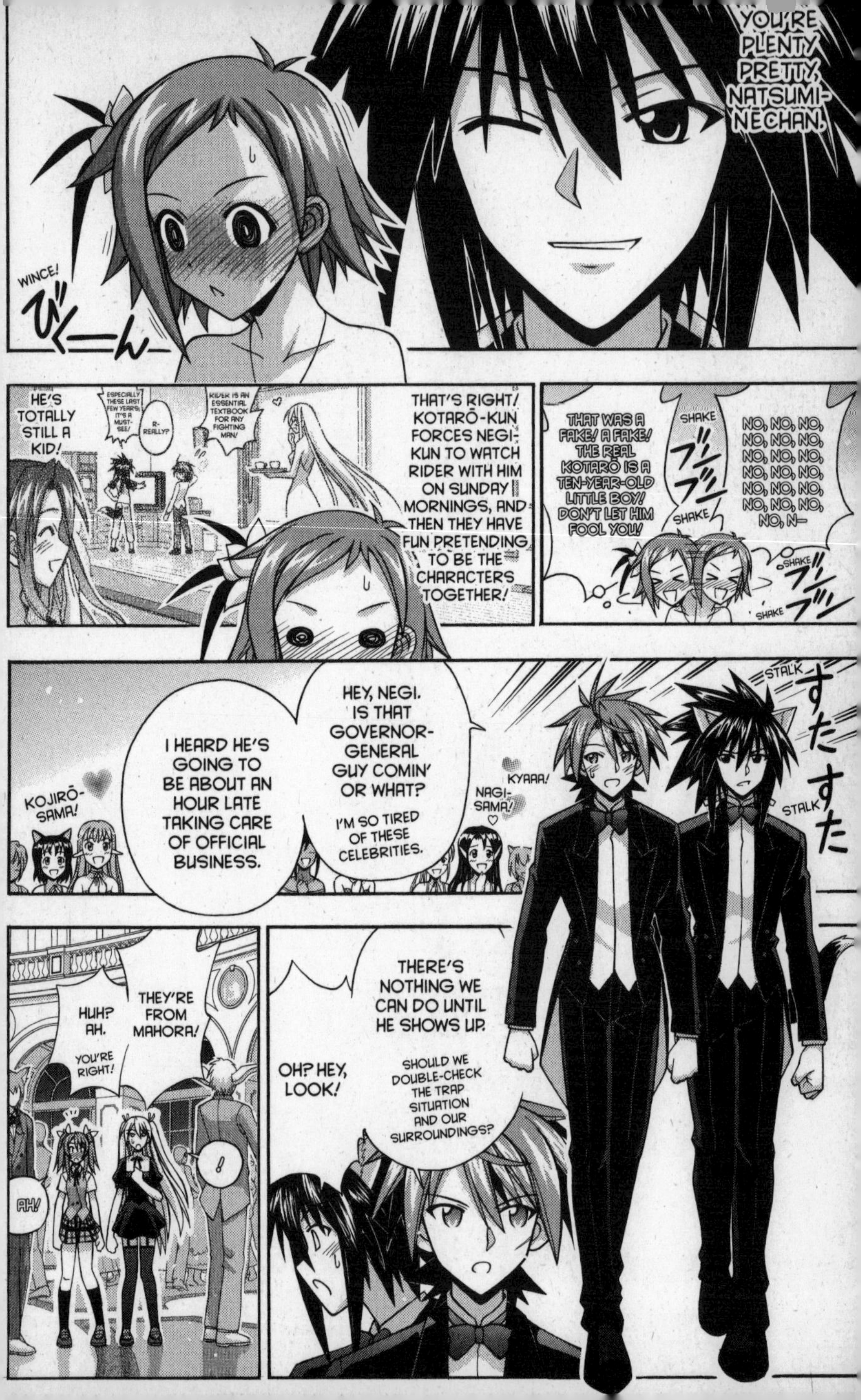
YOU'RE PLENTY PRETTY, NATSUMI-NECHAN.
WINCE!
びくーん
NO, NO, NO, NO, NO, NO, NO, NO, NO, NO, NO, NO, NO, NO, NO, NO, NO, NO, NO, N—
SHAKE
SHAKE
THAT WAS A FAKE! A FAKE! THE REAL KOTARŌ IS A TEN-YEAR-OLD LITTLE BOY! DON'T LET HIM FOOL YOU!
SHAKE
SHAKE
THAT'S RIGHT! KOTARŌ-KUN FORCES NEGI-KUN TO WATCH RIDER WITH HIM ON SUNDAY MORNINGS, AND THEN THEY HAVE FUN PRETENDING TO BE THE CHARACTERS TOGETHER!
RIDER IS AN ESSENTIAL TEXTBOOK FOR ANY FIGHTING MAN!
R-REALLY?
ESPECIALLY THESE LAST FEW YEARS, IT'S A MUST-SEE!
HE'S TOTALLY STILL A KID!
STALK
すたすた
STALK
KYAAA!
NAGI-SAMA!
HEY, NEGI. IS THAT GOVERNOR-GENERAL GUY COMIN' OR WHAT?
I'M SO TIRED OF THESE CELEBRITIES.
I HEARD HE'S GOING TO BE ABOUT AN HOUR LATE TAKING CARE OF OFFICIAL BUSINESS.
KOJIRŌ-SAMA!
THERE'S NOTHING WE CAN DO UNTIL HE SHOWS UP.
SHOULD WE DOUBLE-CHECK THE TRAP SITUATION AND OUR SURROUNDINGS?
OH? HEY, LOOK!
!
THEY'RE FROM MAHORA!
HUH? AH.
YOU'RE RIGHT!
AH!

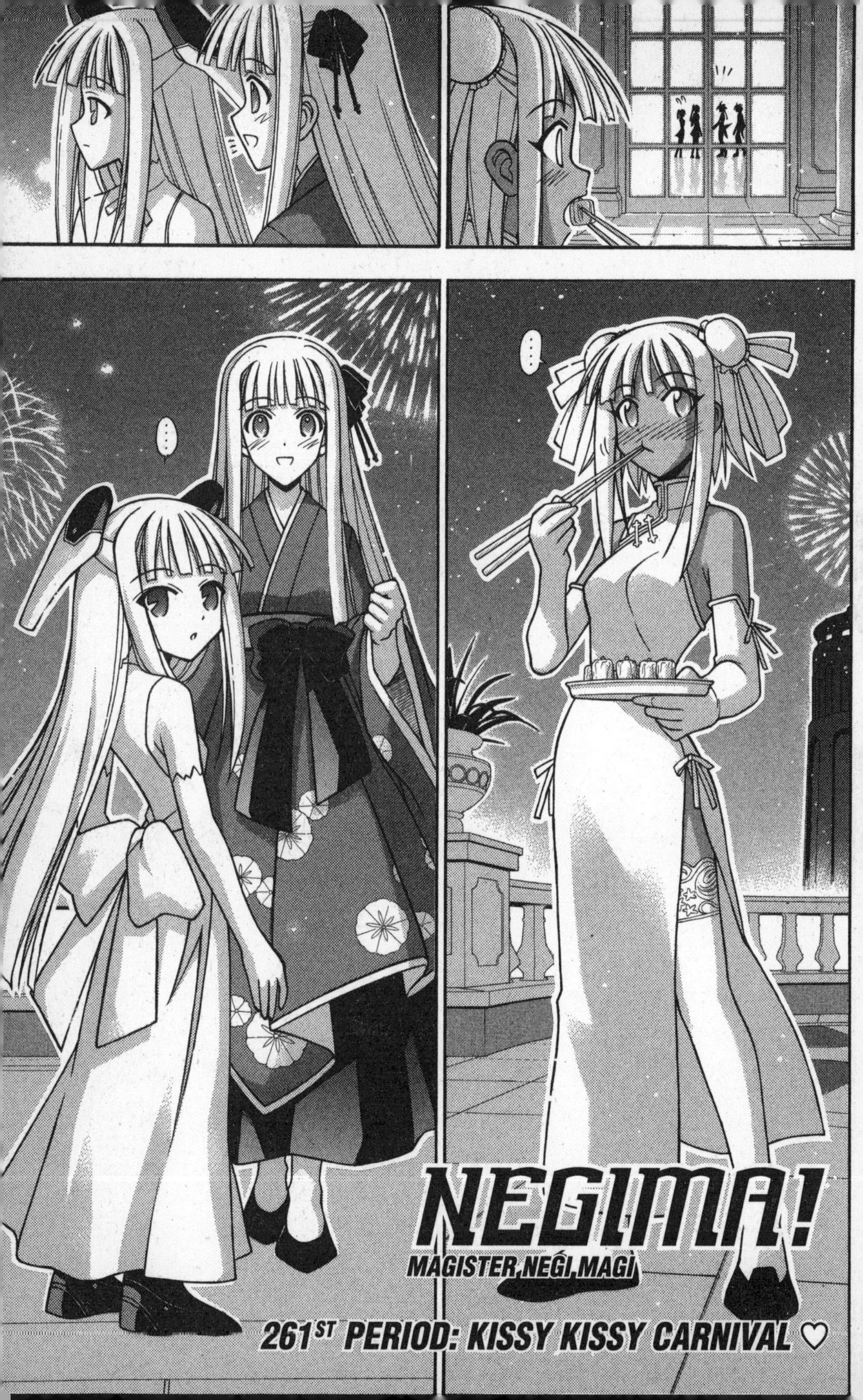
…
NEGIMA!
MAGISTER NEGI MAGI
261ST PERIOD: KISSY KISSY CARNIVAL ♡
…

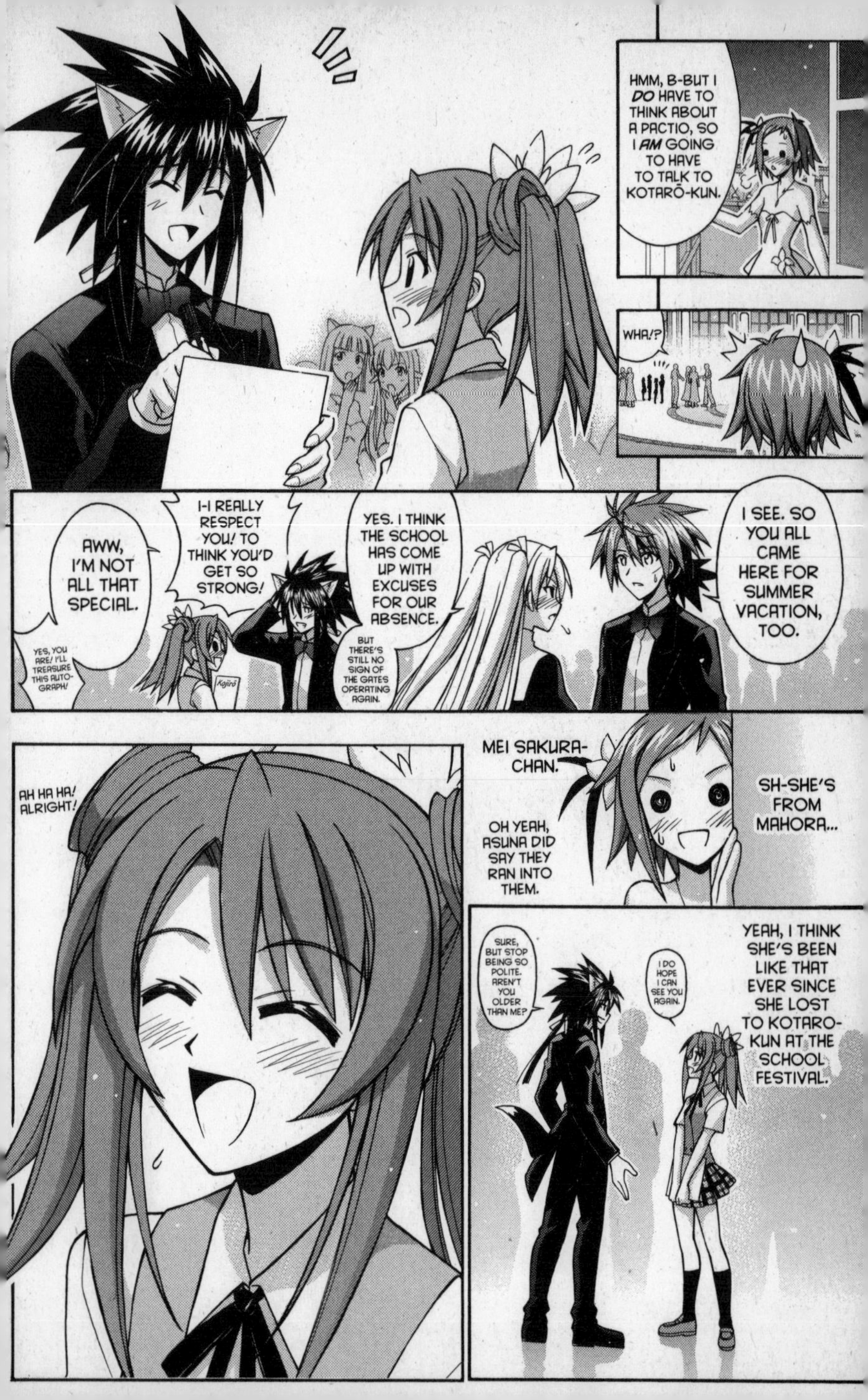
HMM, B-BUT I DO HAVE TO THINK ABOUT A PACTIO, SO I AM GOING TO HAVE TO TALK TO KOTARŌ-KUN.
WHA!?
I SEE. SO YOU ALL CAME HERE FOR SUMMER VACATION, TOO.
YES. I THINK THE SCHOOL HAS COME UP WITH EXCUSES FOR OUR ABSENCE.
BUT THERE'S STILL NO SIGN OF THE GATES OPERATING AGAIN.
I-I REALLY RESPECT YOU! TO THINK YOU'D GET SO STRONG!
AWW, I'M NOT ALL THAT SPECIAL.
YES, YOU ARE! I'LL TREASURE THIS AUTOGRAPH!
Kojirō
SH-SHE'S FROM MAHORA...
MEI SAKURA-CHAN.
OH YEAH, ASUNA DID SAY THEY RAN INTO THEM.
YEAH, I THINK SHE'S BEEN LIKE THAT EVER SINCE SHE LOST TO KOTARO-KUN AT THE SCHOOL FESTIVAL.
I DO HOPE I CAN SEE YOU AGAIN.
SURE, BUT STOP BEING SO POLITE. AREN'T YOU OLDER THAN ME?
AH HA HA! ALRIGHT!

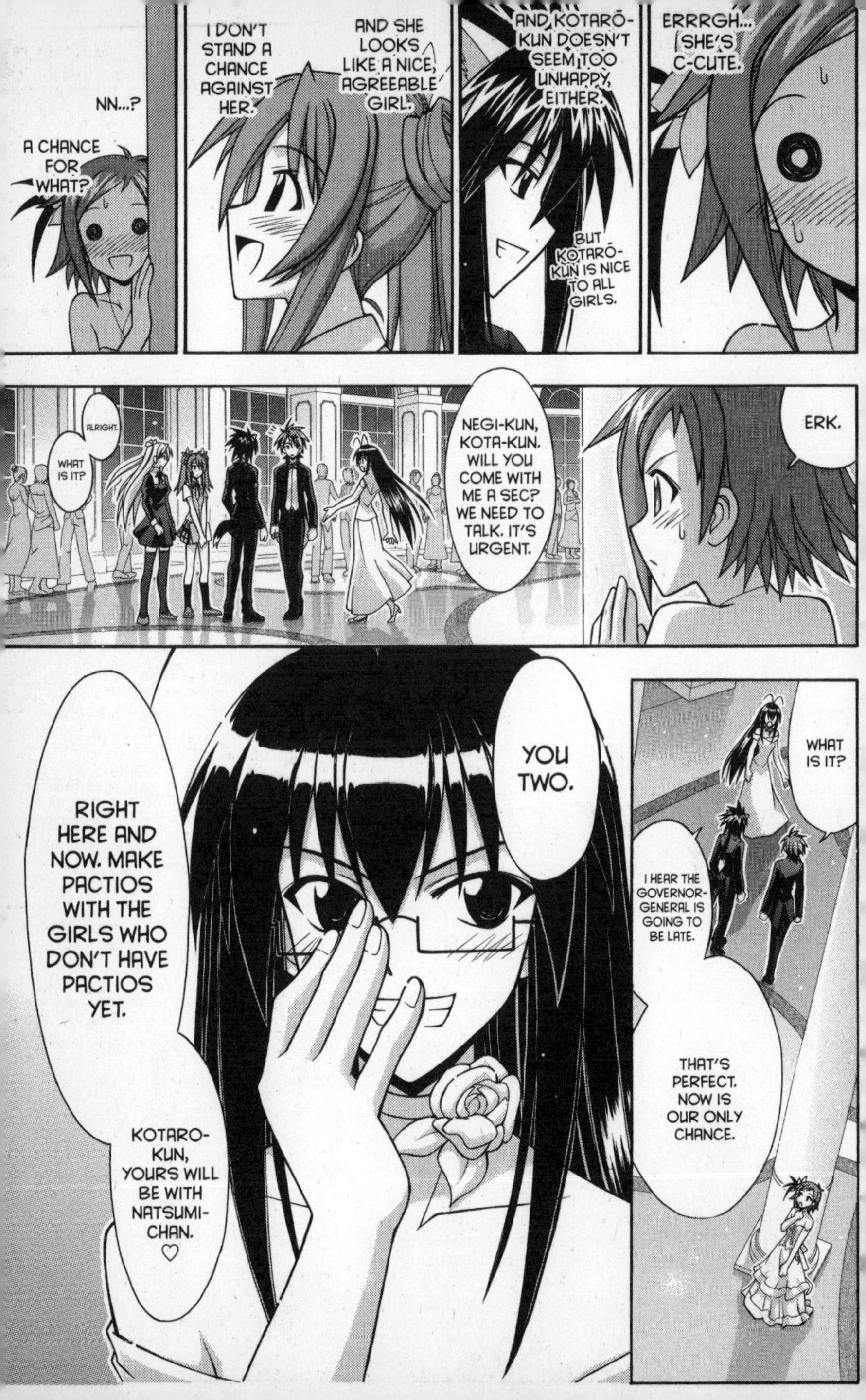
ERRRGH... SHE'S C-CUTE.
AND KOTARŌ-KUN DOESN'T SEEM TOO UNHAPPY, EITHER.
BUT KOTARŌ-KUN IS NICE TO ALL GIRLS.
AND SHE LOOKS LIKE A NICE, AGREEABLE GIRL.
I DON'T STAND A CHANCE AGAINST HER.
NN...?
A CHANCE FOR WHAT?
ERK.
NEGI-KUN, KOTA-KUN. WILL YOU COME WITH ME A SEC? WE NEED TO TALK. IT'S URGENT.
ALRIGHT.
WHAT IS IT?
WHAT IS IT?
I HEAR THE GOVERNOR-GENERAL IS GOING TO BE LATE.
THAT'S PERFECT. NOW IS OUR ONLY CHANCE.
YOU TWO.
RIGHT HERE AND NOW. MAKE PACTIOS WITH THE GIRLS WHO DON'T HAVE PACTIOS YET.
KOTARO-KUN, YOURS WILL BE WITH NATSUMI-CHAN. ♡

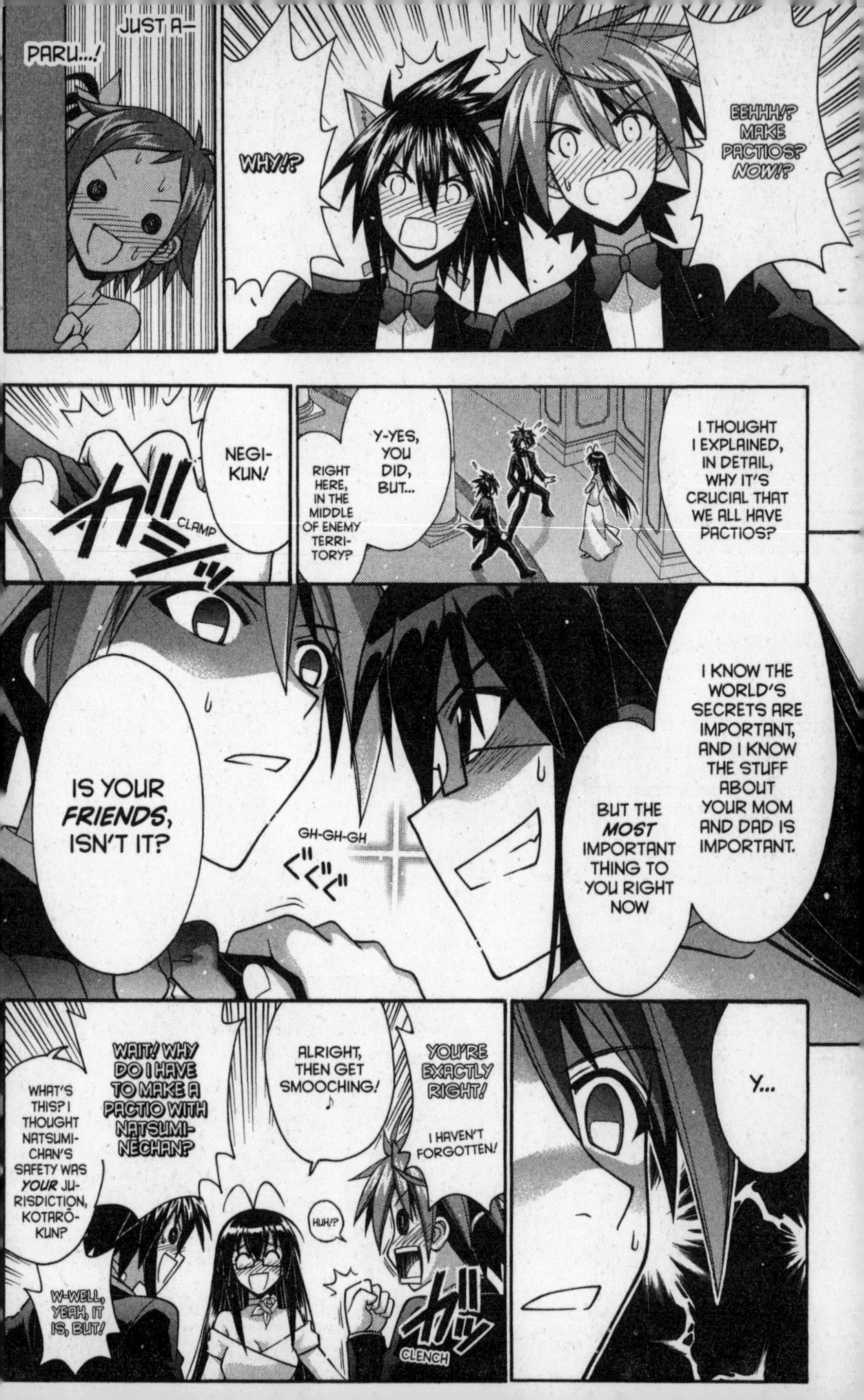
EEHHH!? MAKE PACTIOS? *NOW!?*
WHY!?
JUST A—
PARU...!
I THOUGHT I EXPLAINED, IN DETAIL, WHY IT'S CRUCIAL THAT WE ALL HAVE PACTIOS?
Y-YES, YOU DID, BUT...
RIGHT HERE, IN THE MIDDLE OF ENEMY TERRITORY?
NEGI-KUN!
CLAMP
I KNOW THE WORLD'S SECRETS ARE IMPORTANT, AND I KNOW THE STUFF ABOUT YOUR MOM AND DAD IS IMPORTANT.
BUT THE *MOST* IMPORTANT THING TO YOU RIGHT NOW
GH-GH-GH
IS YOUR *FRIENDS*, ISN'T IT?
Y...
YOU'RE EXACTLY RIGHT!
I HAVEN'T FORGOTTEN!
ALRIGHT, THEN GET SMOOCHING! ♪
HUH!?
CLENCH
WAIT! WHY DO I HAVE TO MAKE A PACTIO WITH NATSUMI-NECHAN?
WHAT'S THIS? I THOUGHT NATSUMI-CHAN'S SAFETY WAS *YOUR* JURISDICTION, KOTARŌ-KUN?
W-WELL, YEAH, IT IS, BUT!

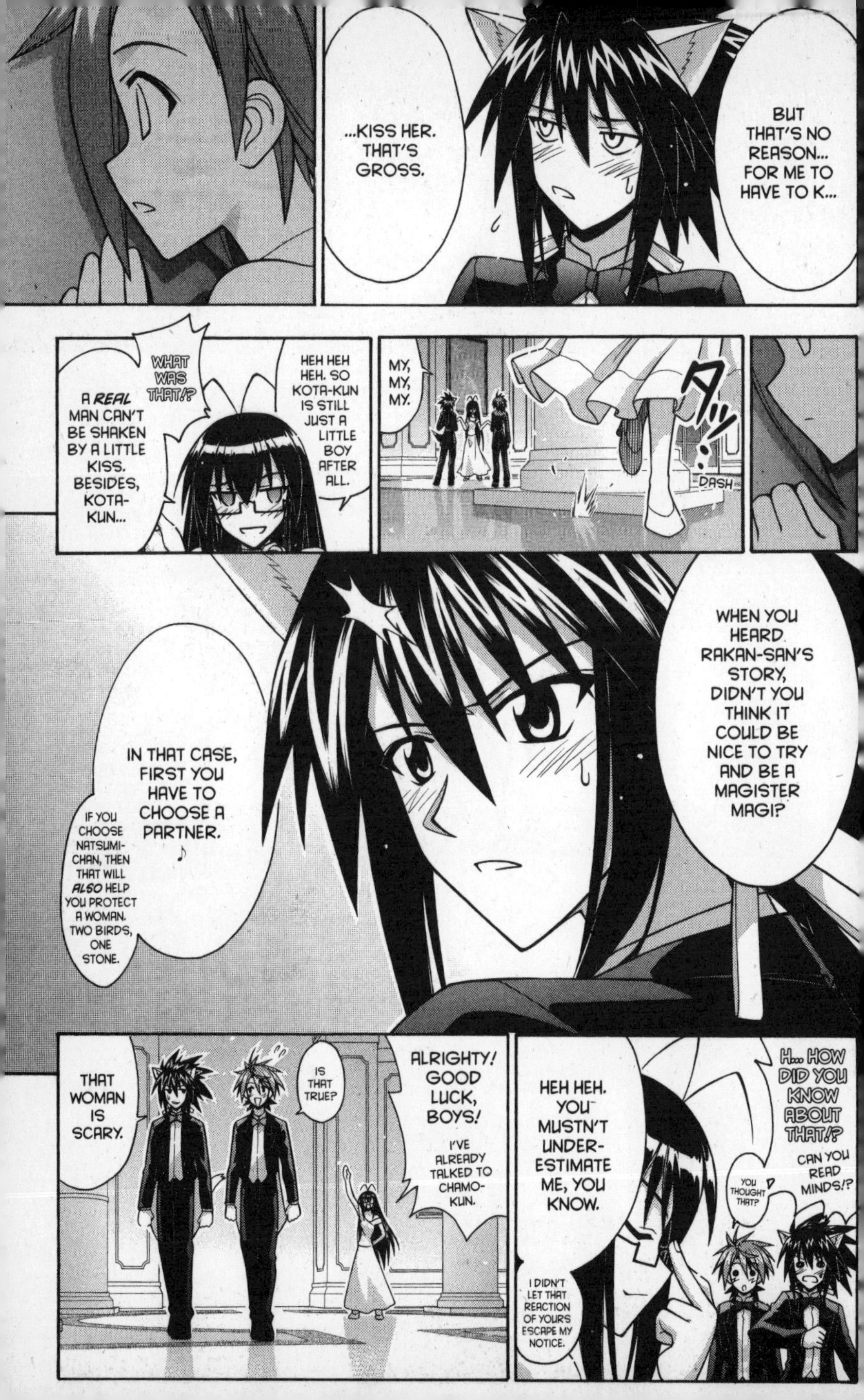
BUT THAT'S NO REASON... FOR ME TO HAVE TO K...
...KISS HER. THAT'S GROSS.
DASH
MY, MY, MY.
HEH HEH HEH. SO KOTA-KUN IS STILL JUST A LITTLE BOY AFTER ALL.
WHAT WAS THAT!?
A *REAL* MAN CAN'T BE SHAKEN BY A LITTLE KISS. BESIDES, KOTA-KUN...
WHEN YOU HEARD RAKAN-SAN'S STORY, DIDN'T YOU THINK IT COULD BE NICE TO TRY AND BE A MAGISTER MAGI?
IN THAT CASE, FIRST YOU HAVE TO CHOOSE A PARTNER. ♪
IF YOU CHOOSE NATSUMI-CHAN, THEN THAT WILL *ALSO* HELP YOU PROTECT A WOMAN. TWO BIRDS, ONE STONE.
H... HOW DID YOU KNOW ABOUT THAT!?
CAN YOU READ MINDS!?
YOU THOUGHT THAT?
HEH HEH. YOU MUSTN'T UNDER-ESTIMATE ME, YOU KNOW.
I DIDN'T LET THAT REACTION OF YOURS ESCAPE MY NOTICE.
ALRIGHTY! GOOD LUCK, BOYS!
I'VE ALREADY TALKED TO CHAMO-KUN.
IS THAT TRUE?
THAT WOMAN IS SCARY.

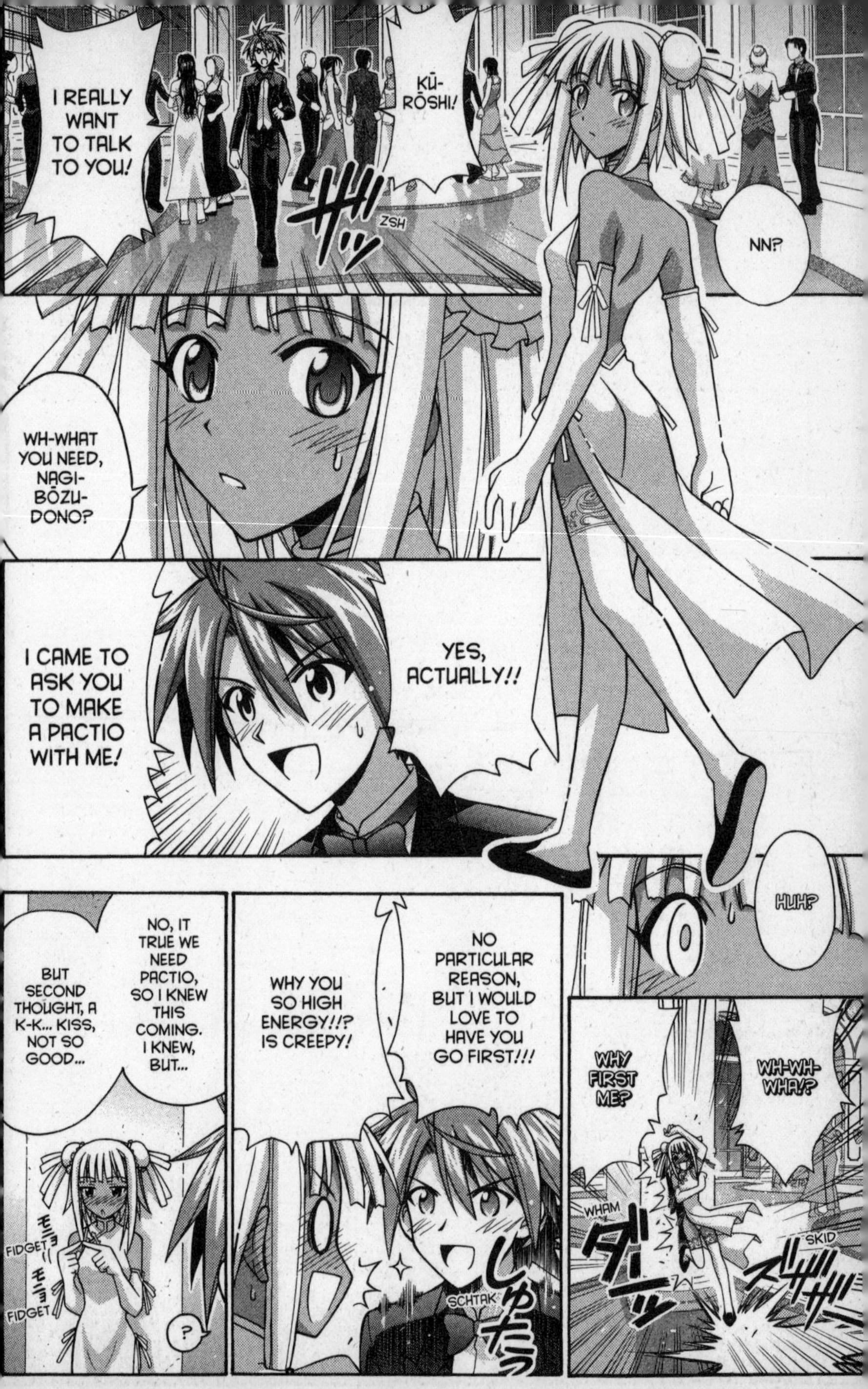
KŪ-RŌSHI!
I REALLY WANT TO TALK TO YOU!
ZSH
NN?
WH-WHAT YOU NEED, NAGI-BŌZU-DONO?
YES, ACTUALLY!!
I CAME TO ASK YOU TO MAKE A PACTIO WITH ME!
HUH?
WH-WH-WHA!?
WHY FIRST ME?
WHAM
SKID
NO PARTICULAR REASON, BUT I WOULD LOVE TO HAVE YOU GO FIRST!!!
WHY YOU SO HIGH ENERGY!!? IS CREEPY!
SCHTAK
NO, IT TRUE WE NEED PACTIO, SO I KNEW THIS COMING. I KNEW, BUT...
BUT SECOND THOUGHT, A K-K... KISS, NOT SO GOOD...
FIDGET
FIDGET
?

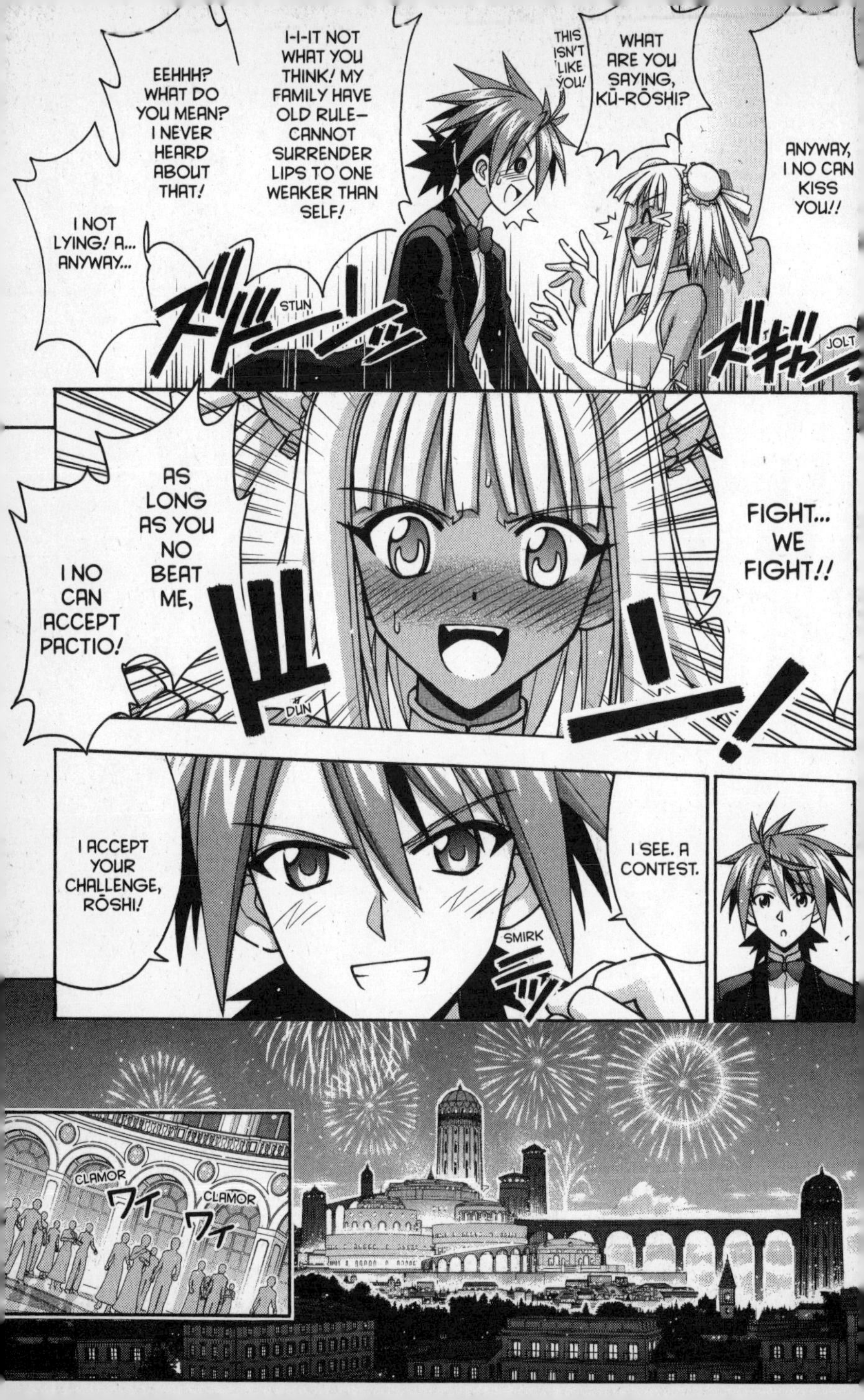
ANYWAY, I NO CAN KISS YOU!!
WHAT ARE YOU SAYING, KŪ-RŌSHI?
THIS ISN'T LIKE YOU!
I-I-IT NOT WHAT YOU THINK! MY FAMILY HAVE OLD RULE— CANNOT SURRENDER LIPS TO ONE WEAKER THAN SELF!
EEHHH? WHAT DO YOU MEAN? I NEVER HEARD ABOUT THAT!
I NOT LYING! A... ANYWAY...
JOLT
STUN
FIGHT... WE FIGHT!!
AS LONG AS YOU NO BEAT ME,
I NO CAN ACCEPT PACTIO!
DUN
I SEE. A CONTEST.
SMIRK
I ACCEPT YOUR CHALLENGE, RŌSHI!
CLAMOR
CLAMOR

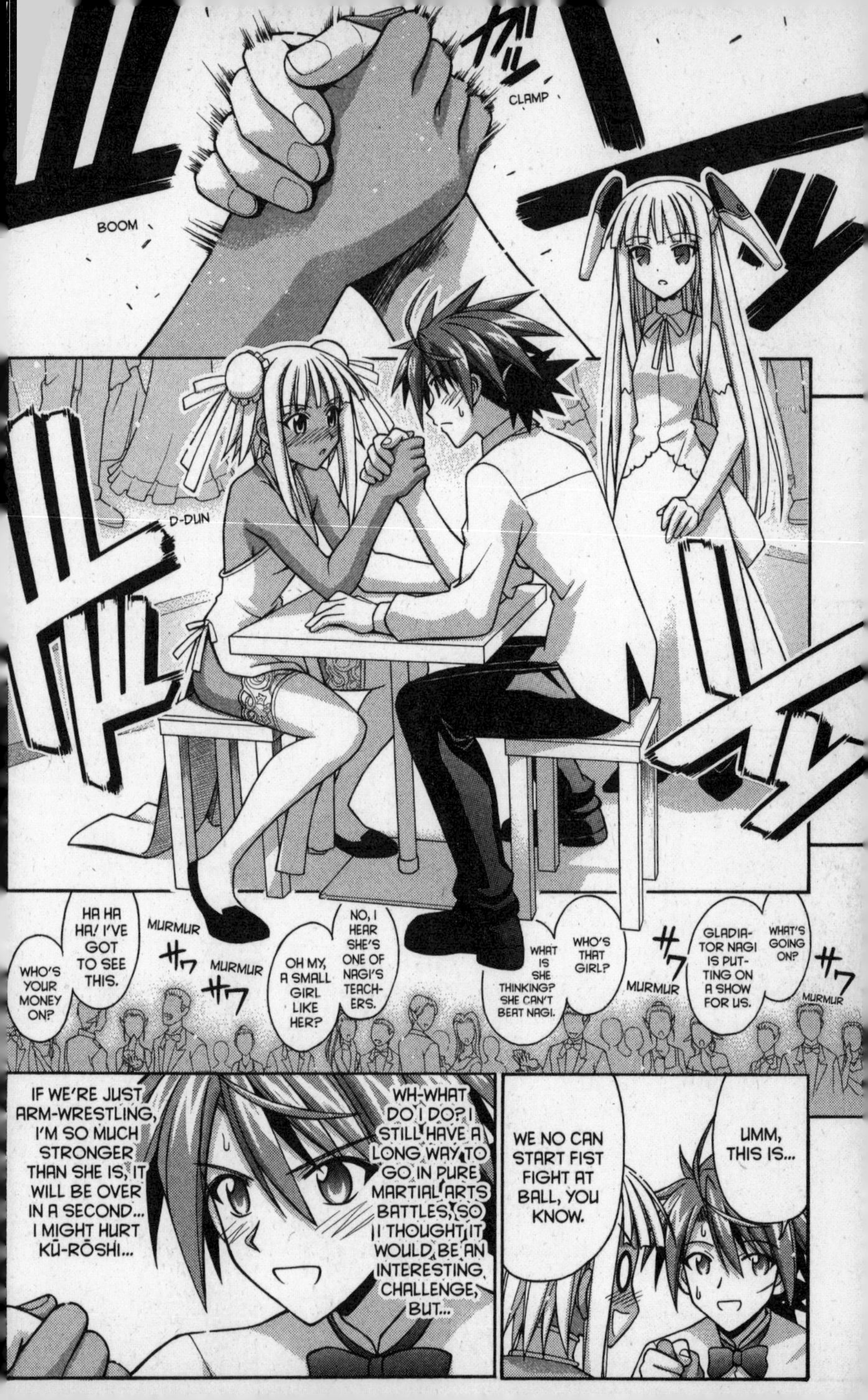
CLAMP
BOOM
D-DUN
WHAT'S GOING ON?
MURMUR
GLADIATOR NAGI IS PUTTING ON A SHOW FOR US.
MURMUR
WHO'S THAT GIRL?
WHAT IS SHE THINKING? SHE CAN'T BEAT NAGI.
NO, I HEAR SHE'S ONE OF NAGI'S TEACHERS.
OH MY, A SMALL GIRL LIKE HER?
MURMUR
MURMUR
HA HA HA! I'VE GOT TO SEE THIS.
WHO'S YOUR MONEY ON?
UMM, THIS IS...
WE NO CAN START FIST FIGHT AT BALL, YOU KNOW.
WH-WHAT DO I DO? I STILL HAVE A LONG WAY TO GO IN PURE MARTIAL ARTS BATTLES, SO I THOUGHT IT WOULD BE AN INTERESTING CHALLENGE, BUT...
IF WE'RE JUST ARM-WRESTLING, I'M SO MUCH STRONGER THAN SHE IS, IT WILL BE OVER IN A SECOND... I MIGHT HURT KŪ-RŌSHI...

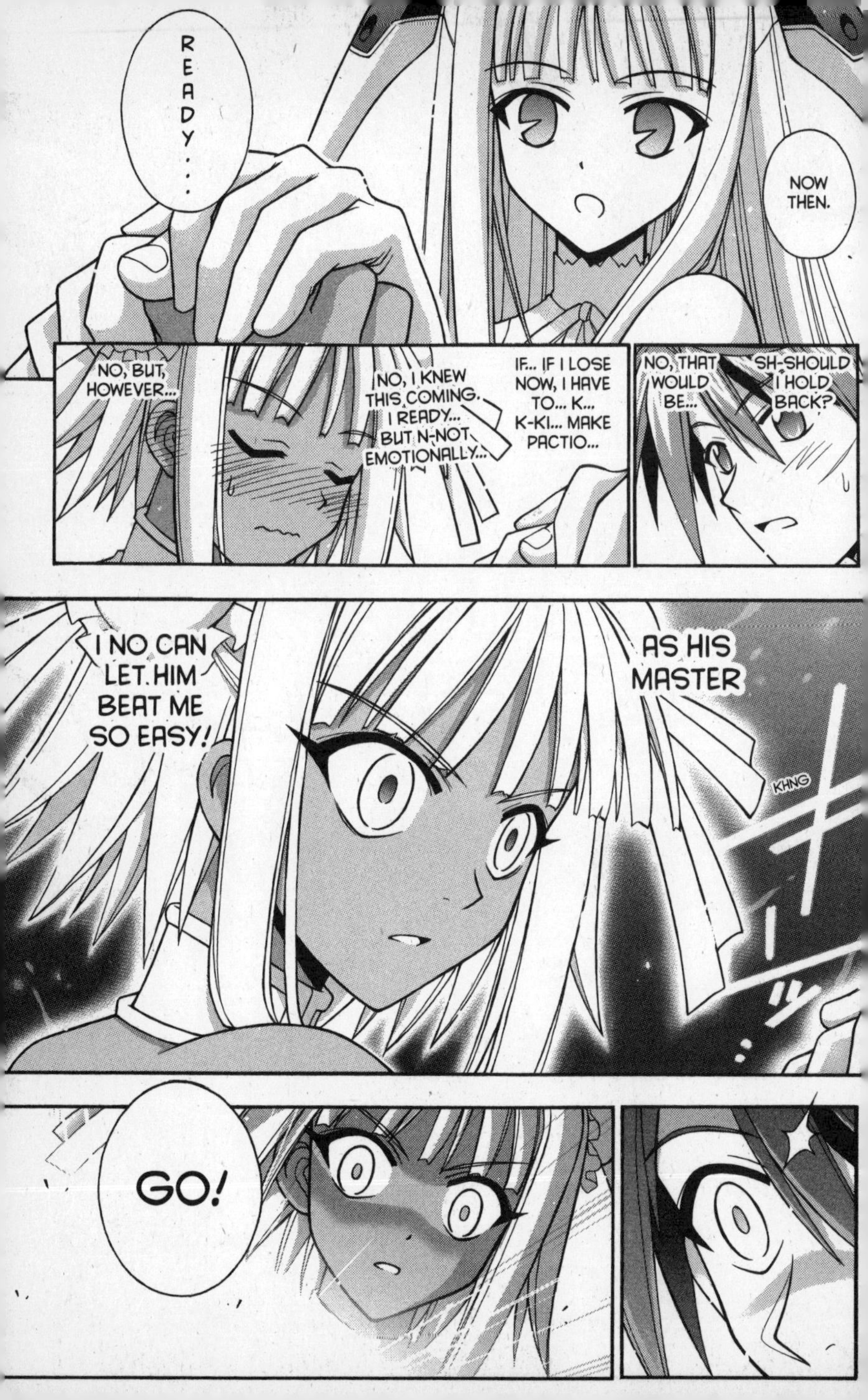
NOW THEN.
READY...
SH-SHOULD I HOLD BACK?
NO, THAT WOULD BE...
IF... IF I LOSE NOW, I HAVE TO... K... K-KI... MAKE PACTIO...
NO, I KNEW THIS COMING. I READY... BUT N-NOT EMOTIONALLY...
NO, BUT, HOWEVER...
AS HIS MASTER
KHNG
I NO CAN LET HIM BEAT ME SO EASY!
GO!

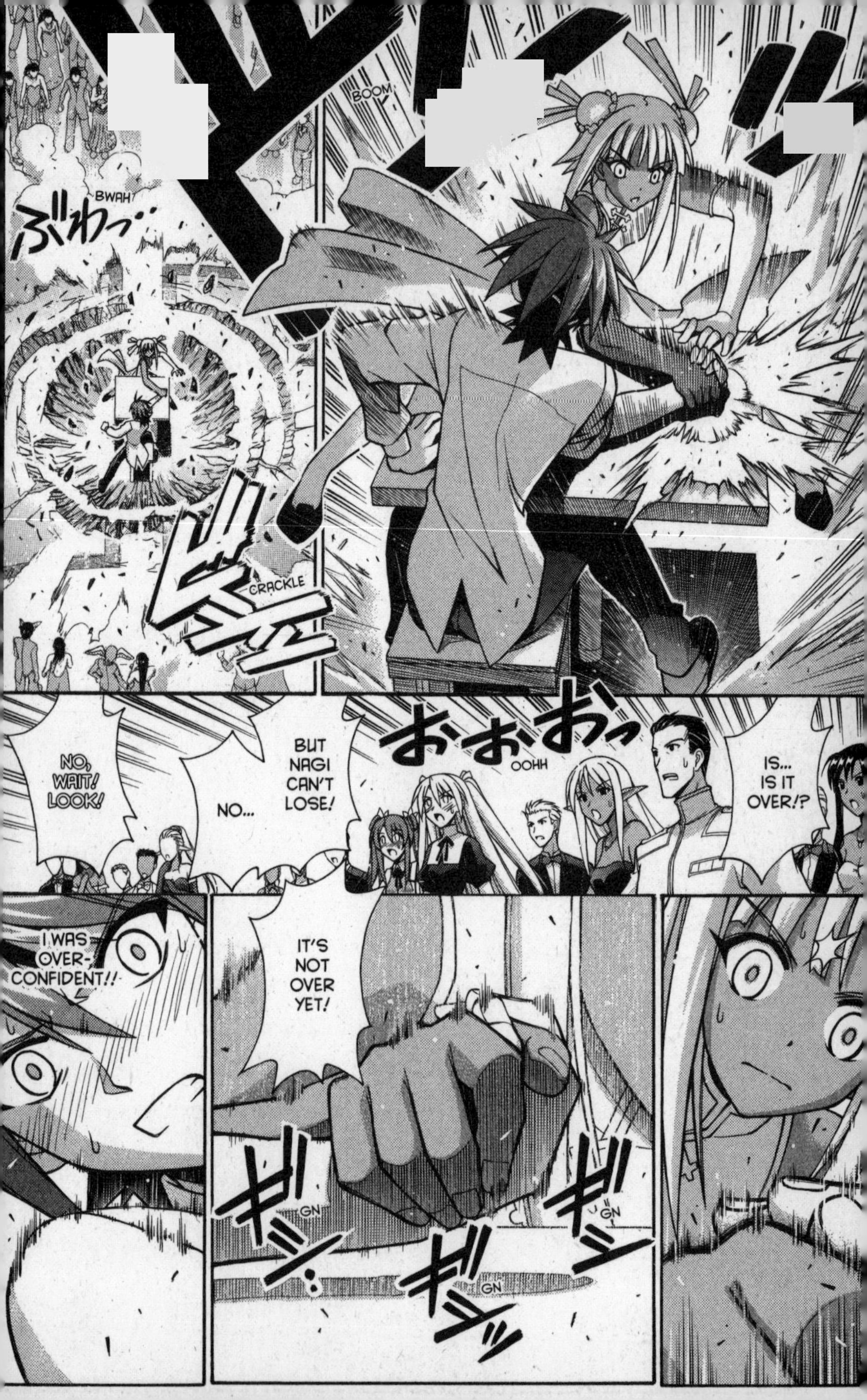
BOOM
BWAH
ぶわっ
CRACKLE
IS... IS IT OVER!?
おぉぉっ
OOHH
BUT NAGI CAN'T LOSE!
NO...
NO, WAIT! LOOK!
IT'S NOT OVER YET!
GN
GN
GN
I WAS OVER-CONFIDENT!!

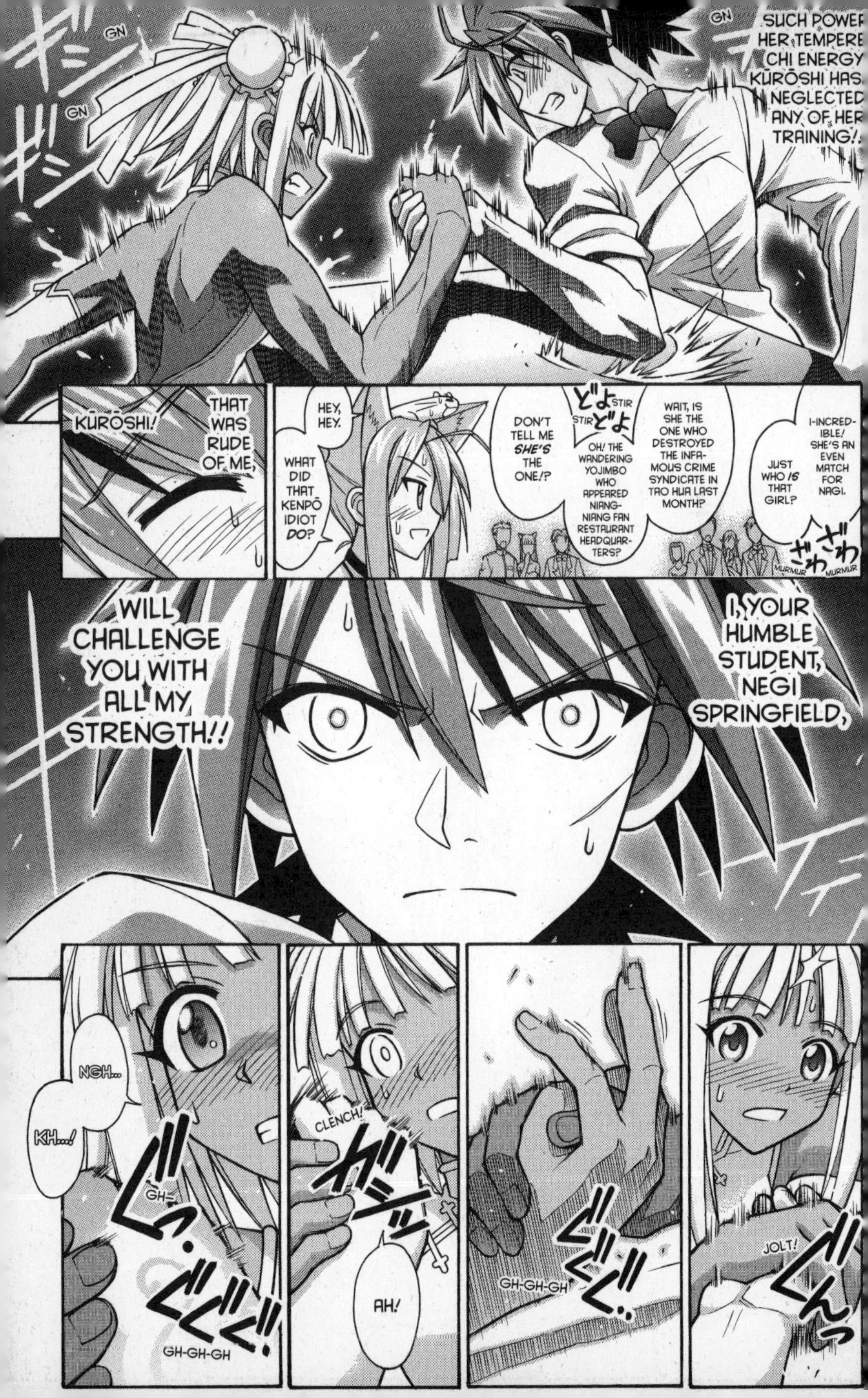
GN
GN
GN
SUCH POWER
HER TEMPERE
CHI ENERGY
KURŌSHI HAS
NEGLECTED
ANY OF HER
TRAINING!!
I-INCREDIBLE! SHE'S AN EVEN MATCH FOR NAGI.
JUST WHO IS THAT GIRL?
ざわざわ
MURMUR MURMUR
WAIT, IS SHE THE ONE WHO DESTROYED THE INFAMOUS CRIME SYNDICATE IN TAO HUA LAST MONTH?
どよ STIR
STIR どよ
OH! THE WANDERING YOJIMBO WHO APPEARED NIANG-NIANG FAN RESTAURANT HEADQUARTERS?
DON'T TELL ME SHE'S THE ONE!?
HEY, HEY.
WHAT DID THAT KENPŌ IDIOT DO?
THAT WAS RUDE OF ME,
KURŌSHI!
I, YOUR HUMBLE STUDENT, NEGI SPRINGFIELD,
WILL CHALLENGE YOU WITH ALL MY STRENGTH!!
JOLT!
GH-GH-GH
CLENCH!
AH!
NGH...
KH...!
GH-
GH-GH-GH

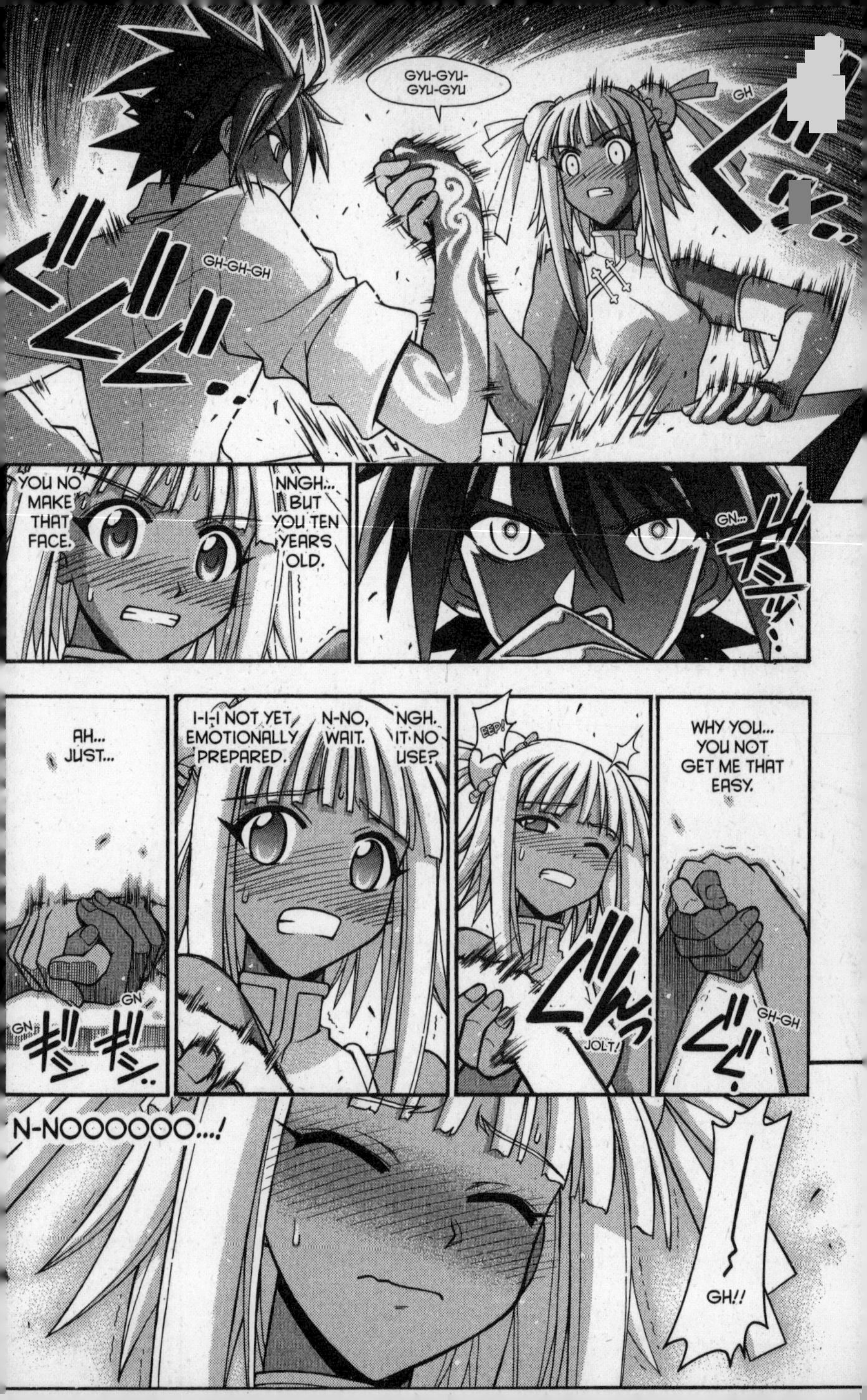
GH
GYU-GYU-GYU-GYU
GH-GH-GH
GN...
NNGH... BUT YOU TEN YEARS OLD.
YOU NO MAKE THAT FACE.
WHY YOU... YOU NOT GET ME THAT EASY.
GH-GH
EEP!
JOLT!
NGH. IT NO USE?
N-NO, WAIT.
I-I-I NOT YET EMOTIONALLY PREPARED.
AH... JUST...
GN
GN
GH!!
N-NOOOOOO...!

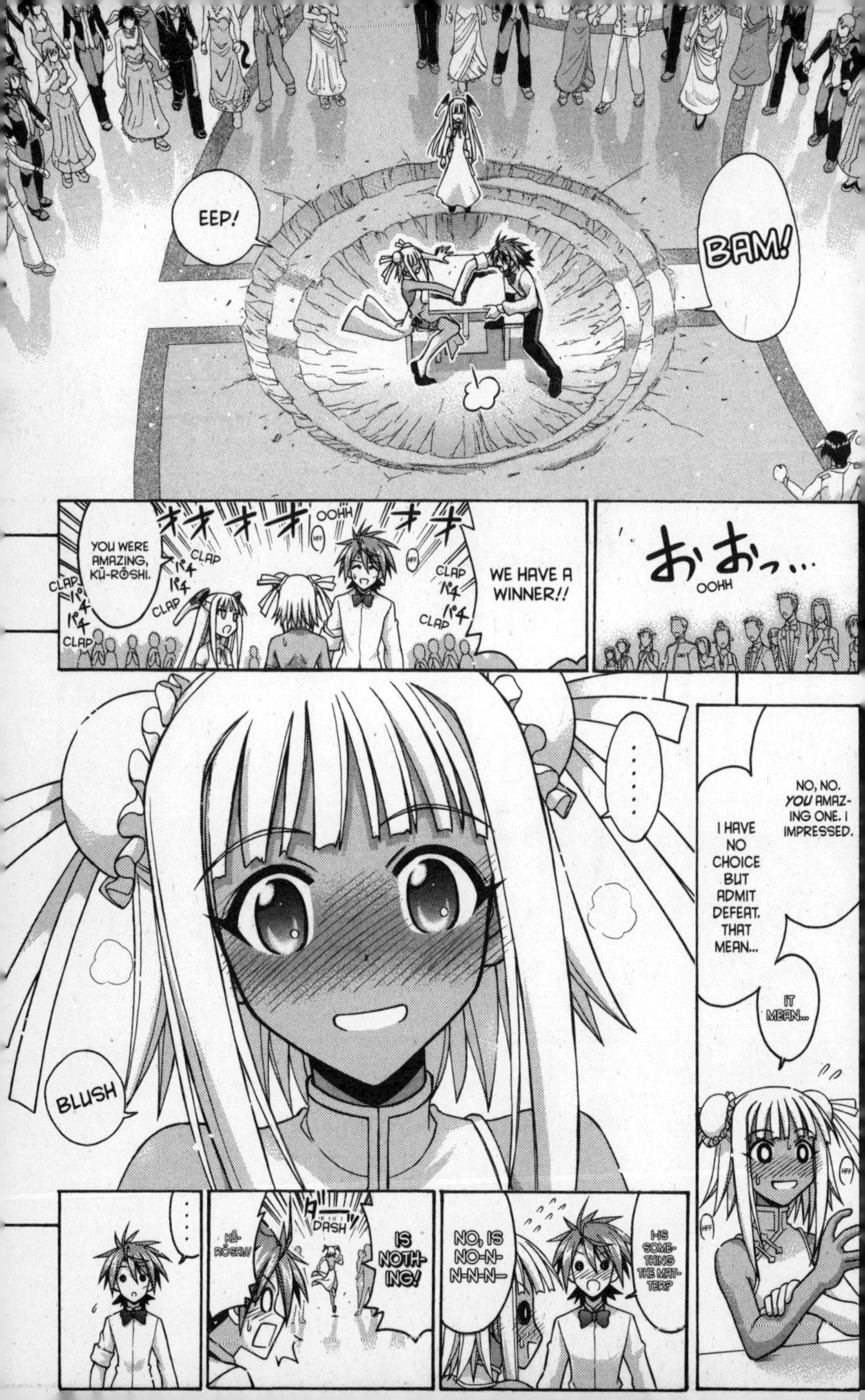
BAM!
EEP!
おおっ…
OOHH
WE HAVE A WINNER!!
オオオオ
OOHH
オオ
HFF
HFF
CLAP
パチ
パチ
CLAP
YOU WERE AMAZING, KŪ-RŌSHI.
CLAP
パチ
パチ
CLAP
CLAP
NO, NO. *YOU* AMAZING ONE. I IMPRESSED.
I HAVE NO CHOICE BUT ADMIT DEFEAT. THAT MEAN...
IT MEAN...
HFF
HFF
......
BLUSH
I-IS SOMETHING THE MATTER?
NO, IS NO-N-N-N-N-N–
IS NOTHING!
ダー
DASH
KŪ-RŌSHI!!
...

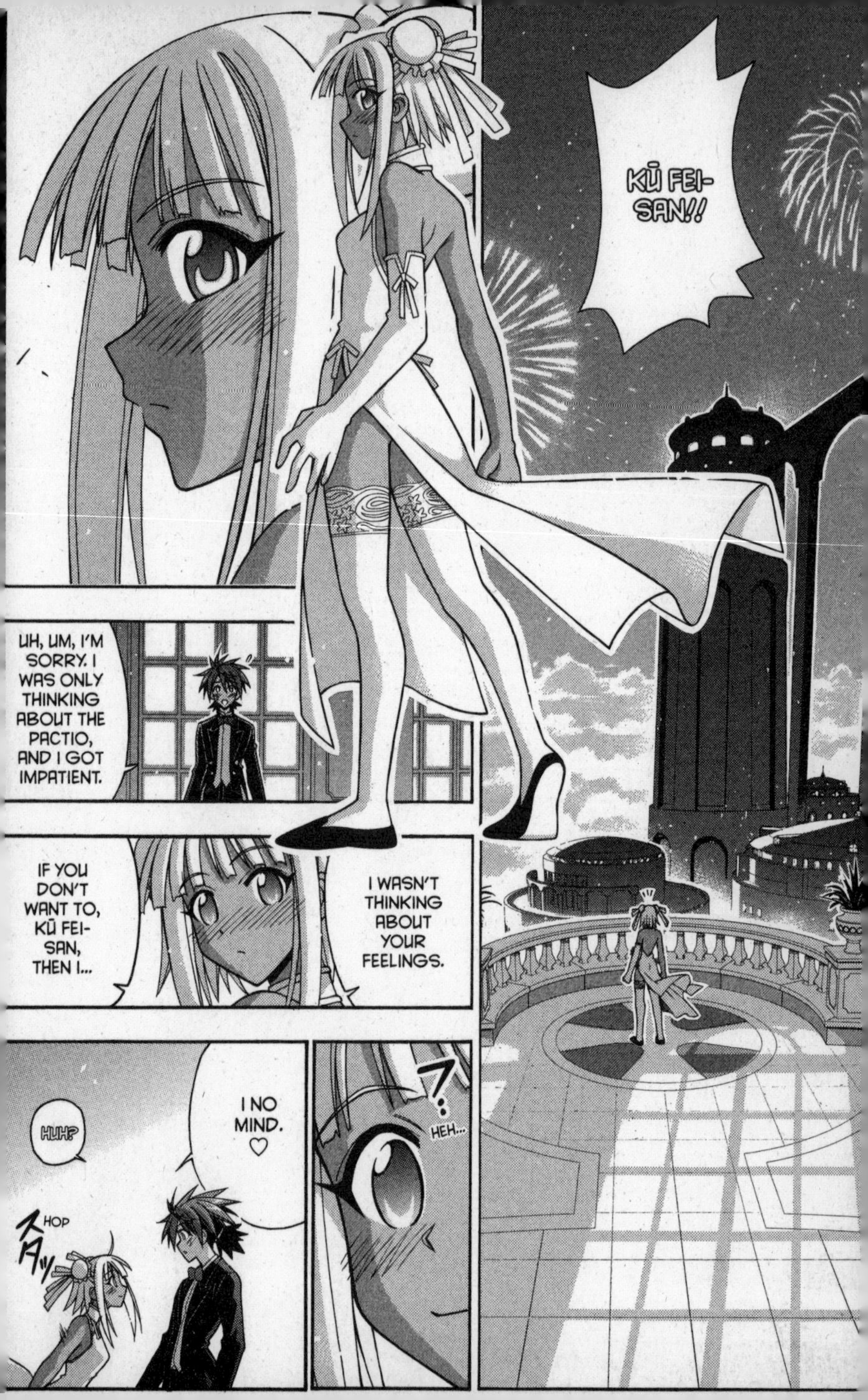
KŪ FEI-SAN!!
UH, UM, I'M SORRY. I WAS ONLY THINKING ABOUT THE PACTIO, AND I GOT IMPATIENT.
I WASN'T THINKING ABOUT YOUR FEELINGS.
IF YOU DON'T WANT TO, KŪ FEI-SAN, THEN I...
HEH...
I NO MIND. ♡
HUH?
HOP

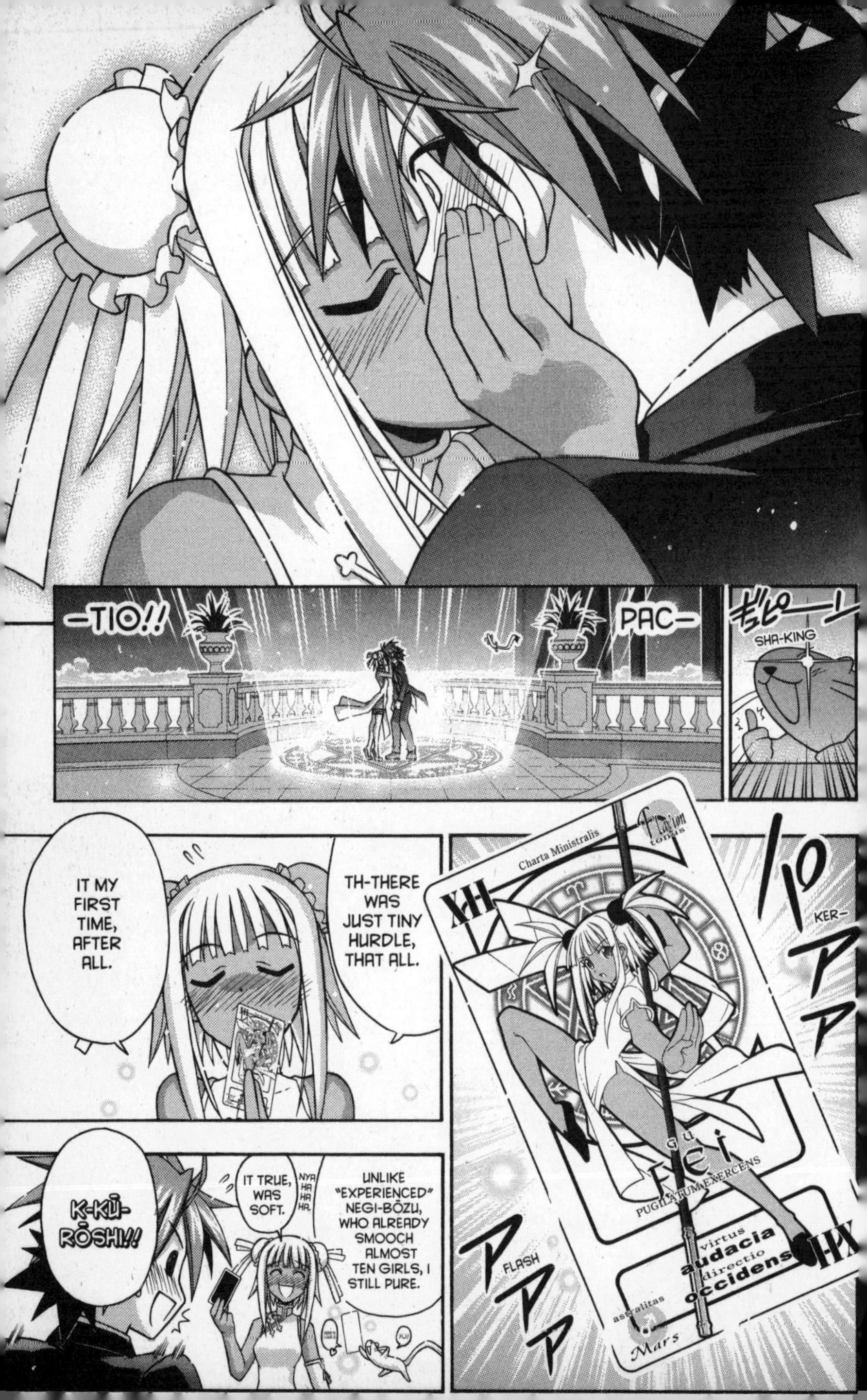
SHA-KING
PAC—
—TIO!!
KER—
Charta Ministralis
XII
PUGILATUM EXERCENS
virtus
audacia
directio
occidens
astralitas
Mars
FLASH
TH-THERE WAS JUST TINY HURDLE, THAT ALL.
IT MY FIRST TIME, AFTER ALL.
UNLIKE "EXPERIENCED" NEGI-BŌZU, WHO ALREADY SMOOCH ALMOST TEN GIRLS, I STILL PURE.
NYA HA HA HA.
IT TRUE, WAS SOFT.
K-KŪ-RŌSHI!!

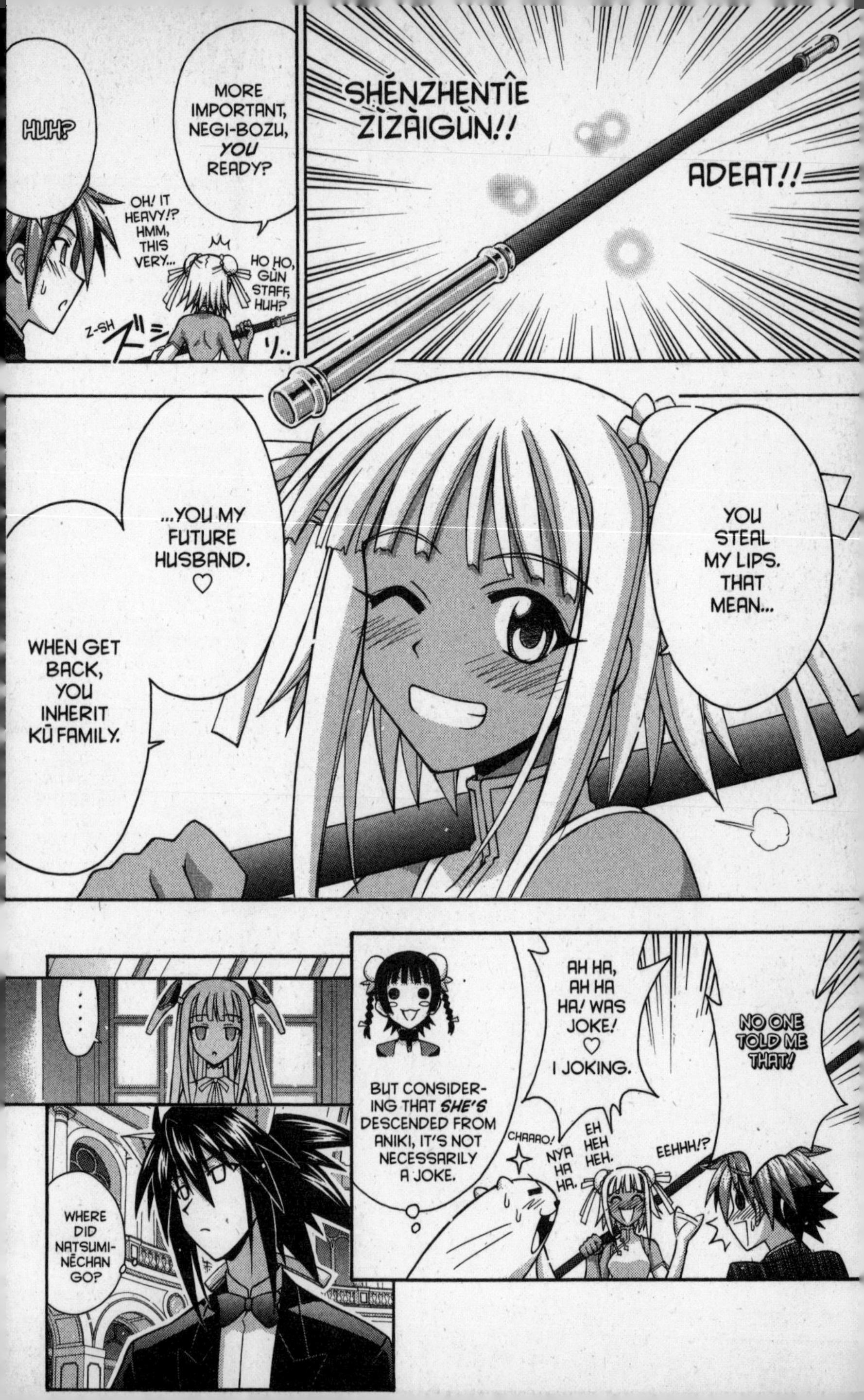

ADEAT!!
SHÉNZHENTÎE ZÌZÀIGÙN!!
MORE IMPORTANT, NEGI-BOZU, *YOU* READY?
HUH?
HO HO, GŪN STAFF, HUH?
OH! IT HEAVY!? HMM, THIS VERY...
Z-SH
YOU STEAL MY LIPS. THAT MEAN...
...YOU MY FUTURE HUSBAND. ♡
WHEN GET BACK, YOU INHERIT KŪ FAMILY.
NO ONE TOLD ME THAT!
AH HA, AH HA HA! WAS JOKE! ♡ I JOKING.
EEHHH!?
EH HEH HEH.
NYA HA HA.
CHAAAO!
BUT CONSIDERING THAT *SHE'S* DESCENDED FROM ANIKI, IT'S NOT NECESSARILY A JOKE.
....
WHERE DID NATSUMI-NĒCHAN GO?

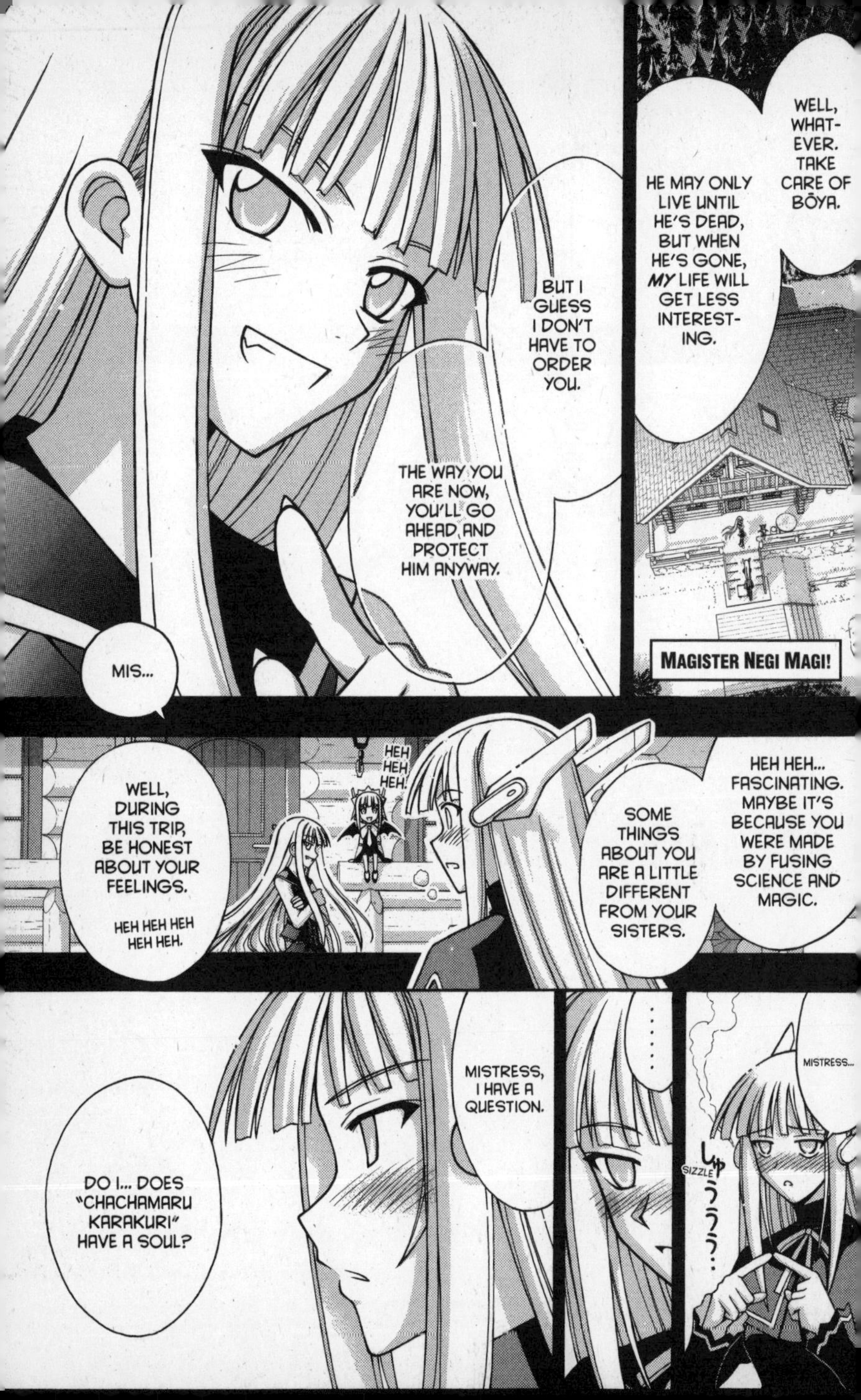
WELL, WHAT-EVER. TAKE CARE OF BŌYA.
HE MAY ONLY LIVE UNTIL HE'S DEAD, BUT WHEN HE'S GONE, *MY* LIFE WILL GET LESS INTEREST-ING.
MAGISTER NEGI MAGI!
BUT I GUESS I DON'T HAVE TO ORDER YOU.
THE WAY YOU ARE NOW, YOU'LL GO AHEAD AND PROTECT HIM ANYWAY.
MIS...
HEH HEH... FASCINATING. MAYBE IT'S BECAUSE YOU WERE MADE BY FUSING SCIENCE AND MAGIC.
SOME THINGS ABOUT YOU ARE A LITTLE DIFFERENT FROM YOUR SISTERS.
HEH HEH HEH!
WELL, DURING THIS TRIP, BE HONEST ABOUT YOUR FEELINGS.
HEH HEH HEH HEH HEH.
MISTRESS...
しゅううう…
SIZZLE
......
MISTRESS, I HAVE A QUESTION.
DO I... DOES "CHACHAMARU KARAKURI" HAVE A SOUL?

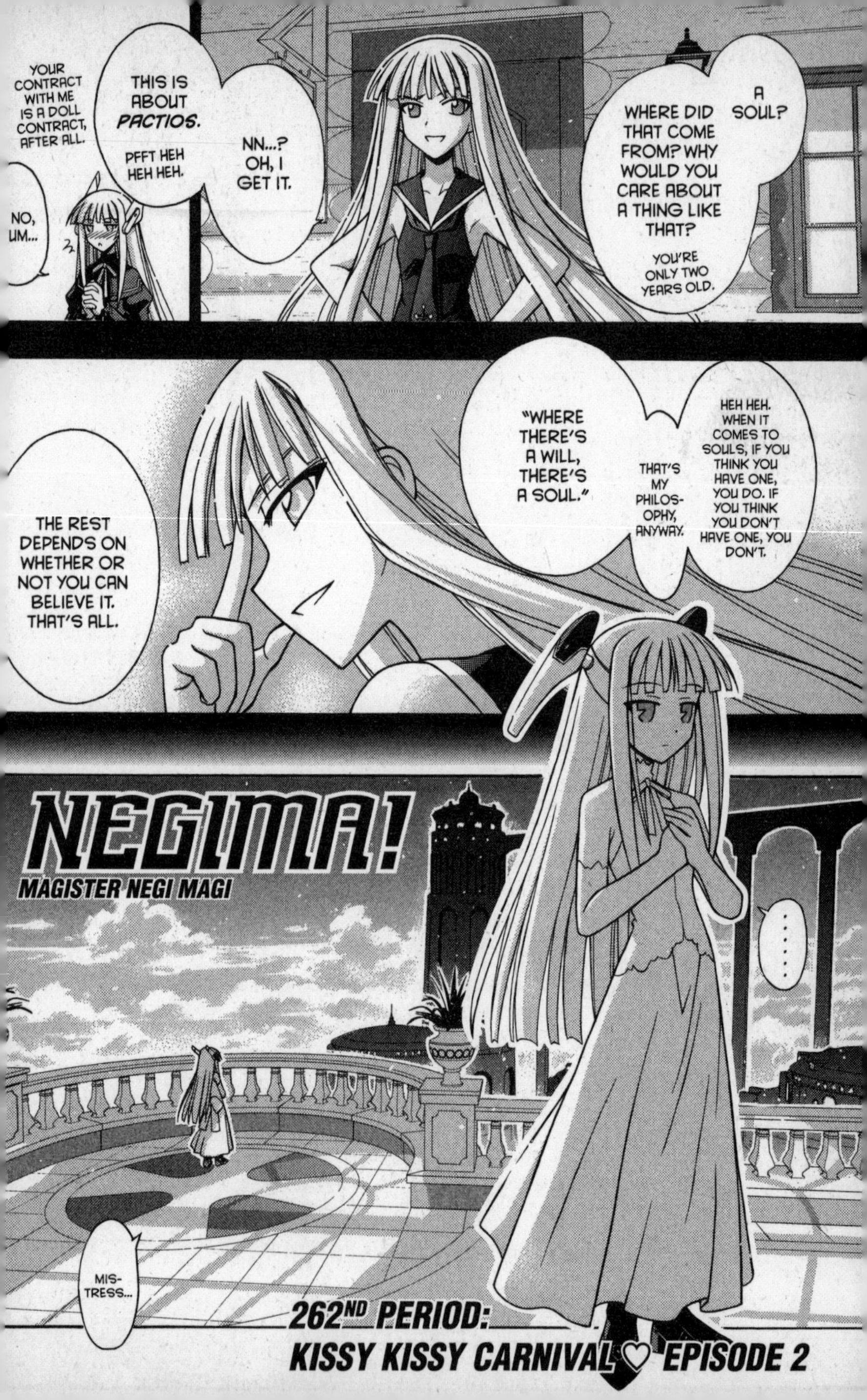
A SOUL?
WHERE DID THAT COME FROM? WHY WOULD YOU CARE ABOUT A THING LIKE THAT?
YOU'RE ONLY TWO YEARS OLD.
NN...? OH, I GET IT.
THIS IS ABOUT PACTIOS.
PFFT HEH HEH HEH.
YOUR CONTRACT WITH ME IS A DOLL CONTRACT, AFTER ALL.
NO, UM...
HEH HEH. WHEN IT COMES TO SOULS, IF YOU THINK YOU HAVE ONE, YOU DO. IF YOU THINK YOU DON'T HAVE ONE, YOU DON'T.
THAT'S MY PHILOSOPHY, ANYWAY.
"WHERE THERE'S A WILL, THERE'S A SOUL."
THE REST DEPENDS ON WHETHER OR NOT YOU CAN BELIEVE IT. THAT'S ALL.
......
NEGIMA!
MAGISTER NEGI MAGI
MISTRESS...
262ND PERIOD:
KISSY KISSY CARNIVAL ♡ EPISODE 2

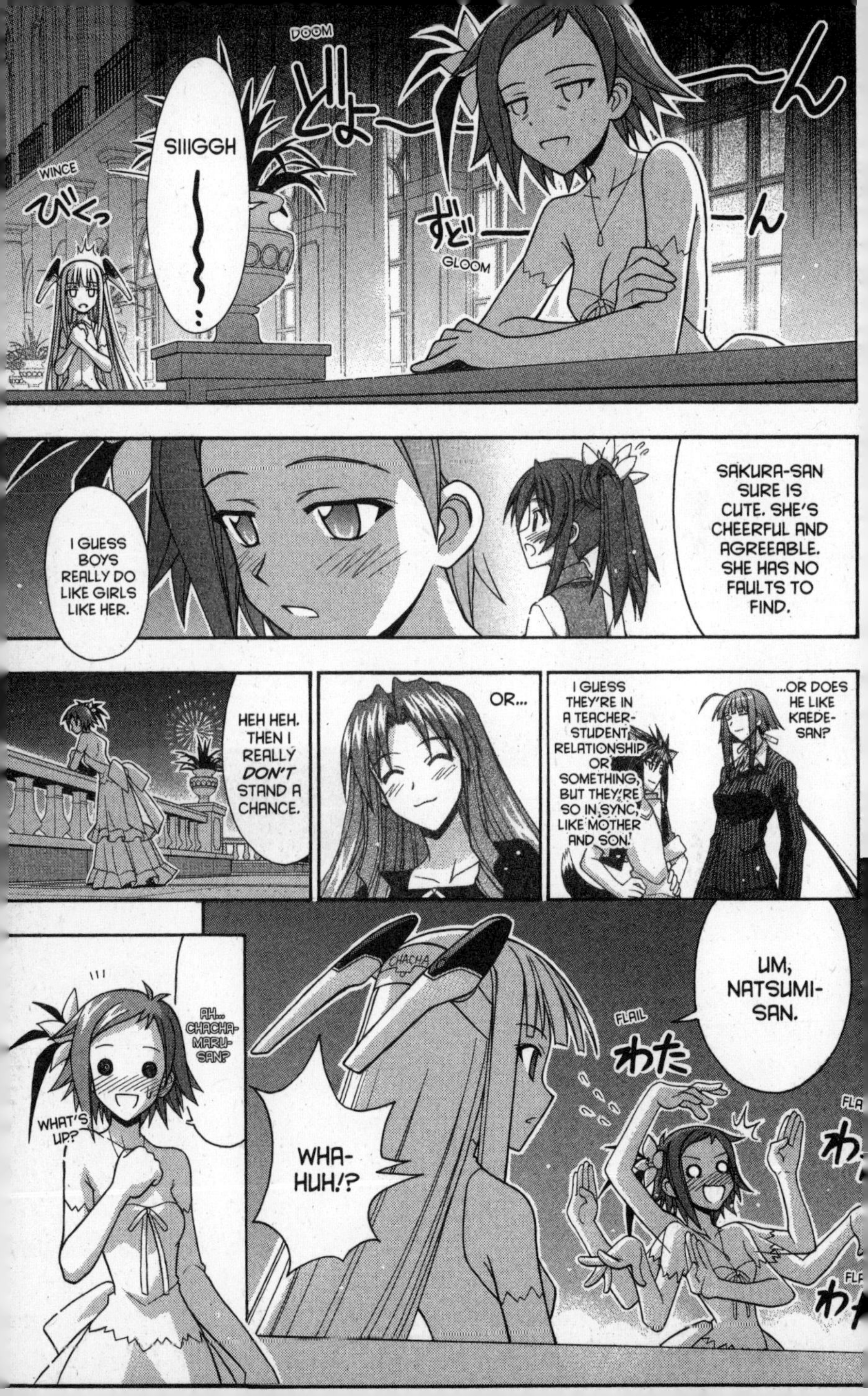
DOOM
どよ～ん
SIIIGGH
ずど～ん
GLOOM
WINCE
びくっ
SAKURA-SAN SURE IS CUTE. SHE'S CHEERFUL AND AGREEABLE. SHE HAS NO FAULTS TO FIND.
I GUESS BOYS REALLY DO LIKE GIRLS LIKE HER.
...OR DOES HE LIKE KAEDE-SAN?
I GUESS THEY'RE IN A TEACHER-STUDENT RELATIONSHIP OR SOMETHING, BUT THEY'RE SO IN SYNC, LIKE MOTHER AND SON.
OR...
HEH HEH. THEN I REALLY *DON'T* STAND A CHANCE.
UM, NATSUMI-SAN.
FLAIL
わた
CHACHA
WHA-HUH!?
AH... CHACHA-MARU-SAN?
WHAT'S UP?

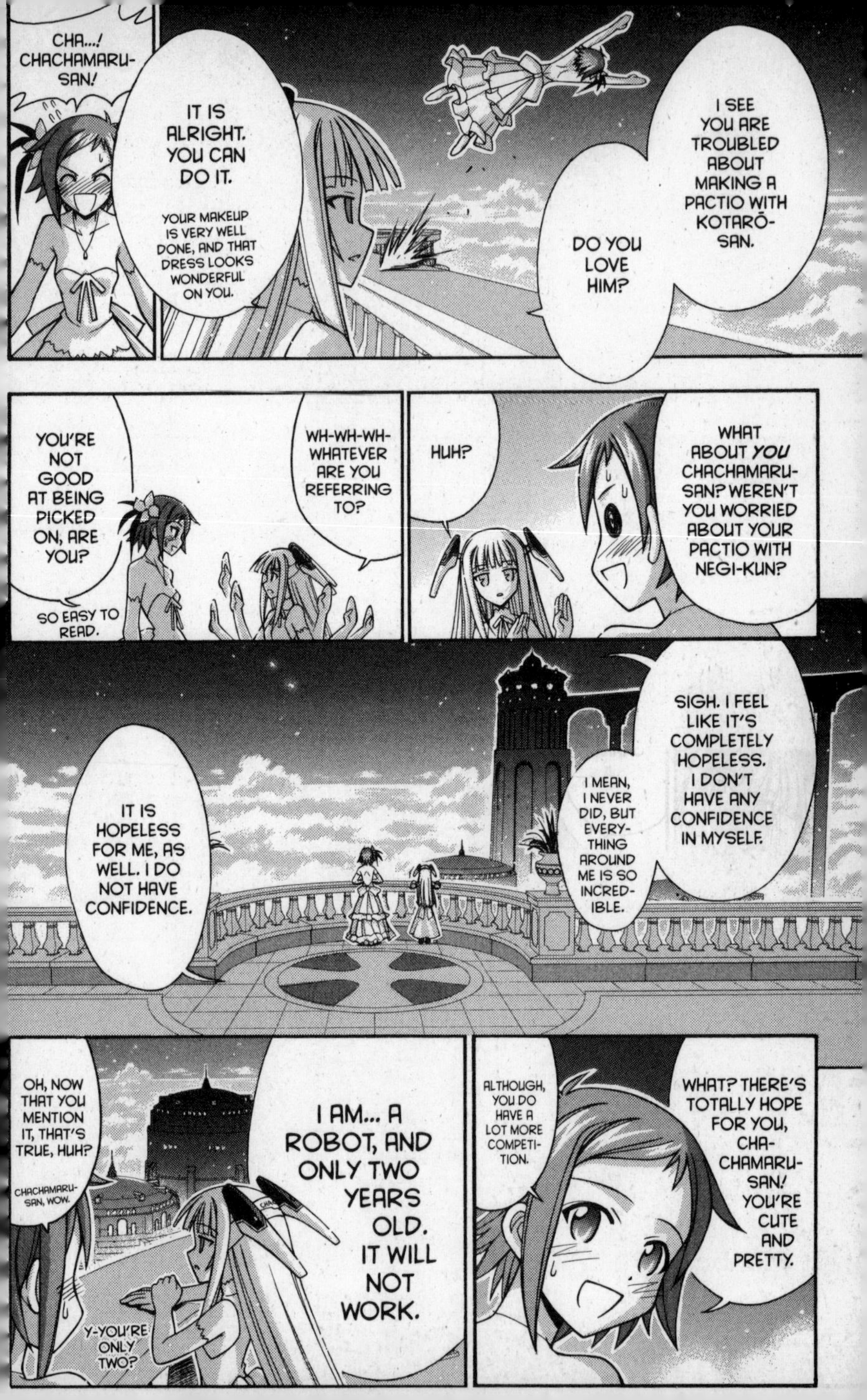

I SEE YOU ARE TROUBLED ABOUT MAKING A PACTIO WITH KOTARŌ-SAN.
DO YOU LOVE HIM?
IT IS ALRIGHT. YOU CAN DO IT.
YOUR MAKEUP IS VERY WELL DONE, AND THAT DRESS LOOKS WONDERFUL ON YOU.
CHA...! CHACHAMARU-SAN!
WHAT ABOUT *YOU* CHACHAMARU-SAN? WEREN'T YOU WORRIED ABOUT YOUR PACTIO WITH NEGI-KUN?
HUH?
WH-WH-WH-WHATEVER ARE YOU REFERRING TO?
YOU'RE NOT GOOD AT BEING PICKED ON, ARE YOU?
SO EASY TO READ.
SIGH. I FEEL LIKE IT'S COMPLETELY HOPELESS. I DON'T HAVE ANY CONFIDENCE IN MYSELF.
I MEAN, I NEVER DID, BUT EVERY-THING AROUND ME IS SO INCRED-IBLE.
IT IS HOPELESS FOR ME, AS WELL. I DO NOT HAVE CONFIDENCE.
WHAT? THERE'S TOTALLY HOPE FOR YOU, CHA-CHAMARU-SAN! YOU'RE CUTE AND PRETTY.
ALTHOUGH, YOU DO HAVE A LOT MORE COMPETI-TION.
I AM... A ROBOT, AND ONLY TWO YEARS OLD. IT WILL NOT WORK.
OH, NOW THAT YOU MENTION IT, THAT'S TRUE, HUH?
CHACHAMARU-SAN, WOW.
Y-YOU'RE ONLY TWO?

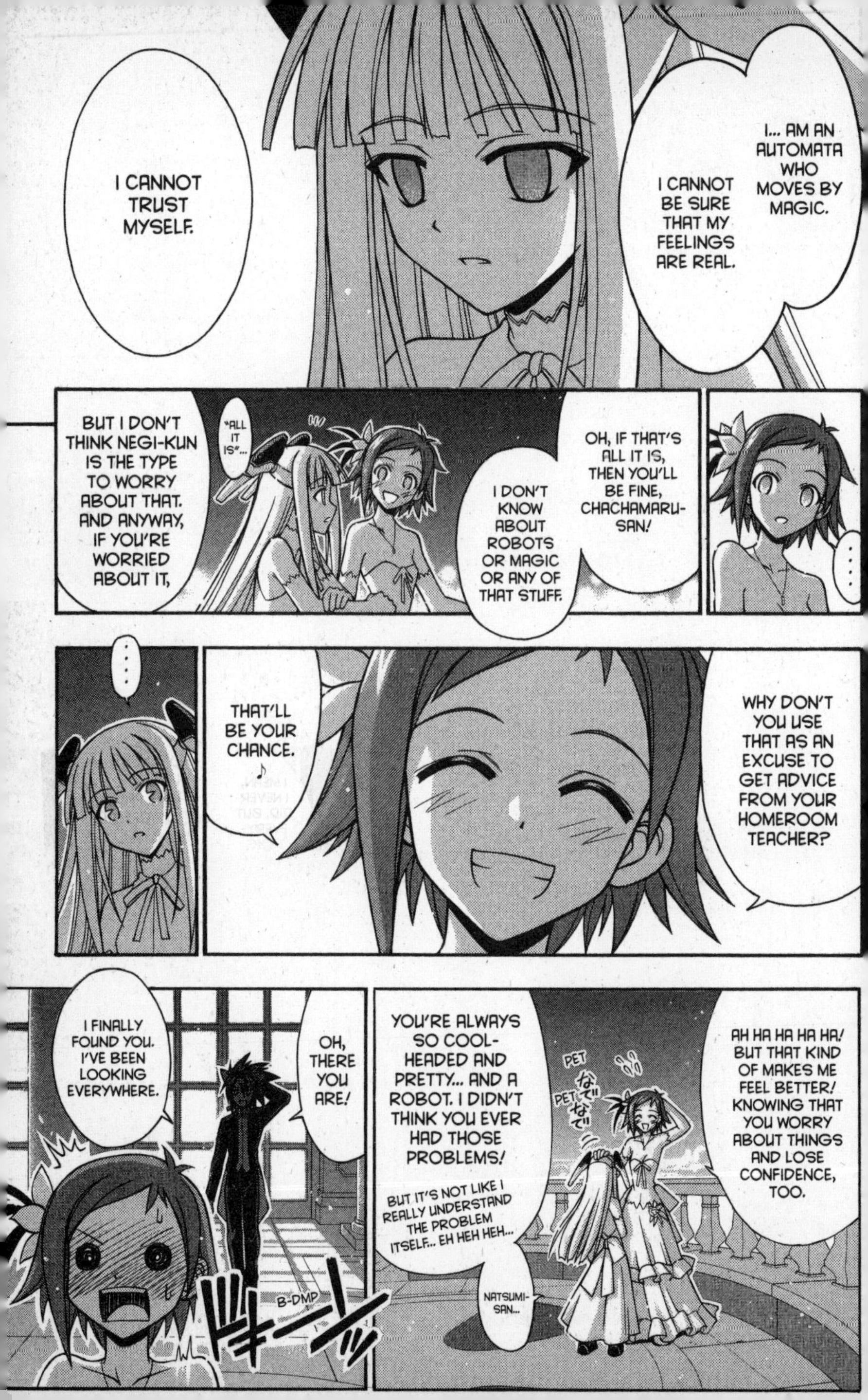

I... AM AN AUTOMATA WHO MOVES BY MAGIC.
I CANNOT BE SURE THAT MY FEELINGS ARE REAL.
I CANNOT TRUST MYSELF.
...
OH, IF THAT'S ALL IT IS, THEN YOU'LL BE FINE, CHACHAMARU-SAN!
I DON'T KNOW ABOUT ROBOTS OR MAGIC OR ANY OF THAT STUFF.
"ALL IT IS"...
BUT I DON'T THINK NEGI-KUN IS THE TYPE TO WORRY ABOUT THAT. AND ANYWAY, IF YOU'RE WORRIED ABOUT IT,
WHY DON'T YOU USE THAT AS AN EXCUSE TO GET ADVICE FROM YOUR HOMEROOM TEACHER?
THAT'LL BE YOUR CHANCE. ♪
...
AH HA HA HA HA! BUT THAT KIND OF MAKES ME FEEL BETTER! KNOWING THAT YOU WORRY ABOUT THINGS AND LOSE CONFIDENCE, TOO.
PET なで
PET なで
YOU'RE ALWAYS SO COOL-HEADED AND PRETTY... AND A ROBOT. I DIDN'T THINK YOU EVER HAD THOSE PROBLEMS!
BUT IT'S NOT LIKE I REALLY UNDERSTAND THE PROBLEM ITSELF... EH HEH HEH...
NATSUMI-SAN...
OH, THERE YOU ARE!
I FINALLY FOUND YOU. I'VE BEEN LOOKING EVERYWHERE.
B-DMP

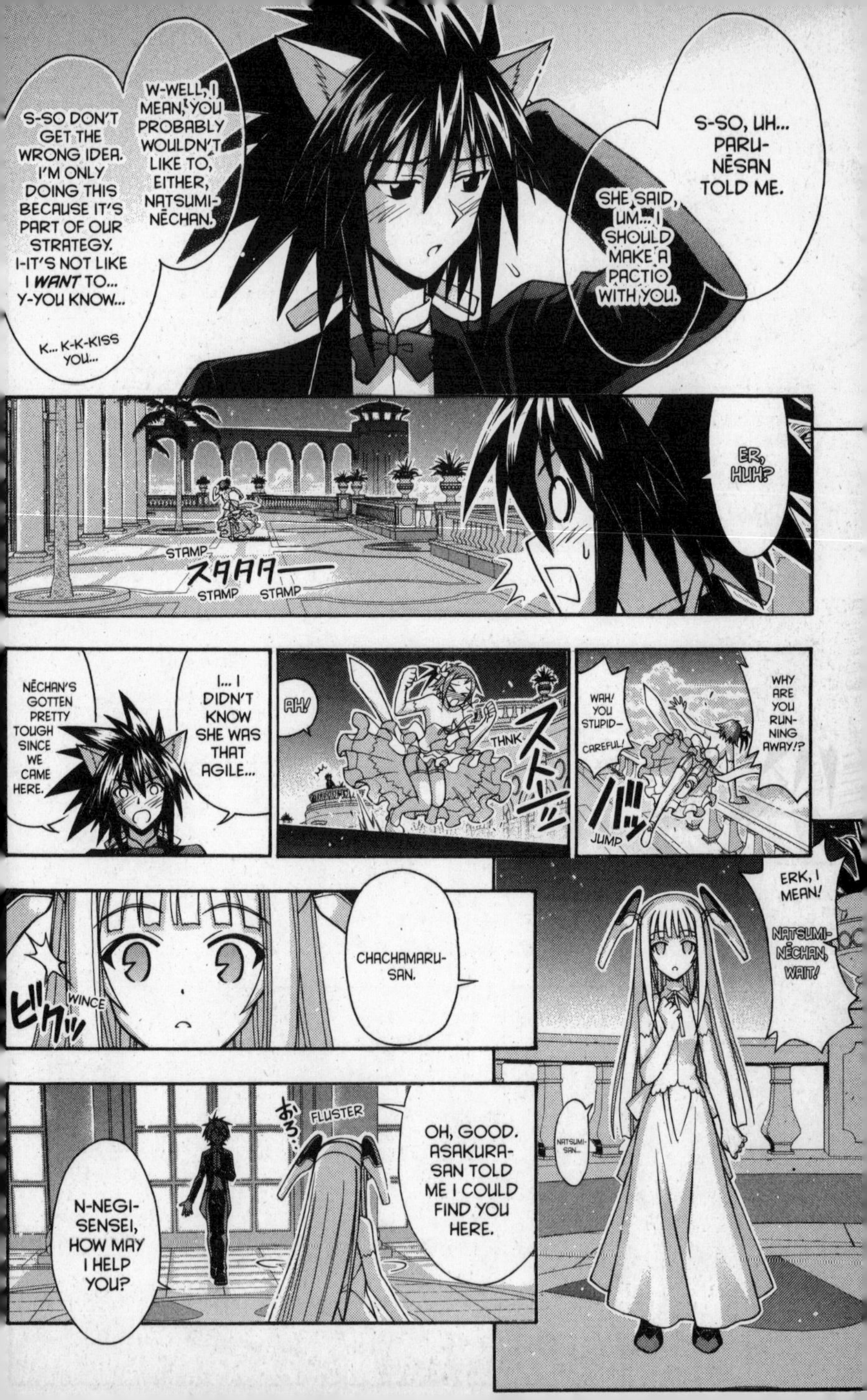
S-SO, UH... PARU-NĒSAN TOLD ME.
SHE SAID, UM... I SHOULD MAKE A PACTIO WITH YOU.
W-WELL, I MEAN, YOU PROBABLY WOULDN'T LIKE TO, EITHER, NATSUMI-NĒCHAN.
S-SO DON'T GET THE WRONG IDEA. I'M ONLY DOING THIS BECAUSE IT'S PART OF OUR STRATEGY. I-IT'S NOT LIKE I *WANT* TO... Y-YOU KNOW...
K... K-K-KISS YOU...
ER, HUH?
スタタター
STAMP STAMP STAMP
WHY ARE YOU RUNNING AWAY!?
WAH! YOU STUPID—
CAREFUL!
バッ
JUMP
ストッ
THNK
AH!
I... I DIDN'T KNOW SHE WAS THAT AGILE...
NĒCHAN'S GOTTEN PRETTY TOUGH SINCE WE CAME HERE.
ERK, I MEAN!
NATSUMI-NĒCHAN, WAIT!
NATSUMI-SAN...
CHACHAMARU-SAN.
ビクッ
WINCE
OH, GOOD. ASAKURA-SAN TOLD ME I COULD FIND YOU HERE.
おろ
FLUSTER
N-NEGI-SENSEI, HOW MAY I HELP YOU?

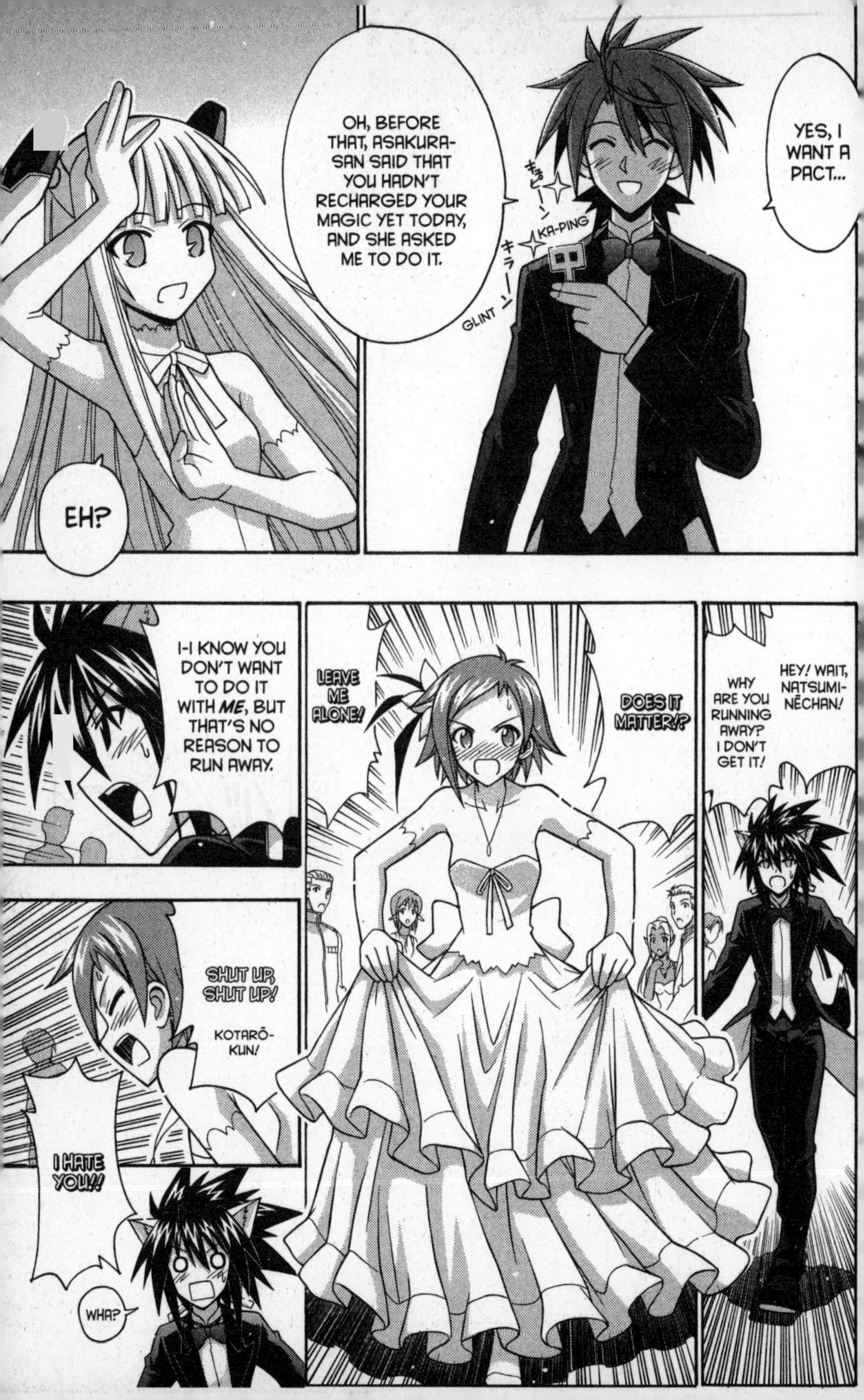
YES, I WANT A PACT...
OH, BEFORE THAT, ASAKURA-SAN SAID THAT YOU HADN'T RECHARGED YOUR MAGIC YET TODAY, AND SHE ASKED ME TO DO IT.
KA-PING
GLINT
EH?
HEY! WAIT, NATSUMI-NĒCHAN!
WHY ARE YOU RUNNING AWAY? I DON'T GET IT!
DOES IT MATTER!?
LEAVE ME ALONE!
I-I KNOW YOU DON'T WANT TO DO IT WITH *ME*, BUT THAT'S NO REASON TO RUN AWAY.
SHUT UP, SHUT UP!
KOTARŌ-KUN!
I HATE YOU!!
WHA?

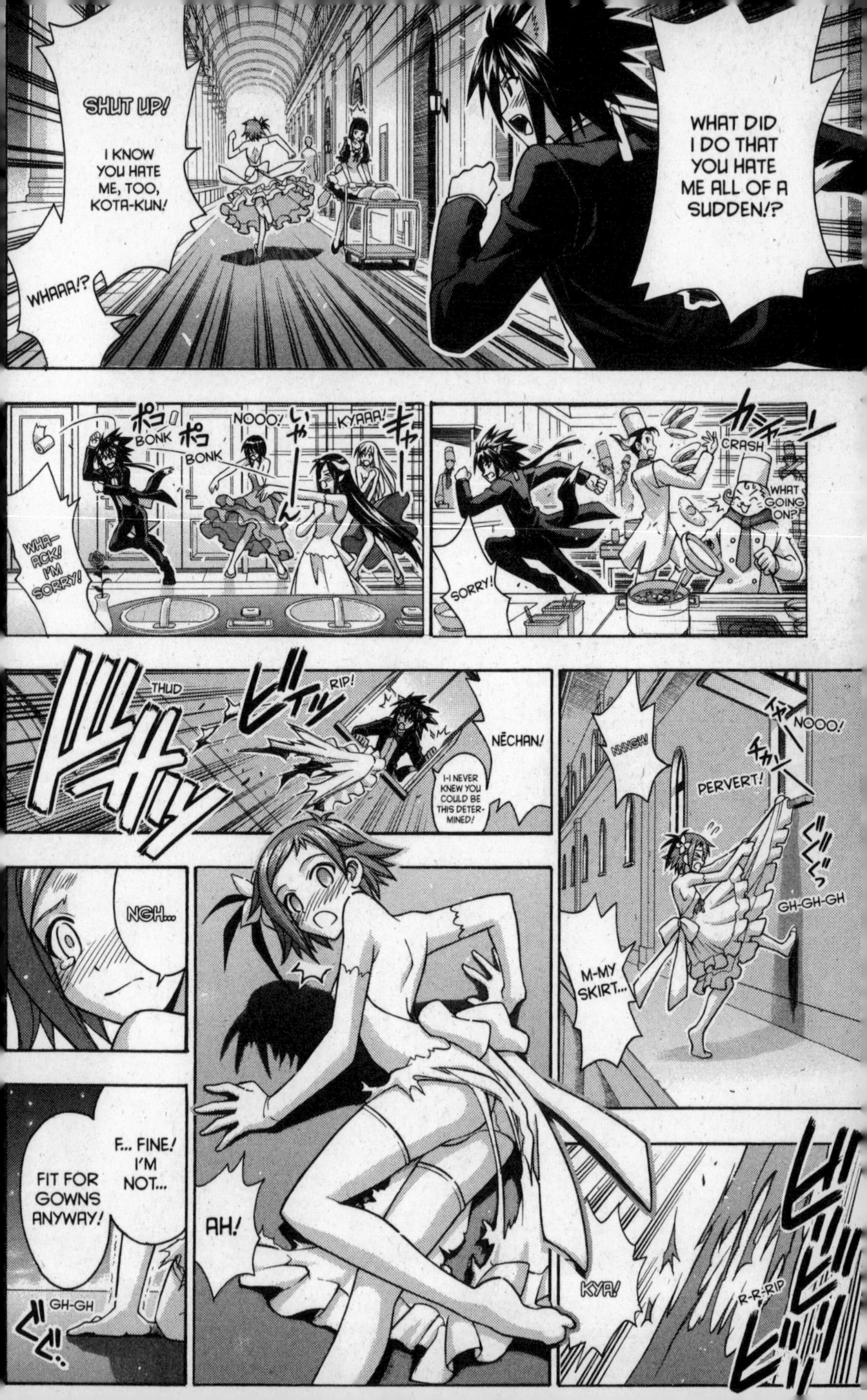
WHAT DID I DO THAT YOU HATE ME ALL OF A SUDDEN!?
SHUT UP!
I KNOW YOU HATE ME, TOO, KOTA-KUN!
WHAAA!?
CRASH
WHAT'S GOING ON?!
SORRY!
KYAAA!
NOOO!
BONK
BONK
WHA-ACK! I'M SORRY!
NOOO!
NNNGH!
PERVERT!
GH-GH-GH
M-MY SKIRT...
RIP!
THUD
NĒCHAN!
I-I NEVER KNEW YOU COULD BE THIS DETERMINED!
R-R-RIP
KYA!
AH!
NGH...
F... FINE! I'M NOT...
FIT FOR GOWNS ANYWAY!
GH-GH

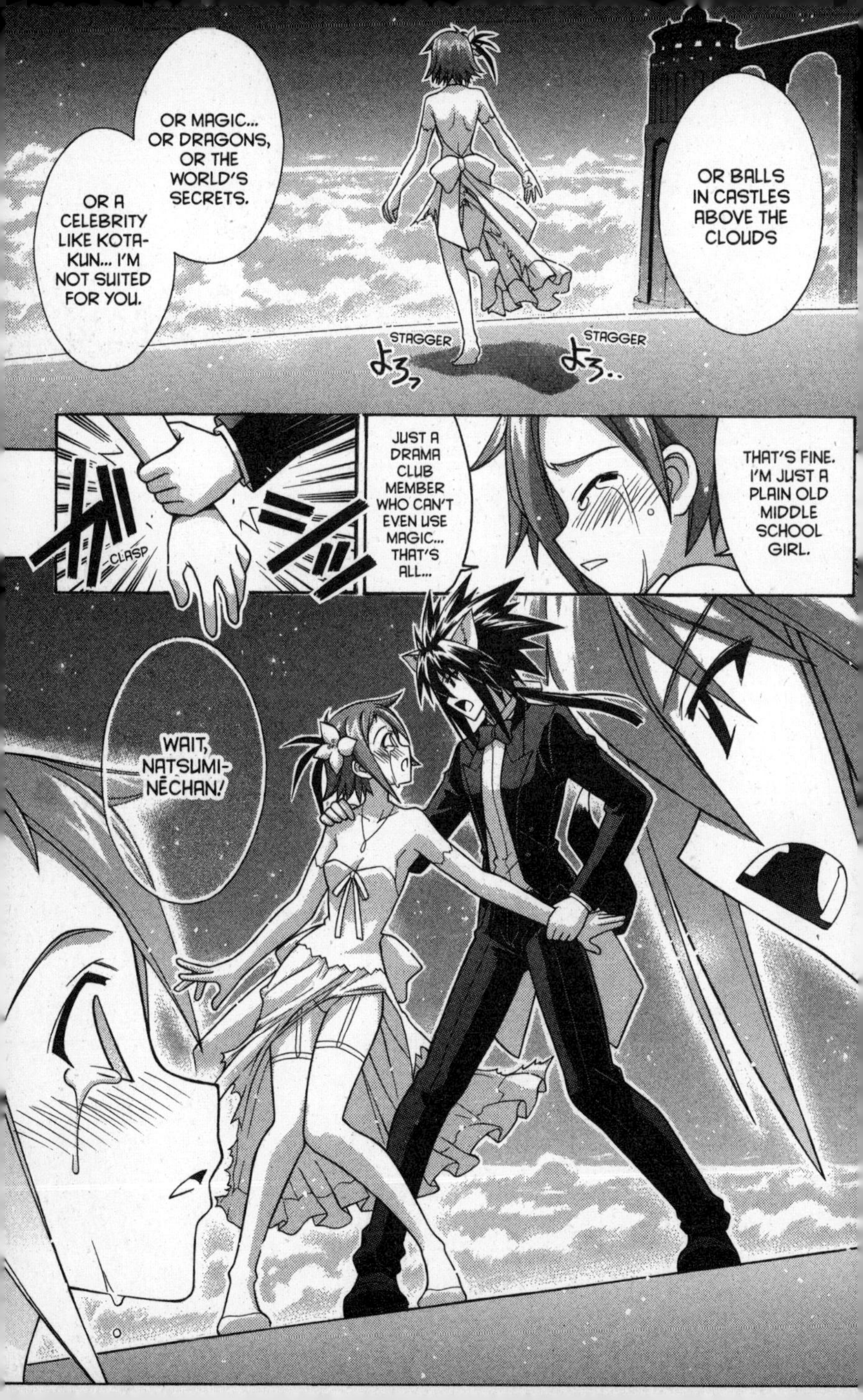
OR BALLS IN CASTLES ABOVE THE CLOUDS
OR MAGIC... OR DRAGONS, OR THE WORLD'S SECRETS.
OR A CELEBRITY LIKE KOTA-KUN... I'M NOT SUITED FOR YOU.
STAGGER
よろ..
STAGGER
よろっ
THAT'S FINE. I'M JUST A PLAIN OLD MIDDLE SCHOOL GIRL.
JUST A DRAMA CLUB MEMBER WHO CAN'T EVEN USE MAGIC... THAT'S ALL...
CLASP
WAIT, NATSUMI-NĒCHAN!

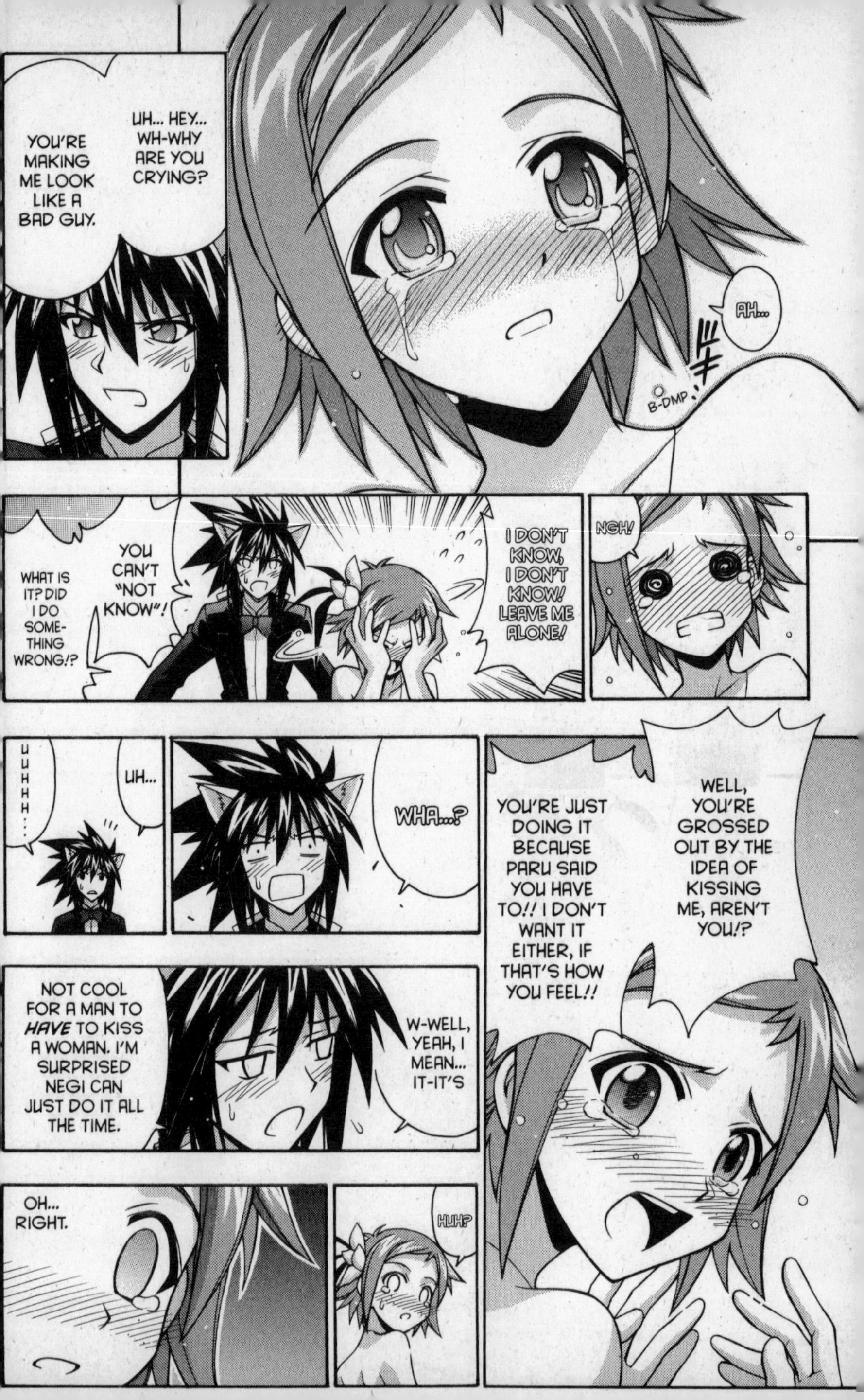
AH...
B-DMP
UH... HEY... WH-WHY ARE YOU CRYING?
YOU'RE MAKING ME LOOK LIKE A BAD GUY.
NGH!
I DON'T KNOW, I DON'T KNOW! LEAVE ME ALONE!
YOU CAN'T "NOT KNOW"!
WHAT IS IT? DID I DO SOMETHING WRONG!?
WELL, YOU'RE GROSSED OUT BY THE IDEA OF KISSING ME, AREN'T YOU!?
YOU'RE JUST DOING IT BECAUSE PARU SAID YOU HAVE TO!! I DON'T WANT IT EITHER, IF THAT'S HOW YOU FEEL!!
WHA...?
UH...
UHHHH...
W-WELL, YEAH, I MEAN... IT-IT'S
NOT COOL FOR A MAN TO *HAVE* TO KISS A WOMAN. I'M SURPRISED NEGI CAN JUST DO IT ALL THE TIME.
HUH?
OH... RIGHT.

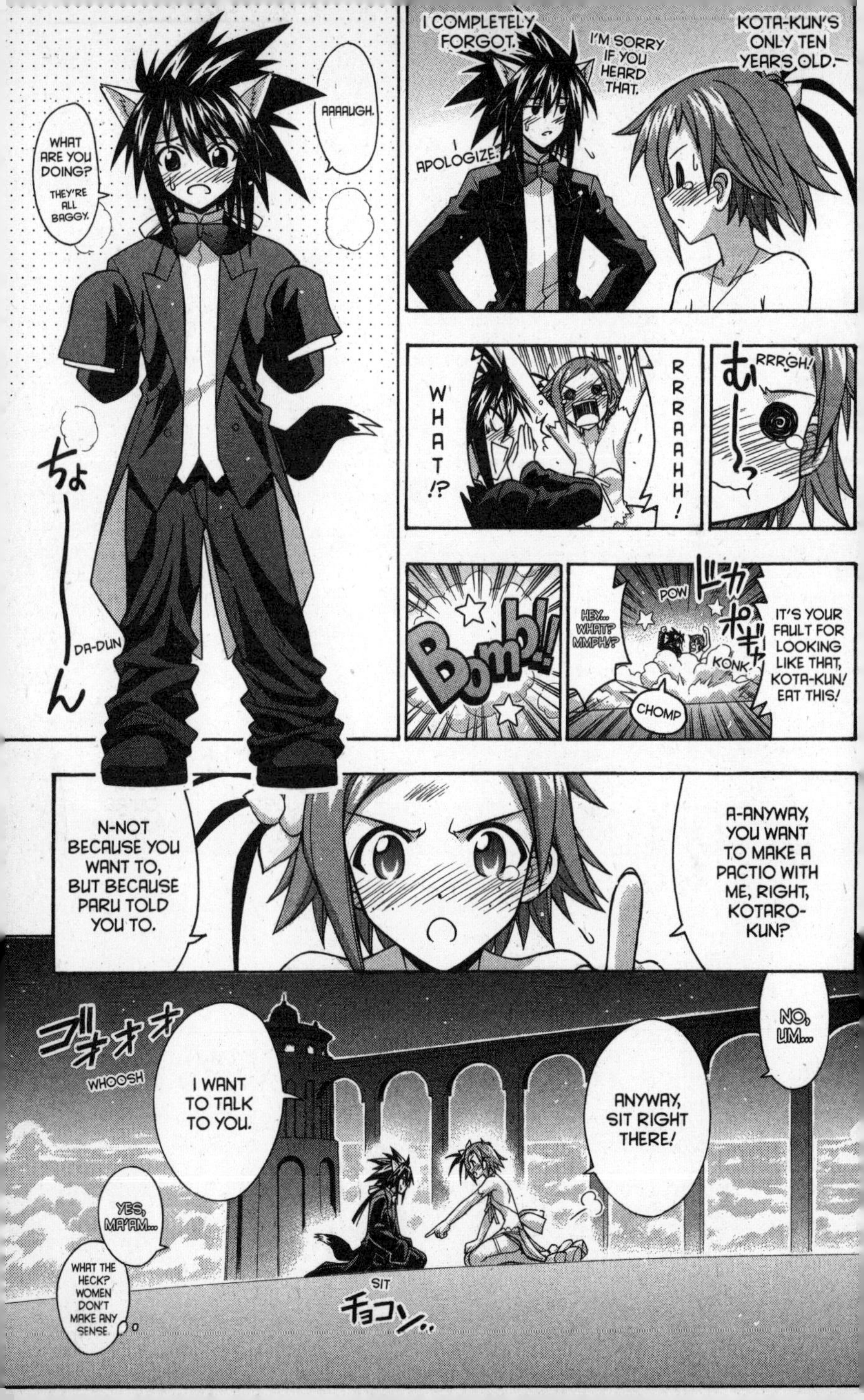
KOTA-KUN'S ONLY TEN YEARS OLD.
I COMPLETELY FORGOT.
I'M SORRY IF YOU HEARD THAT.
I APOLOGIZE.
むーっ
RRRGH!
RRRAAHH!
WHAT!?
ドカ
POW
ポギャ
KONK
IT'S YOUR FAULT FOR LOOKING LIKE THAT, KOTA-KUN! EAT THIS!
HEY... WHAT? MMPH!?
CHOMP
Bomb!!
ちょーん
DA-DUN
RAAAUGH.
WHAT ARE YOU DOING?
THEY'RE ALL BAGGY.
A-ANYWAY, YOU WANT TO MAKE A PACTIO WITH ME, RIGHT, KOTARO-KUN?
N-NOT BECAUSE YOU WANT TO, BUT BECAUSE PARU TOLD YOU TO.
ゴオオオ
WHOOSH
NO, UM...
ANYWAY, SIT RIGHT THERE!
I WANT TO TALK TO YOU.
YES, MA'AM...
WHAT THE HECK? WOMEN DON'T MAKE ANY SENSE.
チョコン
SIT

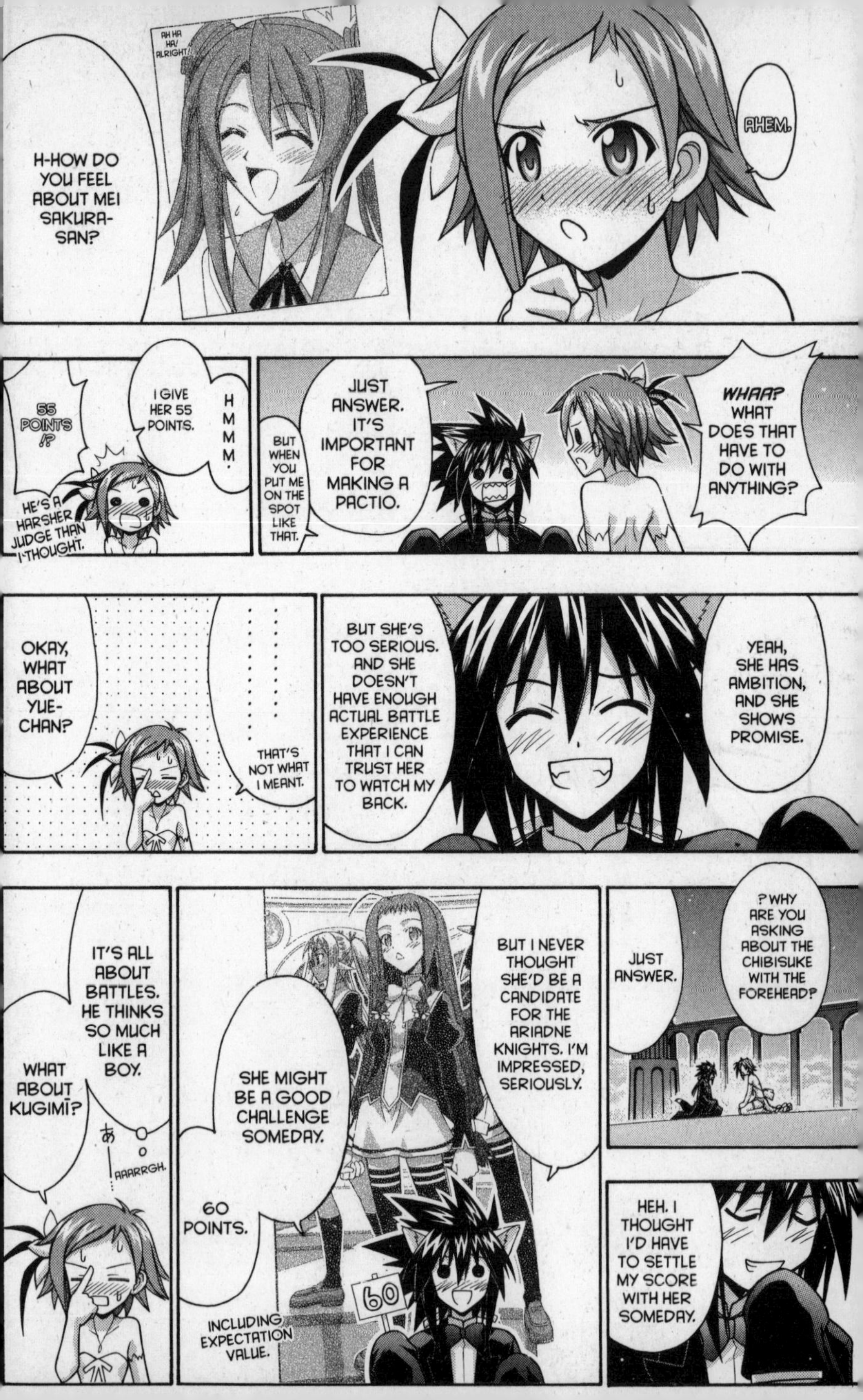
AHEM.
AH HA HA! ALRIGHT!
H-HOW DO YOU FEEL ABOUT MEI SAKURA-SAN?
WHAA? WHAT DOES THAT HAVE TO DO WITH ANYTHING?
JUST ANSWER. IT'S IMPORTANT FOR MAKING A PACTIO.
BUT WHEN YOU PUT ME ON THE SPOT LIKE THAT.
HMMM.
I GIVE HER 55 POINTS.
55 POINTS!?
HE'S A HARSHER JUDGE THAN I THOUGHT.
YEAH, SHE HAS AMBITION, AND SHE SHOWS PROMISE.
BUT SHE'S TOO SERIOUS. AND SHE DOESN'T HAVE ENOUGH ACTUAL BATTLE EXPERIENCE THAT I CAN TRUST HER TO WATCH MY BACK.
THAT'S NOT WHAT I MEANT.
OKAY, WHAT ABOUT YUE-CHAN?
?WHY ARE YOU ASKING ABOUT THE CHIBISUKE WITH THE FOREHEAD?
JUST ANSWER.
HEH. I THOUGHT I'D HAVE TO SETTLE MY SCORE WITH HER SOMEDAY.
BUT I NEVER THOUGHT SHE'D BE A CANDIDATE FOR THE ARIADNE KNIGHTS. I'M IMPRESSED, SERIOUSLY.
SHE MIGHT BE A GOOD CHALLENGE SOMEDAY.
60 POINTS.
60
INCLUDING EXPECTATION VALUE.
IT'S ALL ABOUT BATTLES. HE THINKS SO MUCH LIKE A BOY.
WHAT ABOUT KUGIMĪ?
あ
AAARRGH.

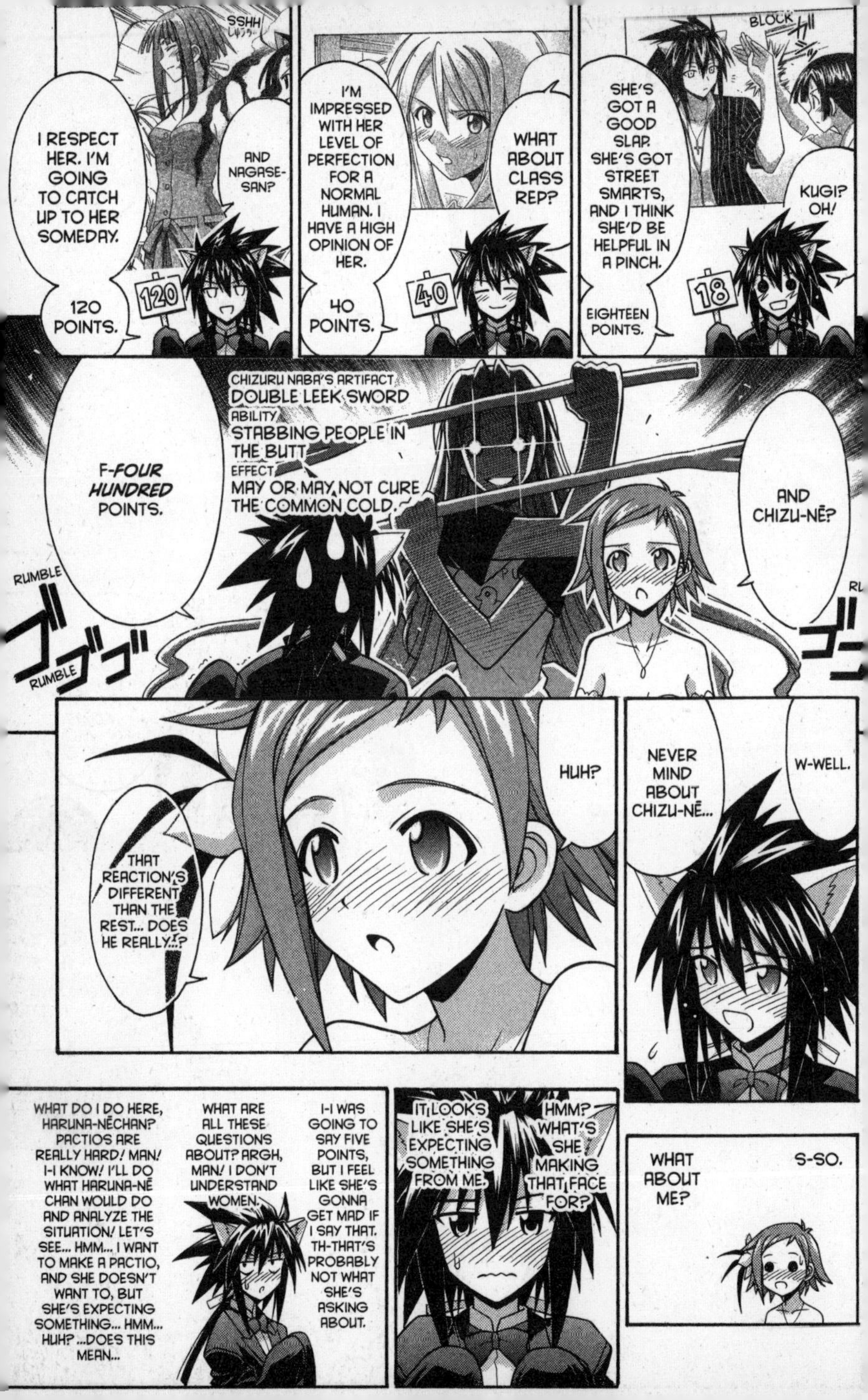
BLOCK
KUGI? OH!
SHE'S GOT A GOOD SLAP. SHE'S GOT STREET SMARTS, AND I THINK SHE'D BE HELPFUL IN A PINCH.
18
EIGHTEEN POINTS.
WHAT ABOUT CLASS REP?
I'M IMPRESSED WITH HER LEVEL OF PERFECTION FOR A NORMAL HUMAN. I HAVE A HIGH OPINION OF HER.
40
40 POINTS.
SSHH
AND NAGASE-SAN?
I RESPECT HER. I'M GOING TO CATCH UP TO HER SOMEDAY.
120
120 POINTS.
AND CHIZU-NĒ?
CHIZURU NABA'S ARTIFACT DOUBLE LEEK SWORD ABILITY STABBING PEOPLE IN THE BUTT EFFECT MAY OR MAY NOT CURE THE COMMON COLD.
F-FOUR HUNDRED POINTS.
RUMBLE
RUMBLE
W-WELL.
NEVER MIND ABOUT CHIZU-NĒ...
HUH?
THAT REACTION'S DIFFERENT THAN THE REST... DOES HE REALLY...!?
S-SO.
WHAT ABOUT ME?
HMM? WHAT'S SHE MAKING THAT FACE FOR?
IT LOOKS LIKE SHE'S EXPECTING SOMETHING FROM ME.
I-I WAS GOING TO SAY FIVE POINTS, BUT I FEEL LIKE SHE'S GONNA GET MAD IF I SAY THAT. TH-THAT'S PROBABLY NOT WHAT SHE'S ASKING ABOUT.
WHAT ARE ALL THESE QUESTIONS ABOUT? ARGH, MAN! I DON'T UNDERSTAND WOMEN.
WHAT DO I DO HERE, HARUNA-NĒCHAN? PACTIOS ARE REALLY HARD! MAN! I-I KNOW! I'LL DO WHAT HARUNA-NĒ CHAN WOULD DO AND ANALYZE THE SITUATION! LET'S SEE... HMM... I WANT TO MAKE A PACTIO, AND SHE DOESN'T WANT TO, BUT SHE'S EXPECTING SOMETHING... HMM... HUH? ...DOES THIS MEAN...

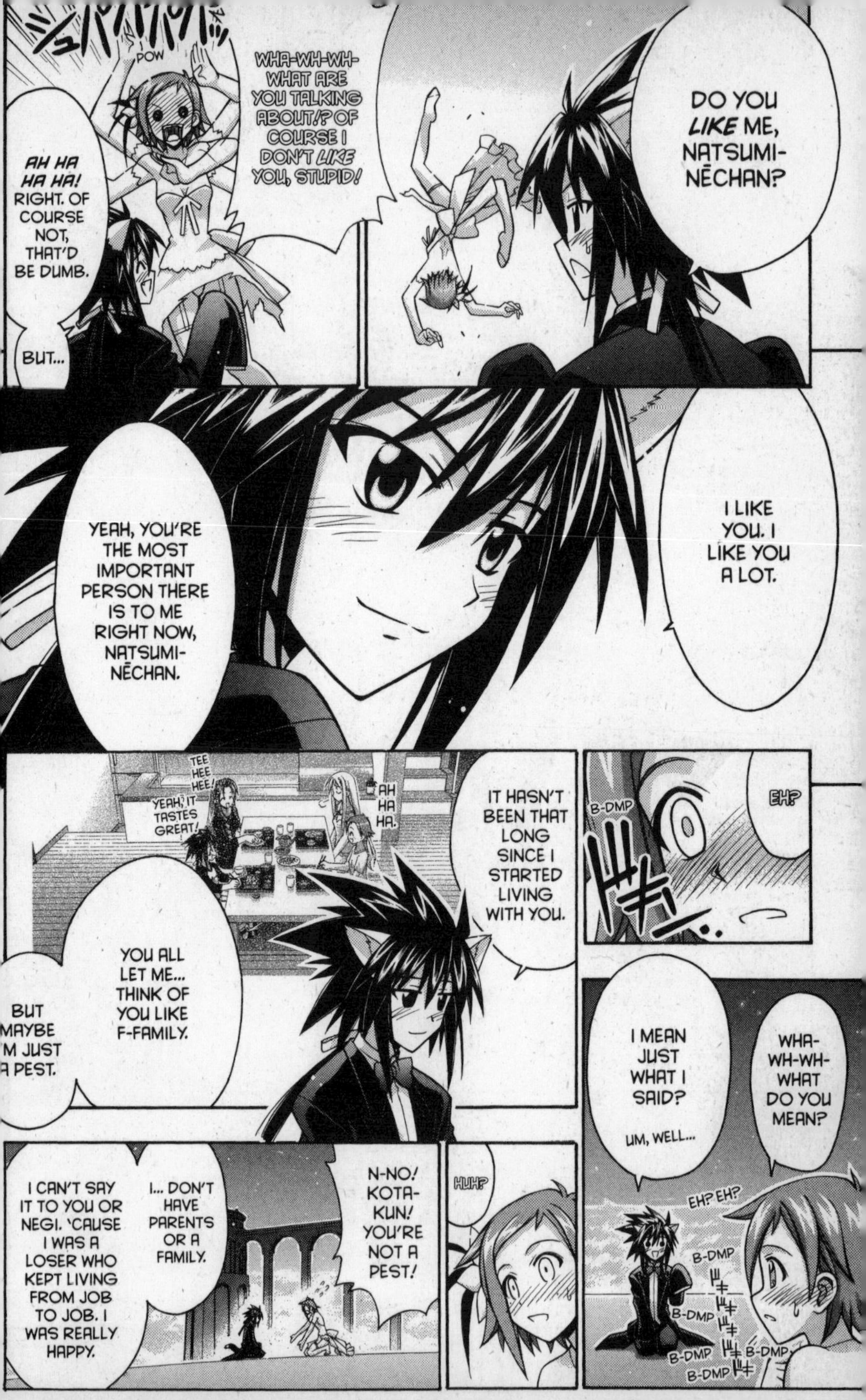
DO YOU LIKE ME, NATSUMI-NĒCHAN?
POW
WHA-WH-WH-WHAT ARE YOU TALKING ABOUT!? OF COURSE I DON'T LIKE YOU, STUPID!
AH HA HA HA! RIGHT. OF COURSE NOT, THAT'D BE DUMB.
BUT...
I LIKE YOU. I LIKE YOU A LOT.
YEAH, YOU'RE THE MOST IMPORTANT PERSON THERE IS TO ME RIGHT NOW, NATSUMI-NĒCHAN.
EH?
B-DMP
WHA-WH-WH-WHAT DO YOU MEAN?
I MEAN JUST WHAT I SAID?
UM, WELL...
EH? EH?
B-DMP
B-DMP
B-DMP
B-DMP
B-DMP
TEE HEE HEE!
YEAH, IT TASTES GREAT!
AH HA HA.
IT HASN'T BEEN THAT LONG SINCE I STARTED LIVING WITH YOU.
YOU ALL LET ME... THINK OF YOU LIKE F-FAMILY.
BUT MAYBE I'M JUST A PEST.
HUH?
N-NO! KOTA-KUN! YOU'RE NOT A PEST!
I... DON'T HAVE PARENTS OR A FAMILY.
I CAN'T SAY IT TO YOU OR NEGI. 'CAUSE I WAS A LOSER WHO KEPT LIVING FROM JOB TO JOB. I WAS REALLY HAPPY.

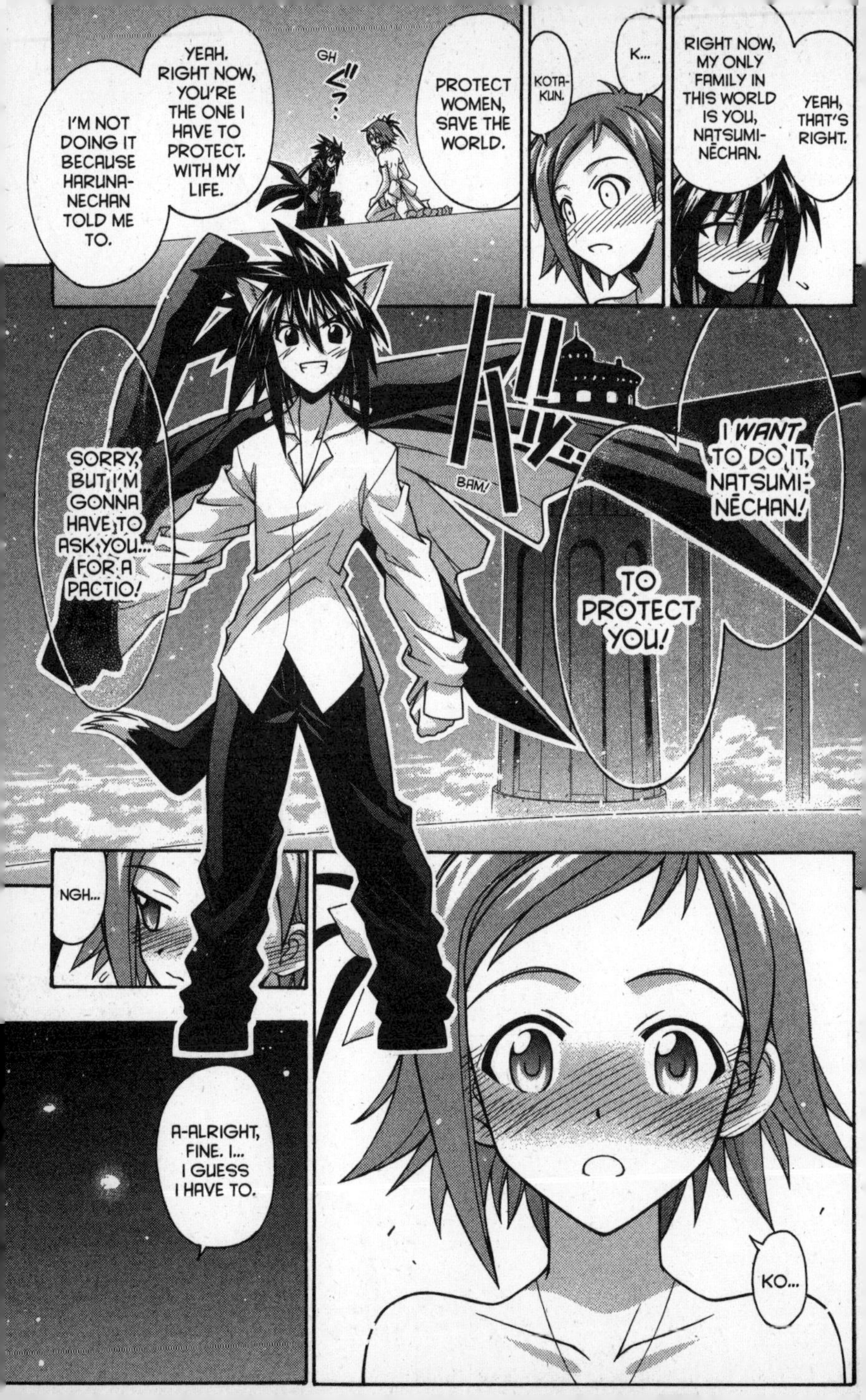
RIGHT NOW, MY ONLY FAMILY IN THIS WORLD IS YOU, NATSUMI-NĒCHAN.
YEAH, THAT'S RIGHT.
K...
KOTA-KUN.
PROTECT WOMEN, SAVE THE WORLD.
GH
YEAH. RIGHT NOW, YOU'RE THE ONE I HAVE TO PROTECT. WITH MY LIFE.
I'M NOT DOING IT BECAUSE HARUNA-NECHAN TOLD ME TO.
I WANT TO DO IT, NATSUMI-NĒCHAN!
TO PROTECT YOU!
BAM!
SORRY, BUT I'M GONNA HAVE TO ASK YOU... FOR A PACTIO!
KO...
NGH...
A-ALRIGHT, FINE. I... I GUESS I HAVE TO.

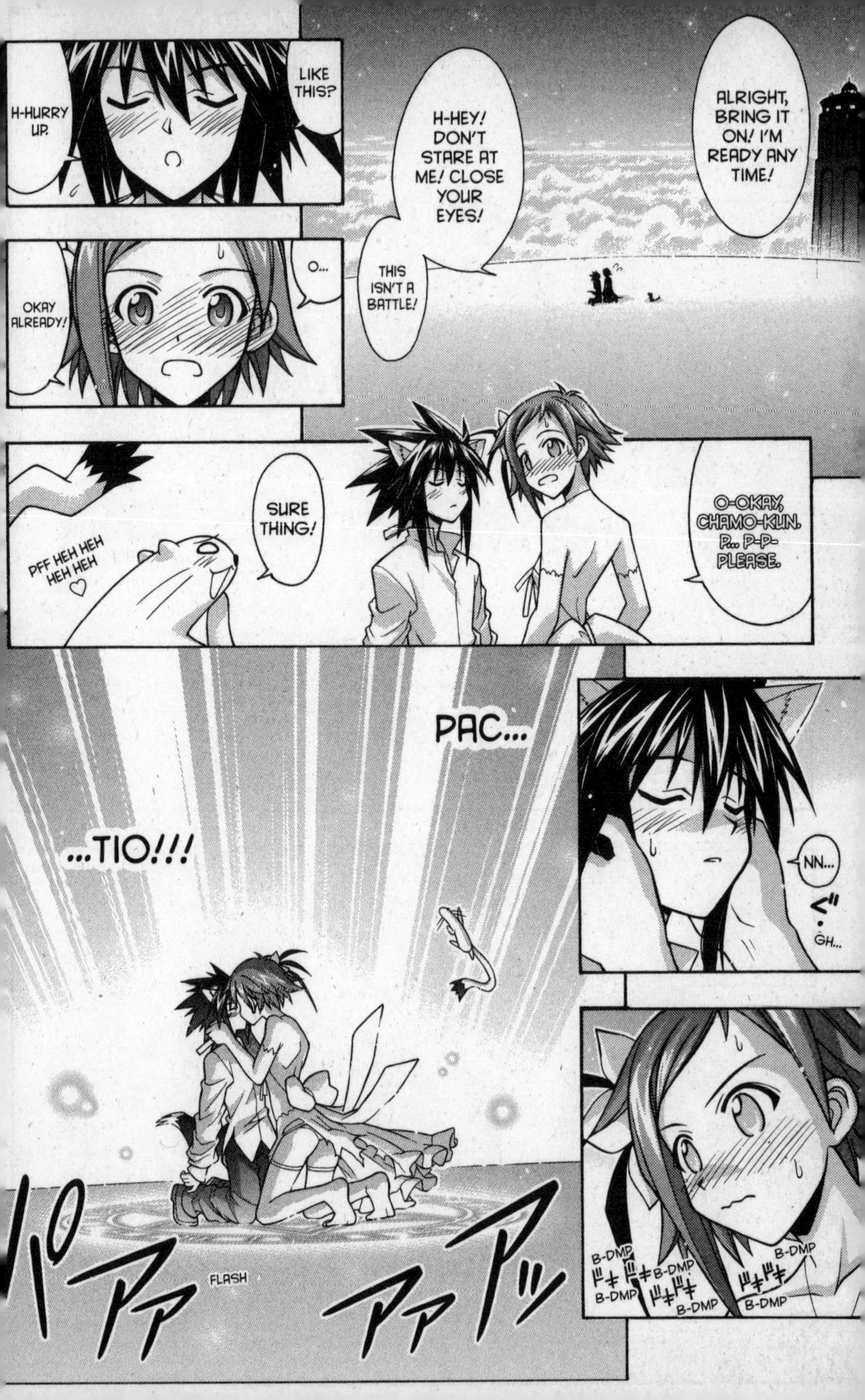
ALRIGHT, BRING IT ON! I'M READY ANY TIME!
H-HEY! DON'T STARE AT ME! CLOSE YOUR EYES!
THIS ISN'T A BATTLE!
LIKE THIS?
H-HURRY UP.
O...
OKAY ALREADY!
O-OKAY, CHAMO-KUN. P... P-P-PLEASE.
SURE THING!
PFF HEH HEH HEH HEH ♡
NN...
ぐ
GH...
ドキドキ
B-DMP
B-DMP
ドキドキ
B-DMP
B-DMP
ドキドキ
B-DMP
B-DMP
PAC...
...TIO!!!
パァァアッ
FLASH

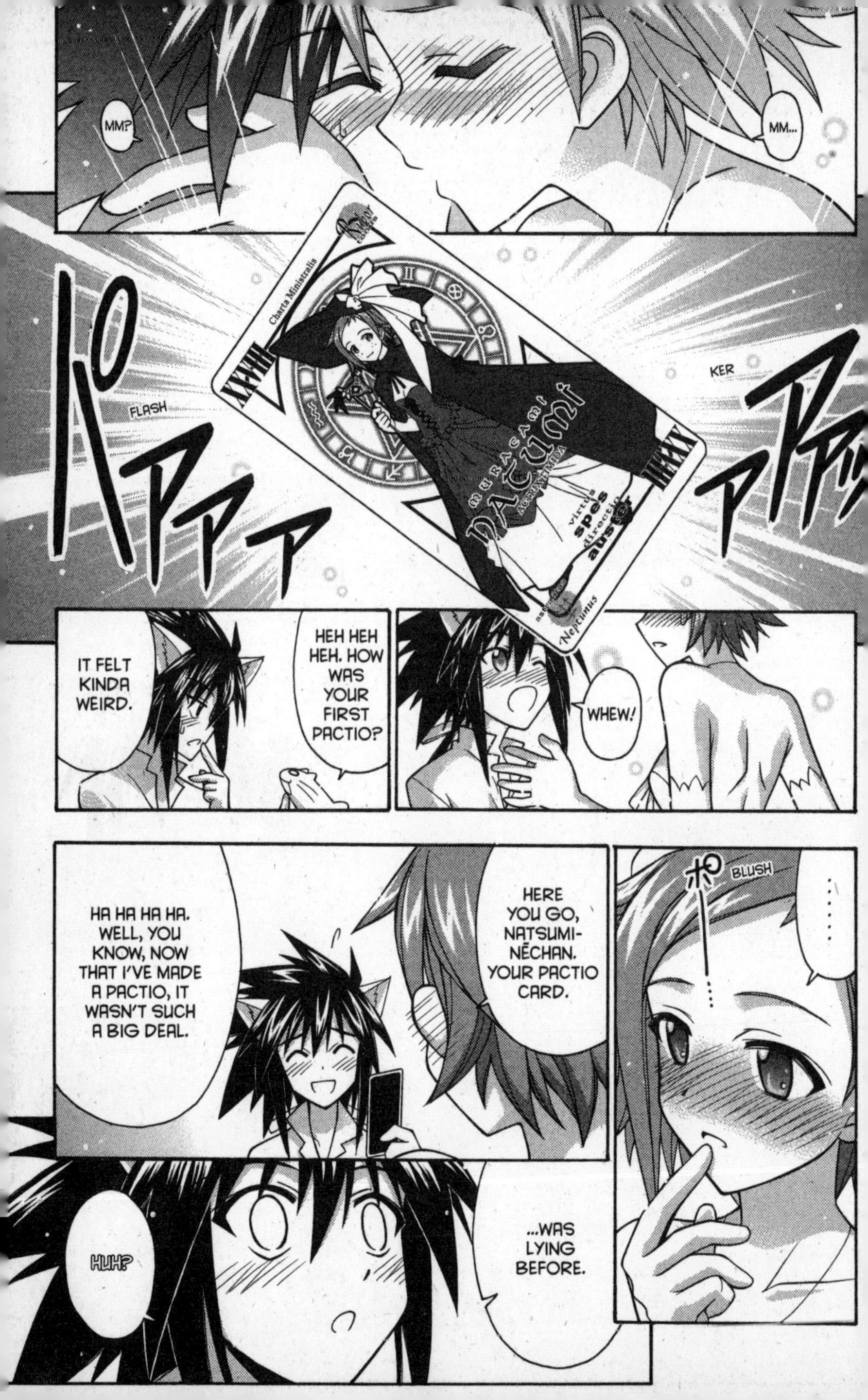
MM...
MM?
KER
FLASH
Charta Ministralis
virtus
spes
directio
auster
Neptunus
WHEW!
HEH HEH HEH. HOW WAS YOUR FIRST PACTIO?
IT FELT KINDA WEIRD.
......
BLUSH
HERE YOU GO, NATSUMI-NĒCHAN. YOUR PACTIO CARD.
HA HA HA HA. WELL, YOU KNOW, NOW THAT I'VE MADE A PACTIO, IT WASN'T SUCH A BIG DEAL.
...WAS LYING BEFORE.
HUH?

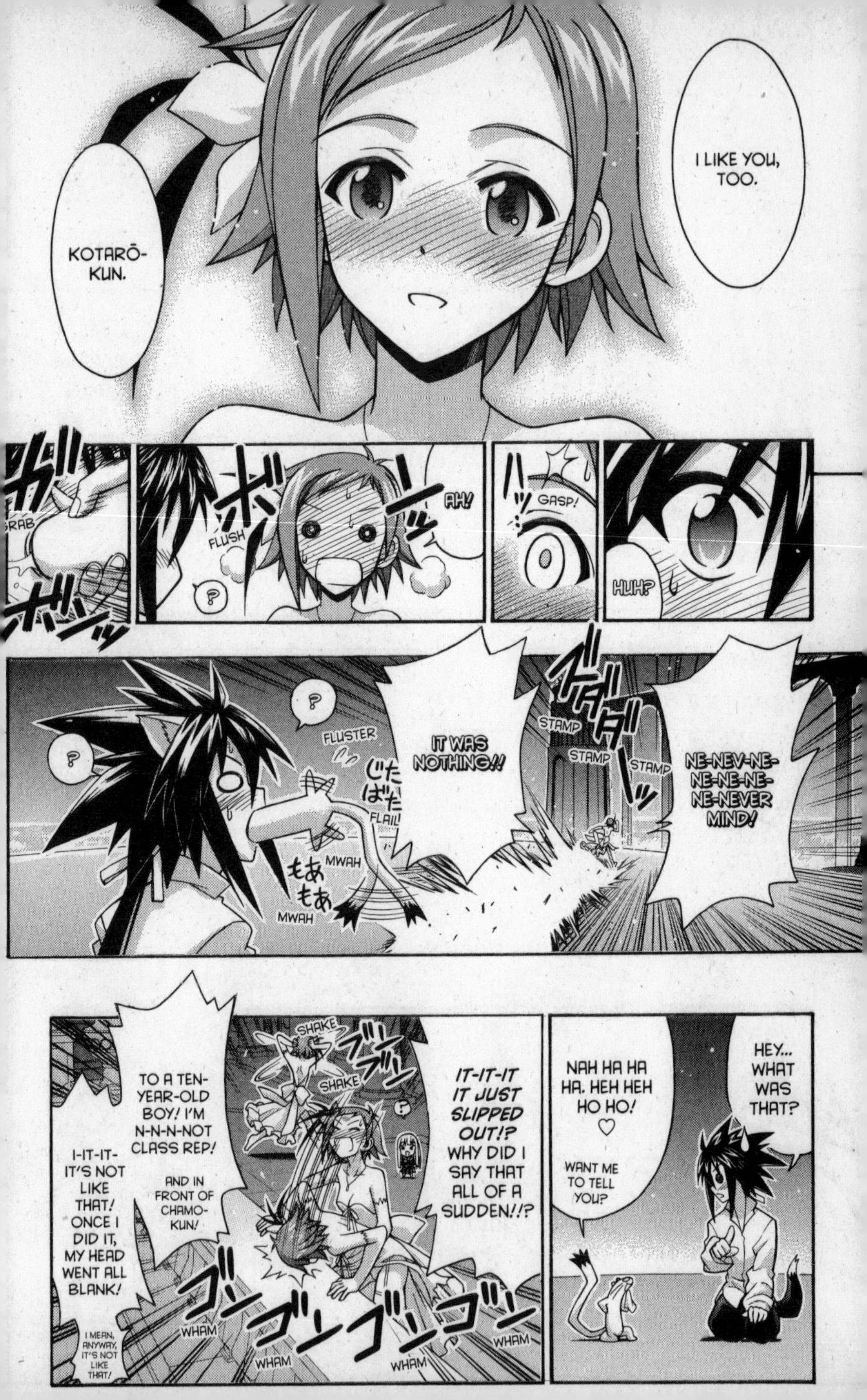
I LIKE YOU, TOO.
KOTARŌ-KUN.
HUH?
GASP!
AH!
FLUSH
?
GRAB
NE-NEV-NE-NE-NE-NE-NE-NEVER MIND!
STAMP
STAMP
STAMP
IT WAS NOTHING!!
FLUSTER
じたばた
FLAIL
?
?
もあもあ
MWAH
MWAH
HEY... WHAT WAS THAT?
NAH HA HA HA. HEH HEH HO HO! ♡
WANT ME TO TELL YOU?
IT-IT-IT IT JUST SLIPPED OUT!? WHY DID I SAY THAT ALL OF A SUDDEN!!?
SHAKE
SHAKE
?
TO A TEN-YEAR-OLD BOY! I'M N-N-N-NOT CLASS REP!
AND IN FRONT OF CHAMO-KUN!
I-IT-IT-IT'S NOT LIKE THAT! ONCE I DID IT, MY HEAD WENT ALL BLANK!
WHAM
WHAM
WHAM
WHAM
I MEAN, ANYWAY, IT'S NOT LIKE THAT!

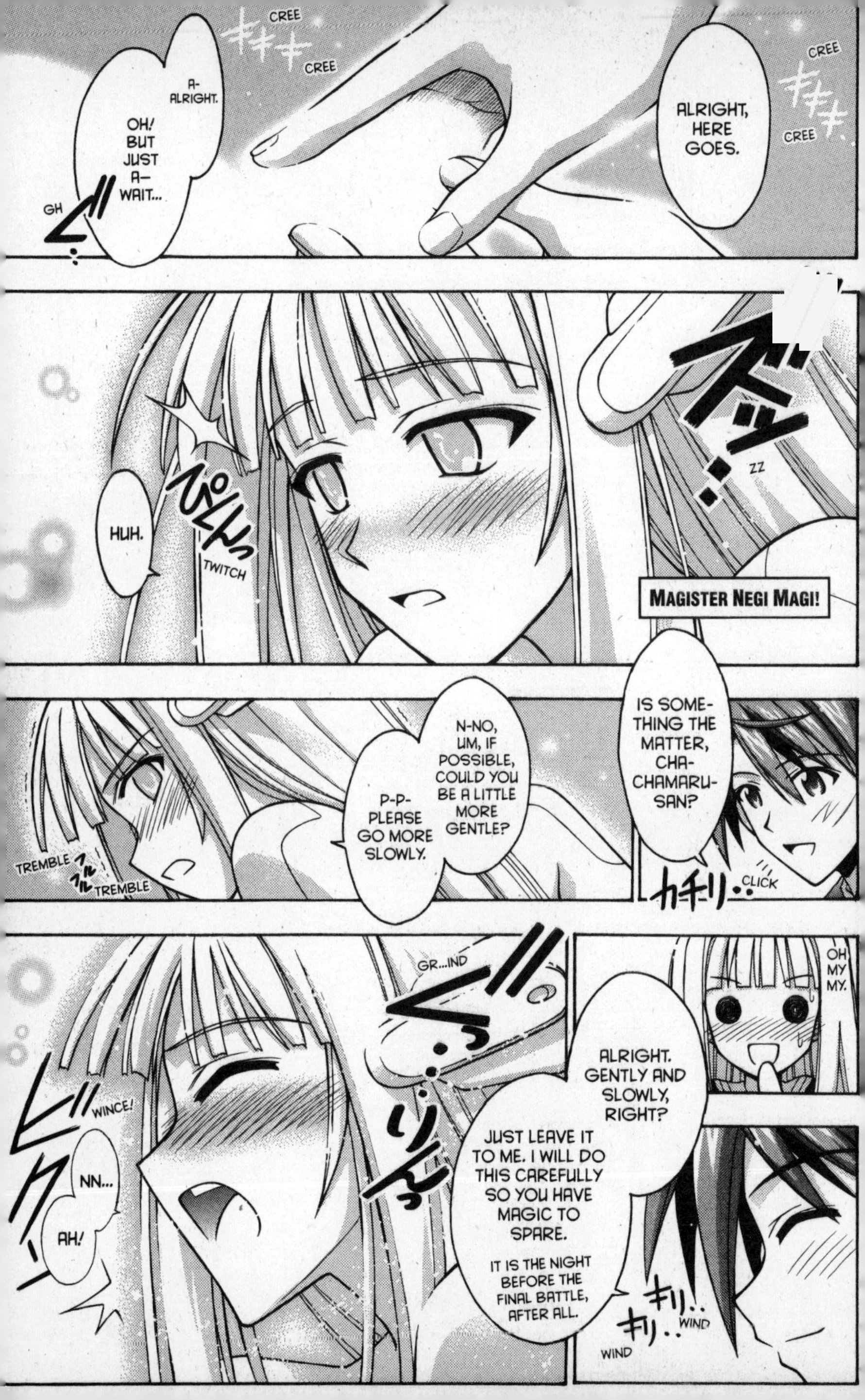
CREE
CREE
ALRIGHT, HERE GOES.
CREE
CREE
A-ALRIGHT.
OH! BUT JUST A— WAIT...
GH
MAGISTER NEGI MAGI!
ZZ
HUH.
TWITCH
IS SOME-THING THE MATTER, CHA-CHAMARU-SAN?
CLICK
N-NO, UM, IF POSSIBLE, COULD YOU BE A LITTLE MORE GENTLE?
P-P-PLEASE GO MORE SLOWLY.
TREMBLE
TREMBLE
OH MY MY.
ALRIGHT. GENTLY AND SLOWLY, RIGHT?
JUST LEAVE IT TO ME. I WILL DO THIS CAREFULLY SO YOU HAVE MAGIC TO SPARE.
IT IS THE NIGHT BEFORE THE FINAL BATTLE, AFTER ALL.
WIND
WIND
GR...IND
WINCE!
NN...
AH!

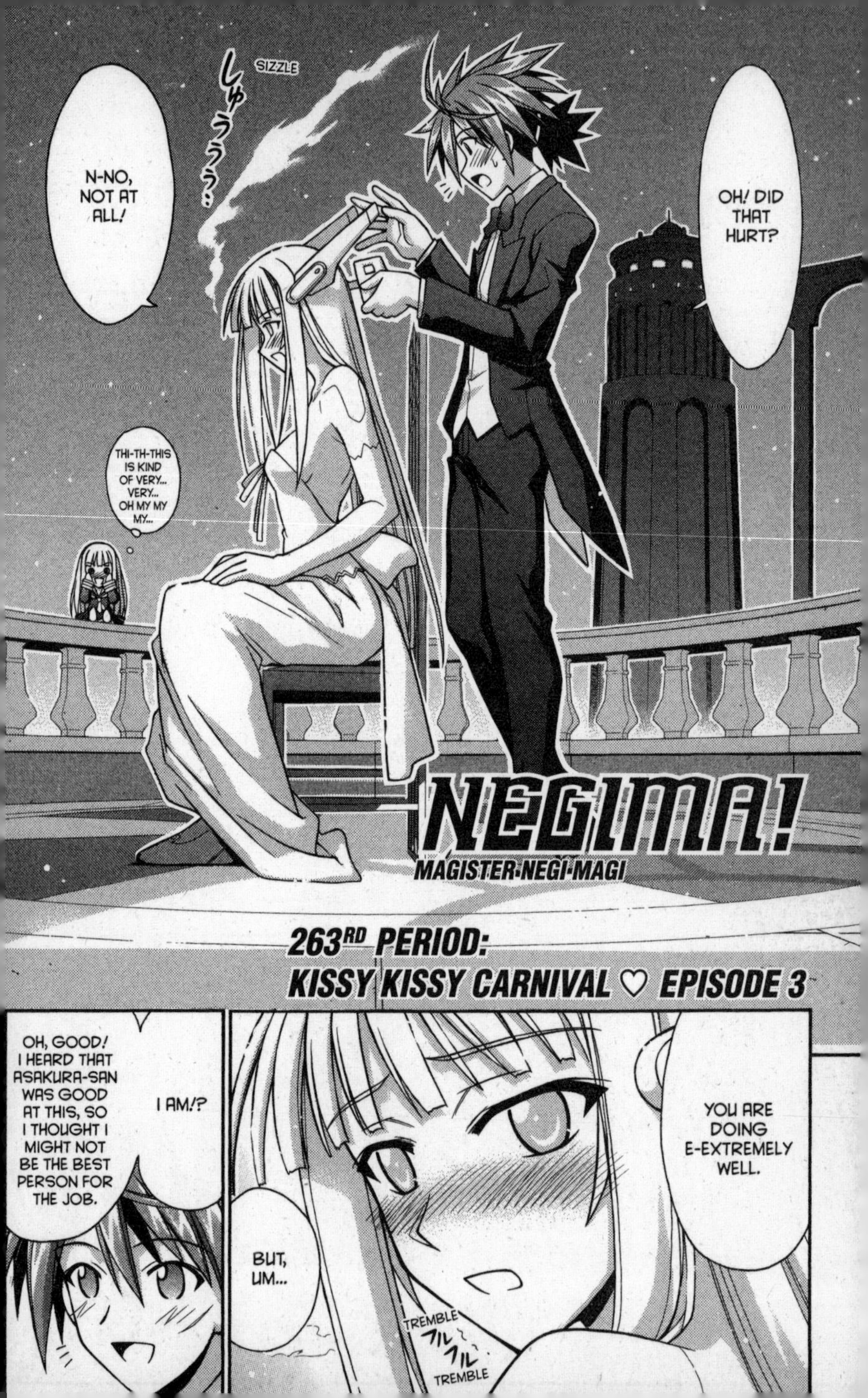
OH! DID THAT HURT?
SIZZLE
N-NO, NOT AT ALL!
THI-TH-THIS IS KIND OF VERY... VERY... OH MY MY MY...
NEGIMA!
MAGISTER NEGI MAGI
263RD PERIOD:
KISSY KISSY CARNIVAL ♡ EPISODE 3
YOU ARE DOING E-EXTREMELY WELL.
BUT, UM...
TREMBLE
TREMBLE
OH, GOOD! I HEARD THAT ASAKURA-SAN WAS GOOD AT THIS, SO I THOUGHT I MIGHT NOT BE THE BEST PERSON FOR THE JOB.
I AM!?

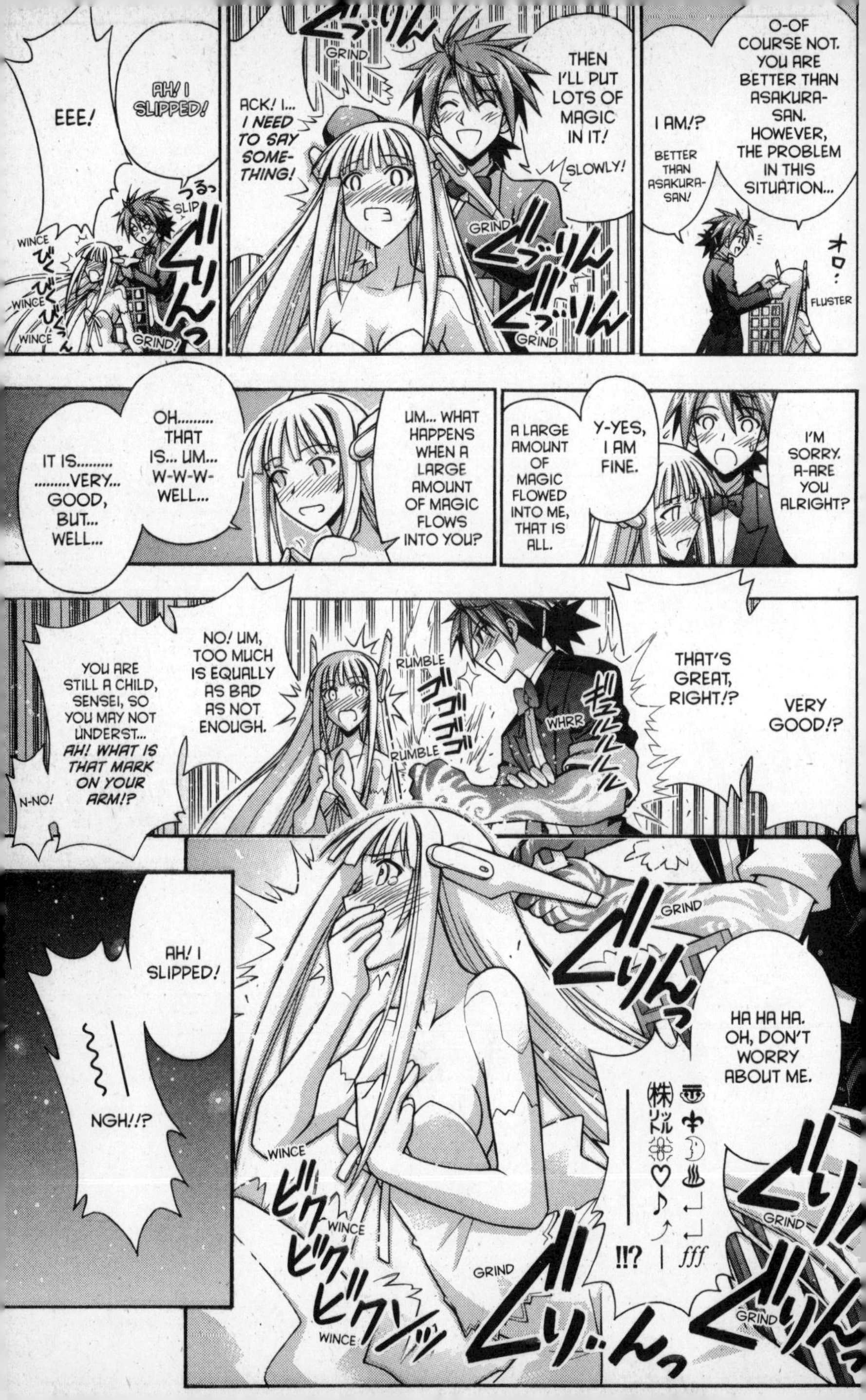
O-OF COURSE NOT. YOU ARE BETTER THAN ASAKURA-SAN. HOWEVER, THE PROBLEM IN THIS SITUATION...
I AM!?
BETTER THAN ASAKURA-SAN!
FLUSTER
THEN I'LL PUT LOTS OF MAGIC IN IT!
SLOWLY!
GRIND
GRIND
ACK! I... I NEED TO SAY SOMETHING!
GRIND
AH! I SLIPPED!
EEE!
SLIP
WINCE
WINCE
WINCE
GRIND!
I'M SORRY. A-ARE YOU ALRIGHT?
Y-YES, I AM FINE.
A LARGE AMOUNT OF MAGIC FLOWED INTO ME, THAT IS ALL.
UM... WHAT HAPPENS WHEN A LARGE AMOUNT OF MAGIC FLOWS INTO YOU?
OH......... THAT IS... UM... W-W-W-WELL...
IT IS......... ....VERY... GOOD, BUT... WELL...
VERY GOOD!?
THAT'S GREAT, RIGHT!?
WHRR
RUMBLE
RUMBLE
NO! UM, TOO MUCH IS EQUALLY AS BAD AS NOT ENOUGH.
YOU ARE STILL A CHILD, SENSEI, SO YOU MAY NOT UNDERST... AH! WHAT IS THAT MARK ON YOUR ARM!?
N-NO!
HA HA HA. OH, DON'T WORRY ABOUT ME.
GRIND
GRIND
GRIND
!!?
GRIND
WINCE
WINCE
WINCE
AH! I SLIPPED!
NGH!!?

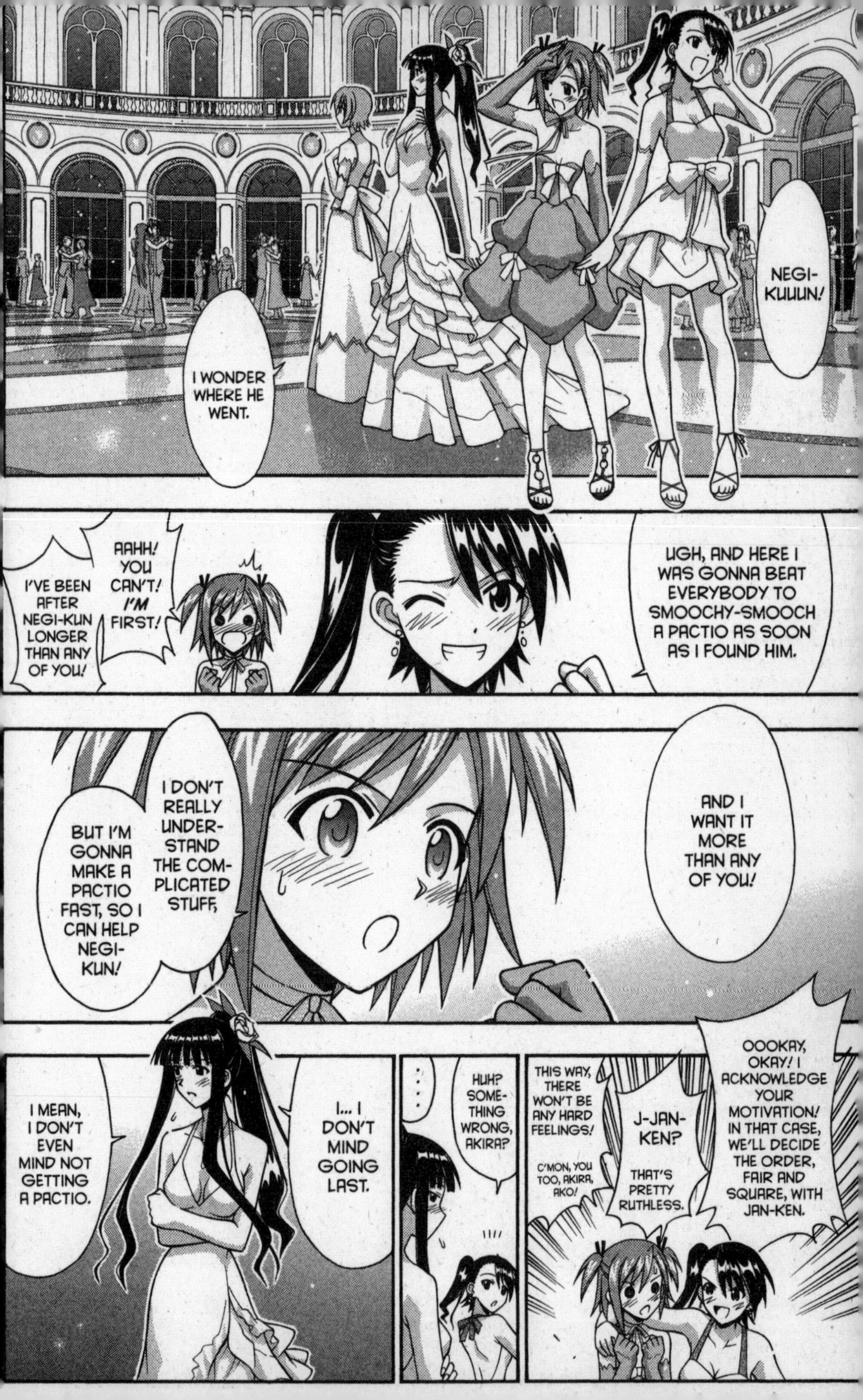

NEGI-KUUUN!
I WONDER WHERE HE WENT.
UGH, AND HERE I WAS GONNA BEAT EVERYBODY TO SMOOCHY-SMOOCH A PACTIO AS SOON AS I FOUND HIM.
AAHH! YOU CAN'T! I'M FIRST!
I'VE BEEN AFTER NEGI-KUN LONGER THAN ANY OF YOU!
AND I WANT IT MORE THAN ANY OF YOU!
I DON'T REALLY UNDERSTAND THE COMPLICATED STUFF,
BUT I'M GONNA MAKE A PACTIO FAST, SO I CAN HELP NEGI-KUN!
OOOKAY, OKAY! I ACKNOWLEDGE YOUR MOTIVATION! IN THAT CASE, WE'LL DECIDE THE ORDER, FAIR AND SQUARE, WITH JAN-KEN.
J-JAN-KEN?
THAT'S PRETTY RUTHLESS.
THIS WAY, THERE WON'T BE ANY HARD FEELINGS!
C'MON, YOU TOO, AKIRA, AKO!
HUH? SOMETHING WRONG, AKIRA?
...
I... I DON'T MIND GOING LAST.
I MEAN, I DON'T EVEN MIND NOT GETTING A PACTIO.

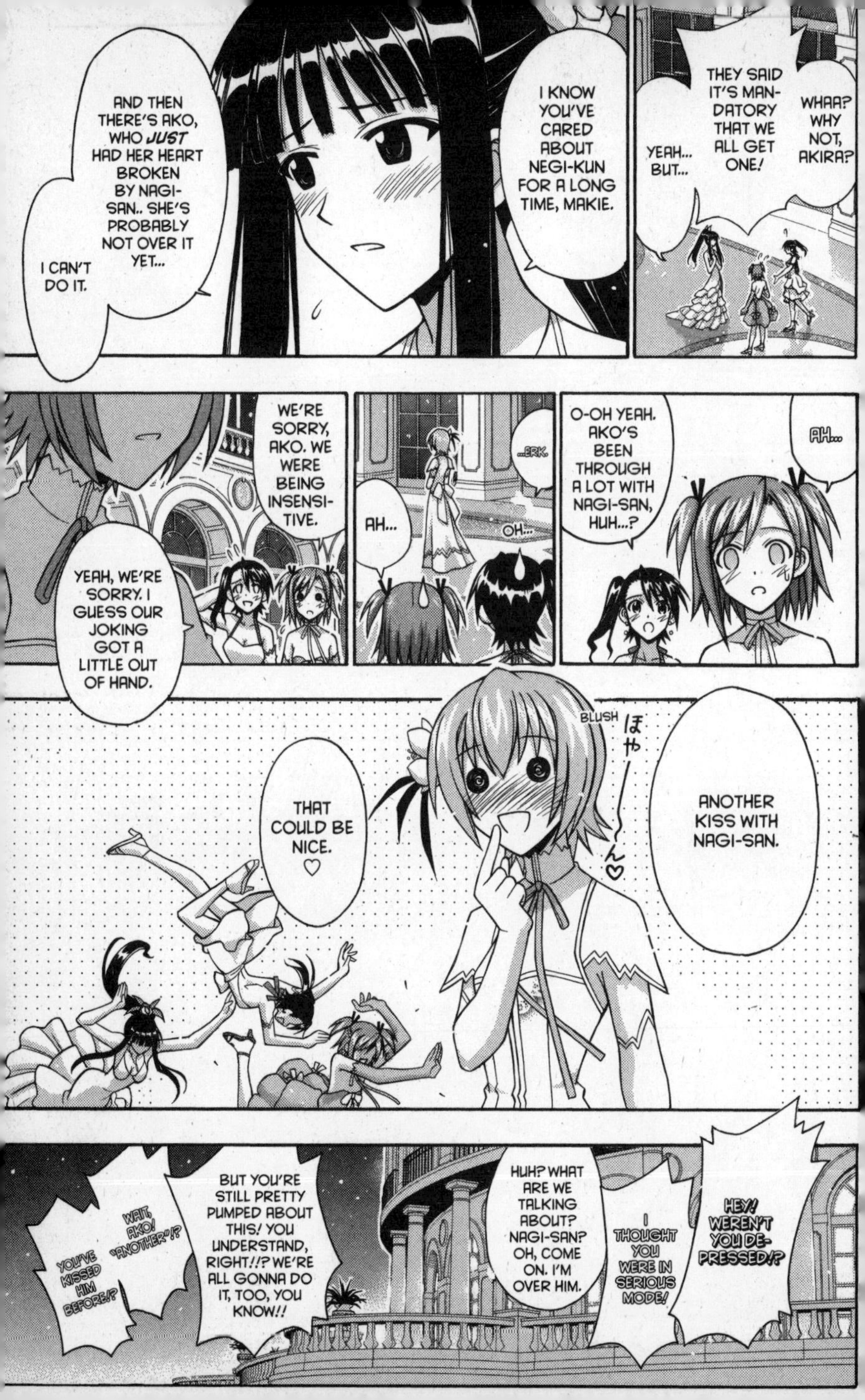
WHAA? WHY NOT, AKIRA?
THEY SAID IT'S MAN-DATORY THAT WE ALL GET ONE!
YEAH... BUT...
I KNOW YOU'VE CARED ABOUT NEGI-KUN FOR A LONG TIME, MAKIE.
AND THEN THERE'S AKO, WHO *JUST* HAD HER HEART BROKEN BY NAGI-SAN.. SHE'S PROBABLY NOT OVER IT YET...
I CAN'T DO IT.
AH...
O-OH YEAH. AKO'S BEEN THROUGH A LOT WITH NAGI-SAN, HUH...?
...ERK.
AH...
OH...
WE'RE SORRY, AKO. WE WERE BEING INSENSI-TIVE.
YEAH, WE'RE SORRY. I GUESS OUR JOKING GOT A LITTLE OUT OF HAND.
ANOTHER KISS WITH NAGI-SAN.
ほや～ん♡
BLUSH
THAT COULD BE NICE. ♡
HEY! WEREN'T YOU DE-PRESSED!?
I THOUGHT YOU WERE IN SERIOUS MODE!
HUH? WHAT ARE WE TALKING ABOUT? NAGI-SAN? OH, COME ON. I'M OVER HIM.
BUT YOU'RE STILL PRETTY PUMPED ABOUT THIS! YOU UNDERSTAND, RIGHT!!? WE'RE ALL GONNA DO IT, TOO, YOU KNOW!!
WAIT, AKO! "ANOTHER"!?
YOU'VE KISSED HIM BEFORE!?

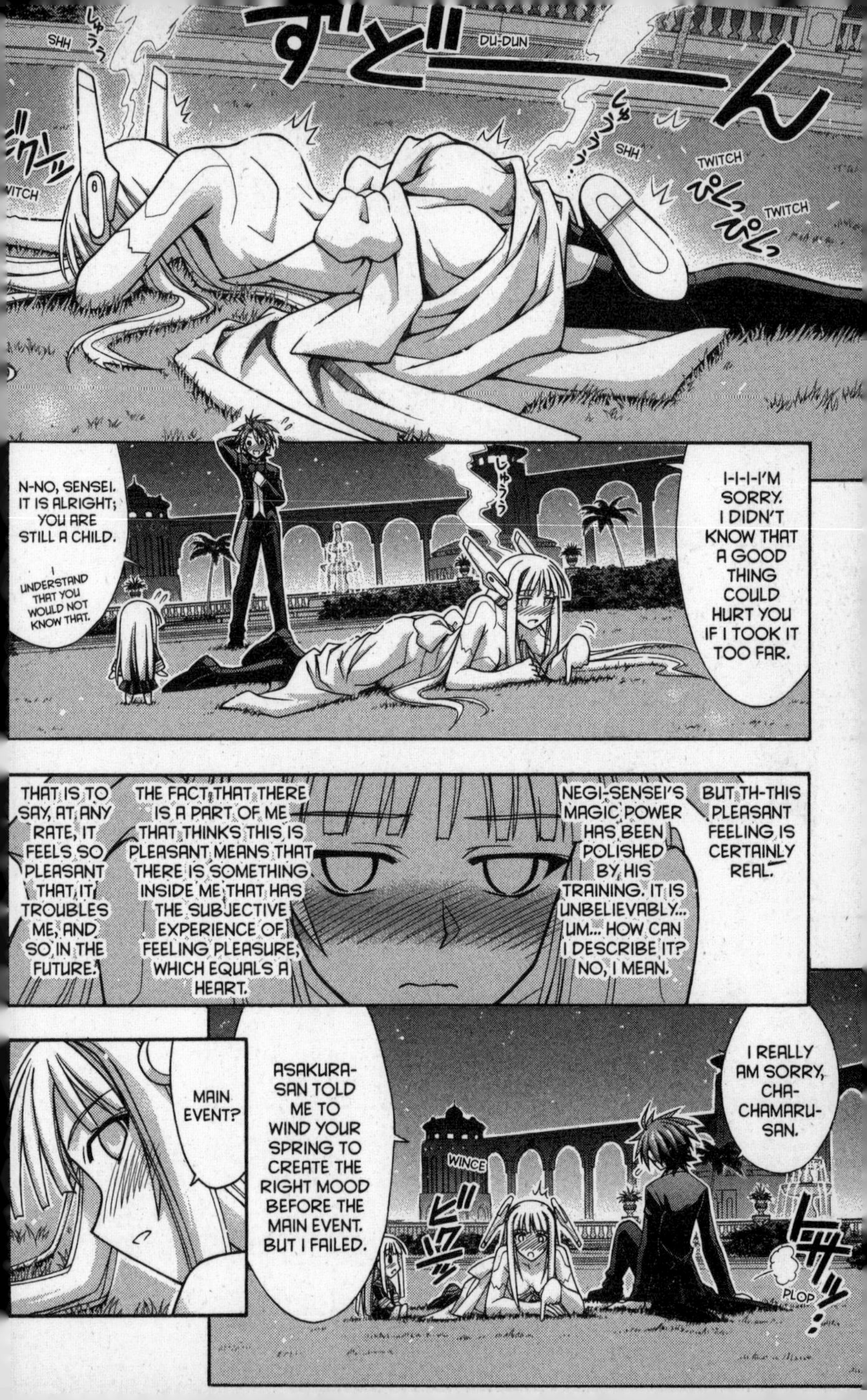

ずど————ん
DU-DUN
SHH
TWITCH
TWITCH
SHH
I-I-I-I'M SORRY. I DIDN'T KNOW THAT A GOOD THING COULD HURT YOU IF I TOOK IT TOO FAR.
N-NO, SENSEI. IT IS ALRIGHT; YOU ARE STILL A CHILD.
I UNDERSTAND THAT YOU WOULD NOT KNOW THAT.
BUT TH-THIS PLEASANT FEELING IS CERTAINLY REAL.
NEGI-SENSEI'S MAGIC POWER HAS BEEN POLISHED BY HIS TRAINING. IT IS UNBELIEVABLY... UM... HOW CAN I DESCRIBE IT? NO, I MEAN.
THE FACT THAT THERE IS A PART OF ME THAT THINKS THIS IS PLEASANT MEANS THAT THERE IS SOMETHING INSIDE ME THAT HAS THE SUBJECTIVE EXPERIENCE OF FEELING PLEASURE, WHICH EQUALS A HEART.
THAT IS TO SAY, AT ANY RATE, IT FEELS SO PLEASANT THAT IT TROUBLES ME, AND SO IN THE FUTURE.
I REALLY AM SORRY, CHA-CHAMARU-SAN.
PLOP
WINCE
ASAKURA-SAN TOLD ME TO WIND YOUR SPRING TO CREATE THE RIGHT MOOD BEFORE THE MAIN EVENT. BUT I FAILED.
MAIN EVENT?

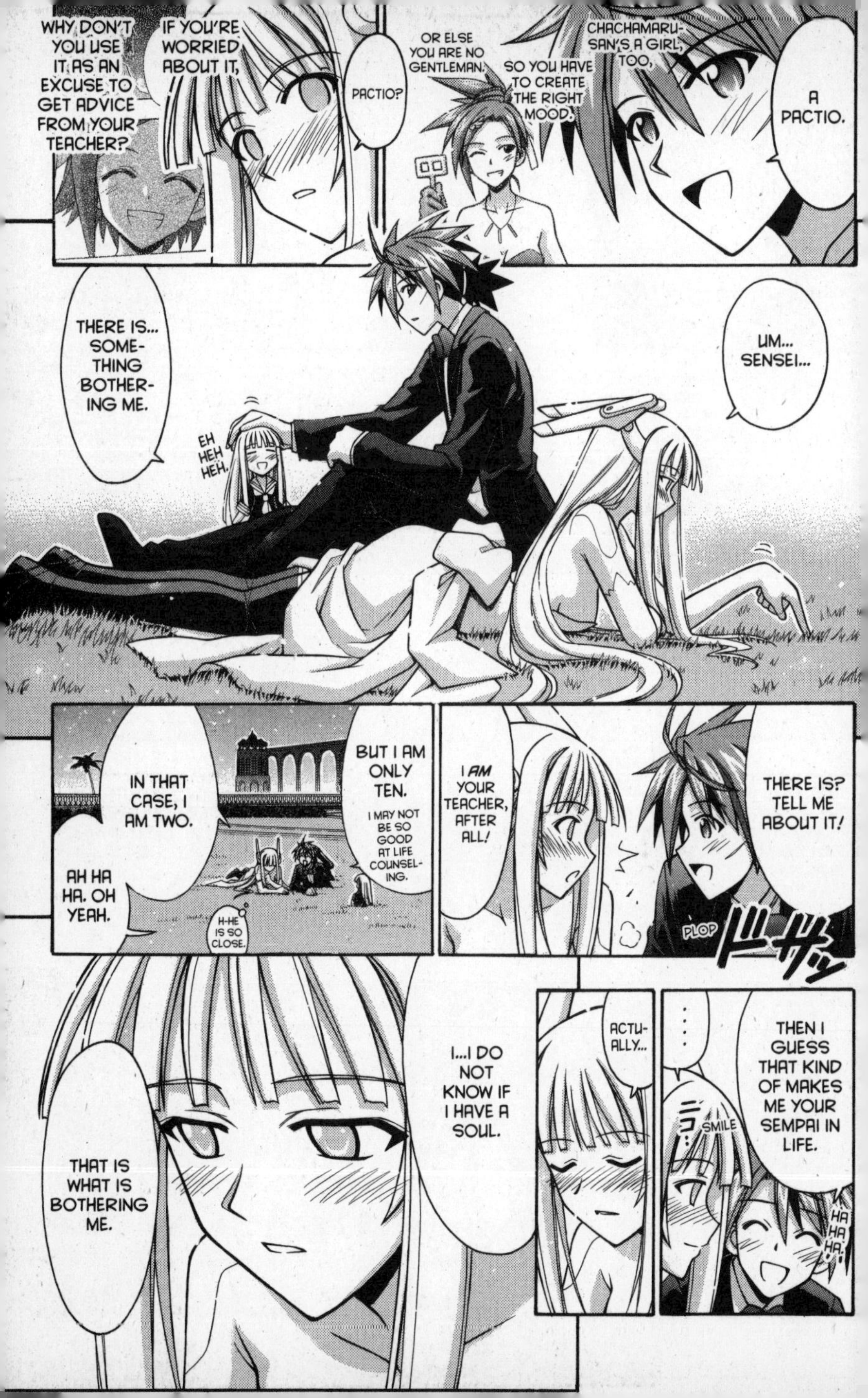
A PACTIO.
CHACHAMARU-SAN'S A GIRL, TOO,
SO YOU HAVE TO CREATE THE RIGHT MOOD.
OR ELSE YOU ARE NO GENTLEMAN.
PACTIO?
IF YOU'RE WORRIED ABOUT IT,
WHY DON'T YOU USE IT AS AN EXCUSE TO GET ADVICE FROM YOUR TEACHER?
UM... SENSEI...
THERE IS... SOME-THING BOTHER-ING ME.
EH HEH HEH.
THERE IS? TELL ME ABOUT IT!
PLOP
I *AM* YOUR TEACHER, AFTER ALL!
BUT I AM ONLY TEN.
I MAY NOT BE SO GOOD AT LIFE COUNSEL-ING.
IN THAT CASE, I AM TWO.
AH HA HA. OH YEAH.
H-HE IS SO CLOSE.
THEN I GUESS THAT KIND OF MAKES ME YOUR SEMPAI IN LIFE.
SMILE
HA HA HA.
....
ACTU-ALLY...
I...I DO NOT KNOW IF I HAVE A SOUL.
THAT IS WHAT IS BOTHERING ME.

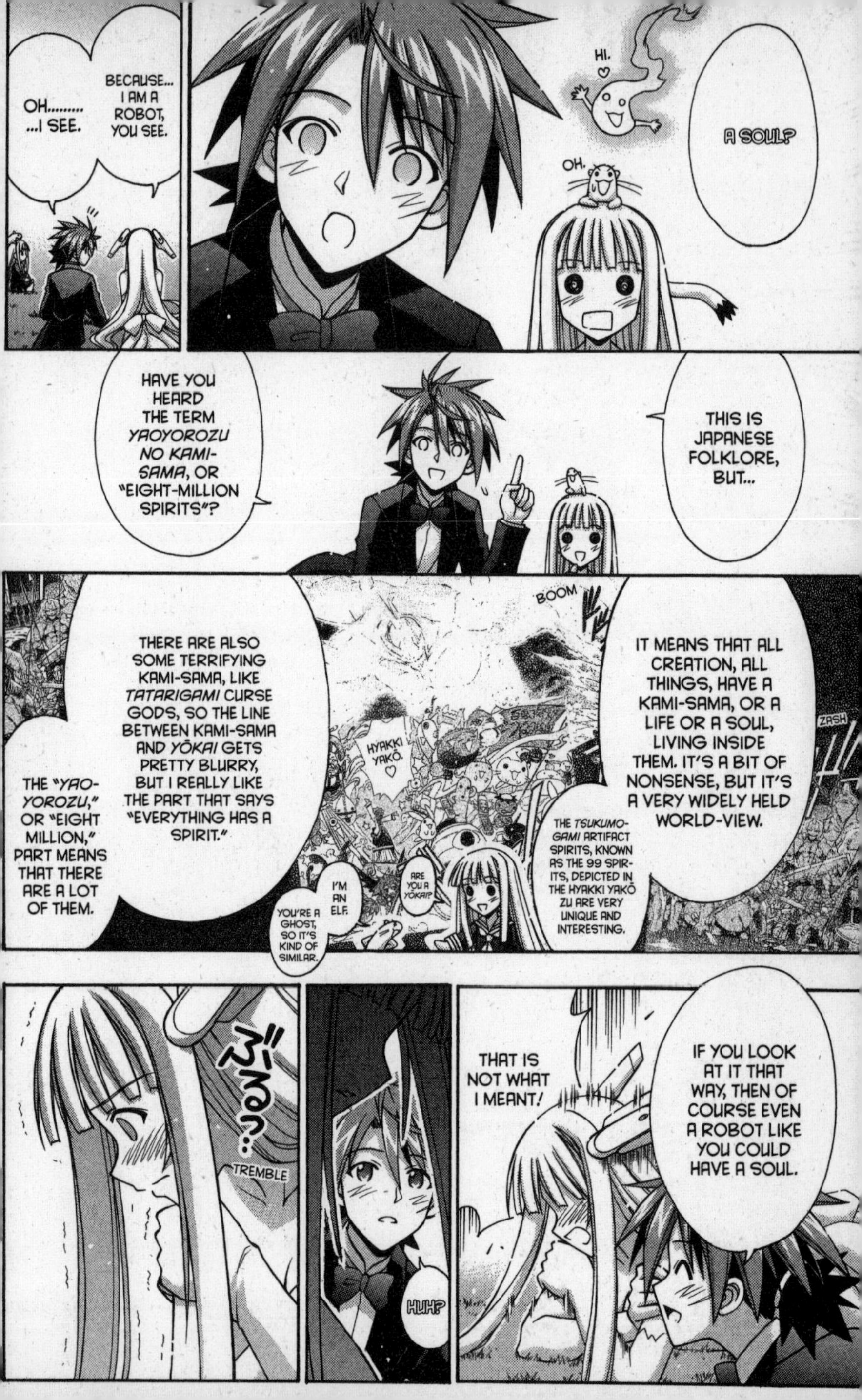
A SOUL?
HI. ♡
OH.
BECAUSE... I AM A ROBOT, YOU SEE.
OH......... ...I SEE.
THIS IS JAPANESE FOLKLORE, BUT...
HAVE YOU HEARD THE TERM *YAOYOROZU NO KAMI-SAMA*, OR "EIGHT-MILLION SPIRITS"?
BOOM
IT MEANS THAT ALL CREATION, ALL THINGS, HAVE A KAMI-SAMA, OR A LIFE OR A SOUL, LIVING INSIDE THEM. IT'S A BIT OF NONSENSE, BUT IT'S A VERY WIDELY HELD WORLD-VIEW.
ZASH
THE *TSUKUMOGAMI* ARTIFACT SPIRITS, KNOWN AS THE 99 SPIRITS, DEPICTED IN THE HYAKKI YAKŌ ZU ARE VERY UNIQUE AND INTERESTING.
HYAKKI YAKŌ. ♡
ARE YOU A *YŌKAI*?
I'M AN ELF.
YOU'RE A GHOST, SO IT'S KIND OF SIMILAR.
THERE ARE ALSO SOME TERRIFYING KAMI-SAMA, LIKE *TATARIGAMI* CURSE GODS, SO THE LINE BETWEEN KAMI-SAMA AND *YŌKAI* GETS PRETTY BLURRY, BUT I REALLY LIKE THE PART THAT SAYS "EVERYTHING HAS A SPIRIT."
THE "*YAO-YOROZU*," OR "EIGHT MILLION," PART MEANS THAT THERE ARE A LOT OF THEM.
IF YOU LOOK AT IT THAT WAY, THEN OF COURSE EVEN A ROBOT LIKE YOU COULD HAVE A SOUL.
THAT IS NOT WHAT I MEANT!
HUH?
ぷるる？
TREMBLE

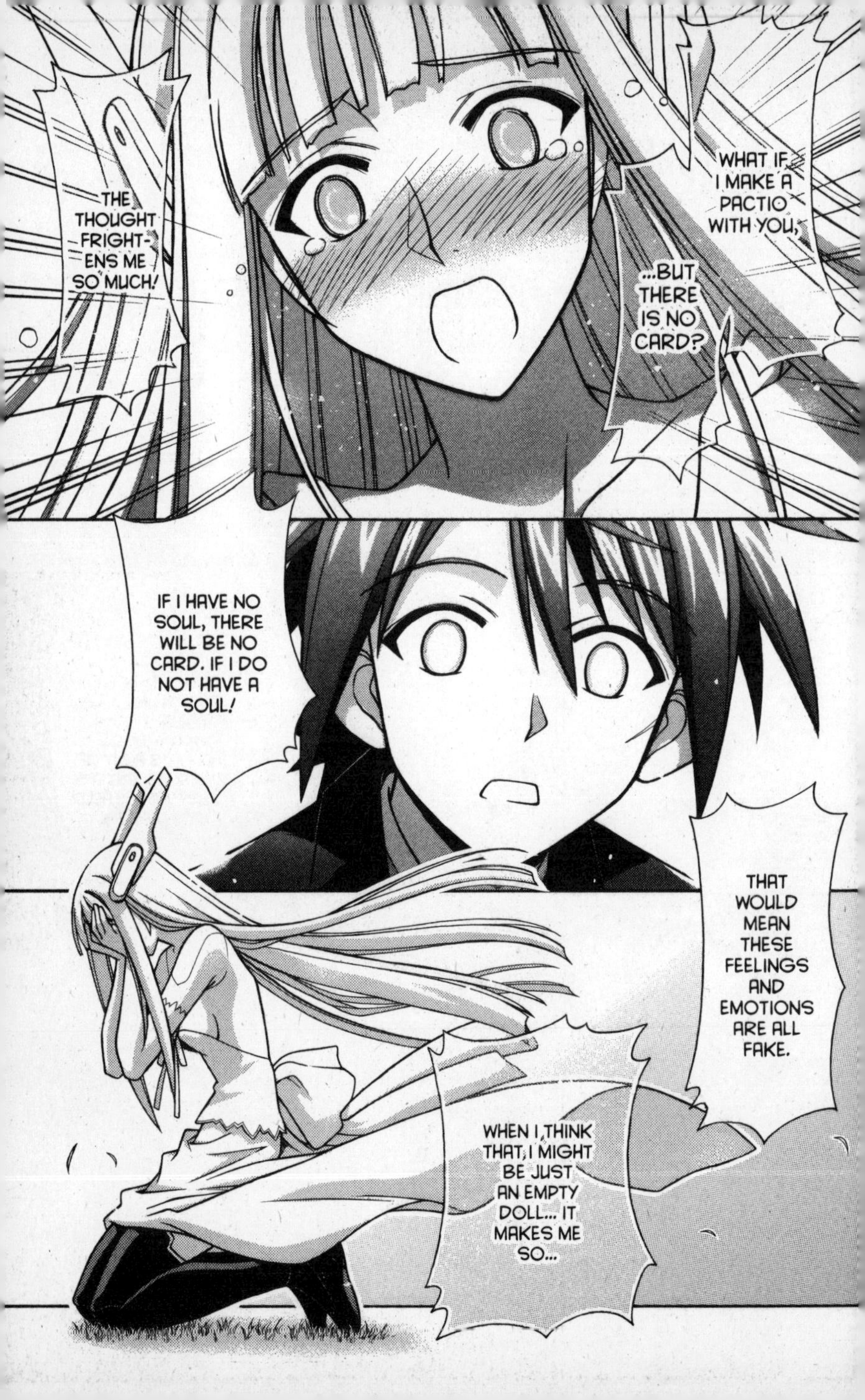
WHAT IF I MAKE A PACTIO WITH YOU,
...BUT THERE IS NO CARD?
THE THOUGHT FRIGHT-ENS ME SO MUCH!
IF I HAVE NO SOUL, THERE WILL BE NO CARD. IF I DO NOT HAVE A SOUL!
THAT WOULD MEAN THESE FEELINGS AND EMOTIONS ARE ALL FAKE.
WHEN I THINK THAT I MIGHT BE JUST AN EMPTY DOLL... IT MAKES ME SO...

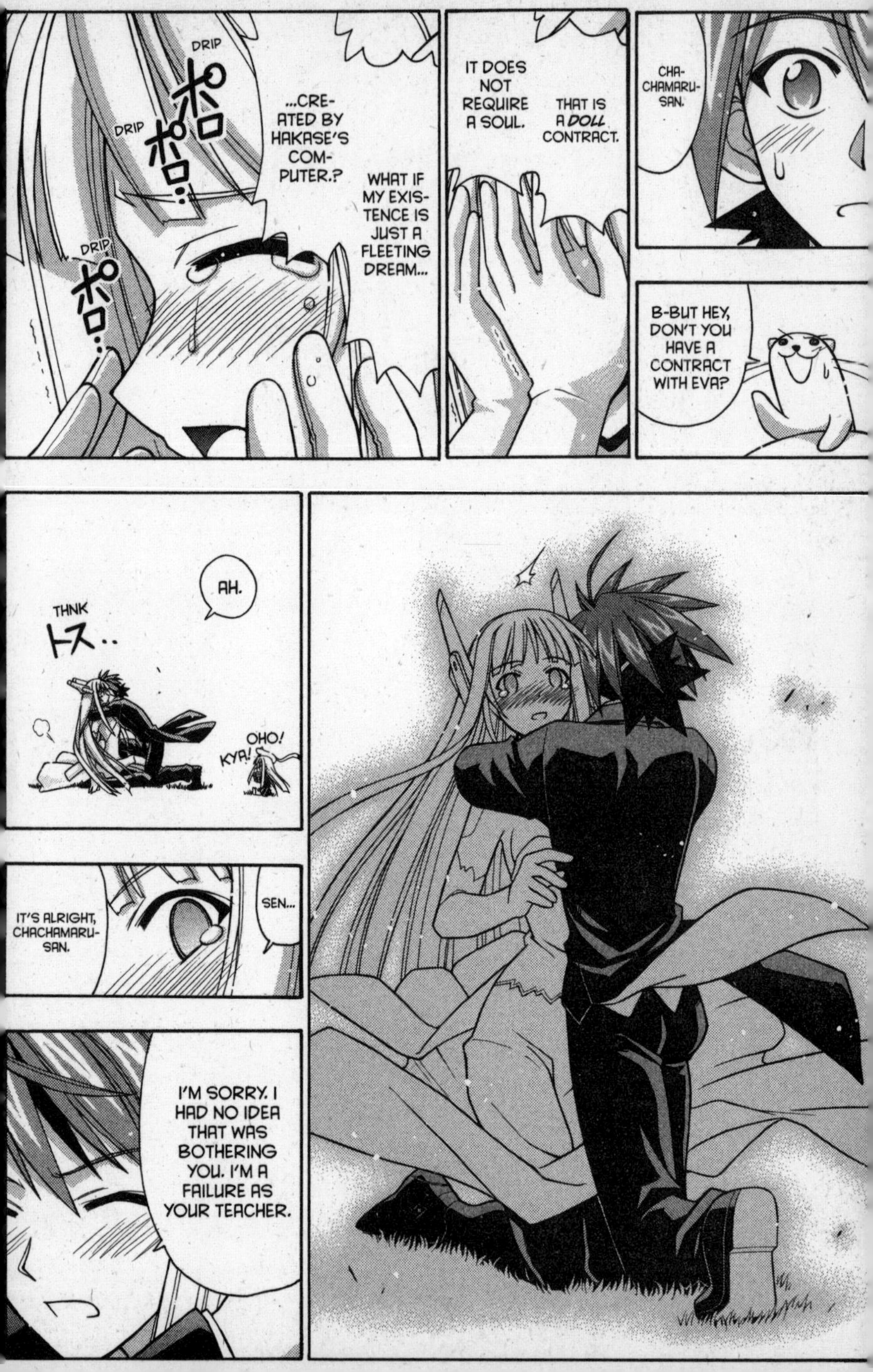

CHA-CHAMARU-SAN.
B-BUT HEY, DON'T YOU HAVE A CONTRACT WITH EVA?
THAT IS A DOLL CONTRACT.
IT DOES NOT REQUIRE A SOUL.
WHAT IF MY EXISTENCE IS JUST A FLEETING DREAM...
...CREATED BY HAKASE'S COMPUTER.?
DRIP
ポロ
DRIP
ポロ...
DRIP
ポロ...
AH.
THNK
トス..
OHO!
KYA!
SEN...
IT'S ALRIGHT, CHACHAMARU-SAN.
I'M SORRY. I HAD NO IDEA THAT WAS BOTHERING YOU. I'M A FAILURE AS YOUR TEACHER.

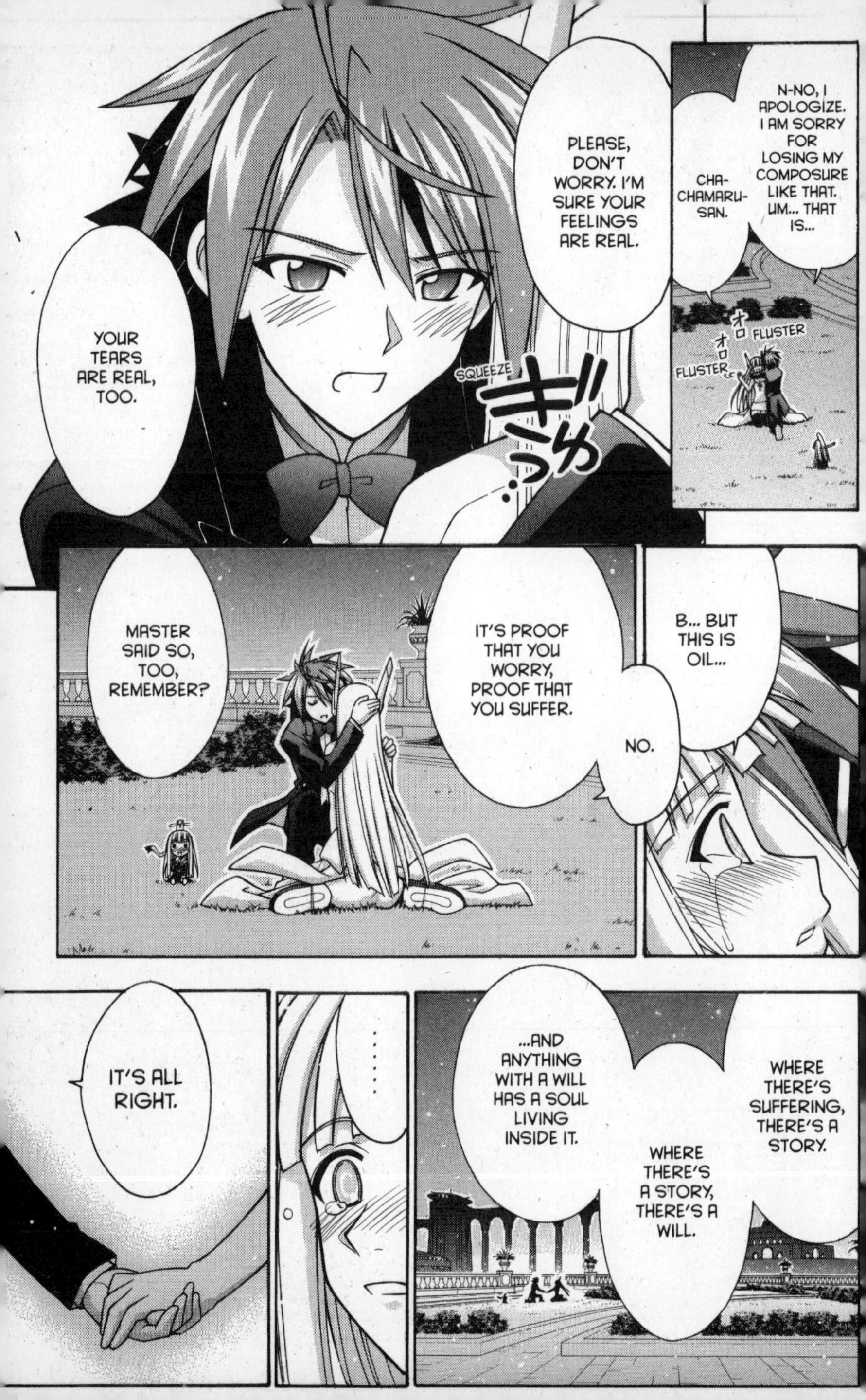

N-NO, I APOLOGIZE. I AM SORRY FOR LOSING MY COMPOSURE LIKE THAT. UM... THAT IS...
CHA-CHAMARU-SAN.
オロ
オロ
FLUSTER
FLUSTER
PLEASE, DON'T WORRY. I'M SURE YOUR FEELINGS ARE REAL.
SQUEEZE
ぎゅっ
YOUR TEARS ARE REAL, TOO.
B... BUT THIS IS OIL...
NO.
IT'S PROOF THAT YOU WORRY, PROOF THAT YOU SUFFER.
MASTER SAID SO, TOO, REMEMBER?
WHERE THERE'S SUFFERING, THERE'S A STORY.
WHERE THERE'S A STORY, THERE'S A WILL.
...AND ANYTHING WITH A WILL HAS A SOUL LIVING INSIDE IT.
......
IT'S ALL RIGHT.

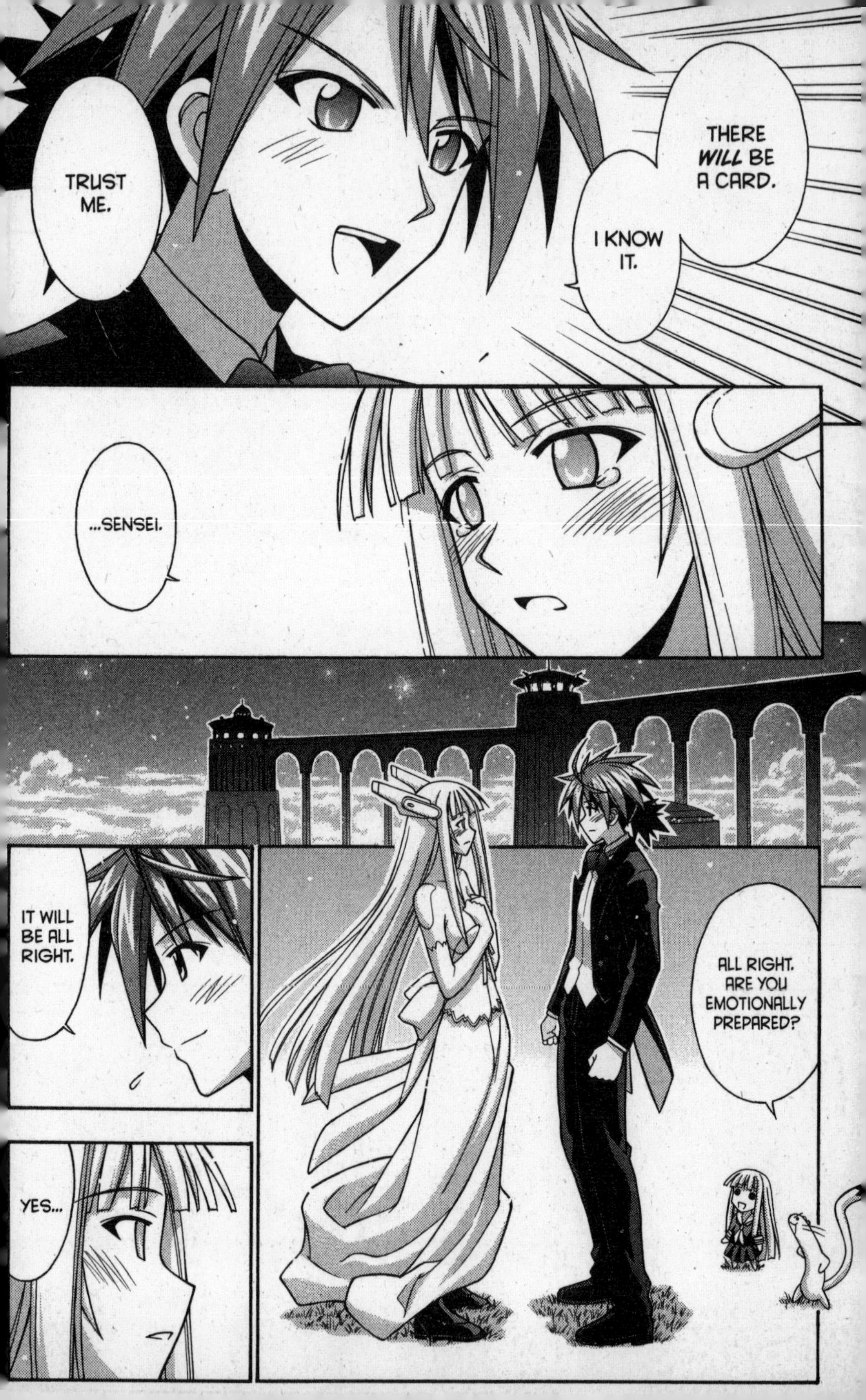
THERE *WILL* BE A CARD.
I KNOW IT.
TRUST ME.
...SENSEI.
ALL RIGHT. ARE YOU EMOTIONALLY PREPARED?
IT WILL BE ALL RIGHT.
YES...

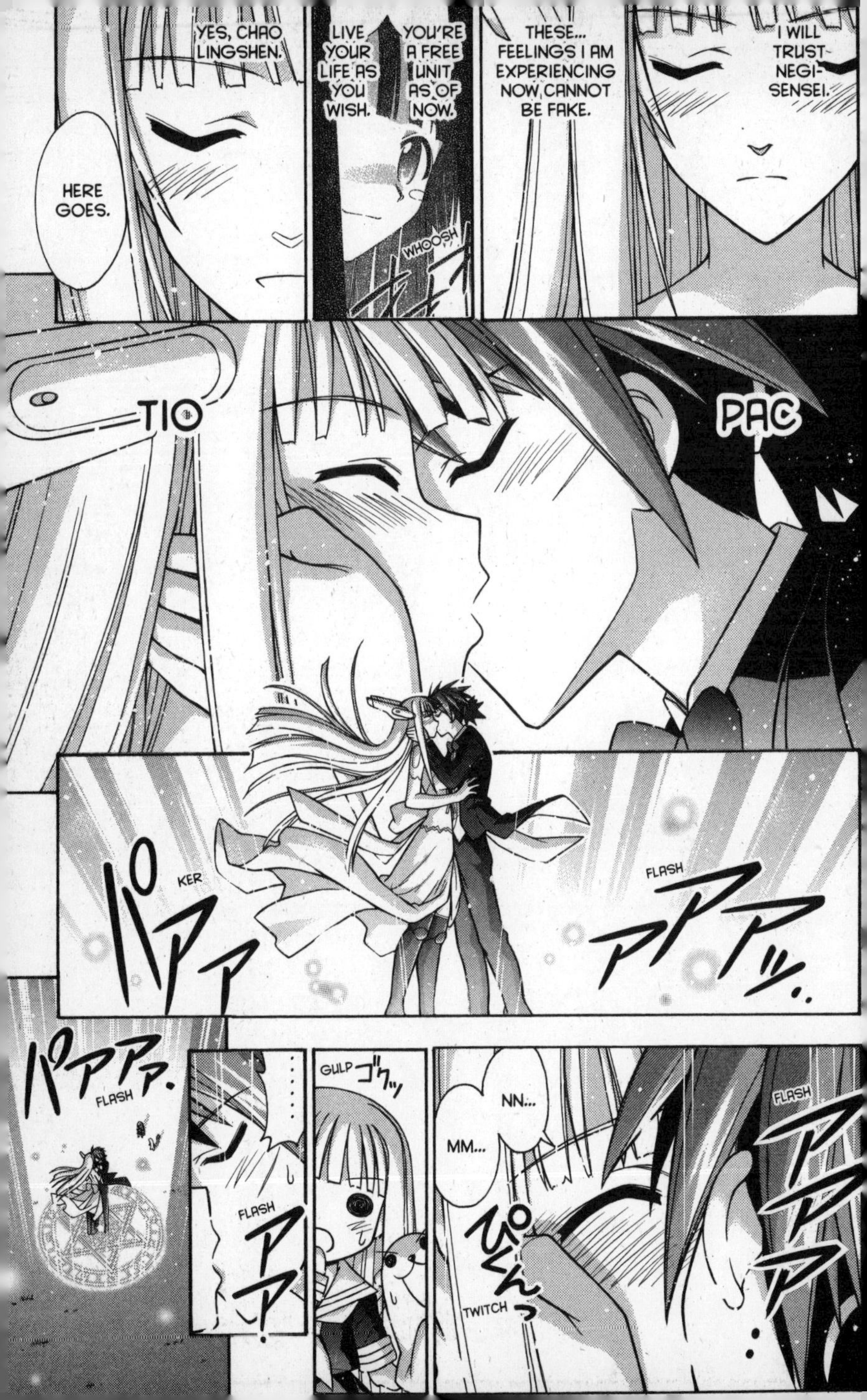

I WILL TRUST NEGI-SENSEI.
THESE... FEELINGS I AM EXPERIENCING NOW CANNOT BE FAKE.
YOU'RE A FREE UNIT AS OF NOW.
LIVE YOUR LIFE AS YOU WISH.
WHOOSH
YES, CHAO LINGSHEN.
HERE GOES.
PAC
TIO
FLASH
KER
FLASH
NN...
MM...
ぴくんっ
TWITCH
GULP ゴクッ
......
FLASH
パアアァ.
FLASH

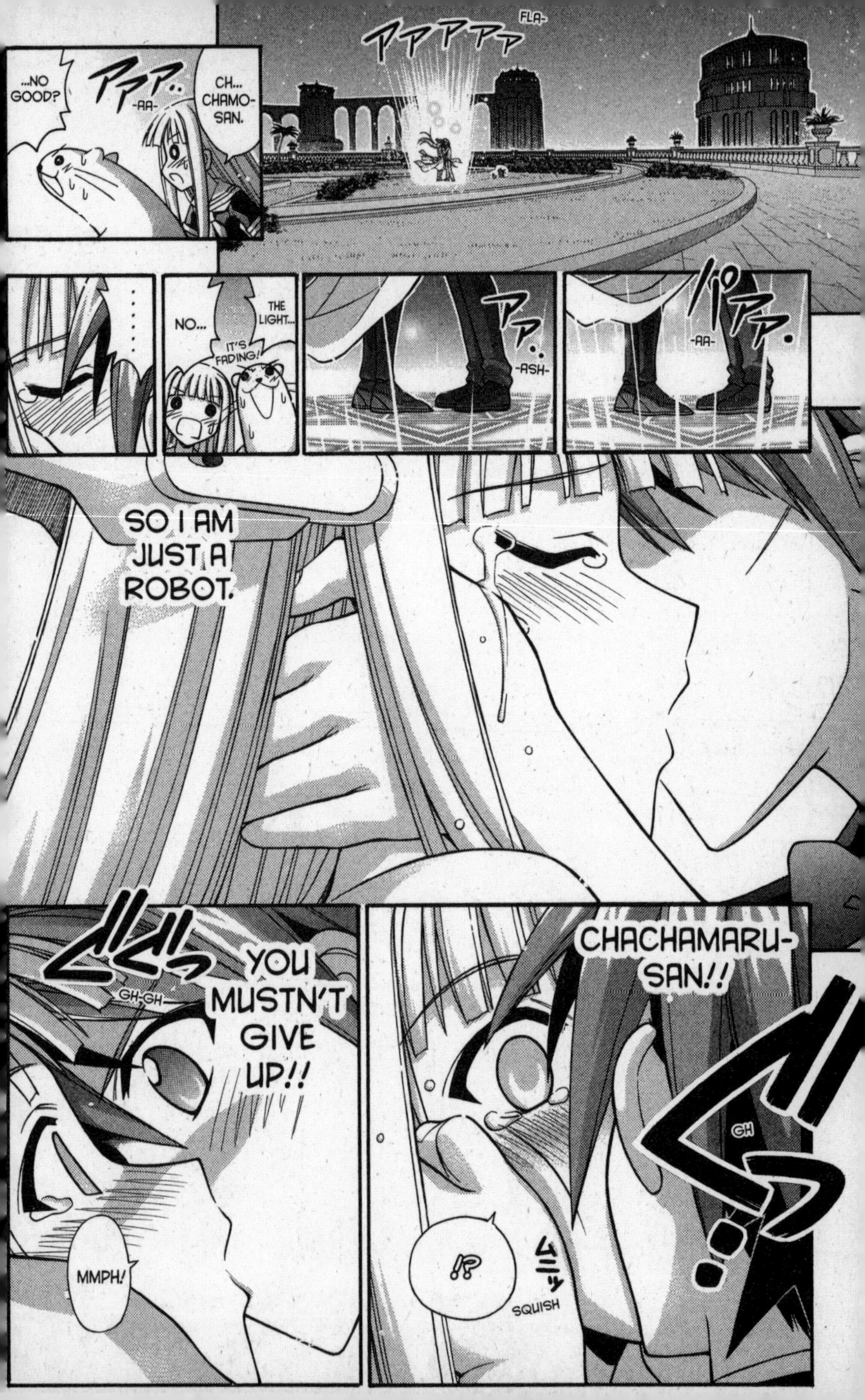
アアアアア
FLA-
CH... CHAMO-SAN.
アアア..
-AA-
...NO GOOD?
パァァ.
-AA-
アァ..
-ASH-
THE LIGHT...
IT'S FADING!
NO...
......
SO I AM JUST A ROBOT.
CHACHAMARU-SAN!!
GH
ムニッ
SQUISH
!?
YOU MUSTN'T GIVE UP!!
GH-GH
MMPH!

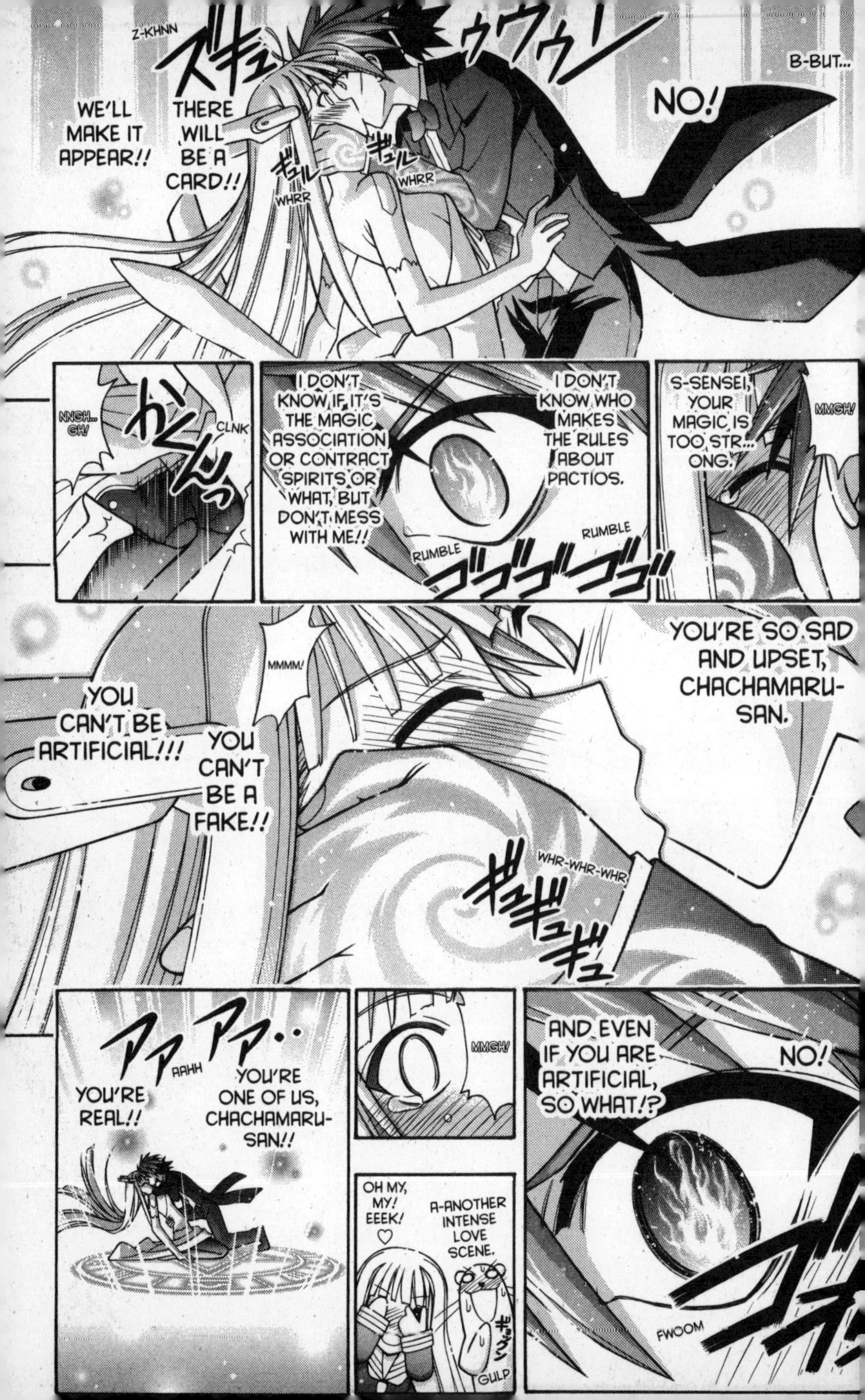
B-BUT...
NO!
Z-KHNN
THERE WILL BE A CARD!!
WE'LL MAKE IT APPEAR!!
WHRR
WHRR
MMGH!
S-SENSEI, YOUR MAGIC IS TOO STR... ONG.
I DON'T KNOW WHO MAKES THE RULES ABOUT PACTIOS.
I DON'T KNOW IF IT'S THE MAGIC ASSOCIATION OR CONTRACT SPIRITS OR WHAT, BUT DON'T MESS WITH ME!!
RUMBLE
RUMBLE
CLNK
NNGH... GH!
YOU'RE SO SAD AND UPSET, CHACHAMARU-SAN.
MMMM!
YOU CAN'T BE A FAKE!!
YOU CAN'T BE ARTIFICIAL!!!
WHR-WHR-WHR
NO!
AND EVEN IF YOU ARE ARTIFICIAL, SO WHAT!?
FWOOM
MMGH!
A-ANOTHER INTENSE LOVE SCENE.
OH MY, MY! EEEK! ♥
GULP
YOU'RE ONE OF US, CHACHAMARU-SAN!!
AAHH
YOU'RE REAL!!

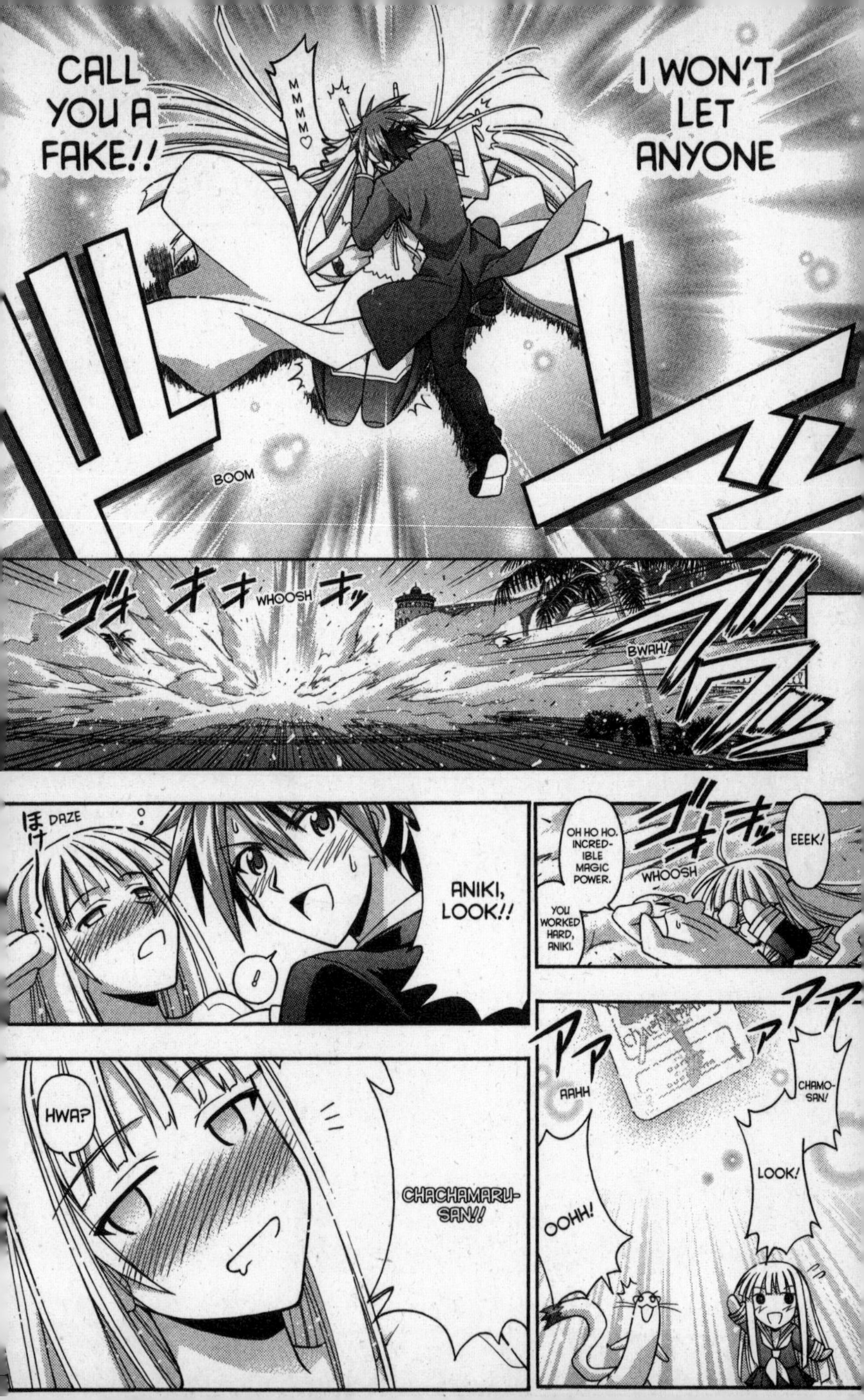
I WON'T LET ANYONE
CALL YOU A FAKE!!
MMMM♡
BOOM
WHOOSH
BWAH!
EEEK!
OH HO HO. INCREDIBLE MAGIC POWER.
WHOOSH
YOU WORKED HARD, ANIKI.
ANIKI, LOOK!!
DAZE
CHAMO-SAN!
LOOK!
AAHH
OOHH!
CHACHAMARU-SAN!!
HWA?

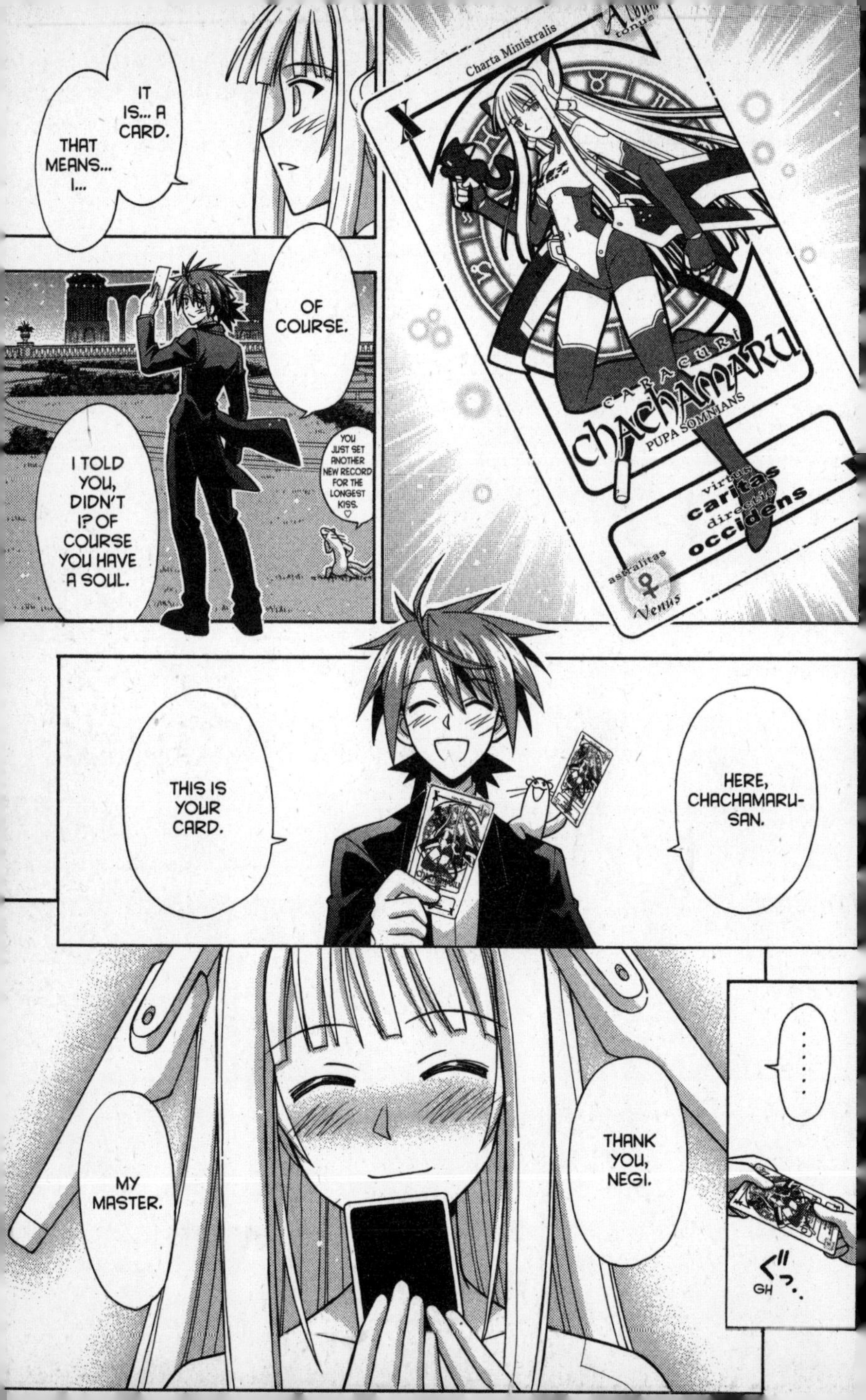
Charta Ministralis
X
CHACHAMARU
PUPA SOMNIANS
virtus caritas
directio occidens
astralitas ♀ Venus
IT IS... A CARD.
THAT MEANS... I...
OF COURSE.
YOU JUST SET ANOTHER NEW RECORD FOR THE LONGEST KISS. ♡
I TOLD YOU, DIDN'T I!? OF COURSE YOU HAVE A SOUL.
HERE, CHACHAMARU-SAN.
THIS IS YOUR CARD.
......
GH
THANK YOU, NEGI.
MY MASTER.

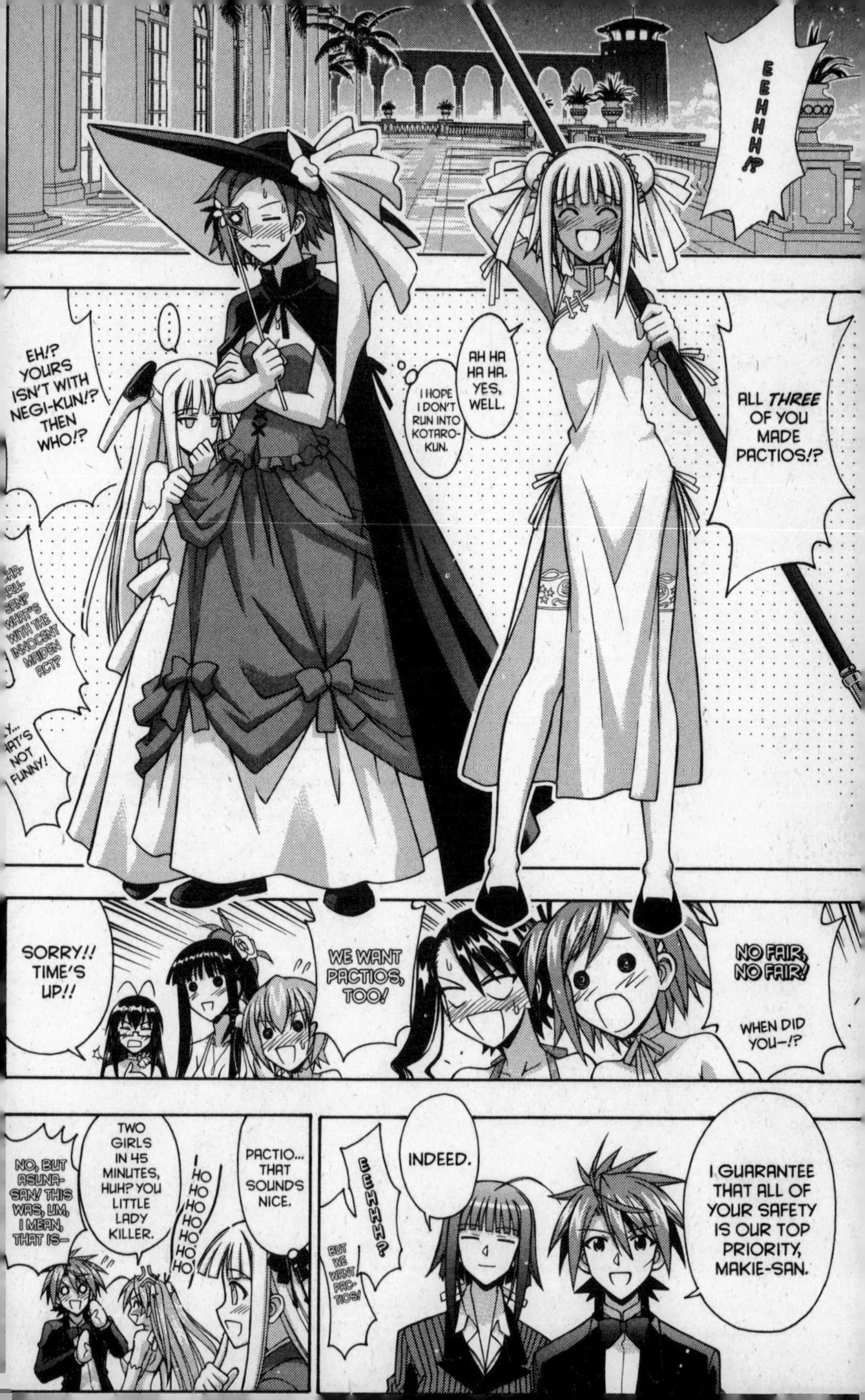
EEHHHH!?
ALL THREE OF YOU MADE PACTIOS!?
AH HA HA HA. YES, WELL.
I HOPE I DON'T RUN INTO KOTARO-KUN.
...
EH!? YOURS ISN'T WITH NEGI-KUN!? THEN WHO!?
SAN? WHAT'S WITH THE INNOCENT MAIDEN ACT?
THAT'S NOT FUNNY!
NO FAIR, NO FAIR!
WHEN DID YOU—!?
WE WANT PACTIOS, TOO!
SORRY!! TIME'S UP!!
I GUARANTEE THAT ALL OF YOUR SAFETY IS OUR TOP PRIORITY, MAKIE-SAN.
INDEED.
EEHHHH!?
BUT WE WANT PAC-TIOS!
PACTIO... THAT SOUNDS NICE.
HO HO HO HO HO HO HO
TWO GIRLS IN 45 MINUTES, HUH? YOU LITTLE LADY KILLER.
NO, BUT ASUNA-SAN! THIS WAS, UM, I MEAN, THAT IS—

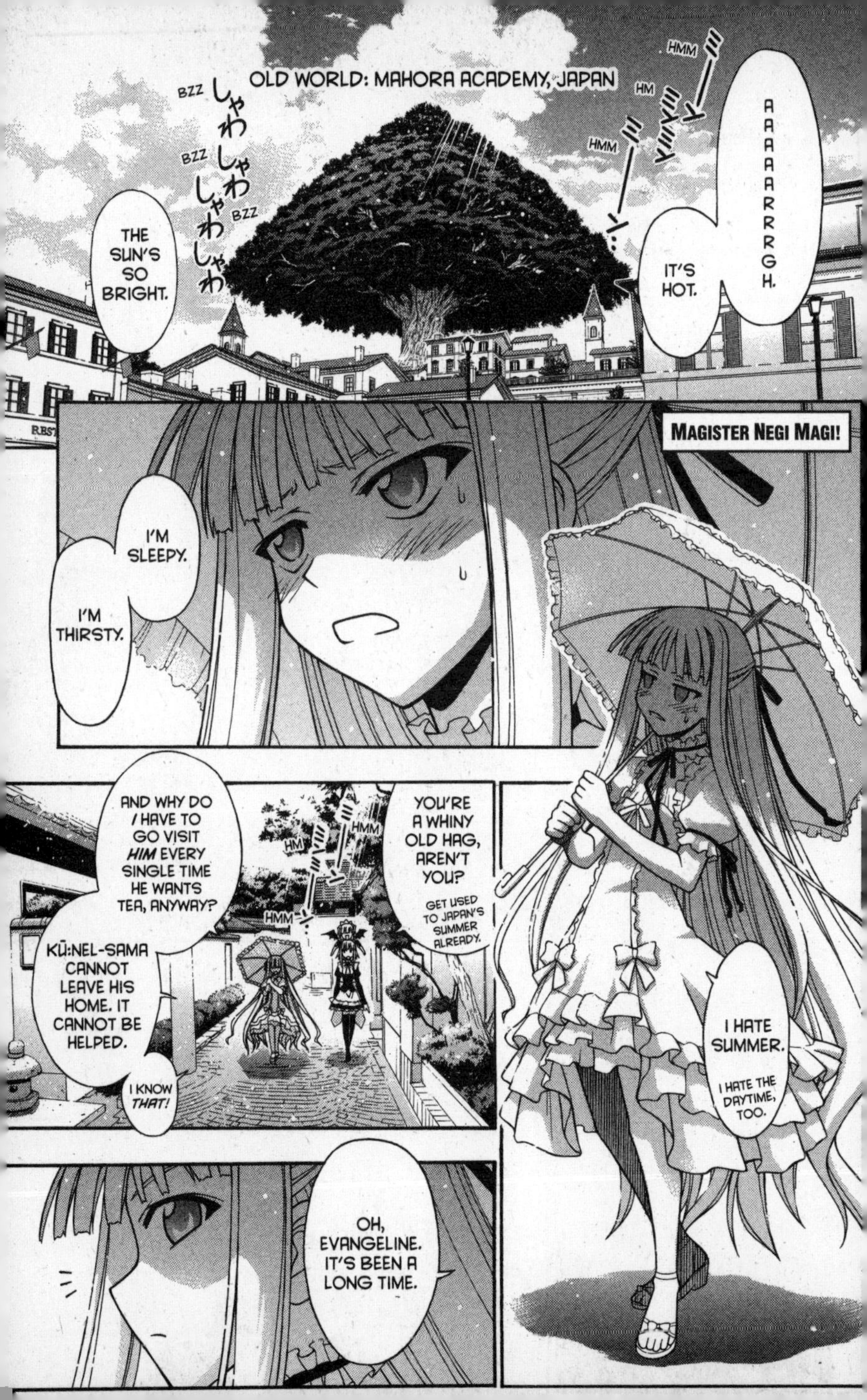
AAAAAARRRGH.
IT'S HOT.
HMM
HM
HMM
OLD WORLD: MAHORA ACADEMY, JAPAN
BZZ BZZ BZZ
しゃわしゃわしゃわしゃわ
THE SUN'S SO BRIGHT.
MAGISTER NEGI MAGI!
I HATE SUMMER.
I HATE THE DAYTIME, TOO.
I'M SLEEPY.
I'M THIRSTY.
YOU'RE A WHINY OLD HAG, AREN'T YOU?
GET USED TO JAPAN'S SUMMER ALREADY.
HMM
HM
HMM
AND WHY DO I HAVE TO GO VISIT HIM EVERY SINGLE TIME HE WANTS TEA, ANYWAY?
KŪ:NEL-SAMA CANNOT LEAVE HIS HOME. IT CANNOT BE HELPED.
I KNOW THAT!
OH, EVANGELINE. IT'S BEEN A LONG TIME.

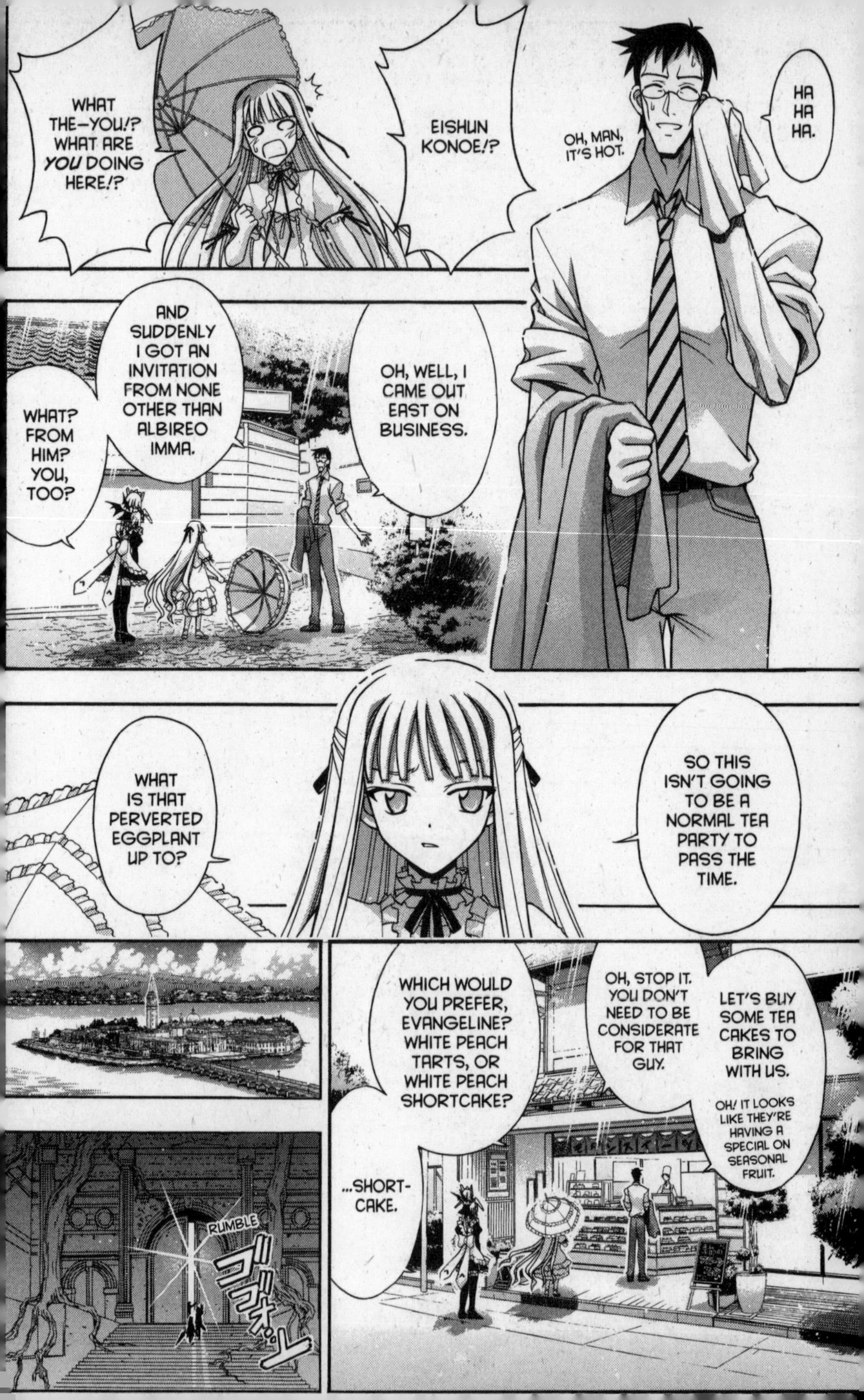
HA HA HA.
OH, MAN, IT'S HOT.
EISHUN KONOE!?
WHAT THE—YOU!? WHAT ARE *YOU* DOING HERE!?
OH, WELL, I CAME OUT EAST ON BUSINESS.
AND SUDDENLY I GOT AN INVITATION FROM NONE OTHER THAN ALBIREO IMMA.
WHAT? FROM HIM? YOU, TOO?
SO THIS ISN'T GOING TO BE A NORMAL TEA PARTY TO PASS THE TIME.
WHAT IS THAT PERVERTED EGGPLANT UP TO?
LET'S BUY SOME TEA CAKES TO BRING WITH US.
OH! IT LOOKS LIKE THEY'RE HAVING A SPECIAL ON SEASONAL FRUIT.
OH, STOP IT. YOU DON'T NEED TO BE CONSIDERATE FOR THAT GUY.
WHICH WOULD YOU PREFER, EVANGELINE? WHITE PEACH TARTS, OR WHITE PEACH SHORTCAKE?
...SHORT-CAKE.
RUMBLE

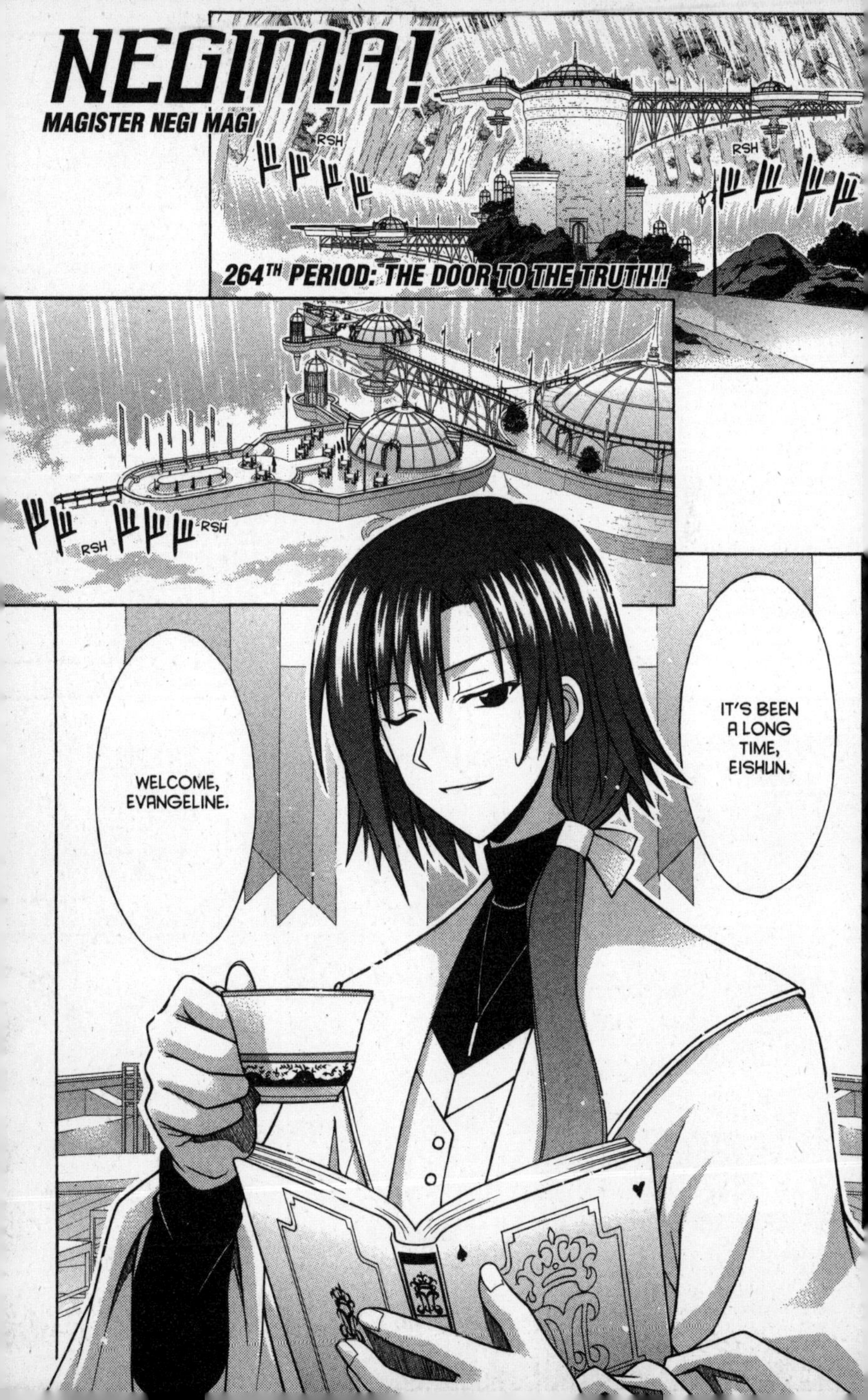
NEGIMA!
MAGISTER NEGI MAGI
ドドドド
RSH
ドドドド
RSH
264TH PERIOD: THE DOOR TO THE TRUTH!!
ドドドド
RSH
ドド
RSH
IT'S BEEN A LONG TIME, EISHUN.
WELCOME, EVANGELINE.

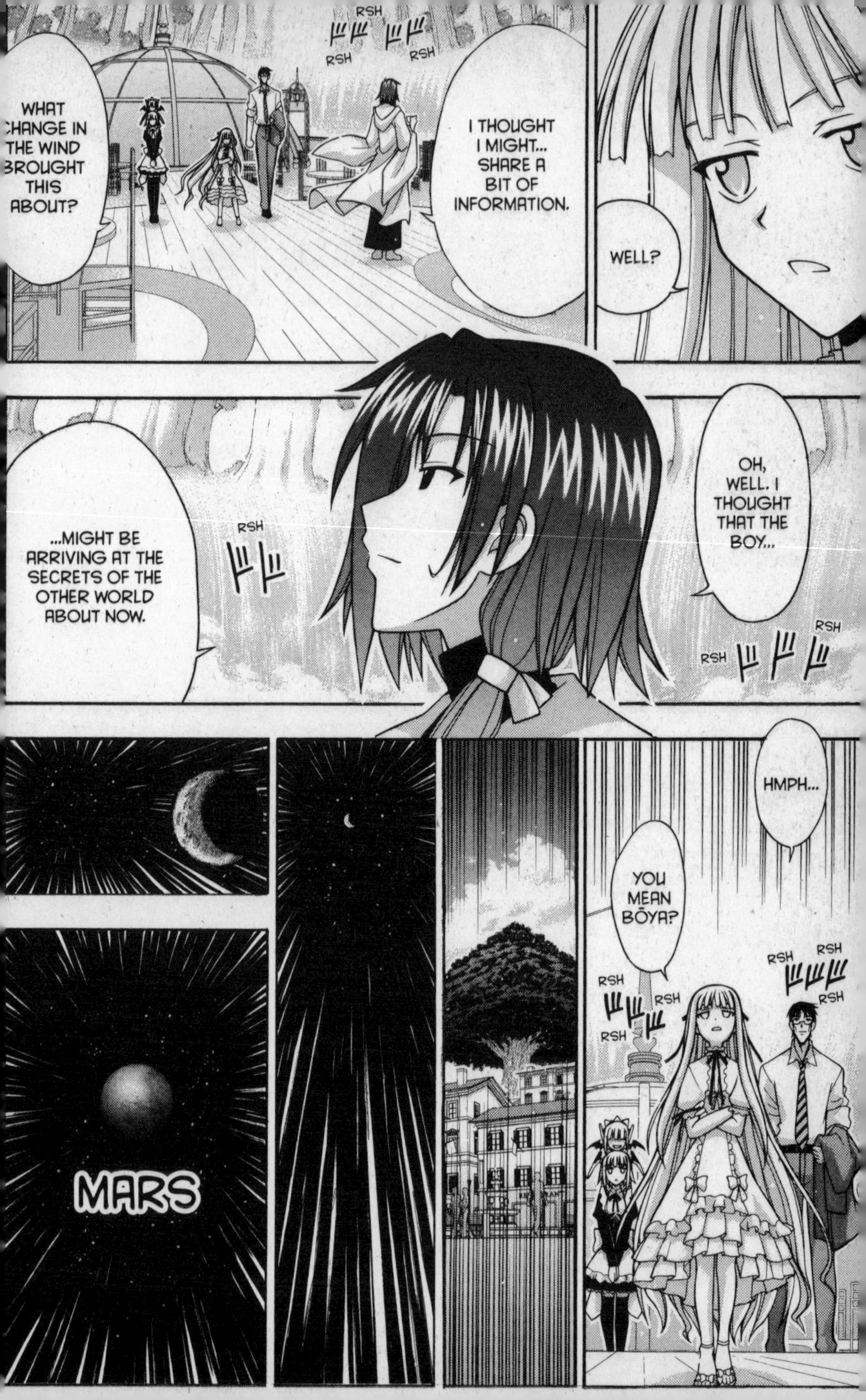
WELL?
I THOUGHT I MIGHT... SHARE A BIT OF INFORMATION.
RSH RSH RSH
WHAT CHANGE IN THE WIND BROUGHT THIS ABOUT?
OH, WELL. I THOUGHT THAT THE BOY...
RSH RSH
...MIGHT BE ARRIVING AT THE SECRETS OF THE OTHER WORLD ABOUT NOW.
RSH
HMPH...
RSH RSH RSH
YOU MEAN BŌYA?
RSH RSH RSH
MARS

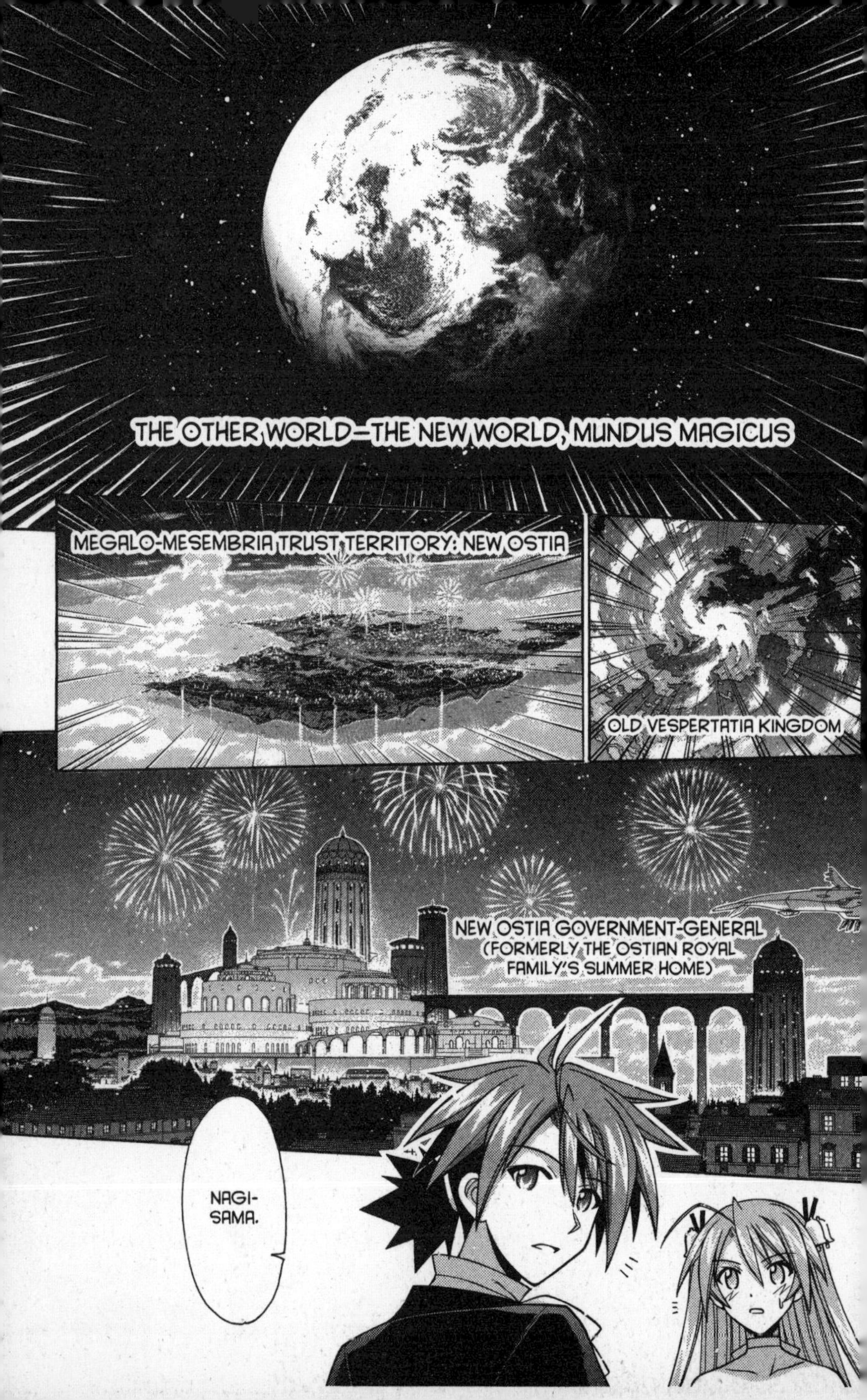
THE OTHER WORLD—THE NEW WORLD, MUNDUS MAGICUS
OLD VESPERTATIA KINGDOM
MEGALO-MESEMBRIA TRUST TERRITORY: NEW OSTIA
NEW OSTIA GOVERNMENT-GENERAL (FORMERLY THE OSTIAN ROYAL FAMILY'S SUMMER HOME)
NAGI-SAMA.

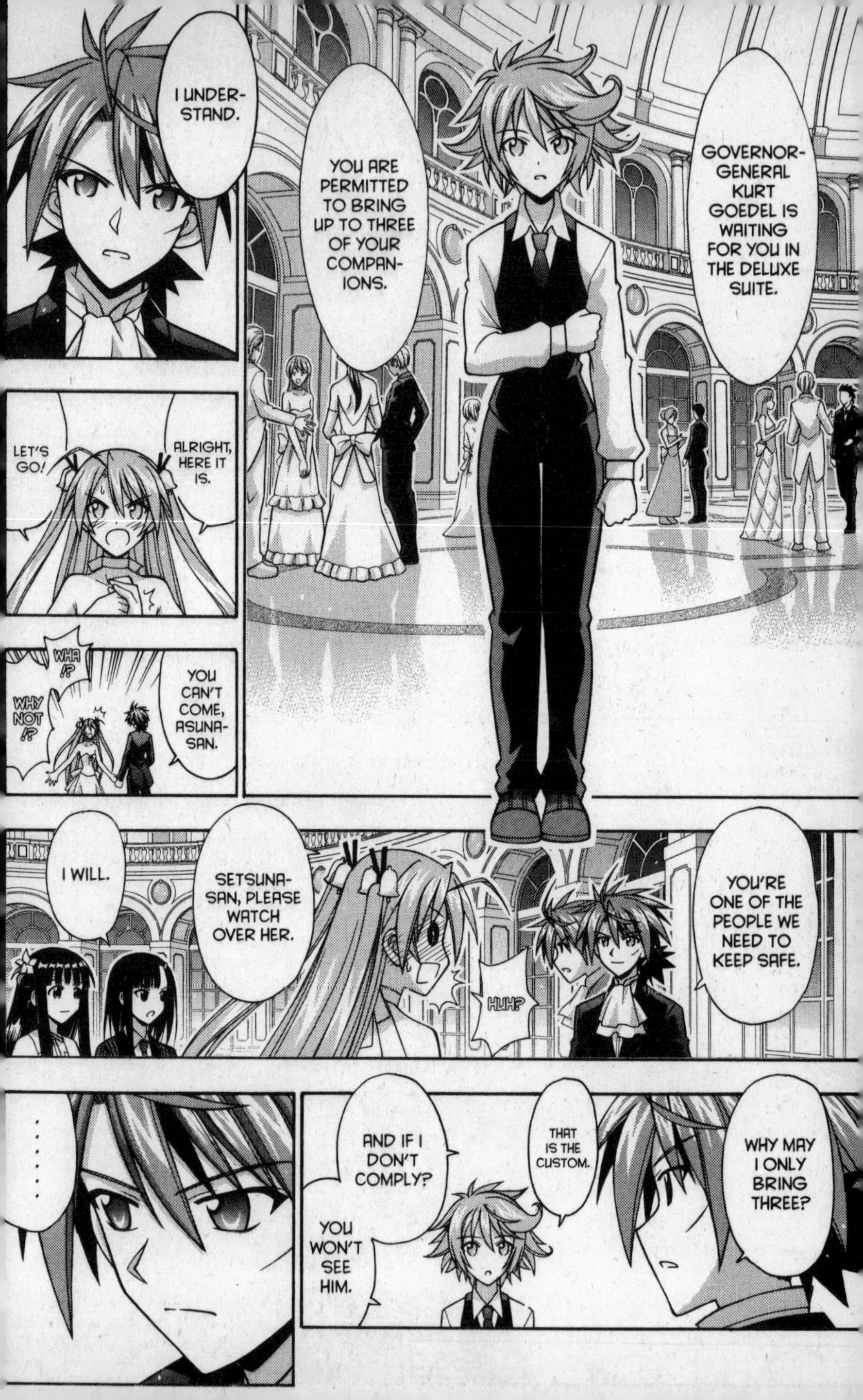
GOVERNOR-GENERAL KURT GOEDEL IS WAITING FOR YOU IN THE DELUXE SUITE.
YOU ARE PERMITTED TO BRING UP TO THREE OF YOUR COMPANIONS.
I UNDER-STAND.
ALRIGHT, HERE IT IS.
LET'S GO!
YOU CAN'T COME, ASUNA-SAN.
WHA!?
WHY NOT!?
YOU'RE ONE OF THE PEOPLE WE NEED TO KEEP SAFE.
HUH?
SETSUNA-SAN, PLEASE WATCH OVER HER.
I WILL.
WHY MAY I ONLY BRING THREE?
THAT IS THE CUSTOM.
AND IF I DON'T COMPLY?
YOU WON'T SEE HIM.
......

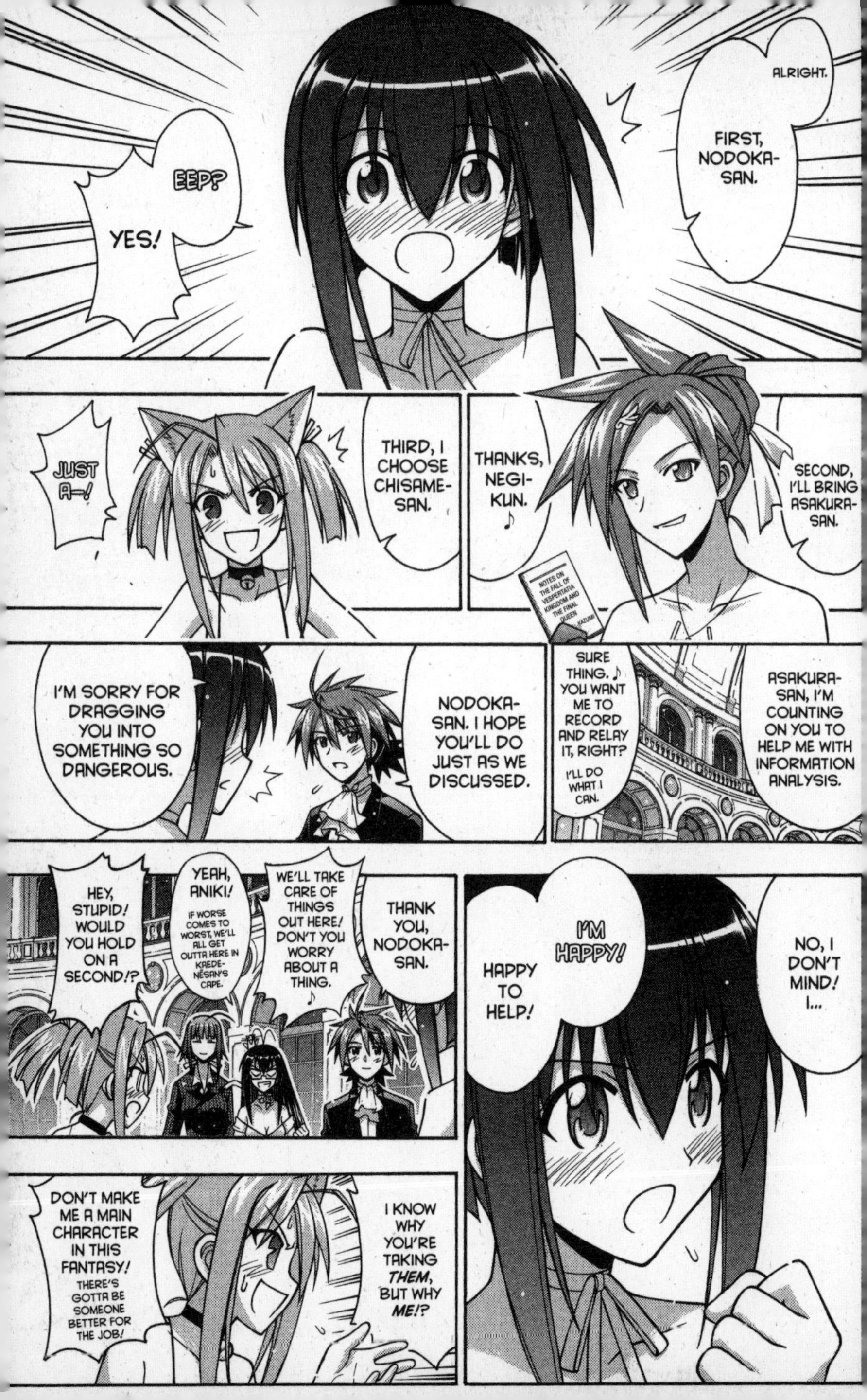
ALRIGHT.
FIRST, NODOKA-SAN.
EEP?
YES!
SECOND, I'LL BRING ASAKURA-SAN.
THANKS, NEGI-KUN. ♪
NOTES ON THE FALL OF VESPERTATIA KINGDOM AND THE FINAL QUEEN
KAZUMI
THIRD, I CHOOSE CHISAME-SAN.
JUST A—!
ASAKURA-SAN, I'M COUNTING ON YOU TO HELP ME WITH INFORMATION ANALYSIS.
SURE THING. ♪ YOU WANT ME TO RECORD AND RELAY IT, RIGHT?
I'LL DO WHAT I CAN.
NODOKA-SAN. I HOPE YOU'LL DO JUST AS WE DISCUSSED.
I'M SORRY FOR DRAGGING YOU INTO SOMETHING SO DANGEROUS.
NO, I DON'T MIND! I...
I'M HAPPY!
HAPPY TO HELP!
THANK YOU, NODOKA-SAN.
WE'LL TAKE CARE OF THINGS OUT HERE! DON'T YOU WORRY ABOUT A THING. ♪
YEAH, ANIKI!
IF WORSE COMES TO WORST, WE'LL ALL GET OUTTA HERE IN KAEDE-NÉSAN'S CAPE.
HEY, STUPID! WOULD YOU HOLD ON A SECOND!?
I KNOW WHY YOU'RE TAKING THEM, BUT WHY ME!?
DON'T MAKE ME A MAIN CHARACTER IN THIS FANTASY!
THERE'S GOTTA BE SOMEONE BETTER FOR THE JOB!

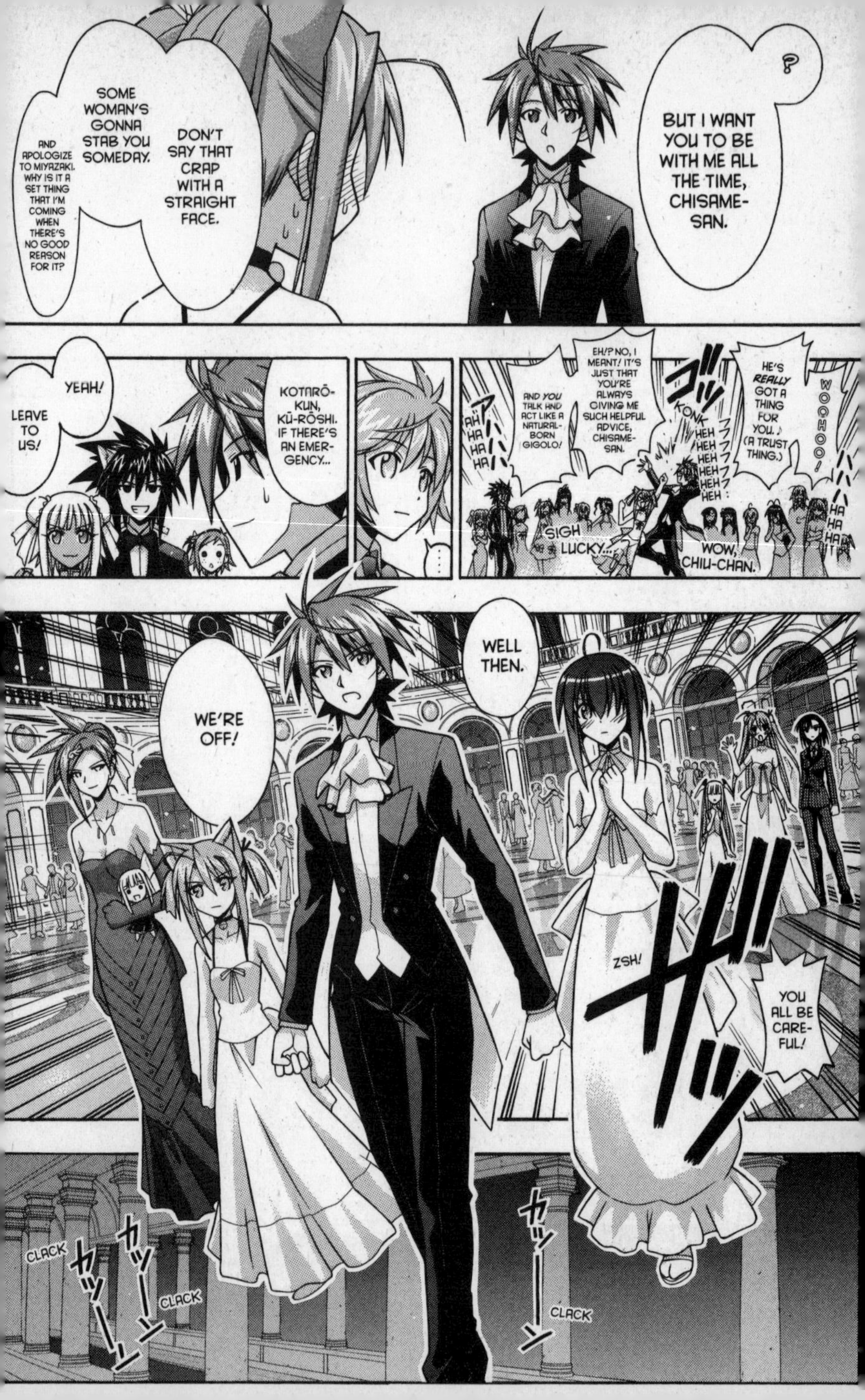
?
BUT I WANT YOU TO BE WITH ME ALL THE TIME, CHISAME-SAN.
DON'T SAY THAT CRAP WITH A STRAIGHT FACE.
SOME WOMAN'S GONNA STAB YOU SOMEDAY.
AND APOLOGIZE TO MIYAZAKI. WHY IS IT A SET THING THAT I'M COMING WHEN THERE'S NO GOOD REASON FOR IT?
WOOHOO!
HE'S REALLY GOT A THING FOR YOU.♪ (A TRUST THING.)
HEH HEH HEH HEH HEH HEH
KONK
EH!? NO, I MEANT! IT'S JUST THAT YOU'RE ALWAYS GIVING ME SUCH HELPFUL ADVICE, CHISAME-SAN.
AND YOU TALK AND ACT LIKE A NATURAL-BORN GIGOLO!
AH HA HA HA
HA HA HA HA
WOW, CHIU-CHAN.
LUCKY...
SIGH
...
KOTARŌ-KUN, KŪ-RŌSHI. IF THERE'S AN EMERGENCY...
YEAH!
LEAVE TO US!
WELL THEN.
WE'RE OFF!
ZSH!
YOU ALL BE CAREFUL!
CLACK
CLACK
CLACK

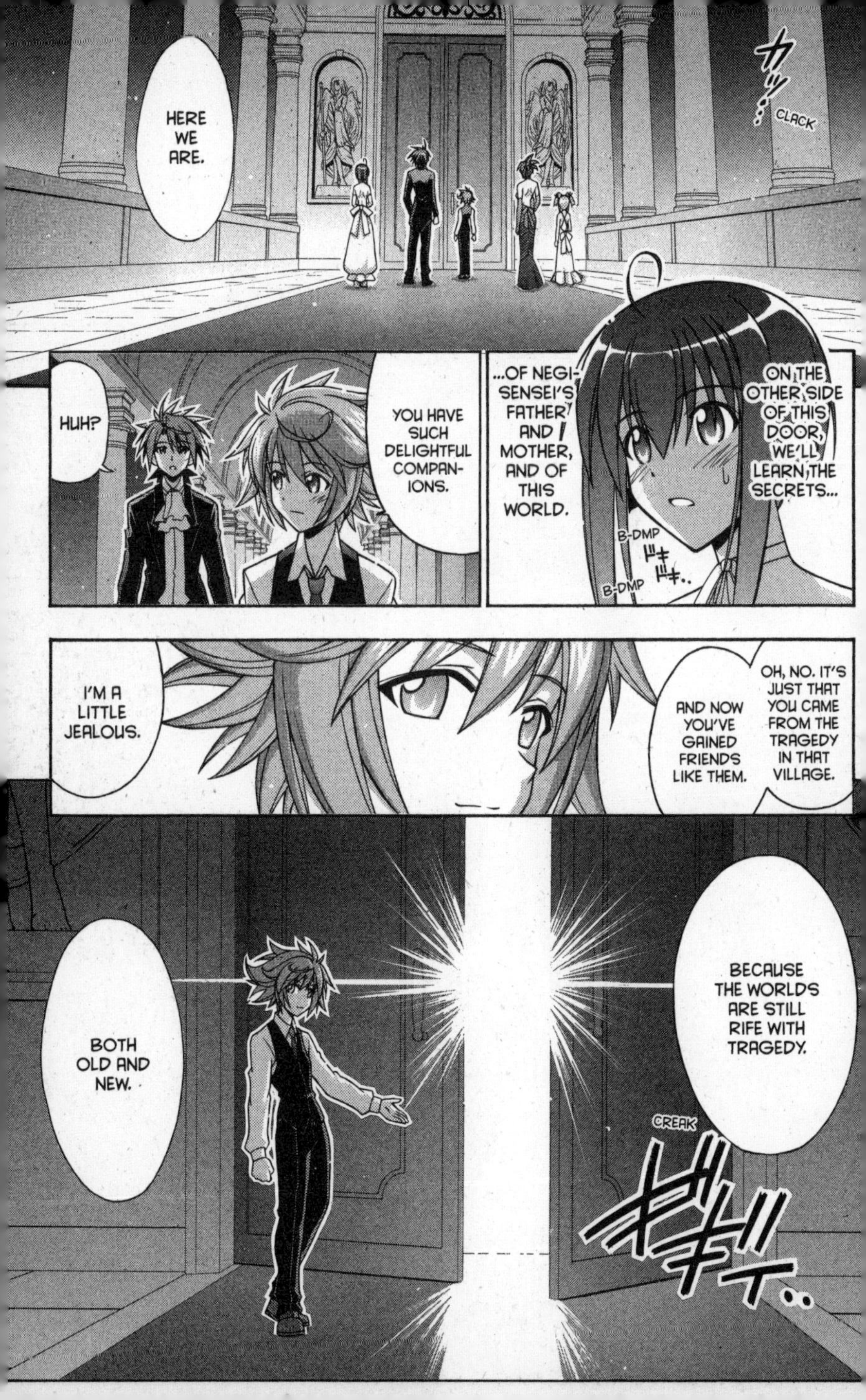
カッ..
CLACK
HERE WE ARE.
ON THE OTHER SIDE OF THIS DOOR, WE'LL LEARN THE SECRETS...
...OF NEGI-SENSEI'S FATHER AND MOTHER, AND OF THIS WORLD.
B-DMP ドキ
B-DMP ドキ..
YOU HAVE SUCH DELIGHTFUL COMPAN-IONS.
HUH?
OH, NO. IT'S JUST THAT YOU CAME FROM THE TRAGEDY IN THAT VILLAGE.
AND NOW YOU'VE GAINED FRIENDS LIKE THEM.
I'M A LITTLE JEALOUS.
BECAUSE THE WORLDS ARE STILL RIFE WITH TRAGEDY.
CREAK
ギギィ..
BOTH OLD AND NEW.

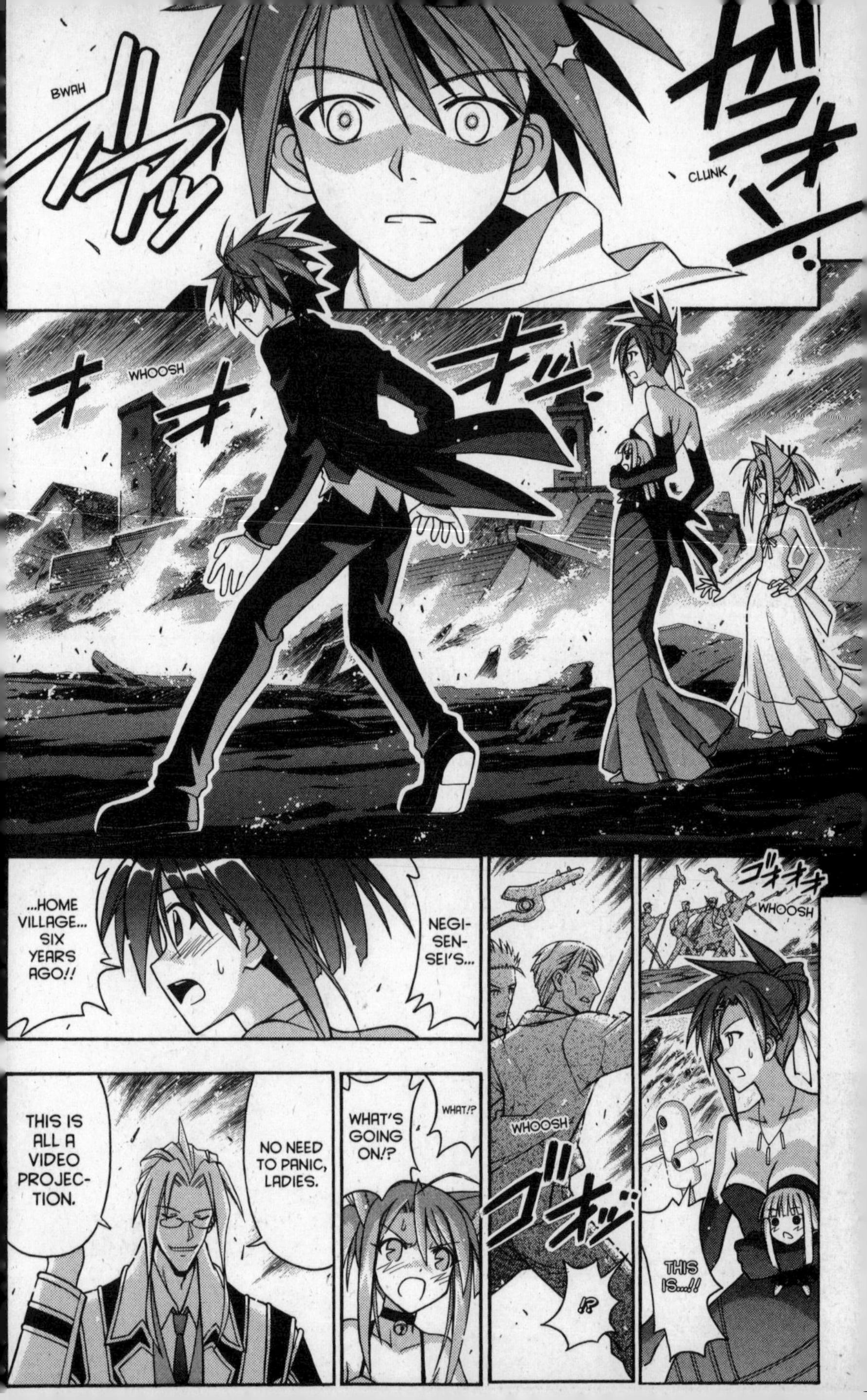
CLUNK
BWAH
WHOOSH
WHOOSH
THIS IS...!!
WHOOSH
!?
NEGI-SEN-SEI'S...
...HOME VILLAGE... SIX YEARS AGO!!
WHAT!?
WHAT'S GOING ON!?
NO NEED TO PANIC, LADIES.
THIS IS ALL A VIDEO PROJECTION.

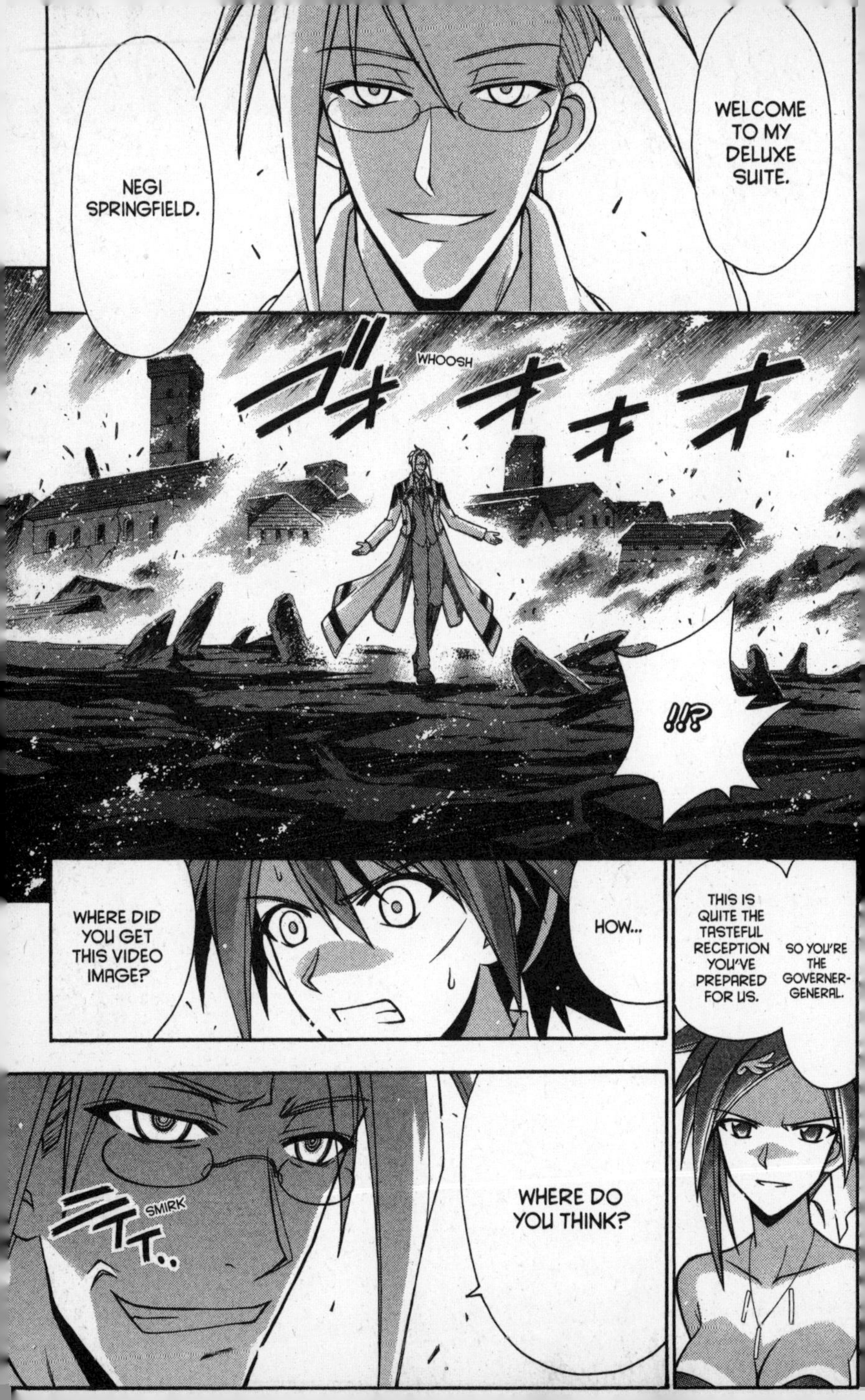
WELCOME TO MY DELUXE SUITE.
NEGI SPRINGFIELD.
WHOOSH
ゴォォォ
!!?
SO YOU'RE THE GOVERNER-GENERAL.
THIS IS QUITE THE TASTEFUL RECEPTION YOU'VE PREPARED FOR US.
HOW...
WHERE DID YOU GET THIS VIDEO IMAGE?
WHERE DO YOU THINK?
SMIRK
ニッ..

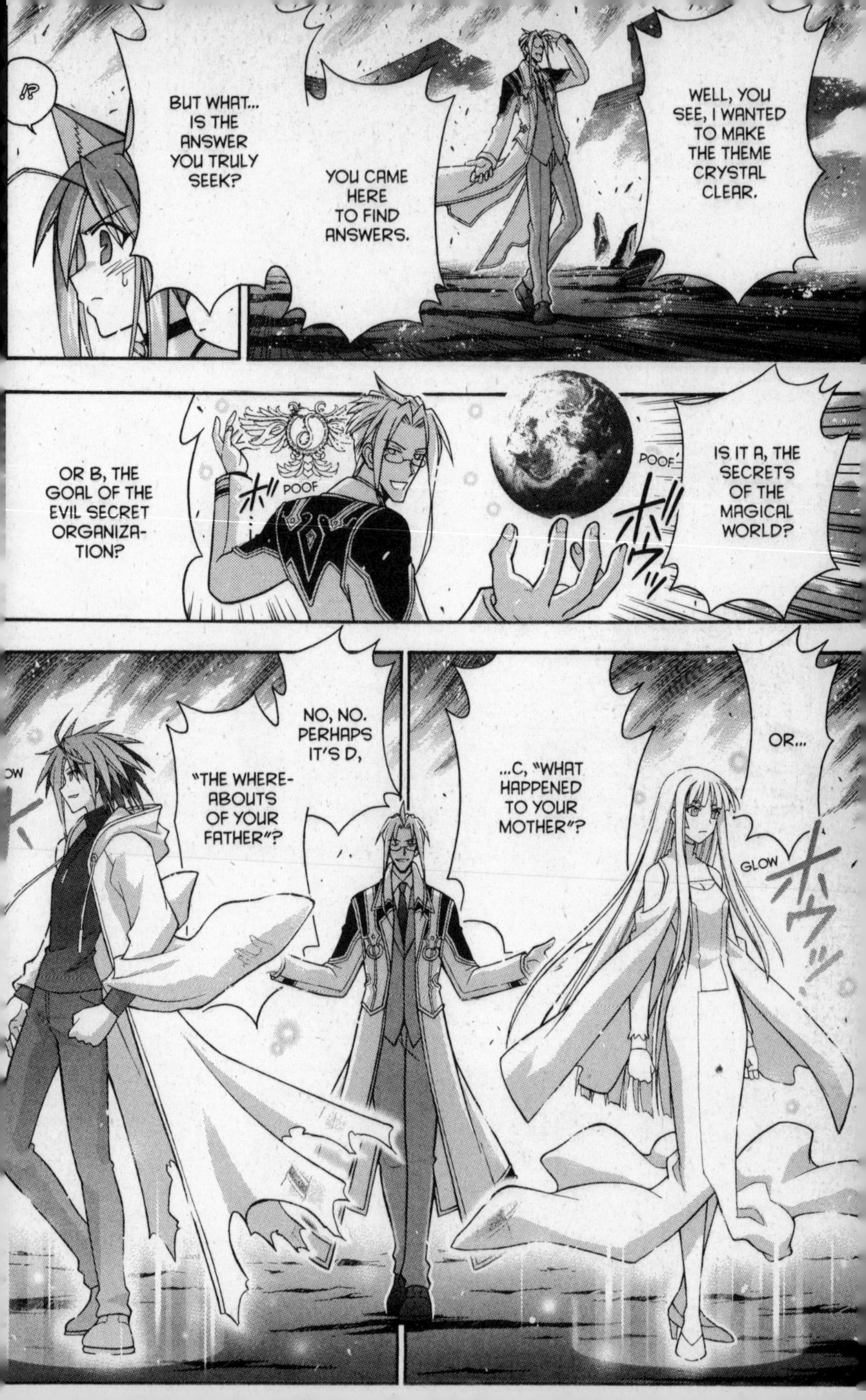
WELL, YOU SEE, I WANTED TO MAKE THE THEME CRYSTAL CLEAR.
YOU CAME HERE TO FIND ANSWERS.
BUT WHAT... IS THE ANSWER YOU TRULY SEEK?
!?
IS IT A, THE SECRETS OF THE MAGICAL WORLD?
POOF
POOF
OR B, THE GOAL OF THE EVIL SECRET ORGANIZATION?
OR...
...C, "WHAT HAPPENED TO YOUR MOTHER"?
GLOW
NO, NO. PERHAPS IT'S D,
"THE WHEREABOUTS OF YOUR FATHER"?

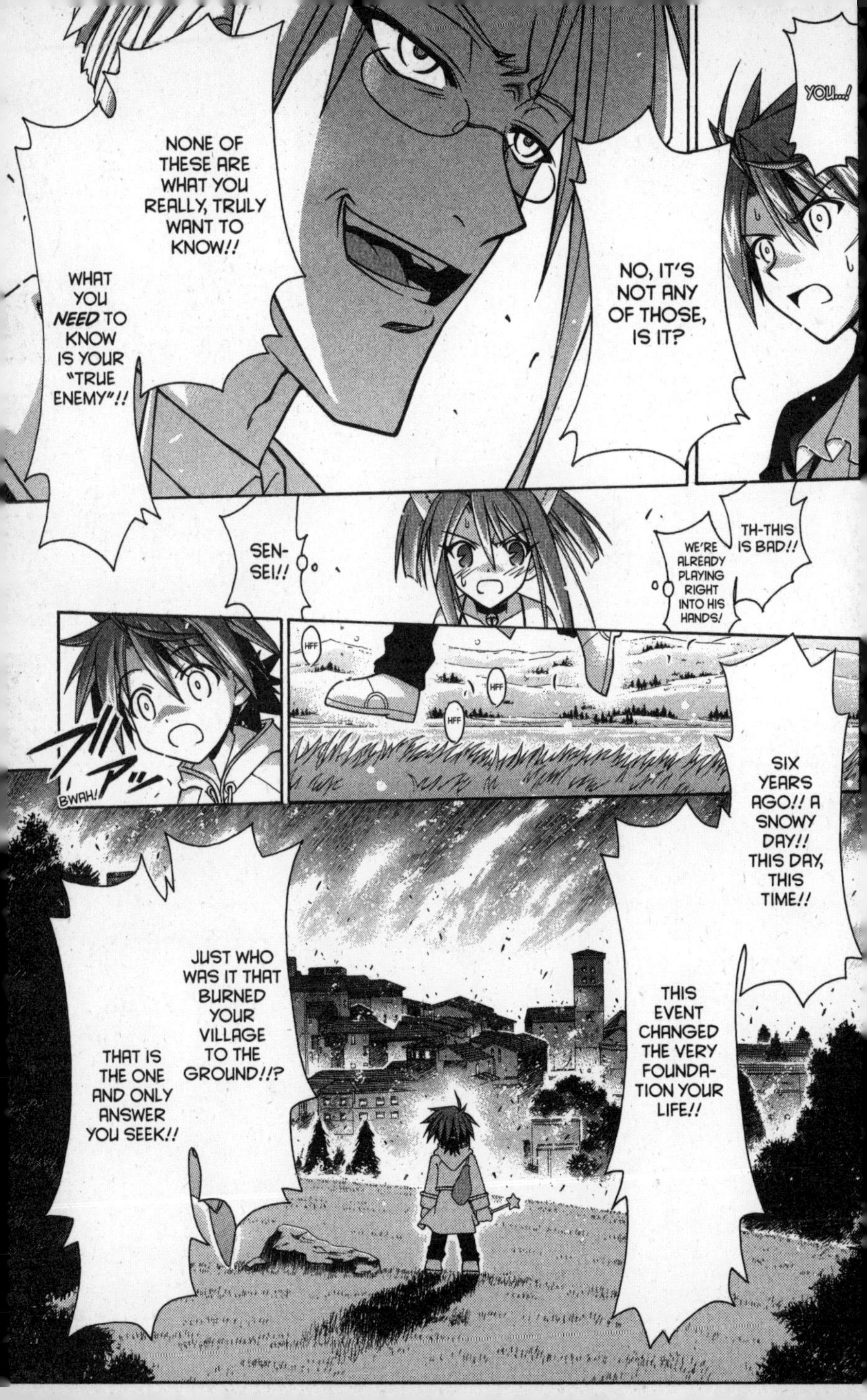
YOU...!
NO, IT'S NOT ANY OF THOSE, IS IT?
NONE OF THESE ARE WHAT YOU REALLY, TRULY WANT TO KNOW!!
WHAT YOU *NEED* TO KNOW IS YOUR "TRUE ENEMY"!!
TH-THIS IS BAD!!
WE'RE ALREADY PLAYING RIGHT INTO HIS HANDS!
SEN-SEI!!
HFF
HFF
HFF
BWAH!
SIX YEARS AGO!! A SNOWY DAY!! THIS DAY, THIS TIME!!
THIS EVENT CHANGED THE VERY FOUNDATION YOUR LIFE!!
JUST WHO WAS IT THAT BURNED YOUR VILLAGE TO THE GROUND!!?
THAT IS THE ONE AND ONLY ANSWER YOU SEEK!!

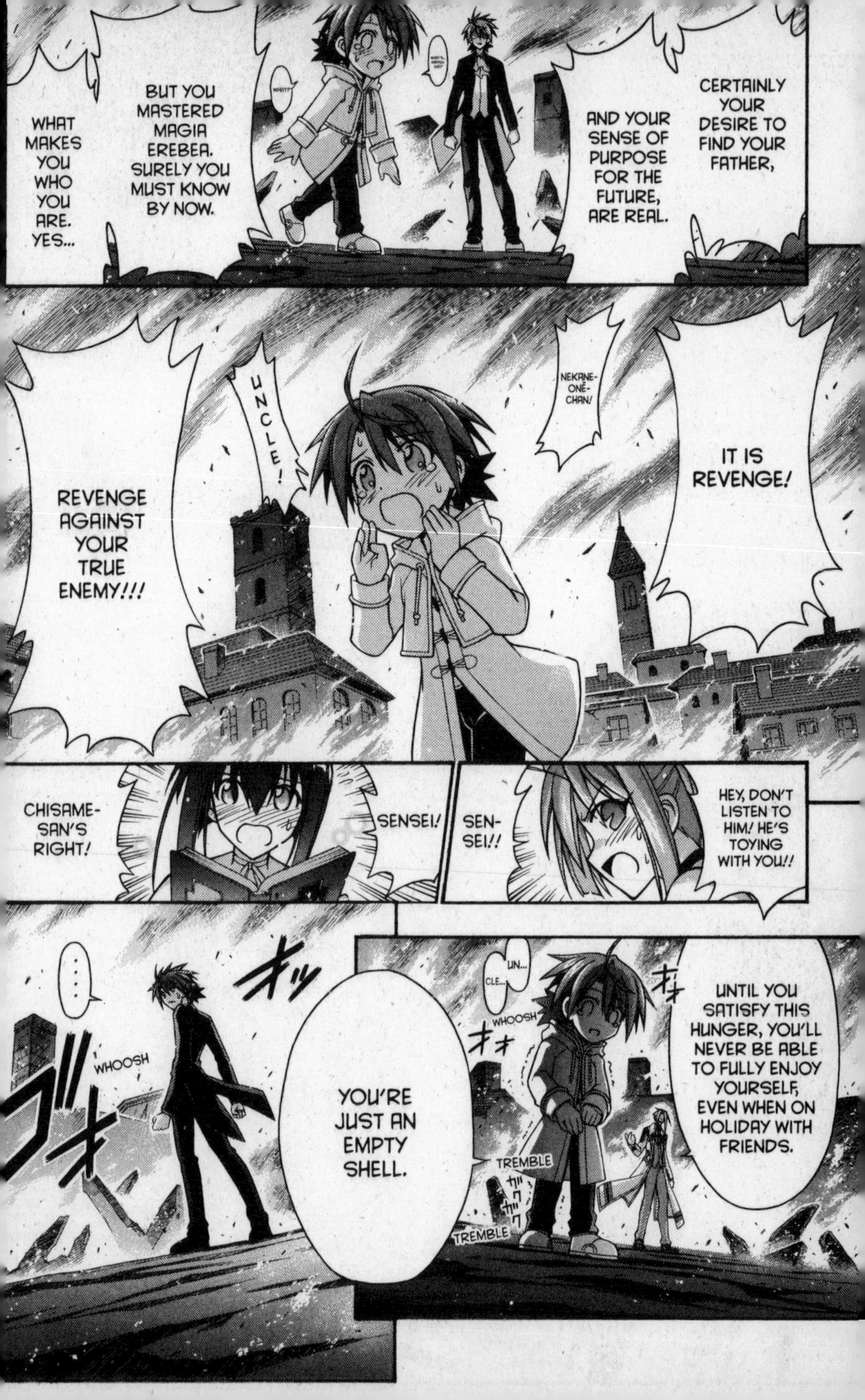
CERTAINLY YOUR DESIRE TO FIND YOUR FATHER,
AND YOUR SENSE OF PURPOSE FOR THE FUTURE, ARE REAL.
WHAT'S... HAPPEN-ING?
WHAT?
BUT YOU MASTERED MAGIA EREBEA. SURELY YOU MUST KNOW BY NOW.
WHAT MAKES YOU WHO YOU ARE. YES...
IT IS REVENGE!
NEKANE-ONÉ-CHAN!
UNCLE!
REVENGE AGAINST YOUR TRUE ENEMY!!!
HEY, DON'T LISTEN TO HIM! HE'S TOYING WITH YOU!!
SEN-SEI!!
SENSEI!
CHISAME-SAN'S RIGHT!
UNTIL YOU SATISFY THIS HUNGER, YOU'LL NEVER BE ABLE TO FULLY ENJOY YOURSELF, EVEN WHEN ON HOLIDAY WITH FRIENDS.
UN...
CLE...
WHOOSH
TREMBLE
TREMBLE
YOU'RE JUST AN EMPTY SHELL.
...
WHOOSH

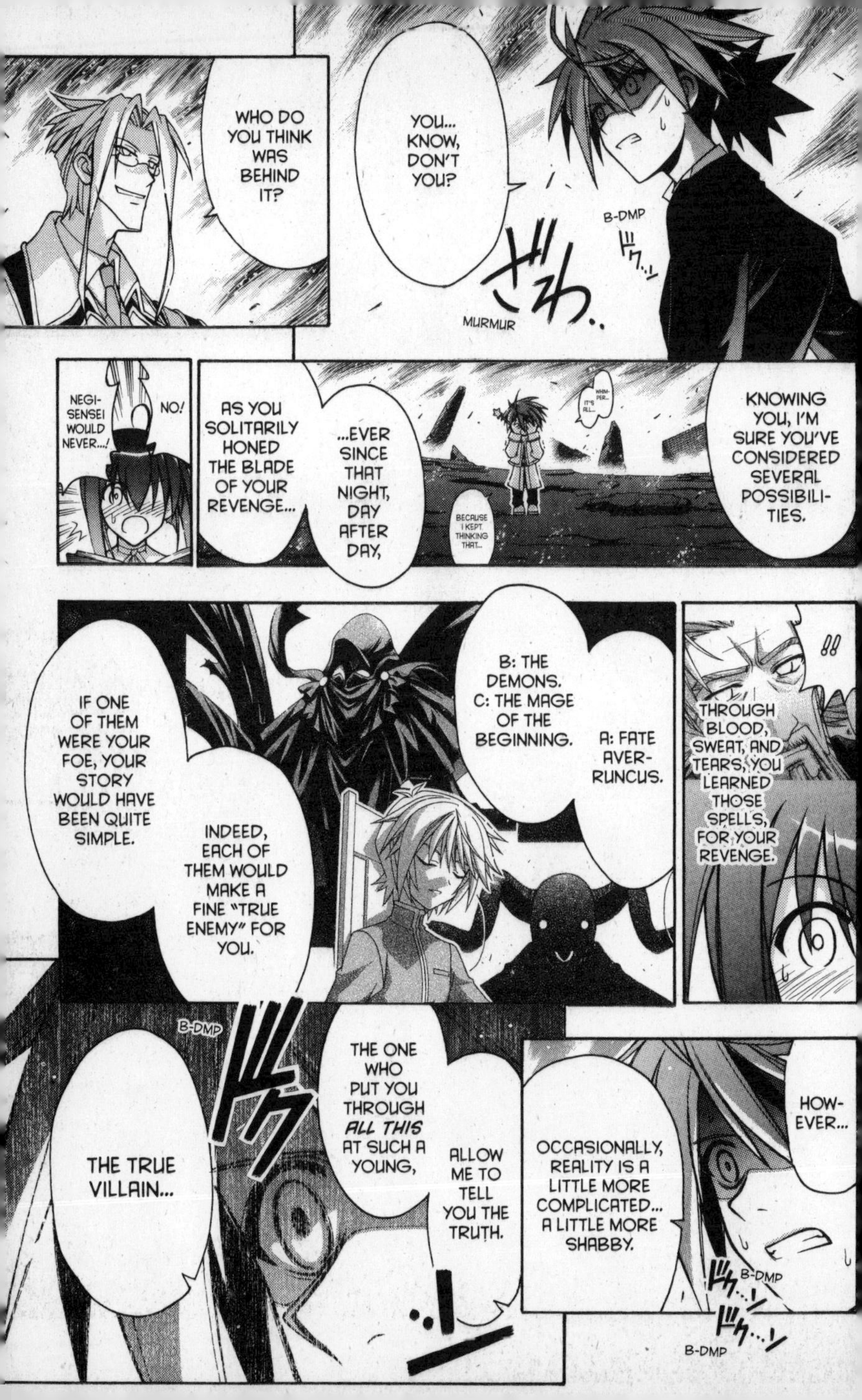
YOU... KNOW, DON'T YOU?
B-DMP
MURMUR
WHO DO YOU THINK WAS BEHIND IT?
KNOWING YOU, I'M SURE YOU'VE CONSIDERED SEVERAL POSSIBILI-TIES.
WHIMPER... IT'S ALL...
BECAUSE I KEPT THINKING THAT...
...EVER SINCE THAT NIGHT, DAY AFTER DAY,
AS YOU SOLITARILY HONED THE BLADE OF YOUR REVENGE...
NO!
NEGI-SENSEI WOULD NEVER...!
!!
THROUGH BLOOD, SWEAT, AND TEARS, YOU LEARNED THOSE SPELLS, FOR YOUR REVENGE.
A: FATE AVER-RUNCUS.
B: THE DEMONS. C: THE MAGE OF THE BEGINNING.
INDEED, EACH OF THEM WOULD MAKE A FINE "TRUE ENEMY" FOR YOU.
IF ONE OF THEM WERE YOUR FOE, YOUR STORY WOULD HAVE BEEN QUITE SIMPLE.
HOW-EVER...
OCCASIONALLY, REALITY IS A LITTLE MORE COMPLICATED... A LITTLE MORE SHABBY.
B-DMP
B-DMP
ALLOW ME TO TELL YOU THE TRUTH.
THE ONE WHO PUT YOU THROUGH *ALL THIS* AT SUCH A YOUNG,
THE TRUE VILLAIN...
B-DMP

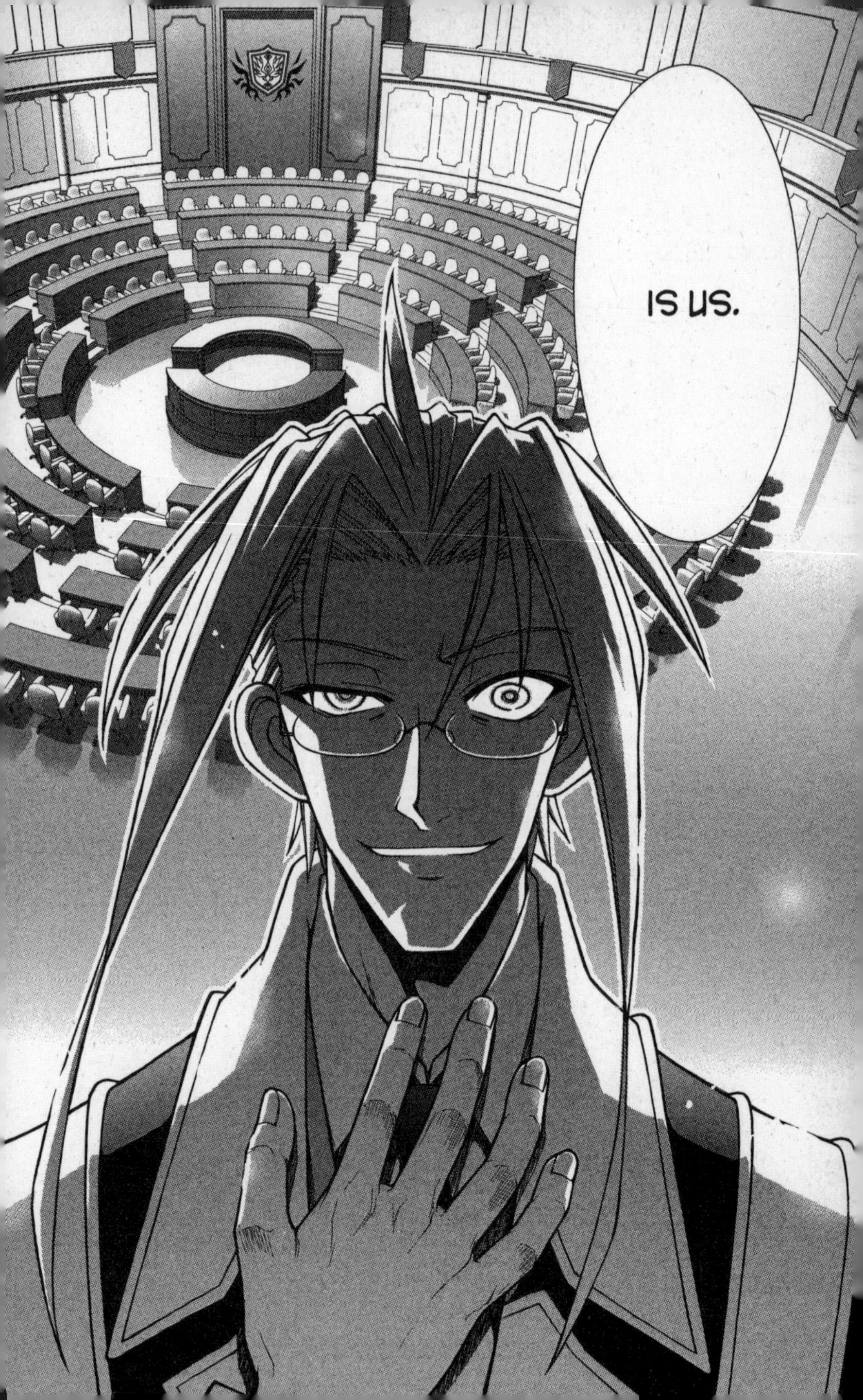
IS US.

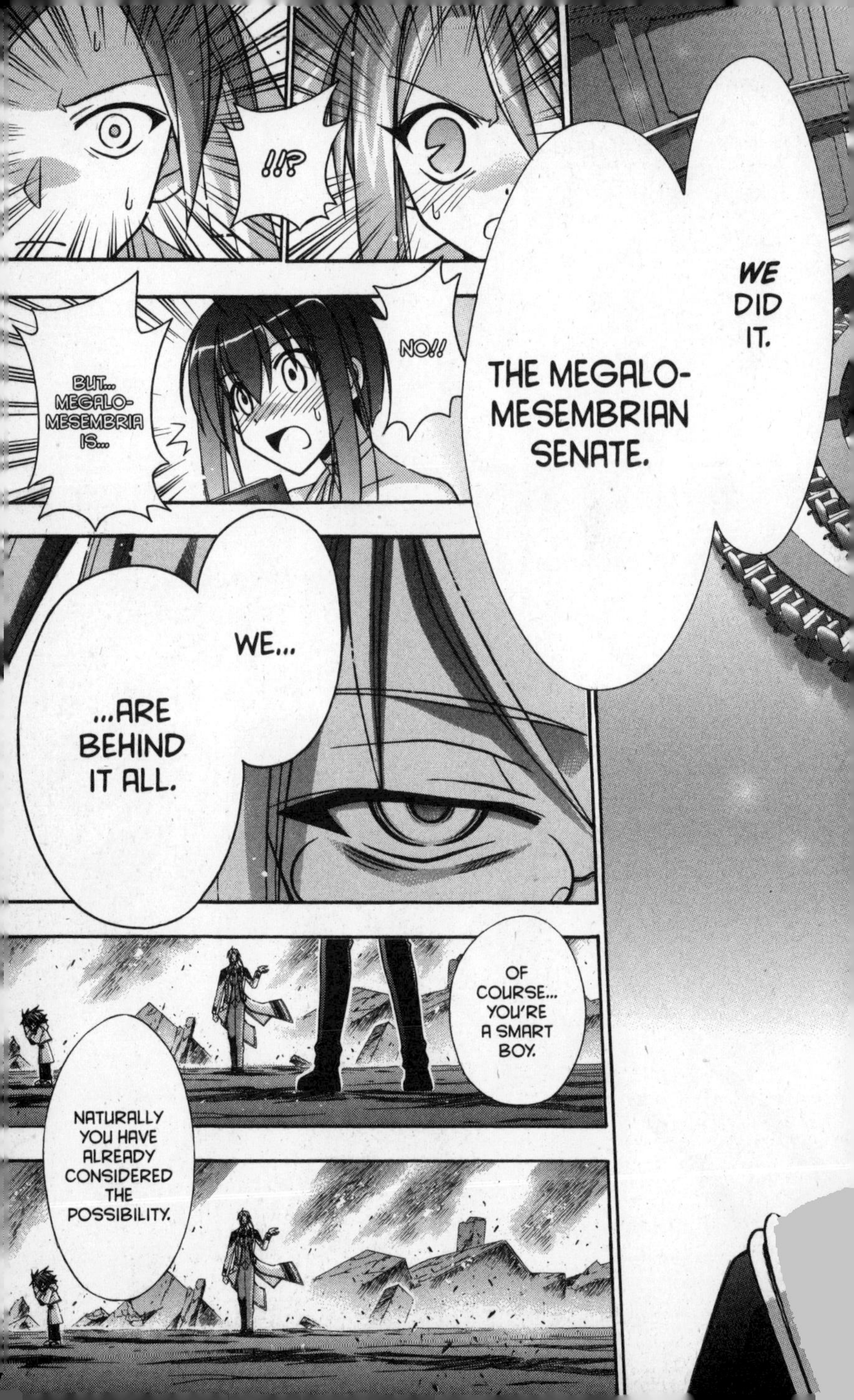
WE DID IT.
THE MEGALO-MESEMBRIAN SENATE.
!!?
NO!!
BUT... MEGALO-MESEMBRIA IS...
WE...
...ARE BEHIND IT ALL.
OF COURSE... YOU'RE A SMART BOY.
NATURALLY YOU HAVE ALREADY CONSIDERED THE POSSIBILITY.

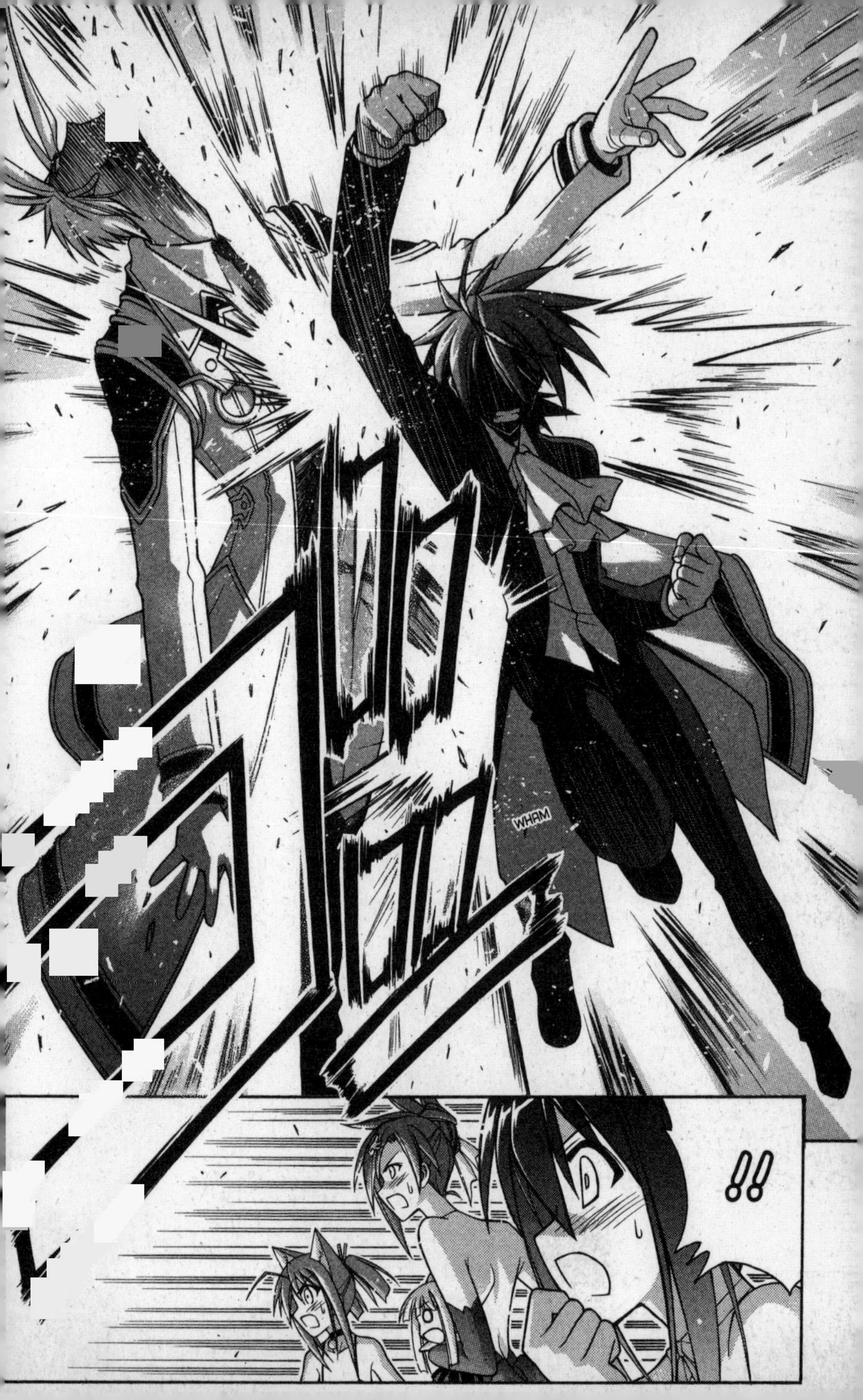
WHAM
!!

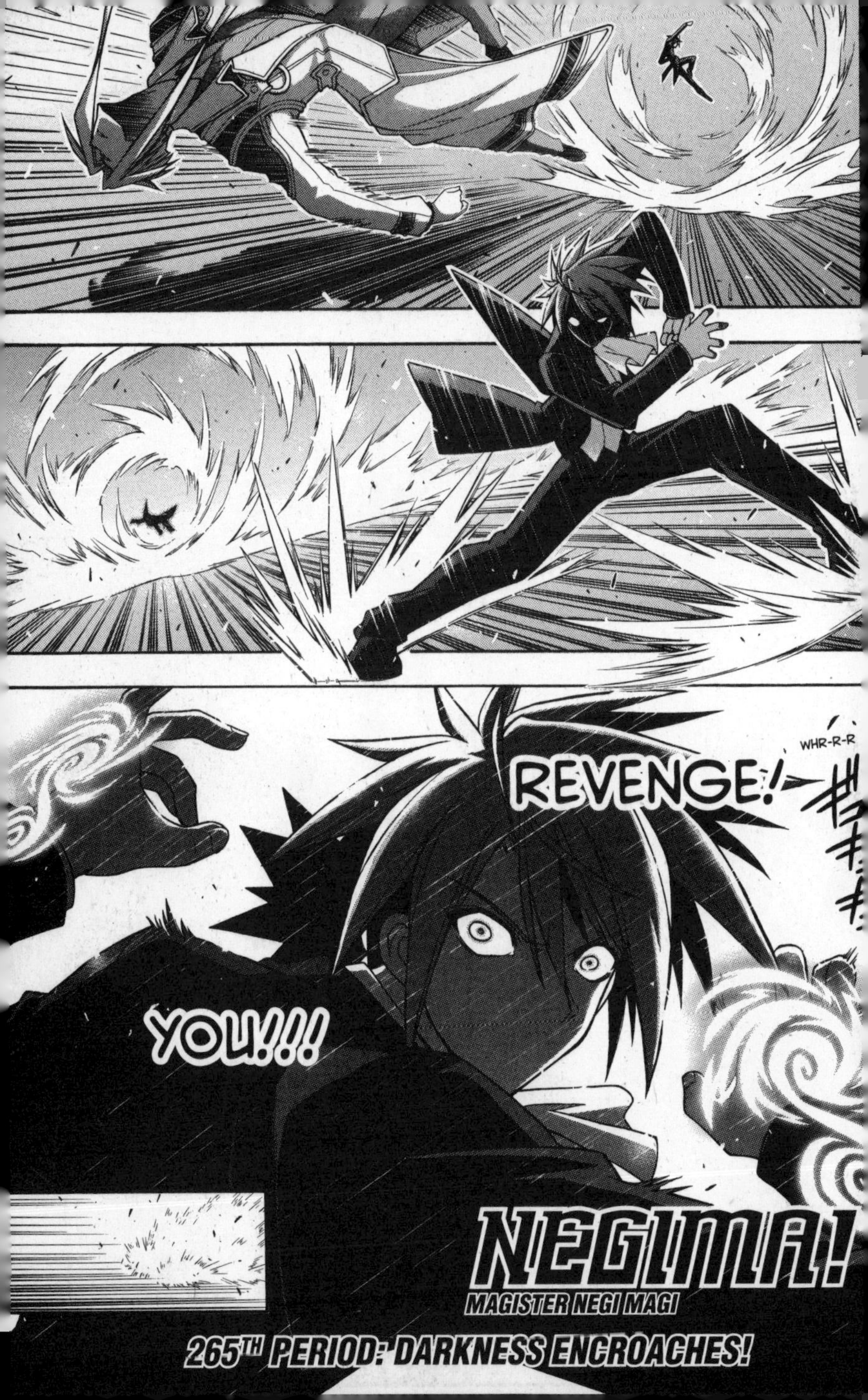
WHR-R-R
REVENGE!
YOU!!!
NEGIMA!
MAGISTER NEGI MAGI
265TH PERIOD: DARKNESS ENCROACHES!

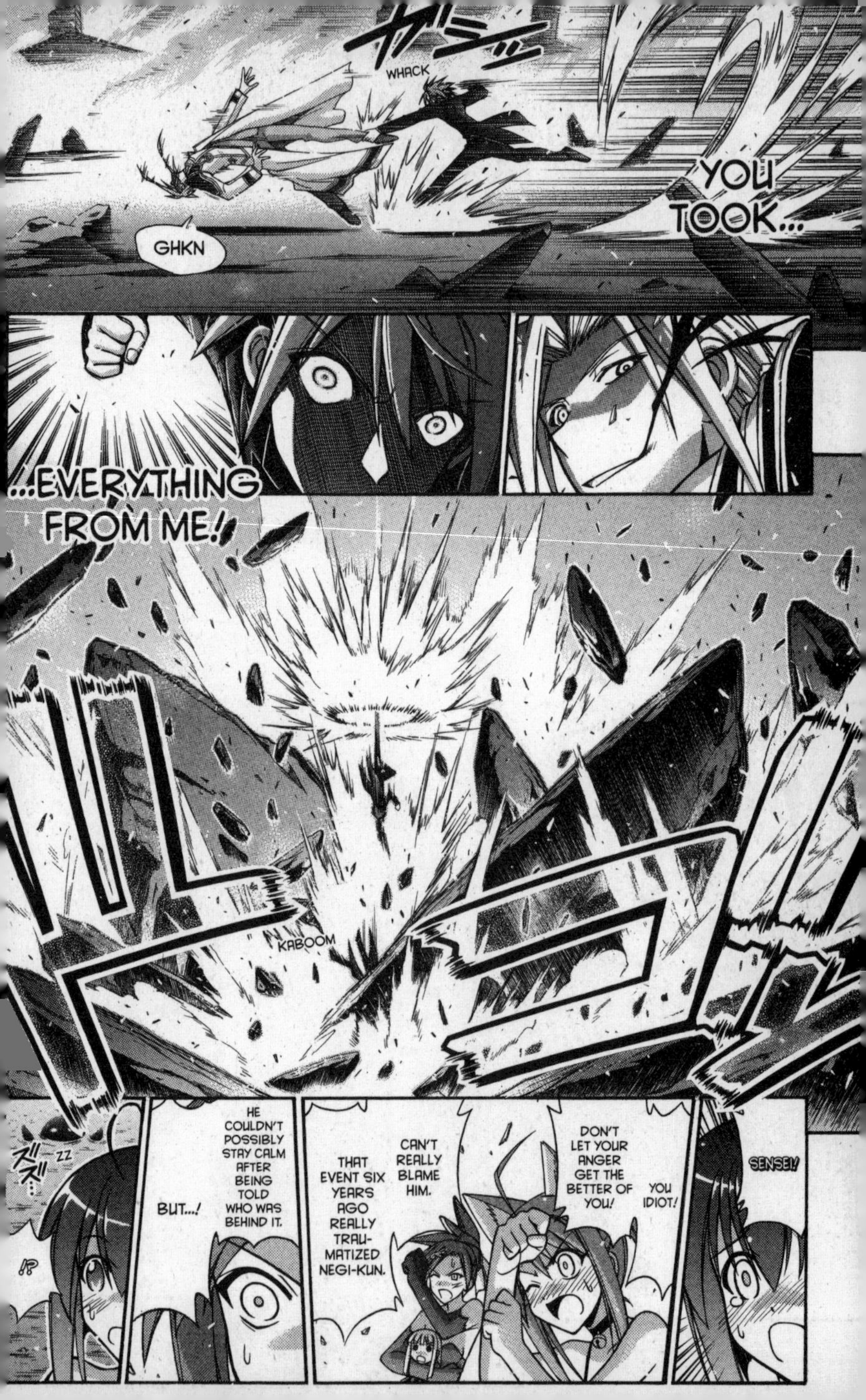
WHACK
YOU TOOK...
GHKN
...EVERYTHING FROM ME!!
KABOOM
SENSEI!
DON'T LET YOUR ANGER GET THE BETTER OF YOU!
YOU IDIOT!
CAN'T REALLY BLAME HIM.
THAT EVENT SIX YEARS AGO REALLY TRAU-MATIZED NEGI-KUN.
HE COULDN'T POSSIBLY STAY CALM AFTER BEING TOLD WHO WAS BEHIND IT.
BUT...!
ZZ
!?

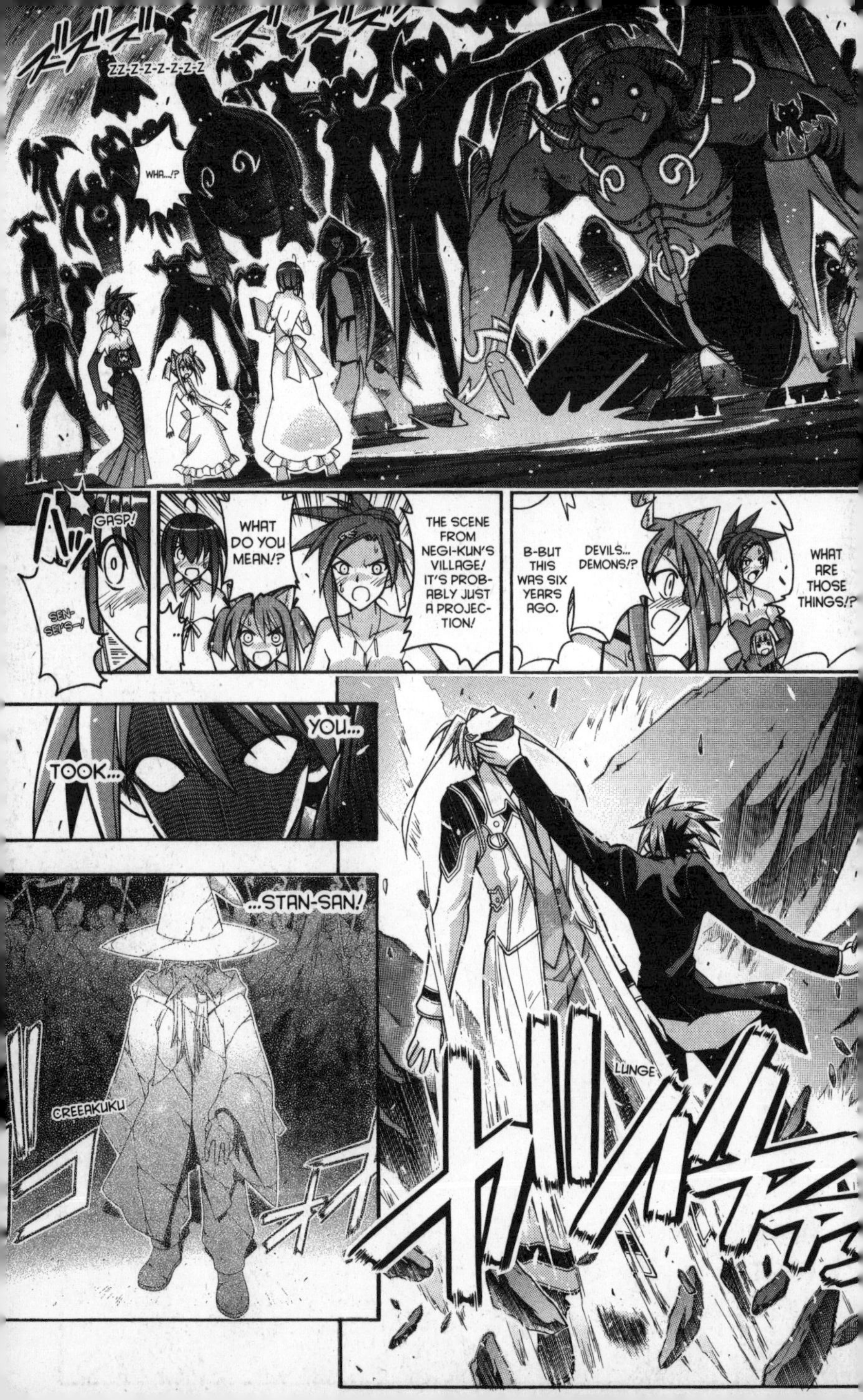
ZZ-Z-Z-Z-Z-Z-Z
WHA...!?
WHAT ARE THOSE THINGS!?
DEVILS... DEMONS!?
B-BUT THIS WAS SIX YEARS AGO.
THE SCENE FROM NEGI-KUN'S VILLAGE! IT'S PROBABLY JUST A PROJECTION!
WHAT DO YOU MEAN!?
...
GASP!
SEN-SEI'S—!
LUNGE
YOU...
TOOK...
...STAN-SAN!
CREEAKUKU

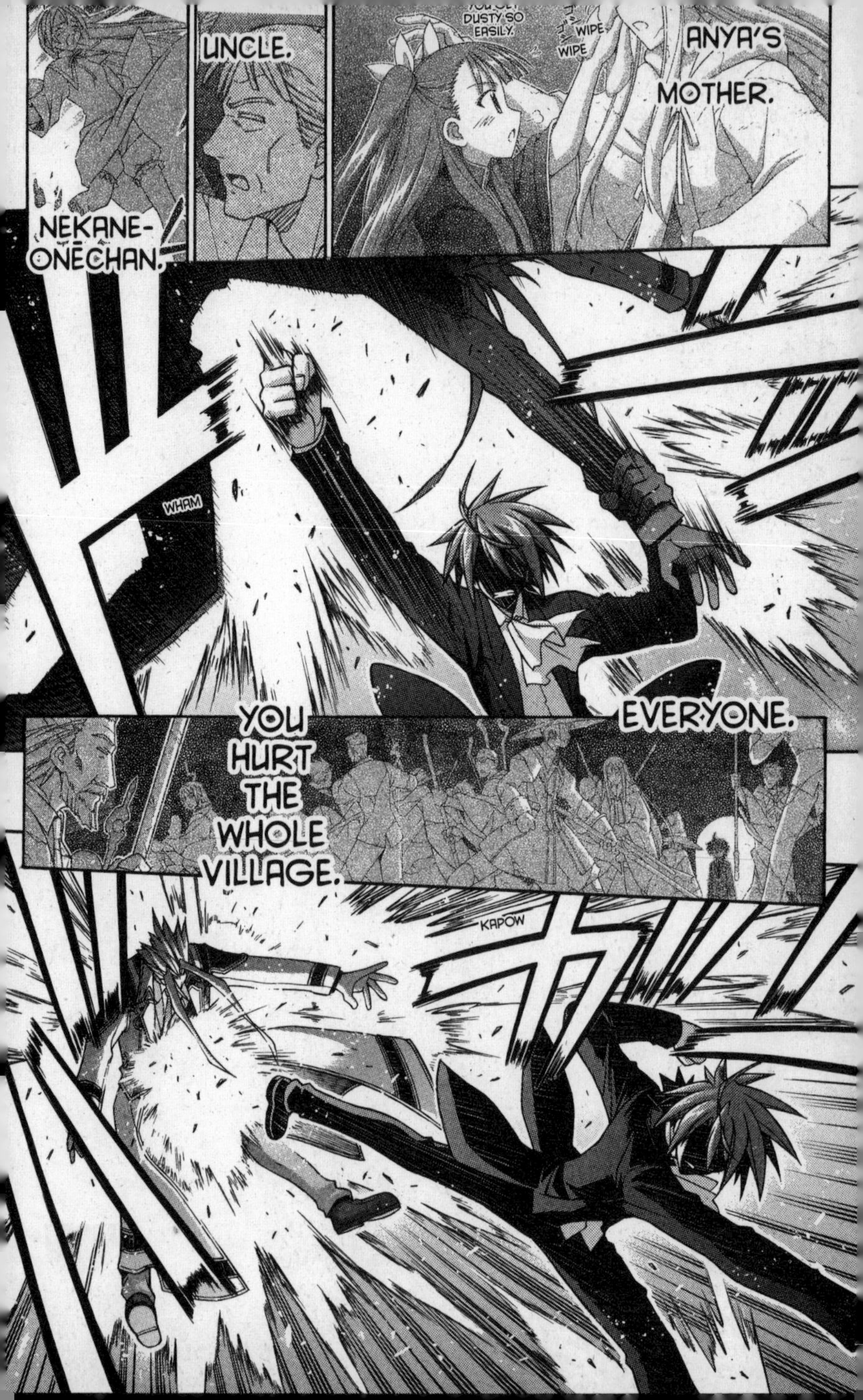
DUSTY SO EASILY.
WIPE
WIPE
ANYA'S MOTHER.
UNCLE.
NEKANE-ONĒCHAN.
WHAM
EVERYONE.
YOU HURT THE WHOLE VILLAGE.
KAPOW

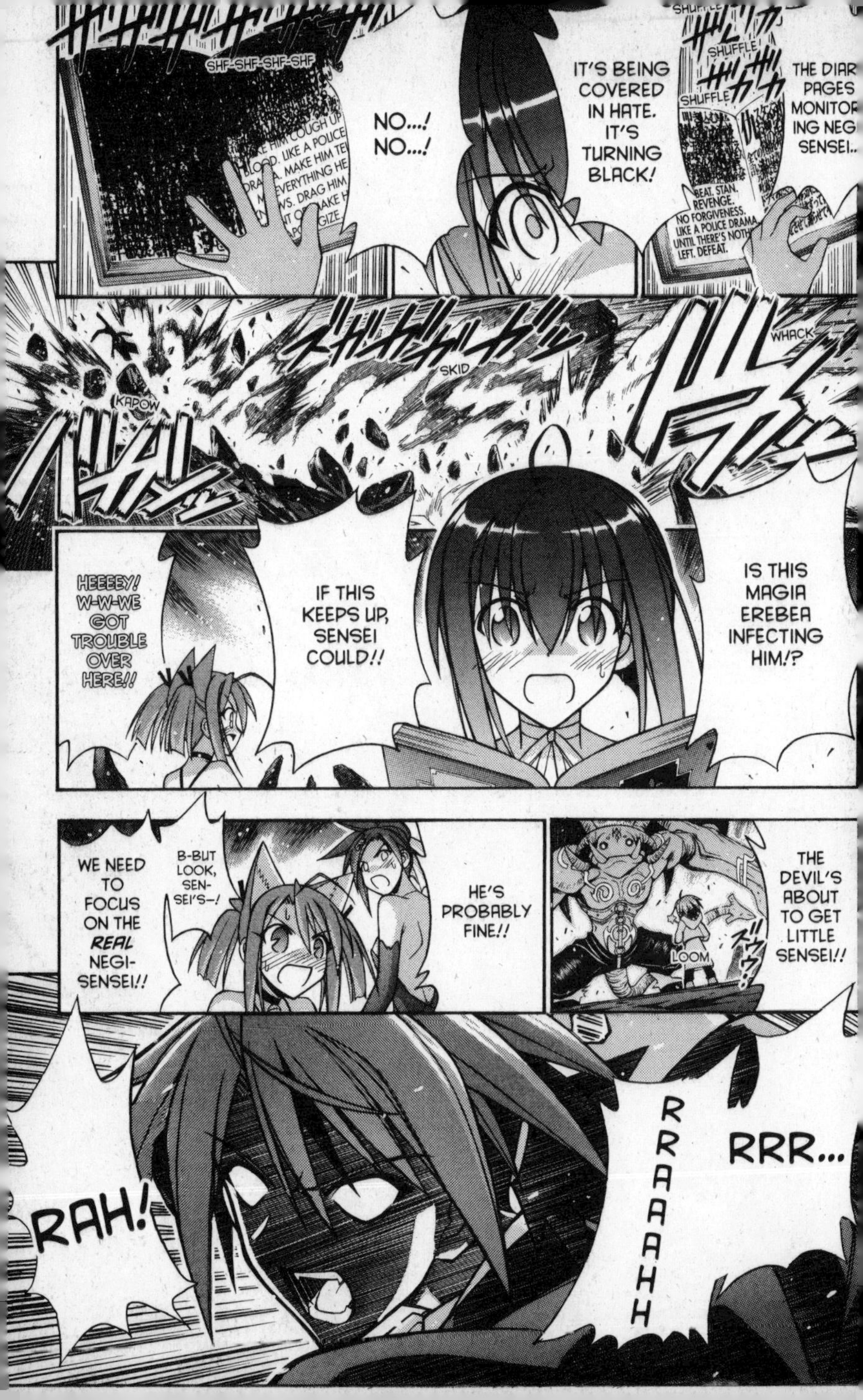
SHUFFLE
SHUFFLE
SHUFFLE
THE DIAR PAGES MONITOR ING NEGI SENSEI...
BEAT. STAN. REVENGE. NO FORGIVENESS. LIKE A POLICE DRAMA. UNTIL THERE'S NOTH LEFT. DEFEAT.
IT'S BEING COVERED IN HATE. IT'S TURNING BLACK!
NO...! NO...!
SHF-SHF-SHF-SHF
BLOOD. LIKE A POLICE
EVERYTHING HE
WHACK
SKID
KAPOW
IS THIS MAGIA EREBEA INFECTING HIM!?
IF THIS KEEPS UP, SENSEI COULD!!
HEEEEY! W-W-WE GOT TROUBLE OVER HERE!!
THE DEVIL'S ABOUT TO GET LITTLE SENSEI!!
LOOM
HE'S PROBABLY FINE!!
B-BUT LOOK, SEN-SEI'S—!
WE NEED TO FOCUS ON THE *REAL* NEGI-SENSEI!!
RRR...
RRAAAAHH
RAH!

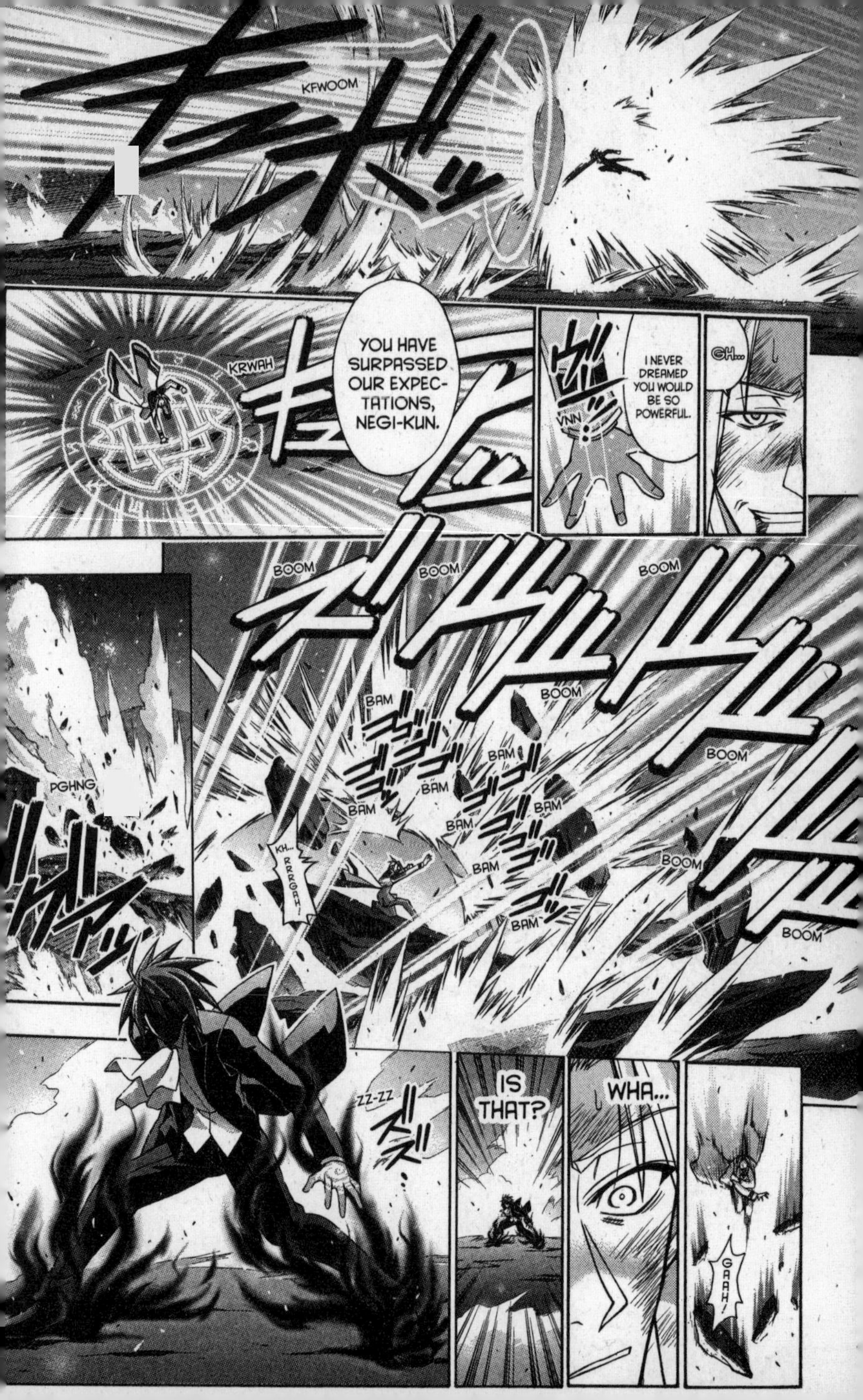
KFWOOM
GH...
VNN
I NEVER DREAMED YOU WOULD BE SO POWERFUL.
YOU HAVE SURPASSED OUR EXPECTATIONS, NEGI-KUN.
KRWAH
BOOM
BOOM
BOOM
BOOM
BOOM
BOOM
BOOM
BAM
BAM
BAM
BAM
BAM
BAM
BAM
BAM
KH... RRRGAH!
PGHNG
GAAH!
WHA...
IS THAT?
ZZ-ZZ

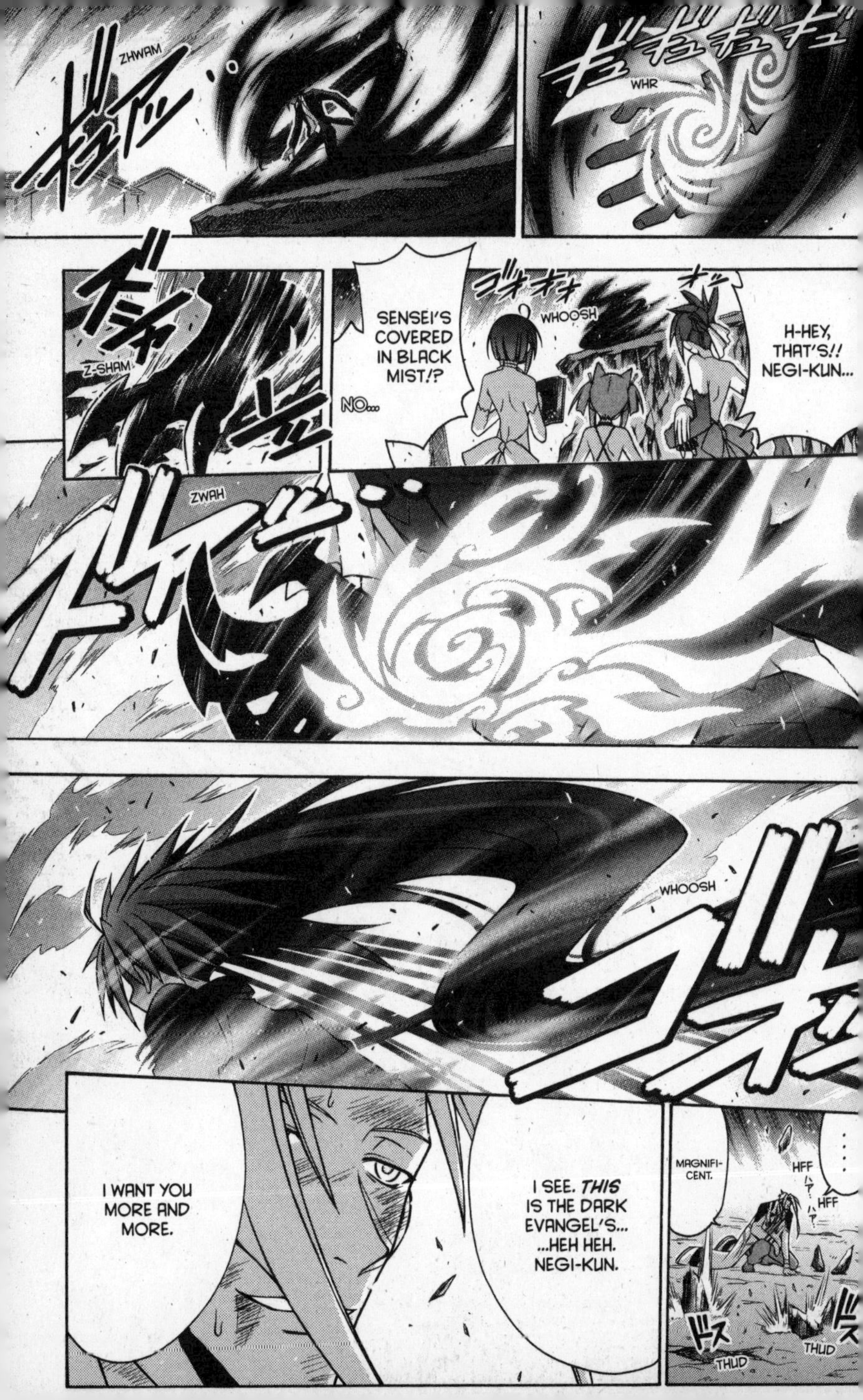
WHR
ZHWAM
H-HEY, THAT'S!! NEGI-KUN...
WHOOSH
SENSEI'S COVERED IN BLACK MIST!?
NO...
Z-SHAM
ZWAH
WHOOSH
MAGNIFI-CENT.
HFF
HFF
THUD
THUD
I SEE. *THIS* IS THE DARK EVANGEL'S... ...HEH HEH. NEGI-KUN.
I WANT YOU MORE AND MORE.

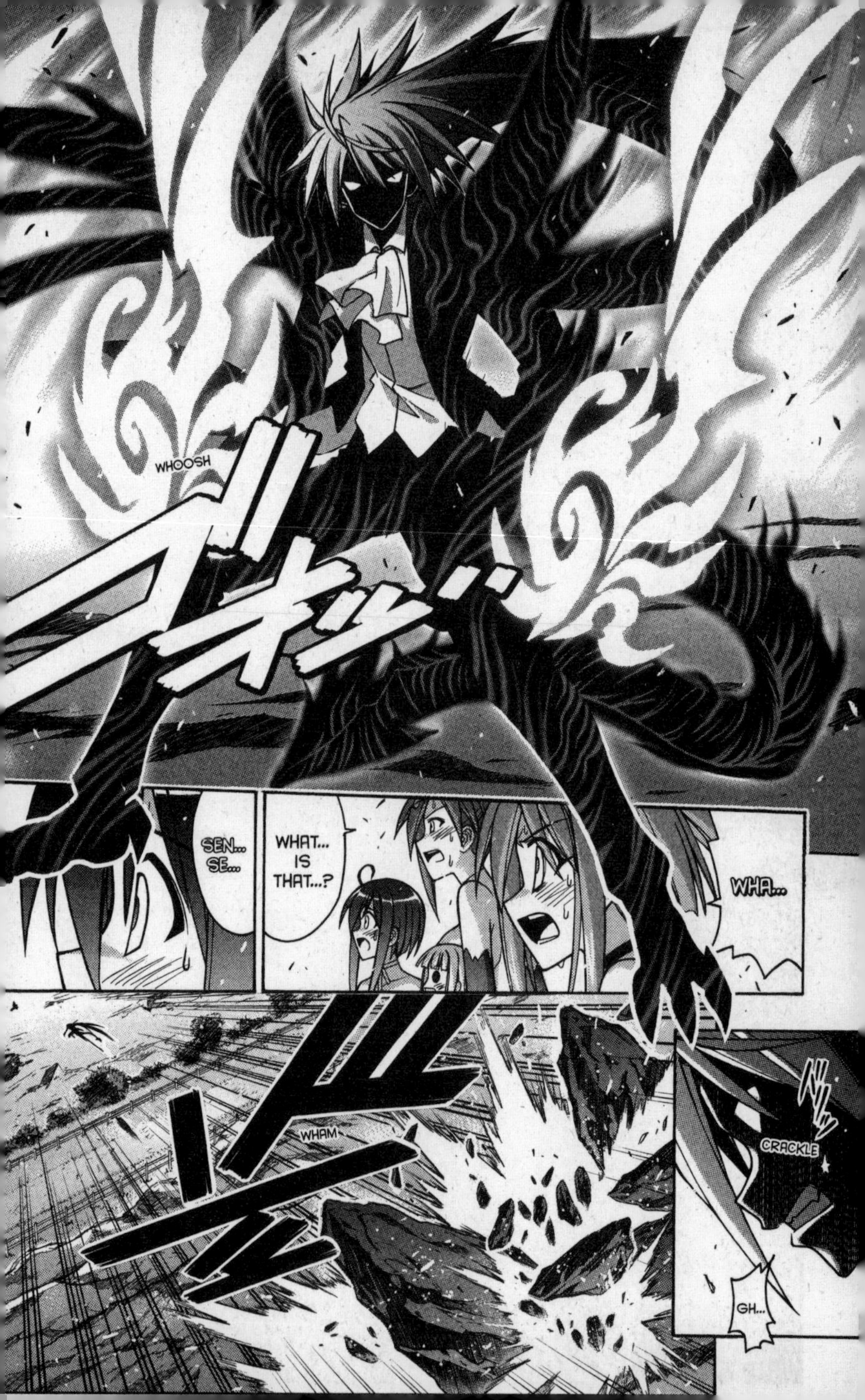
WHOOSH
WHA...
WHAT... IS THAT...?
SEN... SE...
CRACKLE
GH...
WHAM

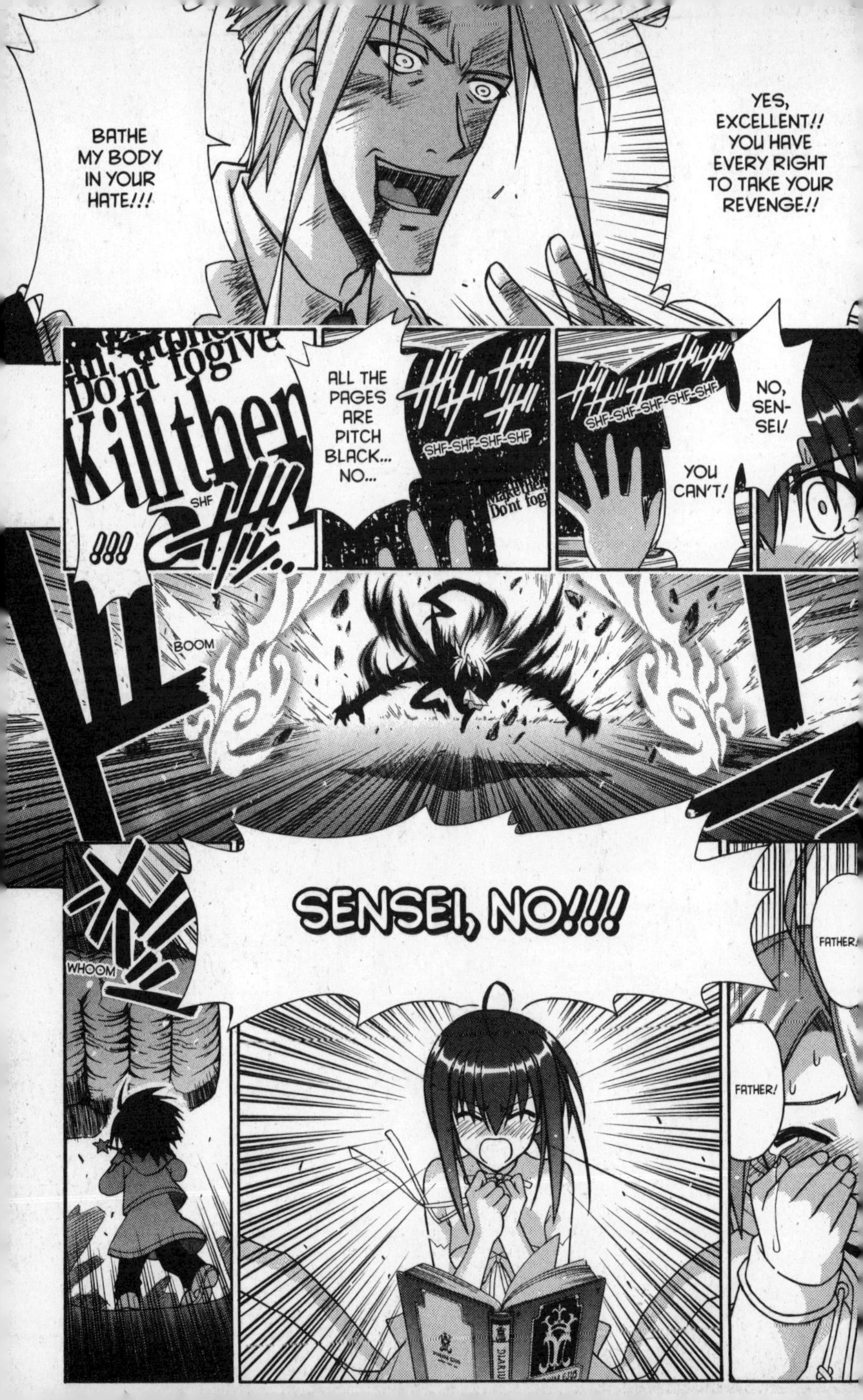
YES, EXCELLENT!! YOU HAVE EVERY RIGHT TO TAKE YOUR REVENGE!!
BATHE MY BODY IN YOUR HATE!!!
SHF-SHF-SHF-SHF-SHF
NO, SEN-SEI!
YOU CAN'T!
SHF-SHF-SHF-SHF
ALL THE PAGES ARE PITCH BLACK... NO...
Don't fogive
Kill then
SHF
!!!
BOOM
FATHER!
FATHER!
SENSEI, NO!!!
WHOOM

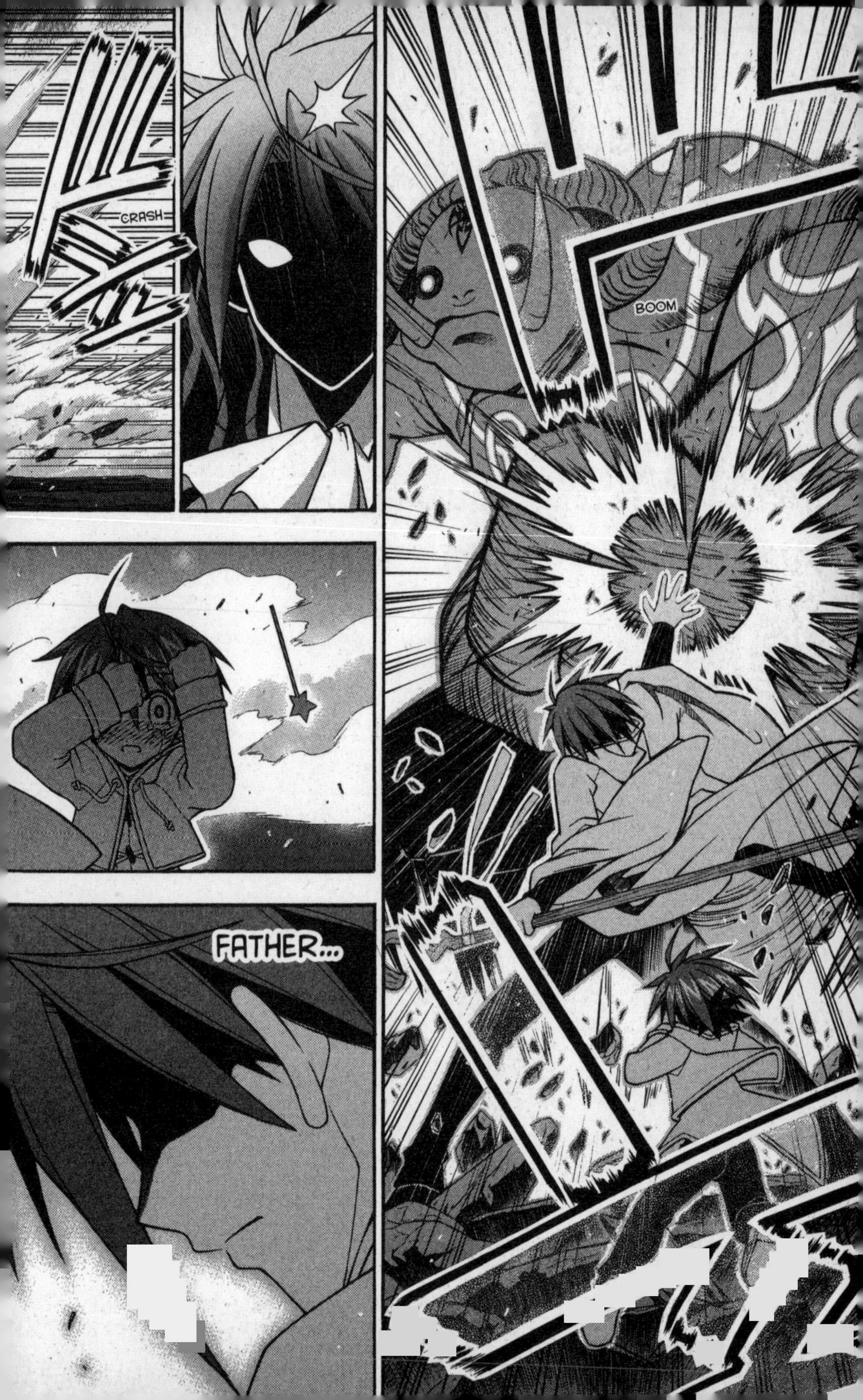
BOOM
CRASH
FATHER...

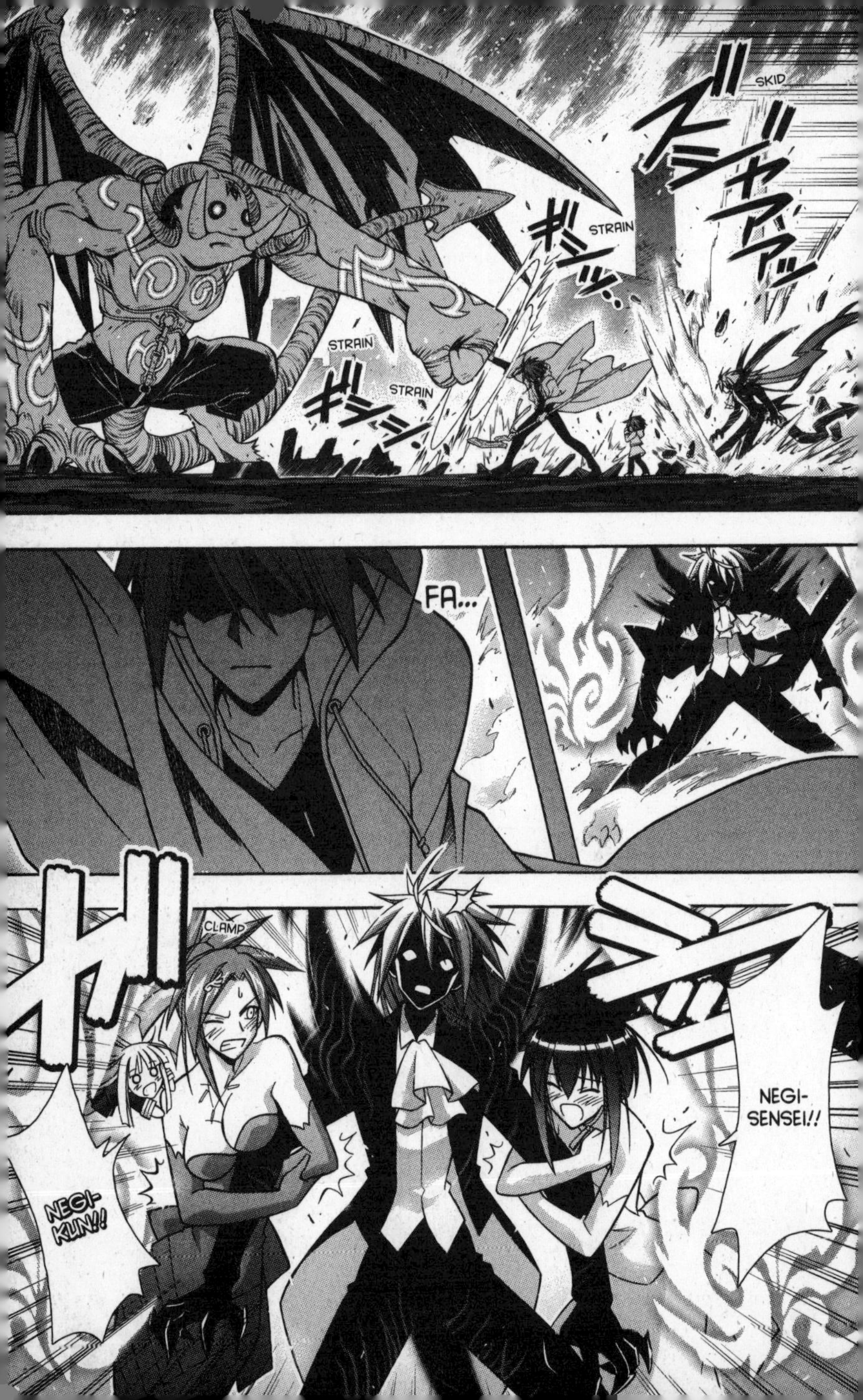
SKID
STRAIN
STRAIN
STRAIN
FA...
NEGI-SENSEI!!
CLAMP
NEGI-KUN!!

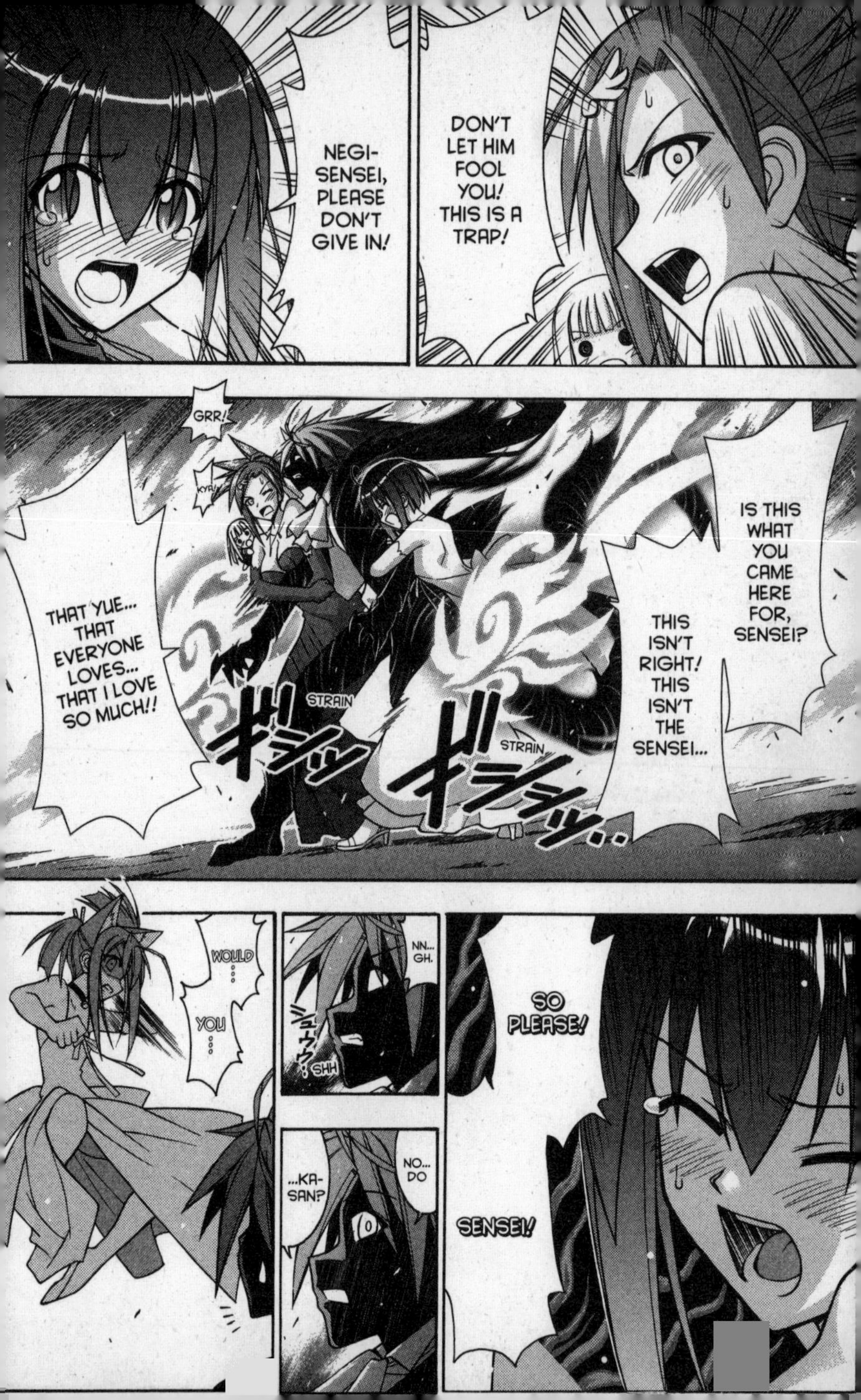
DON'T LET HIM FOOL YOU! THIS IS A TRAP!
NEGI-SENSEI, PLEASE DON'T GIVE IN!
IS THIS WHAT YOU CAME HERE FOR, SENSEI?
THIS ISN'T RIGHT! THIS ISN'T THE SENSEI...
GRR!
KYA!
STRAIN
STRAIN
THAT YUE... THAT EVERYONE LOVES... THAT I LOVE SO MUCH!!
SO PLEASE!
SENSEI!
NN... GH.
SHH
NO... DO
...KA-SAN?
WOULD...
YOU...

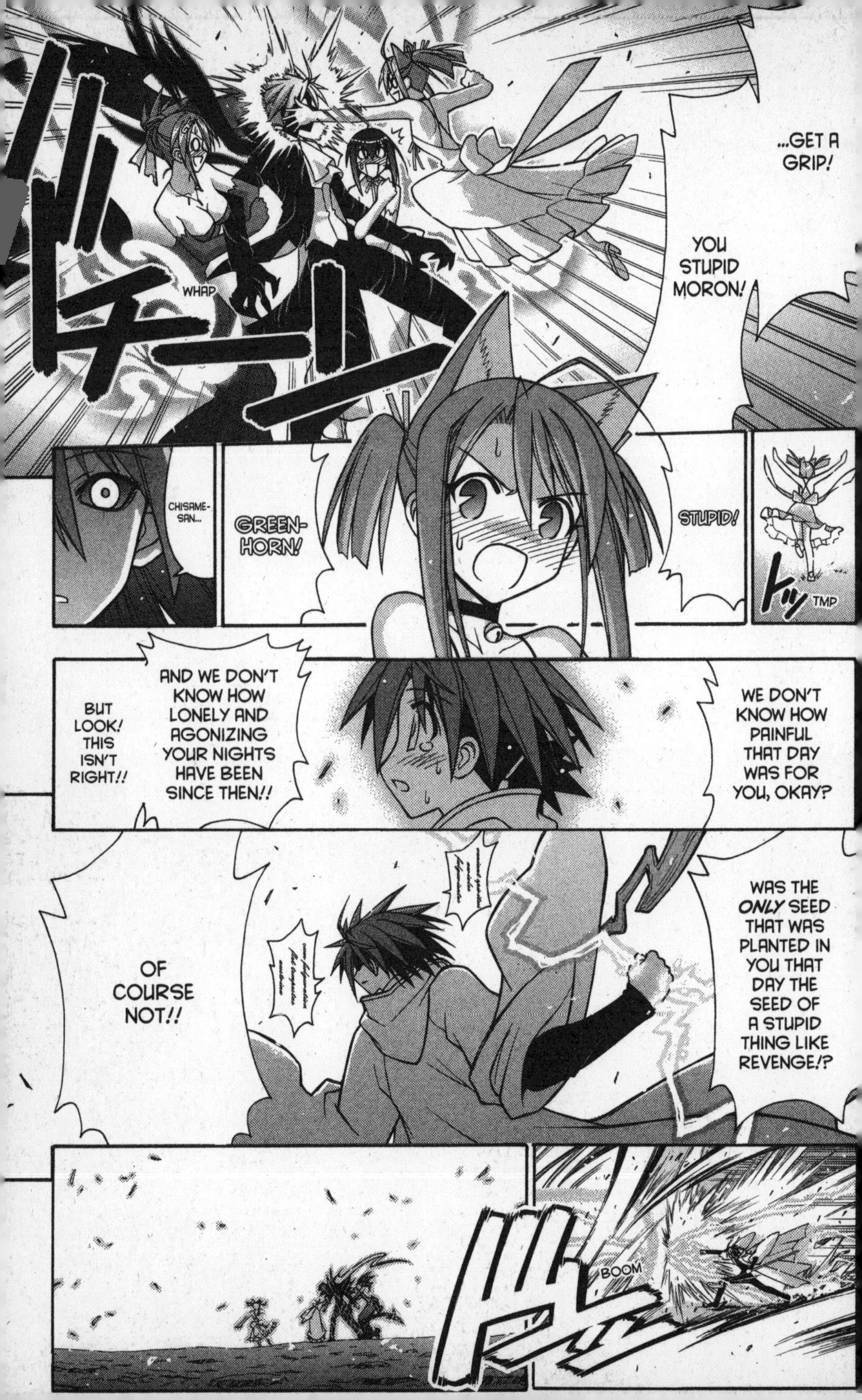

...GET A GRIP!
YOU STUPID MORON!
WHAP
TMP
STUPID!
GREEN-HORN!
CHISAME-SAN...
WE DON'T KNOW HOW PAINFUL THAT DAY WAS FOR YOU, OKAY?
AND WE DON'T KNOW HOW LONELY AND AGONIZING YOUR NIGHTS HAVE BEEN SINCE THEN!!
BUT LOOK! THIS ISN'T RIGHT!!
WAS THE *ONLY* SEED THAT WAS PLANTED IN YOU THAT DAY THE SEED OF A STUPID THING LIKE REVENGE!?
OF COURSE NOT!!
BOOM

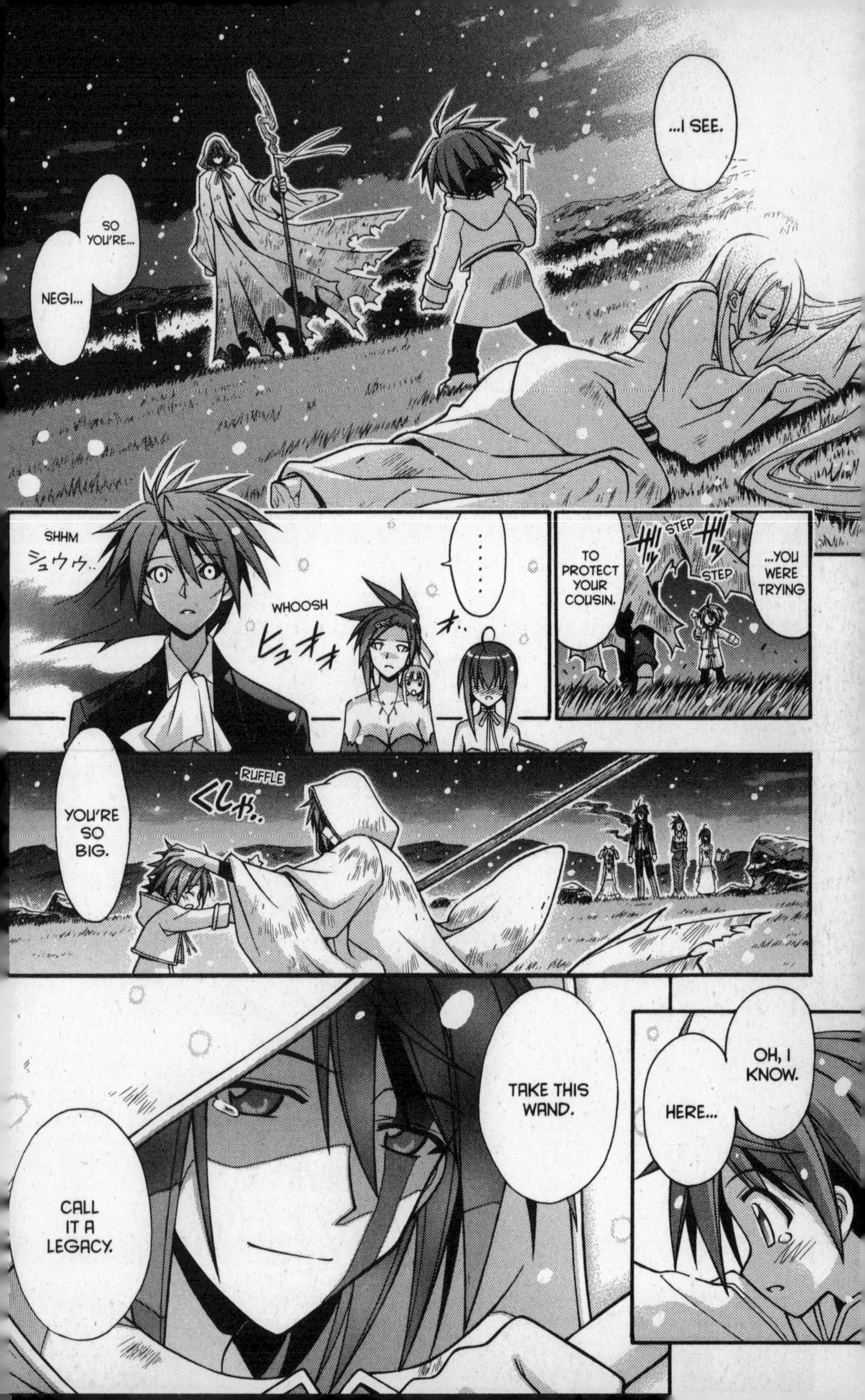
...I SEE.
SO YOU'RE...
NEGI...
...YOU WERE TRYING
STEP
STEP
TO PROTECT YOUR COUSIN.
......
オ..
WHOOSH
ヒュオォ
SHHM
シュウゥ..
RUFFLE
くしゃ..
YOU'RE SO BIG.
OH, I KNOW.
HERE...
TAKE THIS WAND.
CALL IT A LEGACY.

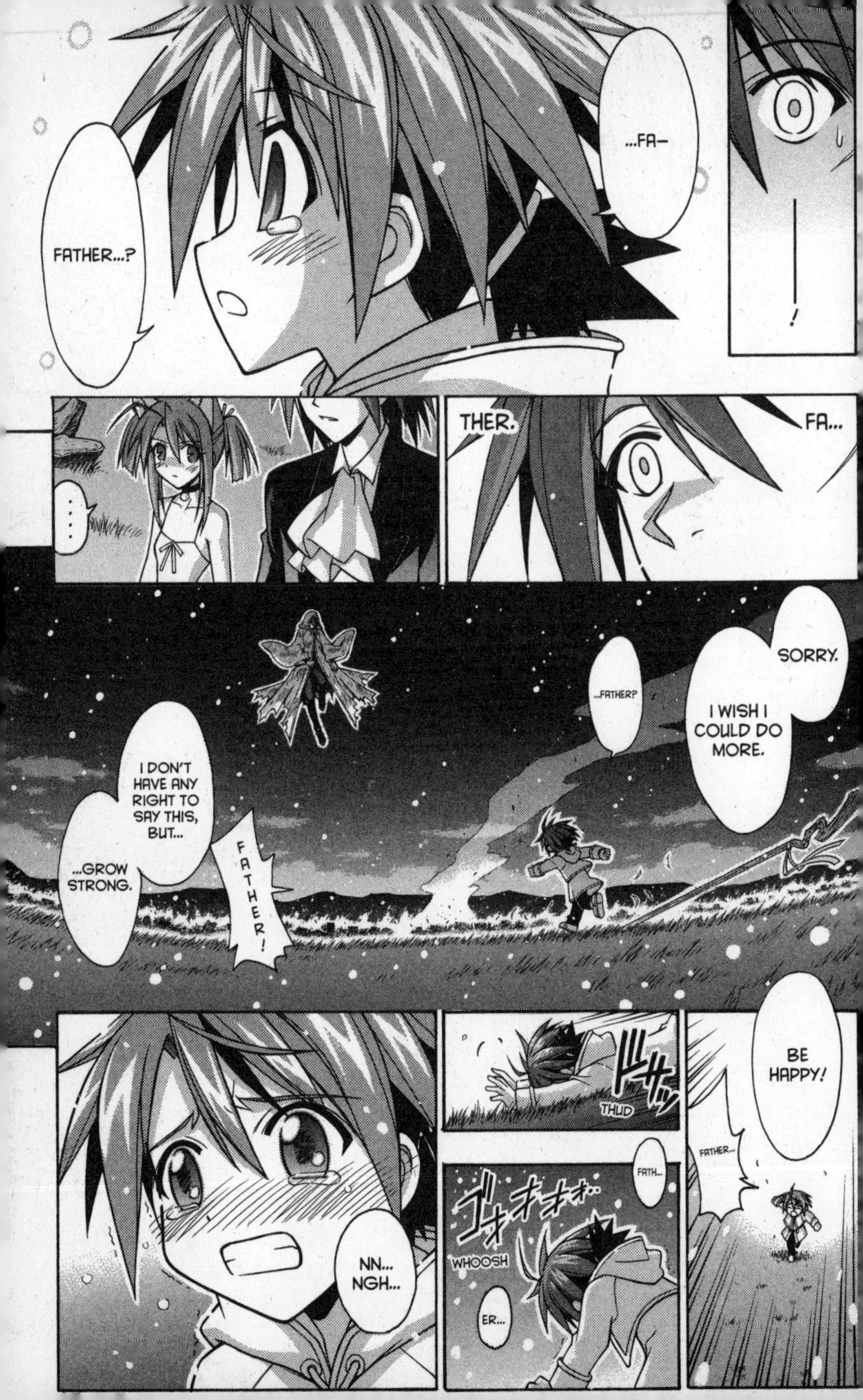
...FA—
FATHER...?
FA...
THER.
....
SORRY.
I WISH I COULD DO MORE.
...FATHER?
I DON'T HAVE ANY RIGHT TO SAY THIS, BUT...
...GROW STRONG.
FATHER!
BE HAPPY!
FATHER...
THUD
FATH...
WHOOSH
ER...
NN... NGH...

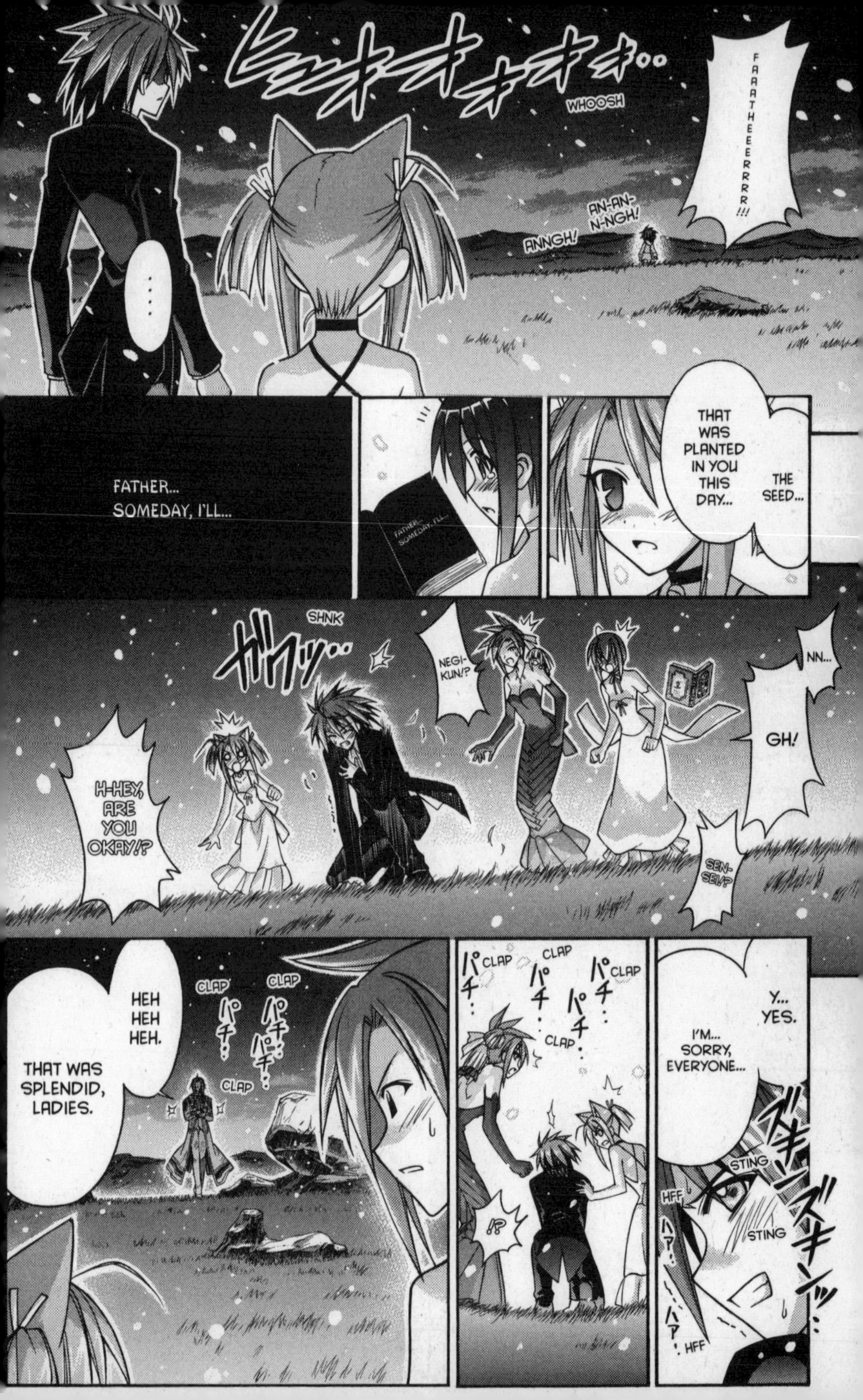
FAAAATHEEEERRRR!!!
ヒュオオオオオ..
WHOOSH
AN-AN-N-NGH!
ANNGH!
....
THE SEED...
THAT WAS PLANTED IN YOU THIS DAY...
FATHER... SOMEDAY, I'LL...
FATHER... SOMEDAY, I'LL...
NN...
GH!
SEN-SEI!?
NEGI-KUN!?
ガクッ..
SHNK
H-HEY, ARE YOU OKAY!?
Y... YES.
I'M... SORRY, EVERYONE...
ズキン
STING
ズキンッ
STING
ハァ..
HFF
ハァ..
HFF
パチ..
CLAP
パチ
CLAP
パチ..
CLAP
パチ..
CLAP
!?
HEH HEH HEH.
THAT WAS SPLENDID, LADIES.
パチ..
CLAP
パチ パチ..
CLAP
CLAP

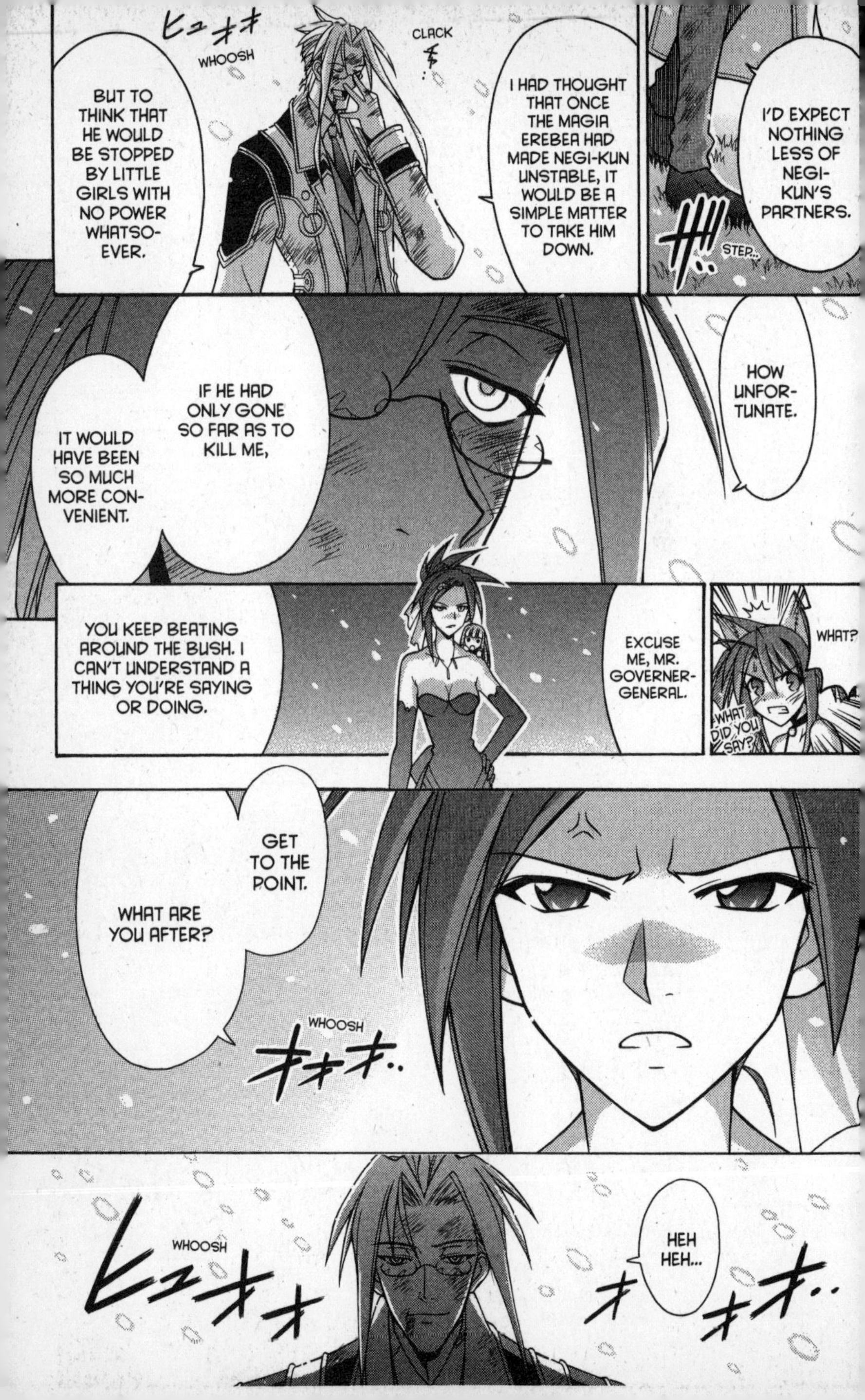
I'D EXPECT NOTHING LESS OF NEGI-KUN'S PARTNERS.
STEP...
CLACK
I HAD THOUGHT THAT ONCE THE MAGIA EREBEA HAD MADE NEGI-KUN UNSTABLE, IT WOULD BE A SIMPLE MATTER TO TAKE HIM DOWN.
WHOOSH
BUT TO THINK THAT HE WOULD BE STOPPED BY LITTLE GIRLS WITH NO POWER WHATSO-EVER.
HOW UNFOR-TUNATE.
IF HE HAD ONLY GONE SO FAR AS TO KILL ME,
IT WOULD HAVE BEEN SO MUCH MORE CON-VENIENT.
WHAT?
WHAT DID YOU SAY?
EXCUSE ME, MR. GOVERNER-GENERAL.
YOU KEEP BEATING AROUND THE BUSH. I CAN'T UNDERSTAND A THING YOU'RE SAYING OR DOING.
GET TO THE POINT.
WHAT ARE YOU AFTER?
WHOOSH
HEH HEH...
WHOOSH

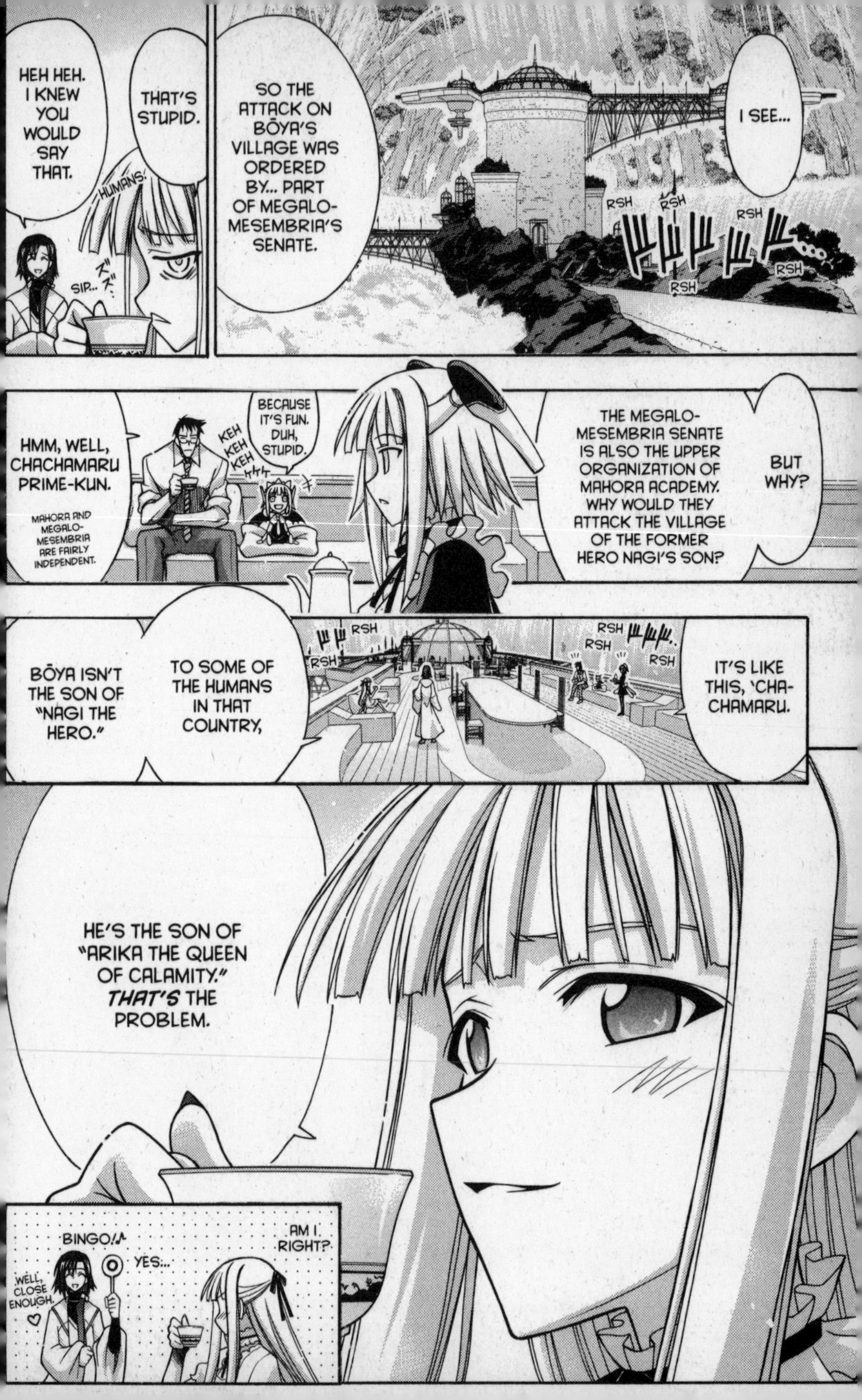
I SEE...
RSH RSH RSH RSH RSH
SO THE ATTACK ON BŌYA'S VILLAGE WAS ORDERED BY... PART OF MEGALO-MESEMBRIA'S SENATE.
THAT'S STUPID.
HUMANS.
HEH HEH. I KNEW YOU WOULD SAY THAT.
SIP...
BUT WHY?
THE MEGALO-MESEMBRIA SENATE IS ALSO THE UPPER ORGANIZATION OF MAHORA ACADEMY. WHY WOULD THEY ATTACK THE VILLAGE OF THE FORMER HERO NAGI'S SON?
BECAUSE IT'S FUN. DUH, STUPID.
KEH KEH KEH
HMM, WELL, CHACHAMARU PRIME-KUN.
MAHORA AND MEGALO-MESEMBRIA ARE FAIRLY INDEPENDENT.
IT'S LIKE THIS, 'CHA-CHAMARU.
RSH RSH RSH RSH RSH
TO SOME OF THE HUMANS IN THAT COUNTRY,
BŌYA ISN'T THE SON OF "NAGI THE HERO."
HE'S THE SON OF "ARIKA THE QUEEN OF CALAMITY." *THAT'S* THE PROBLEM.
AM I RIGHT?
YES...
BINGO!♪
WELL, CLOSE ENOUGH. ♡

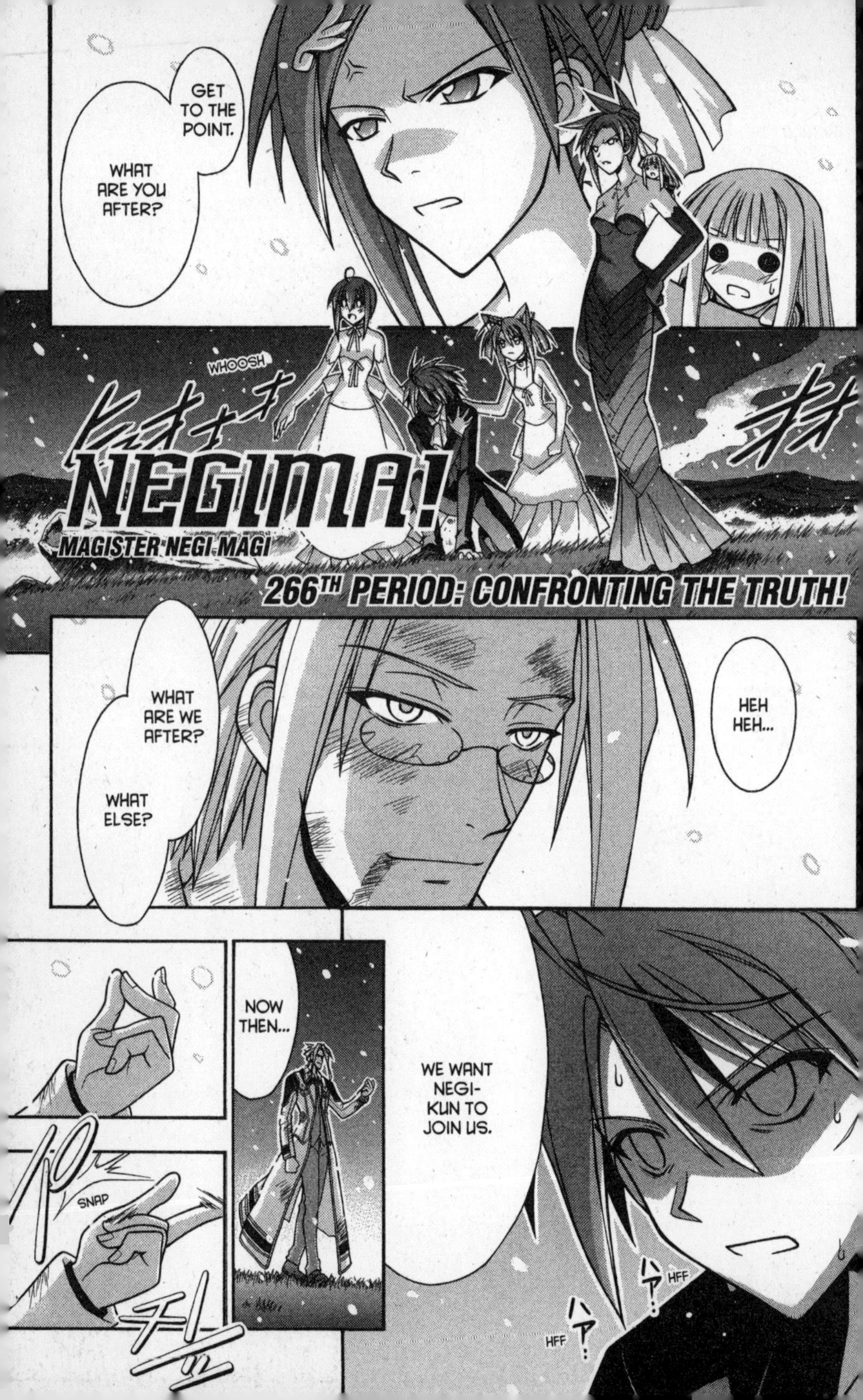

GET TO THE POINT.
WHAT ARE YOU AFTER?
WHOOSH
NEGIMA!
MAGISTER NEGI MAGI
266TH PERIOD: CONFRONTING THE TRUTH!
HEH HEH...
WHAT ARE WE AFTER?
WHAT ELSE?
NOW THEN...
WE WANT NEGI-KUN TO JOIN US.
HFF
HFF
SNAP

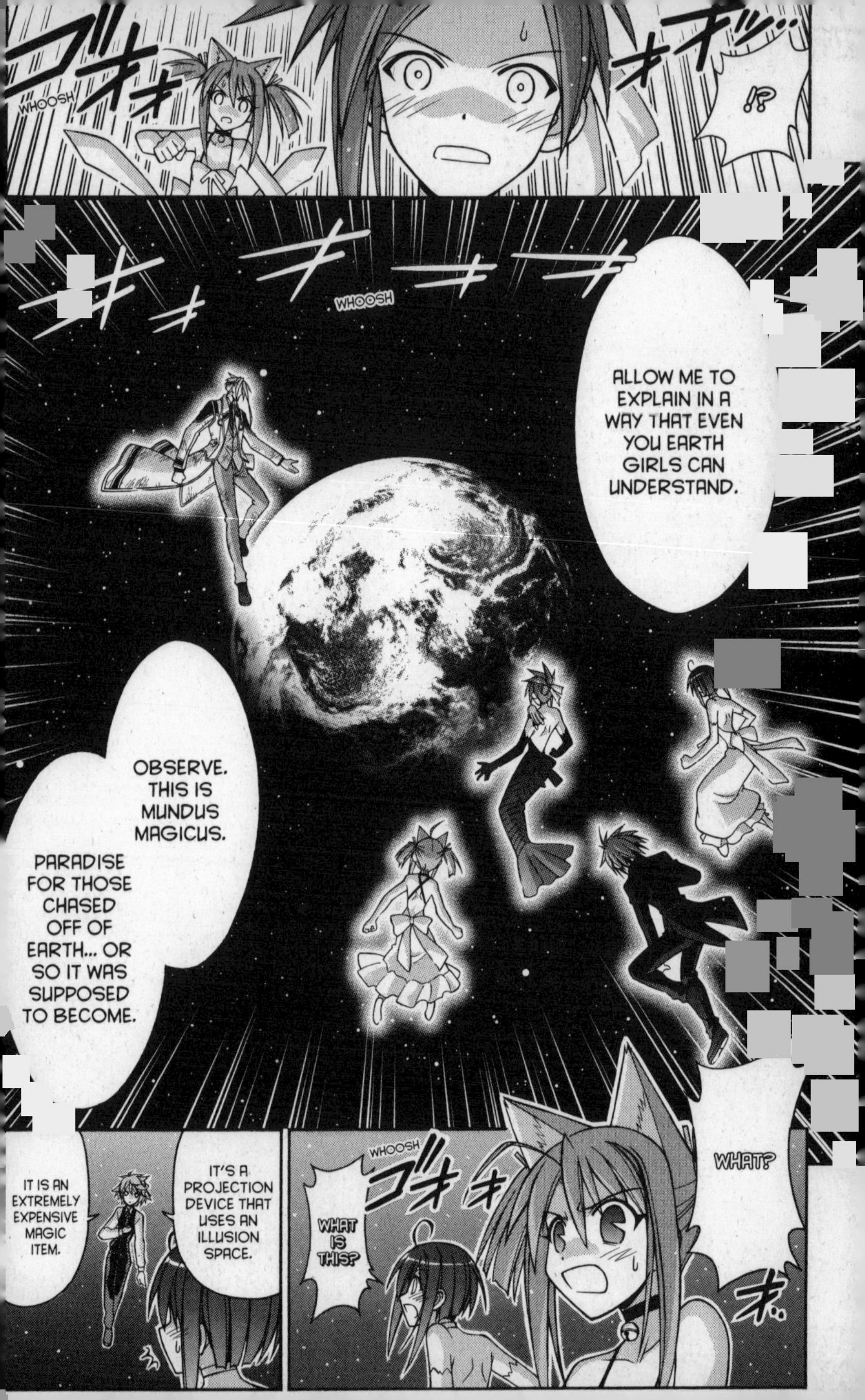
!?
WHOOSH
ALLOW ME TO EXPLAIN IN A WAY THAT EVEN YOU EARTH GIRLS CAN UNDERSTAND.
WHOOSH
OBSERVE. THIS IS MUNDUS MAGICUS.
PARADISE FOR THOSE CHASED OFF OF EARTH... OR SO IT WAS SUPPOSED TO BECOME.
WHAT?
WHOOSH
WHAT IS THIS?
IT'S A PROJECTION DEVICE THAT USES AN ILLUSION SPACE.
IT IS AN EXTREMELY EXPENSIVE MAGIC ITEM.

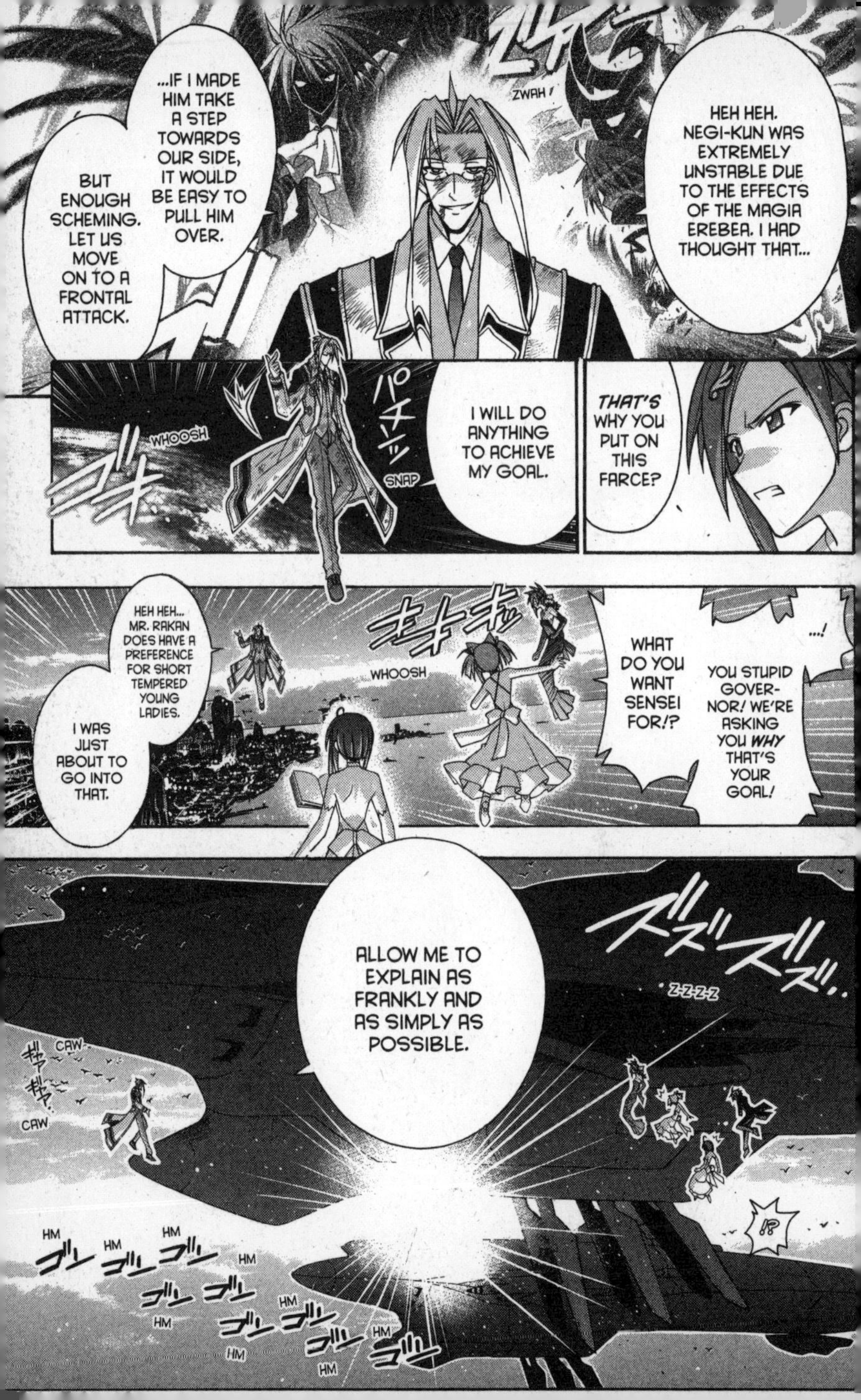
HEH HEH. NEGI-KUN WAS EXTREMELY UNSTABLE DUE TO THE EFFECTS OF THE MAGIA EREBEA. I HAD THOUGHT THAT...
ZWAH!
...IF I MADE HIM TAKE A STEP TOWARDS OUR SIDE, IT WOULD BE EASY TO PULL HIM OVER.
BUT ENOUGH SCHEMING. LET US MOVE ON TO A FRONTAL ATTACK.
THAT'S WHY YOU PUT ON THIS FARCE?
I WILL DO ANYTHING TO ACHIEVE MY GOAL.
SNAP
WHOOSH
...!
YOU STUPID GOVERNOR! WE'RE ASKING YOU *WHY* THAT'S YOUR GOAL!
WHAT DO YOU WANT SENSEI FOR!?
WHOOSH
HEH HEH... MR. RAKAN DOES HAVE A PREFERENCE FOR SHORT TEMPERED YOUNG LADIES.
I WAS JUST ABOUT TO GO INTO THAT.
Z-Z-Z-Z
!?
ALLOW ME TO EXPLAIN AS FRANKLY AND AS SIMPLY AS POSSIBLE.
CAW
CAW
HM HM HM HM HM HM HM HM HM

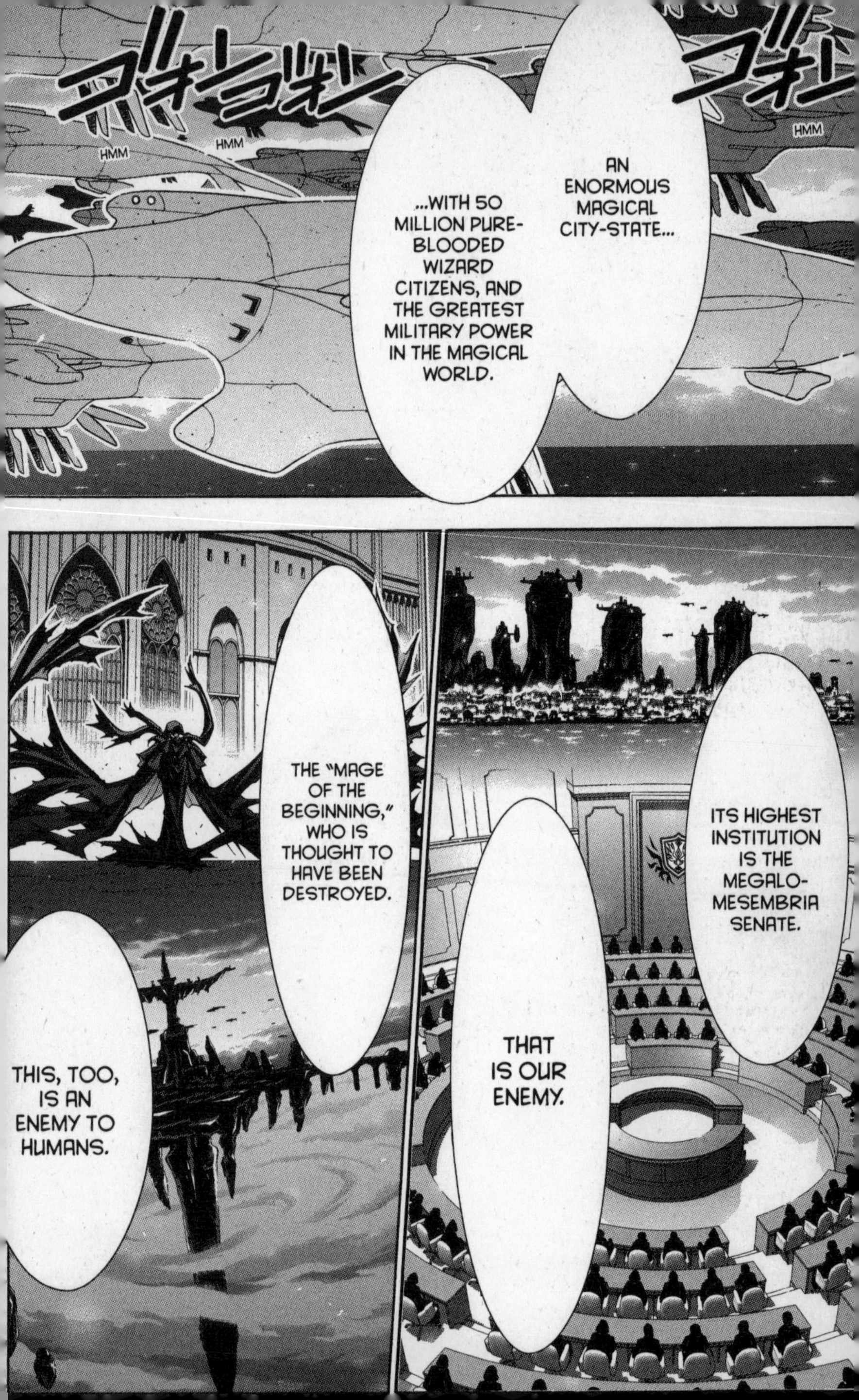
HMM
HMM
HMM
AN ENORMOUS MAGICAL CITY-STATE...
...WITH 50 MILLION PURE-BLOODED WIZARD CITIZENS, AND THE GREATEST MILITARY POWER IN THE MAGICAL WORLD.
ITS HIGHEST INSTITUTION IS THE MEGALO-MESEMBRIA SENATE.
THAT IS OUR ENEMY.
THE "MAGE OF THE BEGINNING," WHO IS THOUGHT TO HAVE BEEN DESTROYED.
THIS, TOO, IS AN ENEMY TO HUMANS.

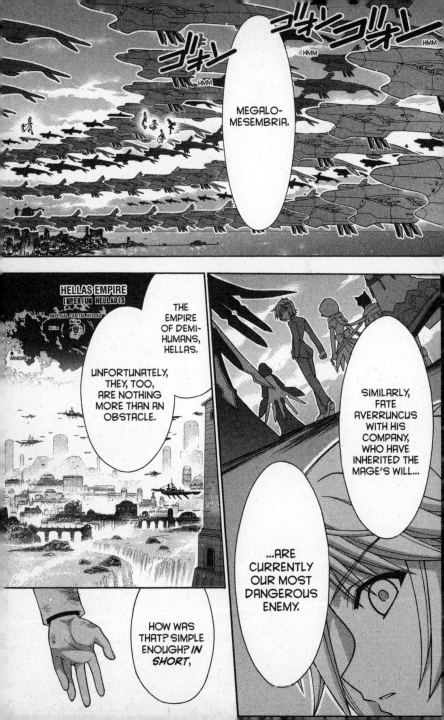

MEGALO-MESEMBRIA.

HELLAS EMPIRE
IMPERIUM HELLADIS

IMPERIAL CAPITAL HELLAS
Hellas

ARIADNE

THE EMPIRE OF DEMI-HUMANS, HELLAS.

UNFORTUNATELY, THEY, TOO, ARE NOTHING MORE THAN AN OBSTACLE.

SIMILARLY, FATE AVERRUNCUS WITH HIS COMPANY, WHO HAVE INHERITED THE MAGE'S WILL...

...ARE CURRENTLY OUR MOST DANGEROUS ENEMY.

HOW WAS THAT? SIMPLE ENOUGH? *IN SHORT,*

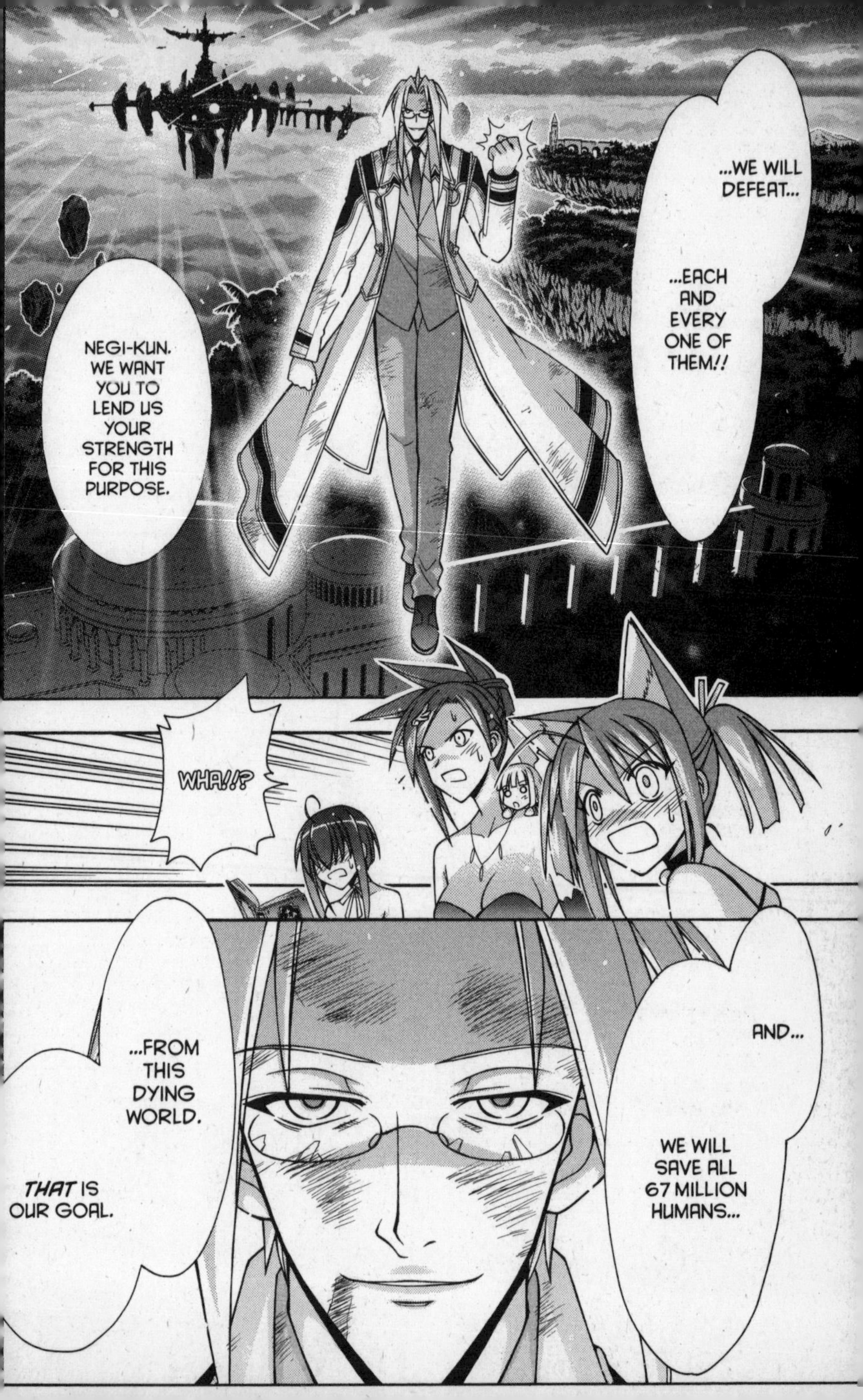
...WE WILL DEFEAT...
...EACH AND EVERY ONE OF THEM!!
NEGI-KUN. WE WANT YOU TO LEND US YOUR STRENGTH FOR THIS PURPOSE.
WHA!!?
AND...
WE WILL SAVE ALL 67 MILLION HUMANS...
...FROM THIS DYING WORLD.
THAT IS OUR GOAL.

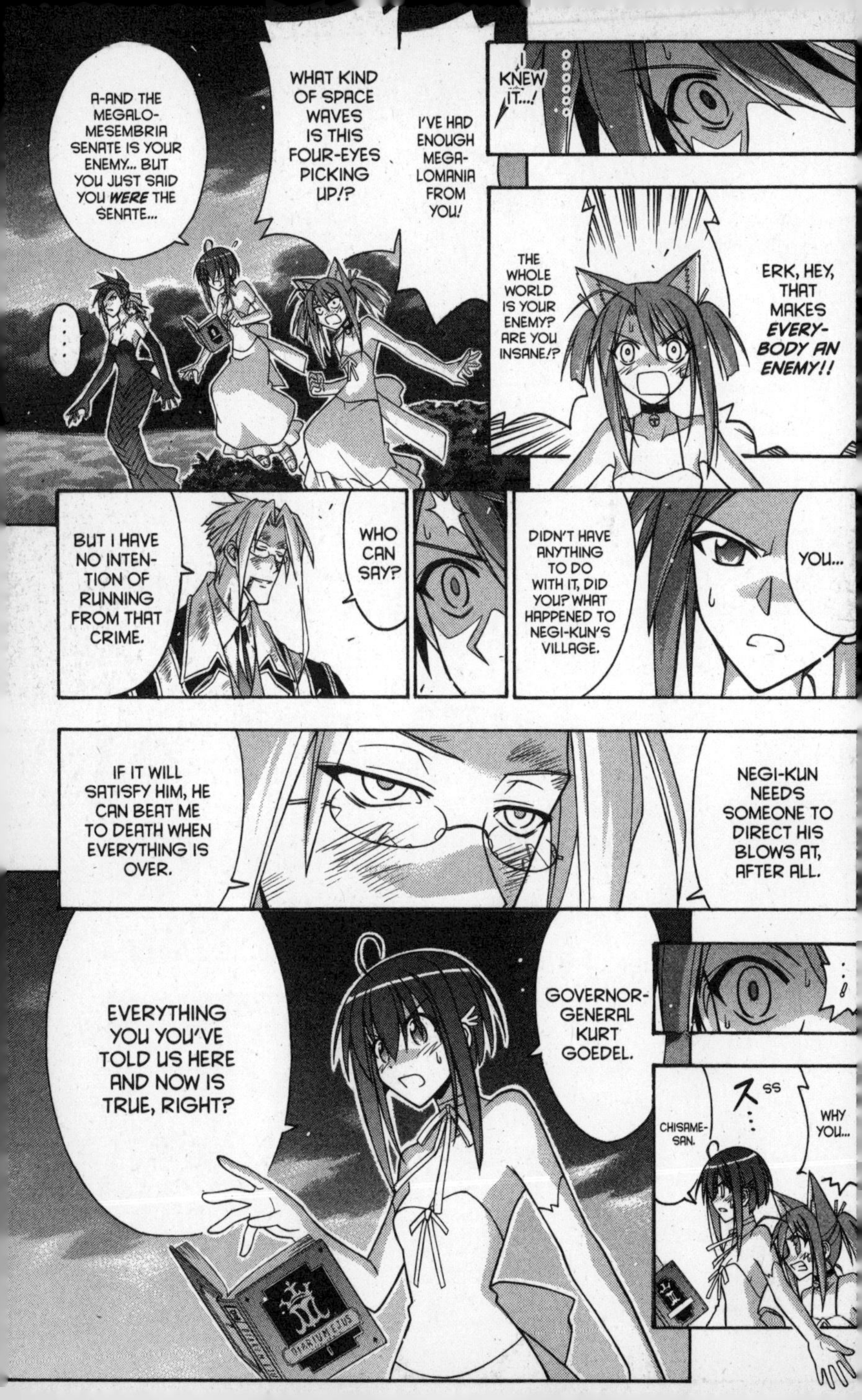
I KNEW IT...!
ERK, HEY, THAT MAKES *EVERY-BODY AN ENEMY!!*
THE WHOLE WORLD IS YOUR ENEMY? ARE YOU INSANE!?
I'VE HAD ENOUGH MEGA-LOMANIA FROM YOU!
WHAT KIND OF SPACE WAVES IS THIS FOUR-EYES PICKING UP!?
A-AND THE MEGALO-MESEMBRIA SENATE IS YOUR ENEMY... BUT YOU JUST SAID YOU *WERE* THE SENATE...
...
YOU...
DIDN'T HAVE ANYTHING TO DO WITH IT, DID YOU? WHAT HAPPENED TO NEGI-KUN'S VILLAGE.
WHO CAN SAY?
BUT I HAVE NO INTEN-TION OF RUNNING FROM THAT CRIME.
NEGI-KUN NEEDS SOMEONE TO DIRECT HIS BLOWS AT, AFTER ALL.
IF IT WILL SATISFY HIM, HE CAN BEAT ME TO DEATH WHEN EVERYTHING IS OVER.
...!
WHY YOU...
ス SS
CHISAME-SAN.
GOVERNOR-GENERAL KURT GOEDEL.
EVERYTHING YOU YOU'VE TOLD US HERE AND NOW IS TRUE, RIGHT?

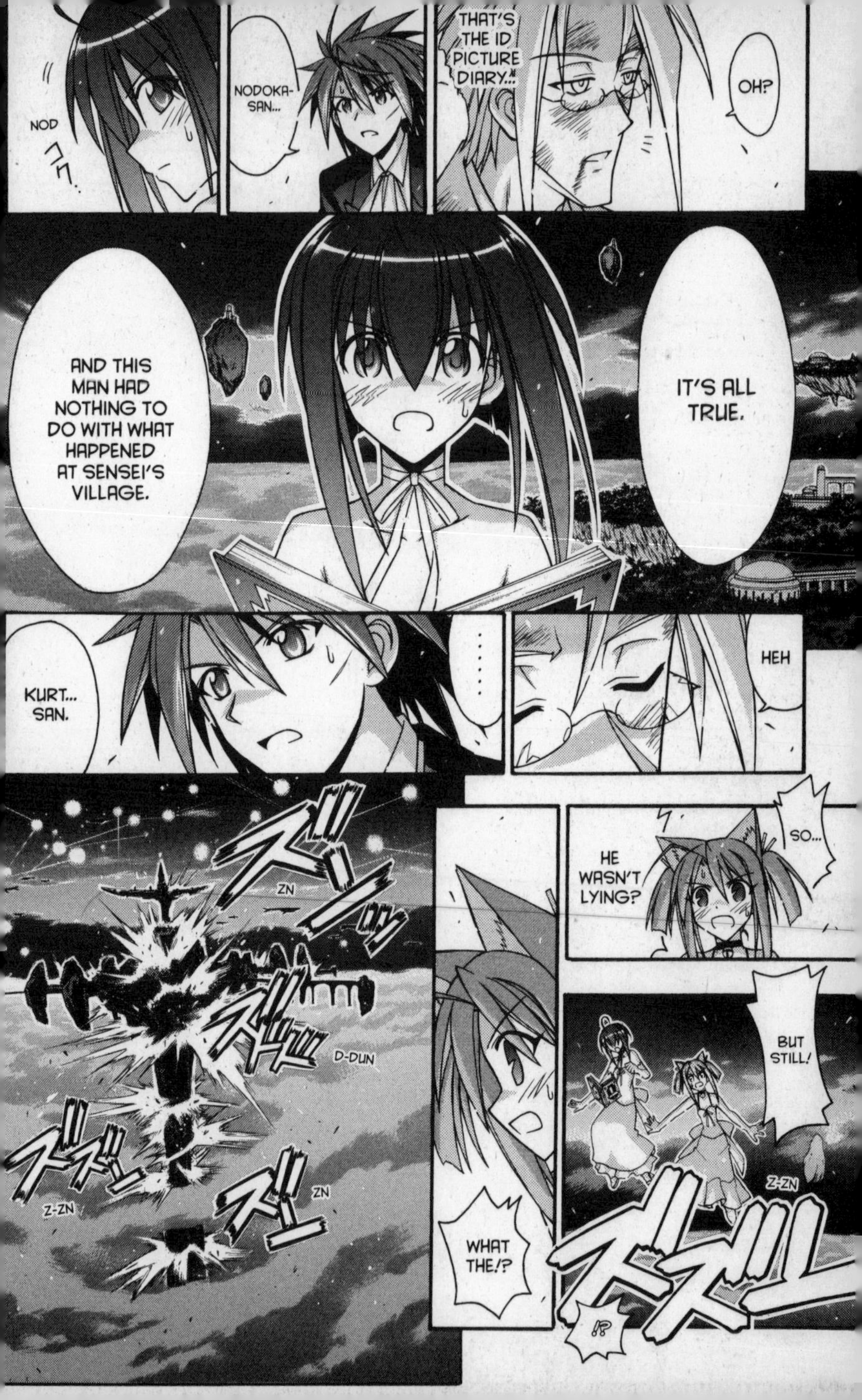
OH?
THAT'S THE ID PICTURE DIARY...!
NODOKA-SAN...
NOD
コク
IT'S ALL TRUE.
AND THIS MAN HAD NOTHING TO DO WITH WHAT HAPPENED AT SENSEI'S VILLAGE.
HEH
......
KURT... SAN.
SO...
HE WASN'T LYING?
BUT STILL!
Z-ZN
!?
WHAT THE!?
ZN
D-DUN
ZN
Z-ZN

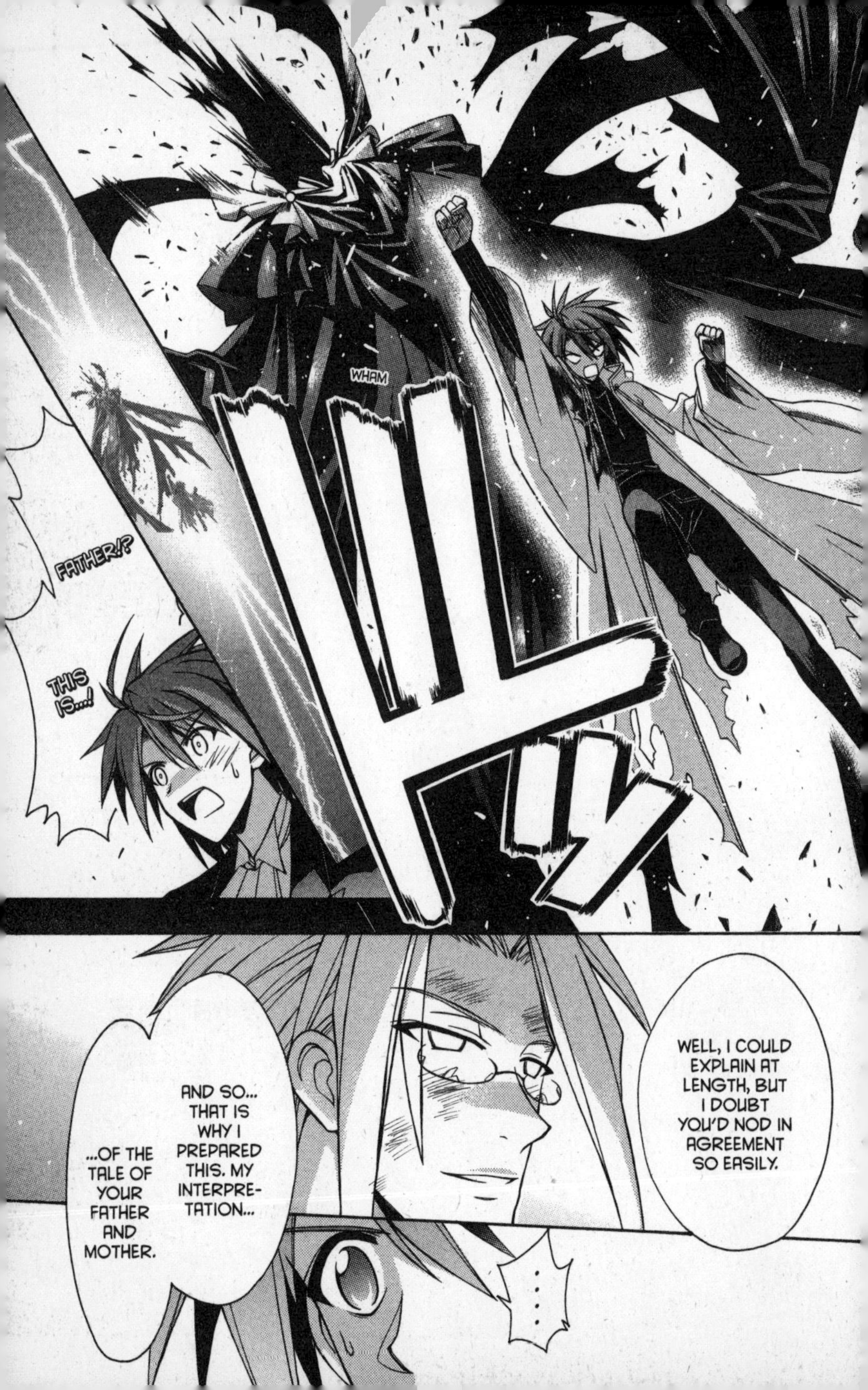
WHAM
FATHER!?
THIS IS...!
WELL, I COULD EXPLAIN AT LENGTH, BUT I DOUBT YOU'D NOD IN AGREEMENT SO EASILY.
AND SO... THAT IS WHY I PREPARED THIS. MY INTERPRE-TATION...
...OF THE TALE OF YOUR FATHER AND MOTHER.
...

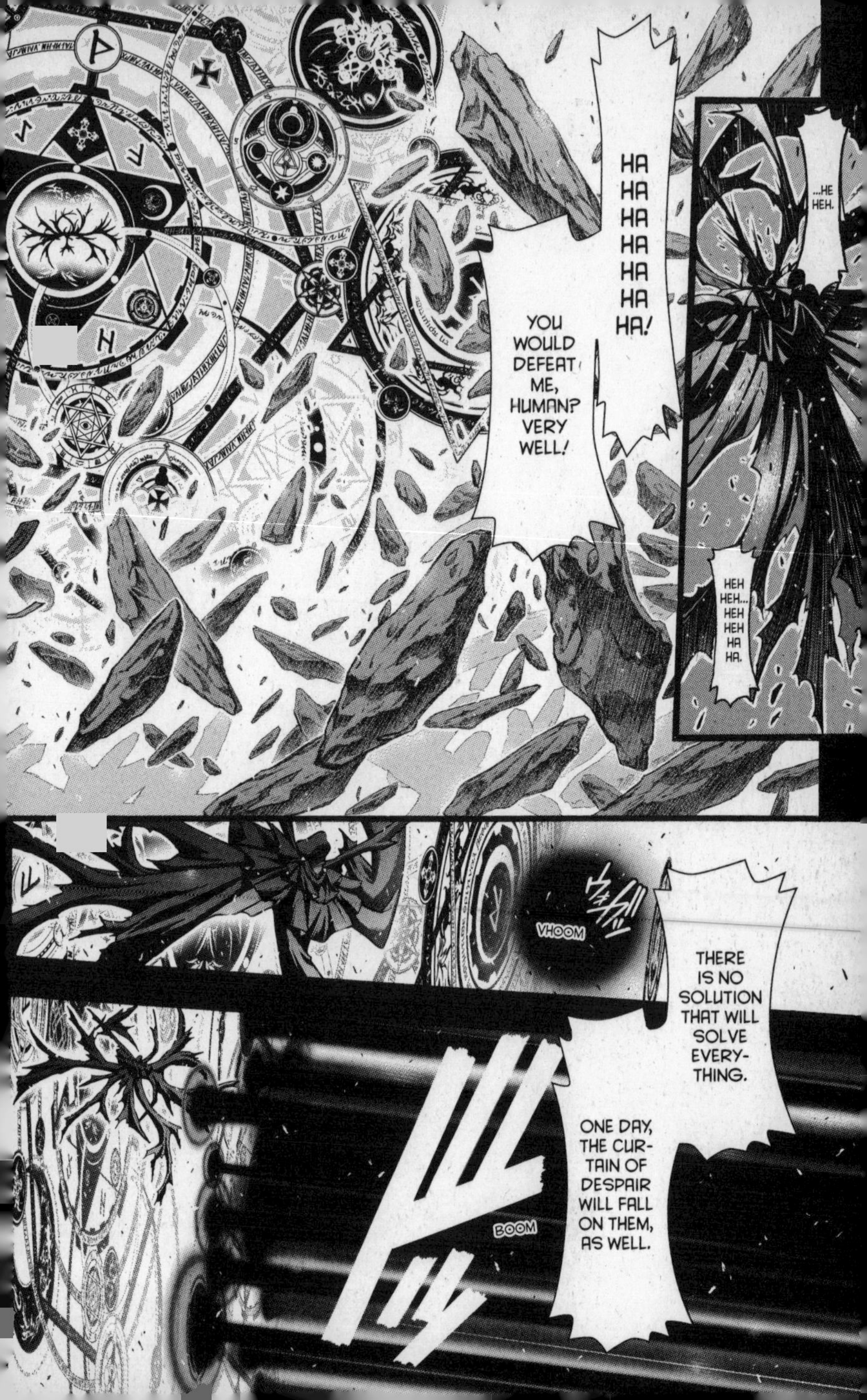
...HE HEH.
HEH HEH... HEH HEH HA HA.
HA HA HA HA HA HA HA!
YOU WOULD DEFEAT ME, HUMAN? VERY WELL!
THERE IS NO SOLUTION THAT WILL SOLVE EVERY-THING.
VHOOM
ONE DAY, THE CUR-TAIN OF DESPAIR WILL FALL ON THEM, AS WELL.
BOOM

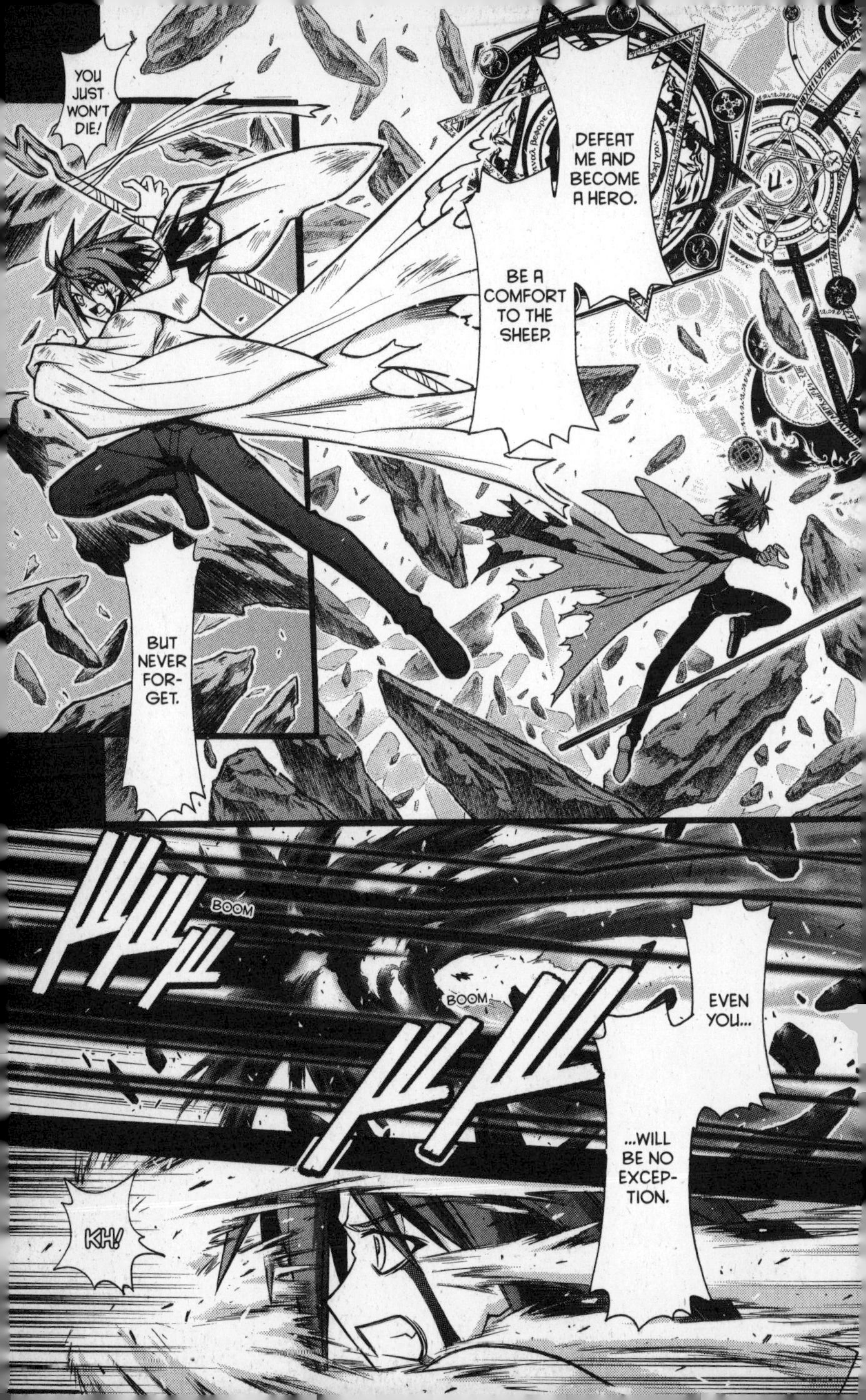
DEFEAT ME AND BECOME A HERO.
BE A COMFORT TO THE SHEEP.
YOU JUST WON'T DIE!
BUT NEVER FOR-GET.
EVEN YOU...
...WILL BE NO EXCEP-TION.
BOOM
BOOM
KH!

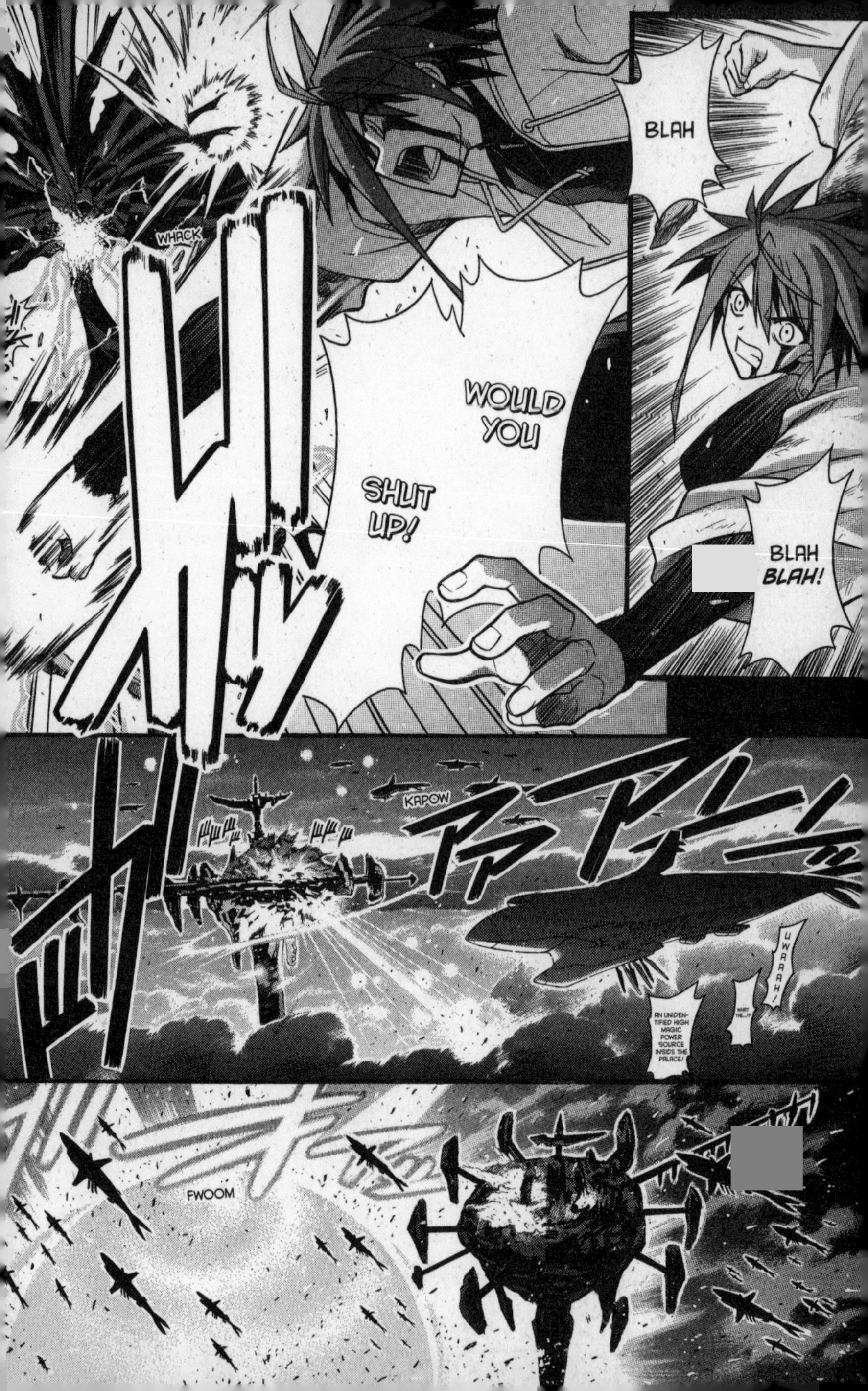
BLAH
BLAH BLAH!
WOULD YOU
SHUT UP!
WHACK
UWAAAAH!
WHAT THE...!?
AN UNIDENTIFIED HIGH MAGIC POWER SOURCE INSIDE THE PALACE!
KAPOW
FWOOM

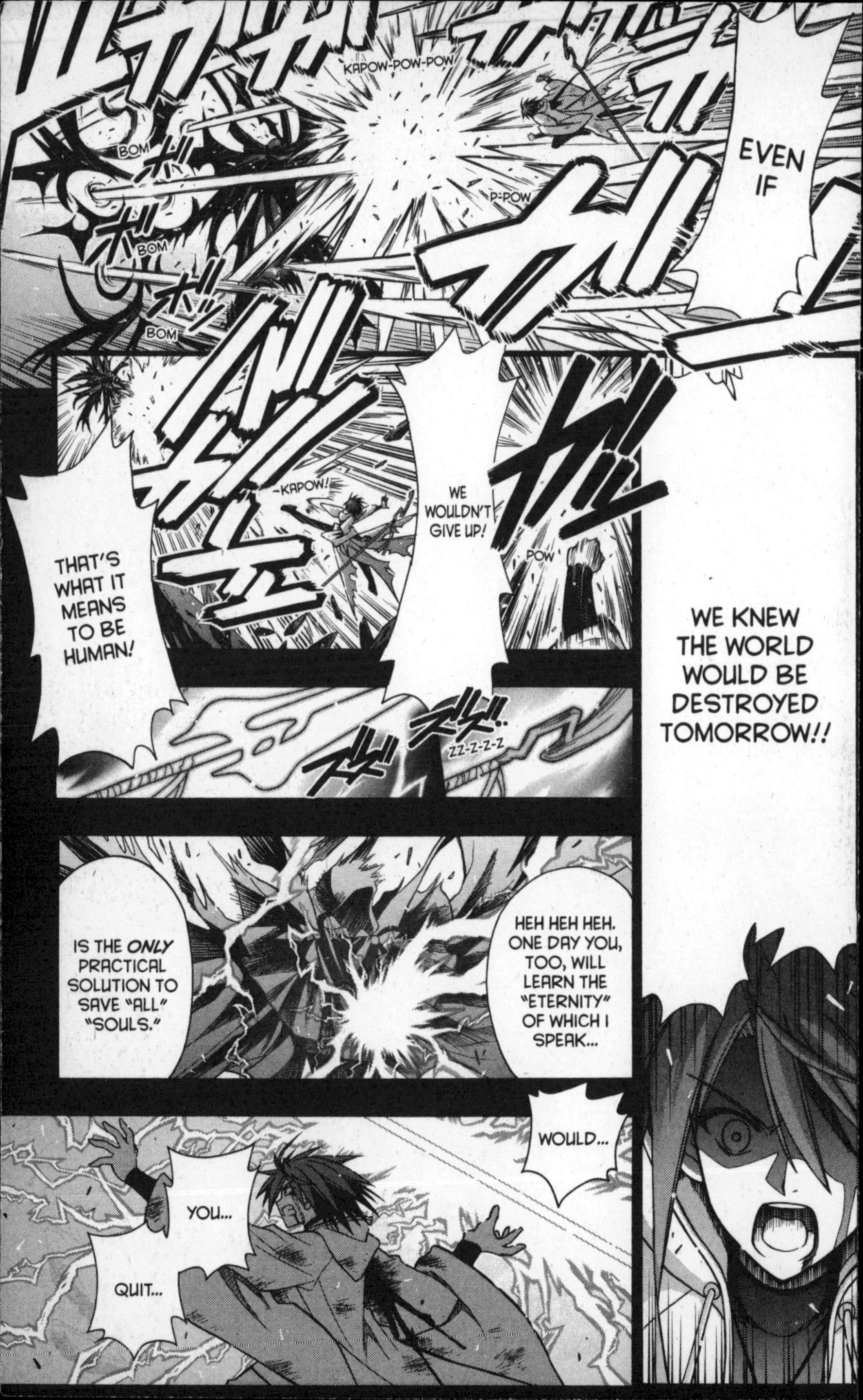
EVEN IF
KAPOW-POW-POW
P-POW
BOM
BOM
BOM
WE KNEW THE WORLD WOULD BE DESTROYED TOMORROW!!
WE WOULDN'T GIVE UP!
POW
-KAPOW!
THAT'S WHAT IT MEANS TO BE HUMAN!
ZZ-Z-Z-Z
HEH HEH HEH. ONE DAY YOU, TOO, WILL LEARN THE "ETERNITY" OF WHICH I SPEAK...
IS THE *ONLY* PRACTICAL SOLUTION TO SAVE "ALL" "SOULS."
WOULD...
YOU...
QUIT...

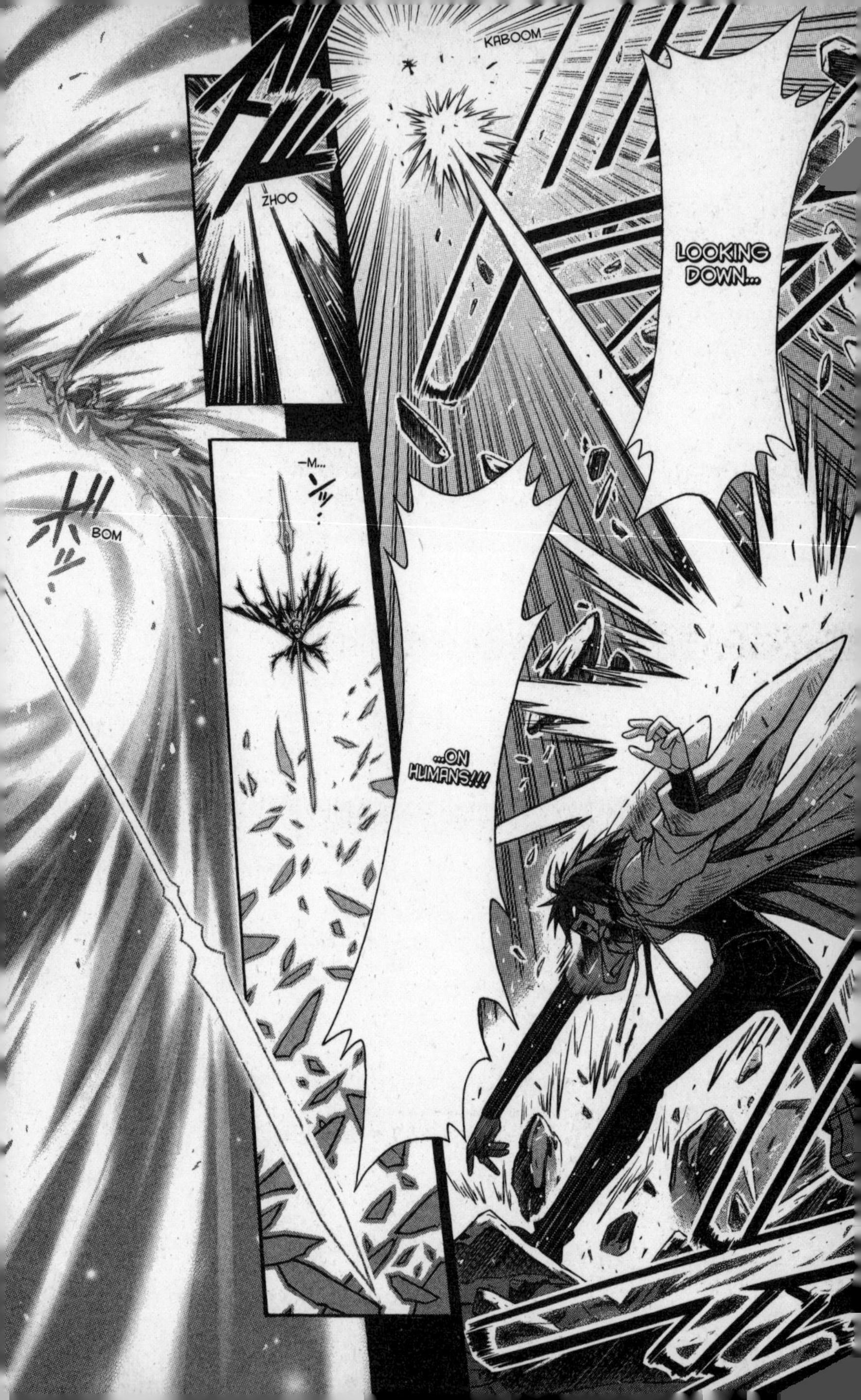
KABOOM
LOOKING DOWN...
ZHOO
...ON HUMANS!!!
—M...
BOM

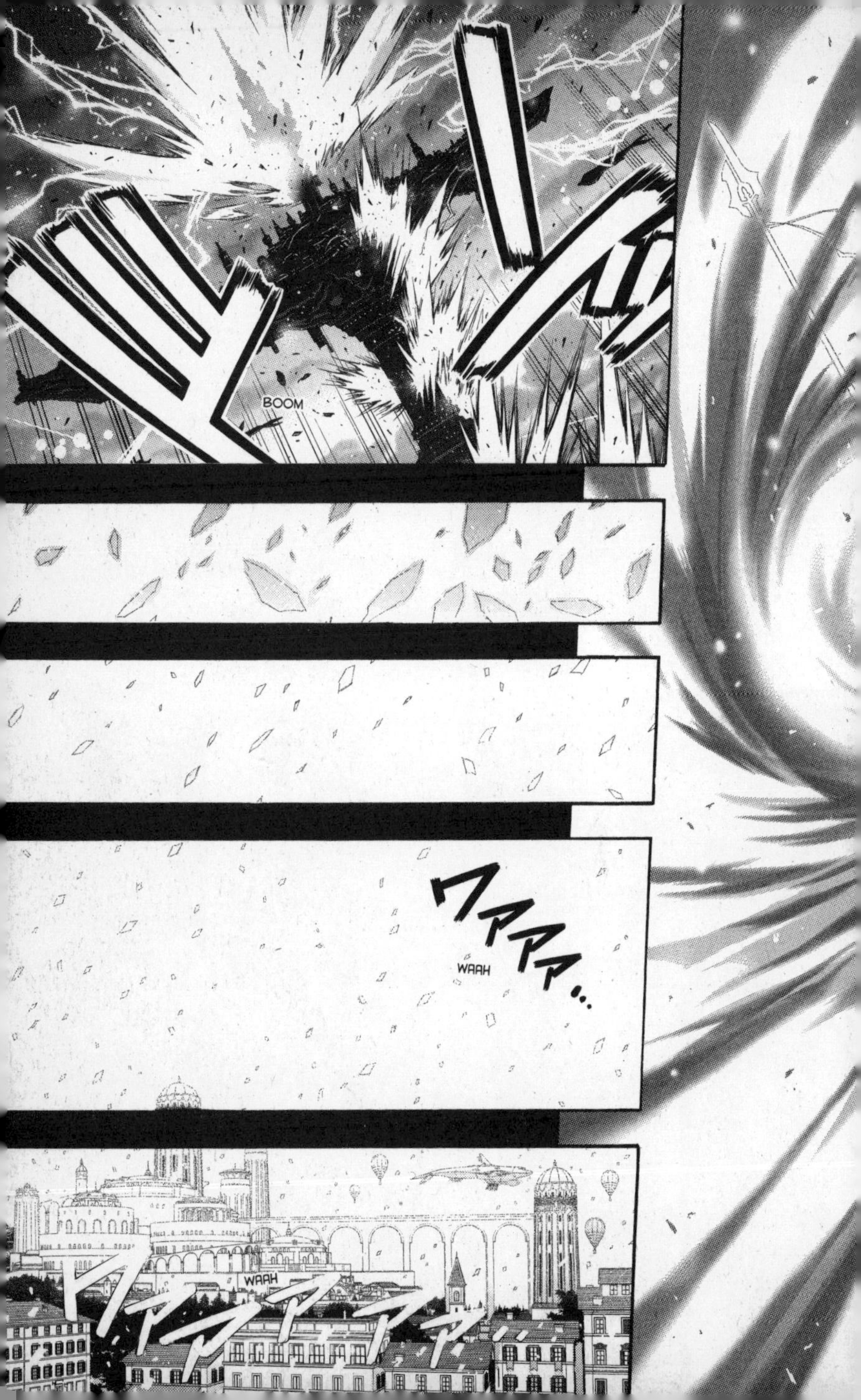
BOOM
ワァァ…
WAAH
WAAH

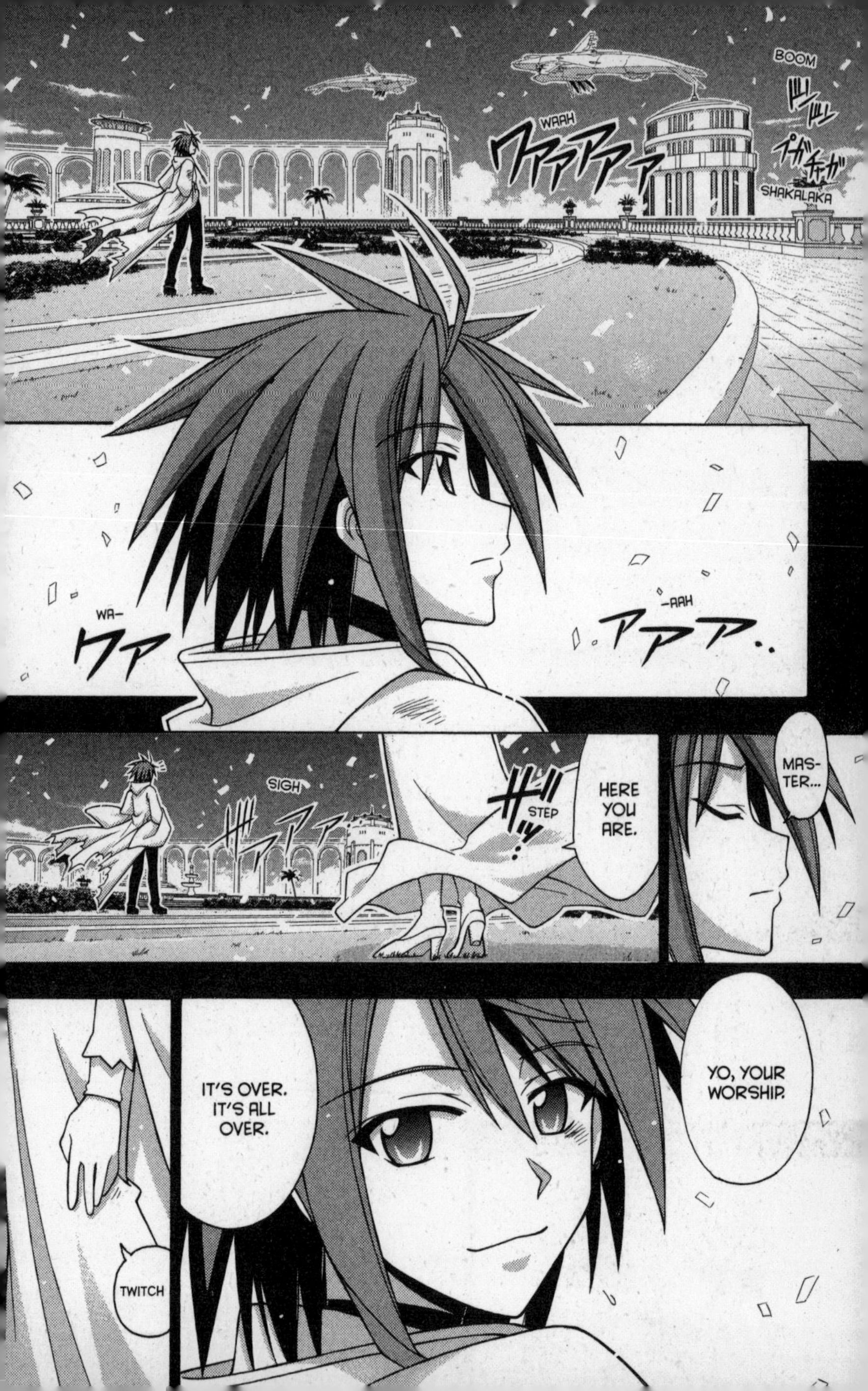
BOOM
WAAH
SHAKALAKA
WA-
-AAH
MAS-
TER...
HERE
YOU
ARE.
STEP
SIGH
YO, YOUR
WORSHIP.
IT'S OVER.
IT'S ALL
OVER.
TWITCH

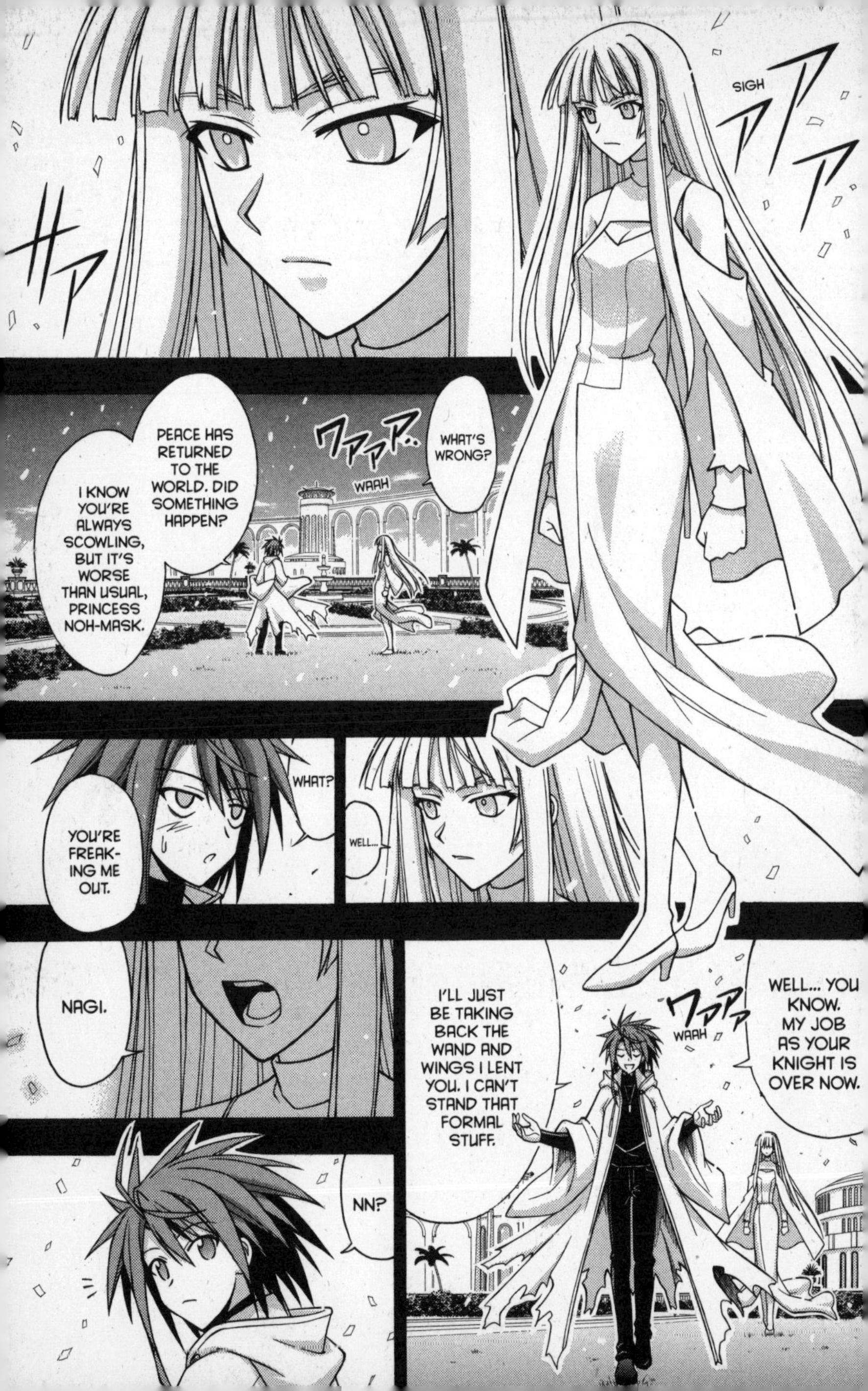

SIGH
アアア
サア
WHAT'S WRONG?
ワァァ..
WAAH
PEACE HAS RETURNED TO THE WORLD. DID SOMETHING HAPPEN?
I KNOW YOU'RE ALWAYS SCOWLING, BUT IT'S WORSE THAN USUAL, PRINCESS NOH-MASK.
WELL...
WHAT?
YOU'RE FREAK-ING ME OUT.
WELL... YOU KNOW. MY JOB AS YOUR KNIGHT IS OVER NOW.
ワァァ
WAAH
I'LL JUST BE TAKING BACK THE WAND AND WINGS I LENT YOU. I CAN'T STAND THAT FORMAL STUFF.
NAGI.
NN?

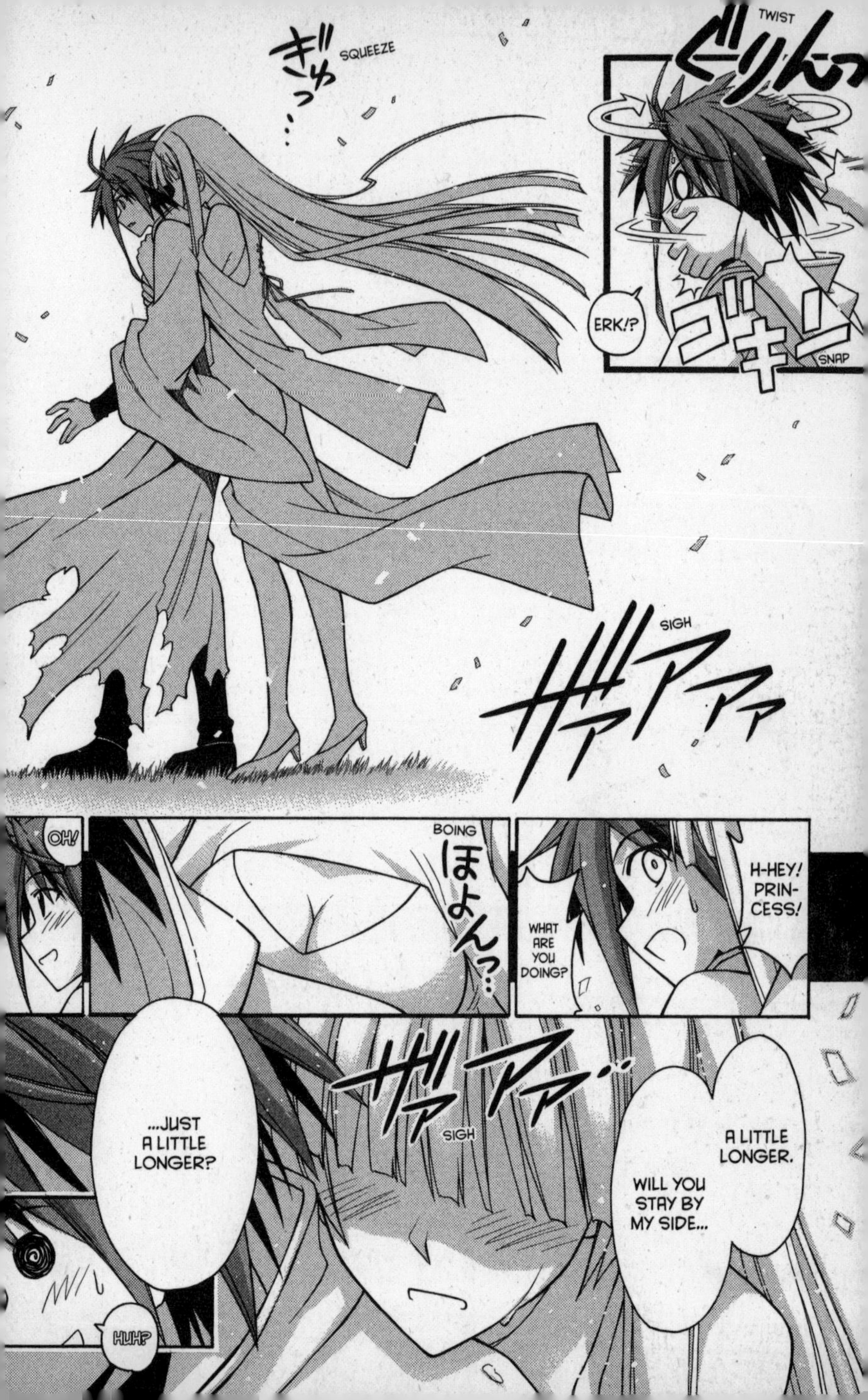
TWIST
ERK!?
SNAP
SQUEEZE
SIGH
H-HEY! PRIN-CESS!
WHAT ARE YOU DOING?
BOING
OH!
A LITTLE LONGER.
WILL YOU STAY BY MY SIDE...
SIGH
...JUST A LITTLE LONGER?
HUH?

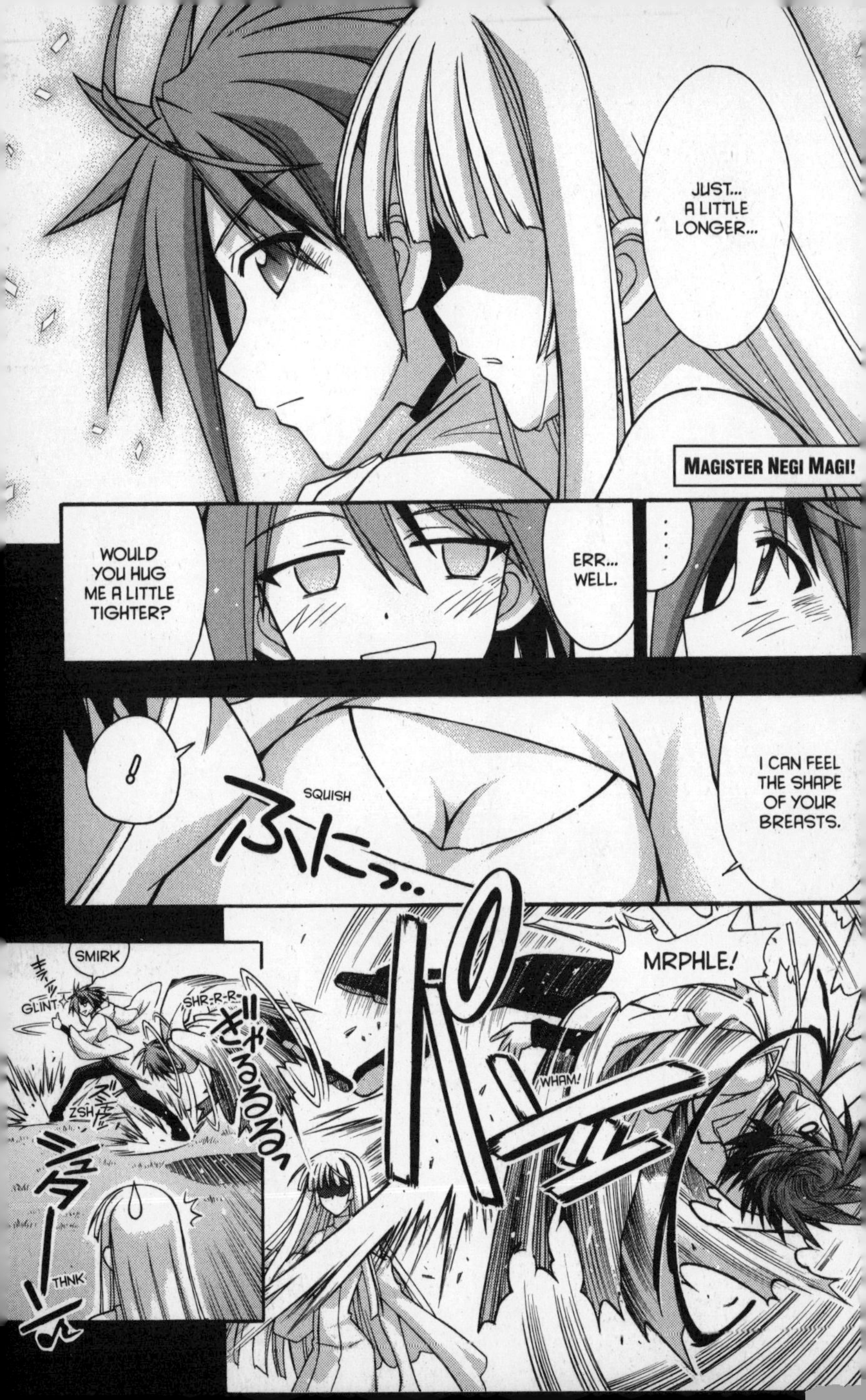
JUST... A LITTLE LONGER...
MAGISTER NEGI MAGI!
....
ERR... WELL.
WOULD YOU HUG ME A LITTLE TIGHTER?
I CAN FEEL THE SHAPE OF YOUR BREASTS.
!
SQUISH
ふにっ..
MRPHLE!
WHAM!
SMIRK
GLINT
SHR-R-R
ZSH
THNK

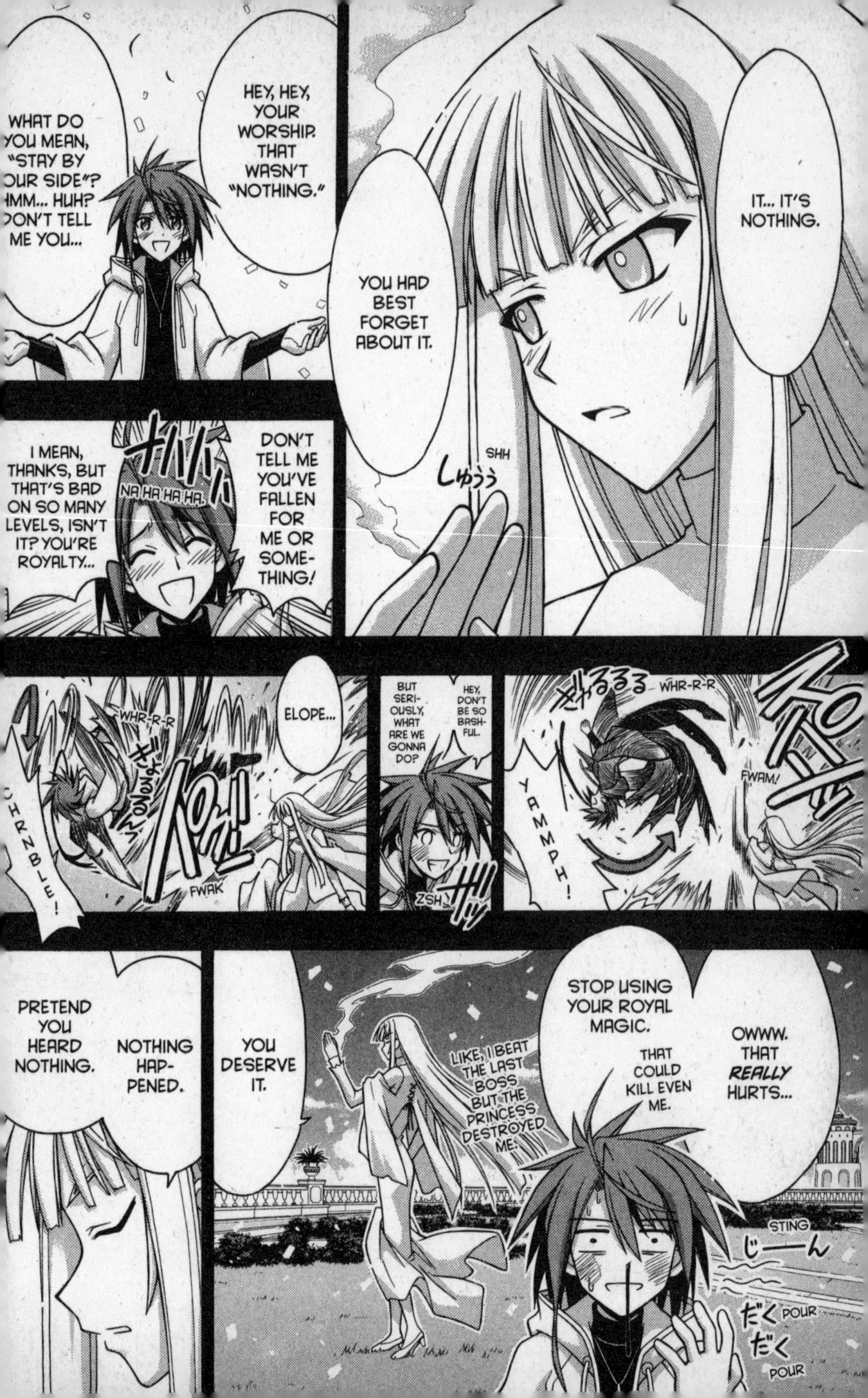
IT... IT'S NOTHING.
YOU HAD BEST FORGET ABOUT IT.
しゅううう
SHH
HEY, HEY, YOUR WORSHIP. THAT WASN'T "NOTHING."
WHAT DO YOU MEAN, "STAY BY OUR SIDE"? MM... HUH? ON'T TELL ME YOU...
DON'T TELL ME YOU'VE FALLEN FOR ME OR SOME-THING!
NA HA HA HA.
I MEAN, THANKS, BUT THAT'S BAD ON SO MANY LEVELS, ISN'T IT? YOU'RE ROYALTY...
ぎゅるるる
WHR-R-R
FWAM!
YAMMPH!
HEY, DON'T BE SO BASH-FUL.
BUT SERI-OUSLY, WHAT ARE WE GONNA DO?
ZSH
ELOPE...
WHR-R-R
FWAK
CHRNBLE!
STOP USING YOUR ROYAL MAGIC.
OWWW. THAT *REALLY* HURTS...
THAT COULD KILL EVEN ME.
LIKE, I BEAT THE LAST BOSS BUT THE PRINCESS DESTROYED ME.
YOU DESERVE IT.
STING
じーん
だく POUR
だく POUR
NOTHING HAP-PENED.
PRETEND YOU HEARD NOTHING.

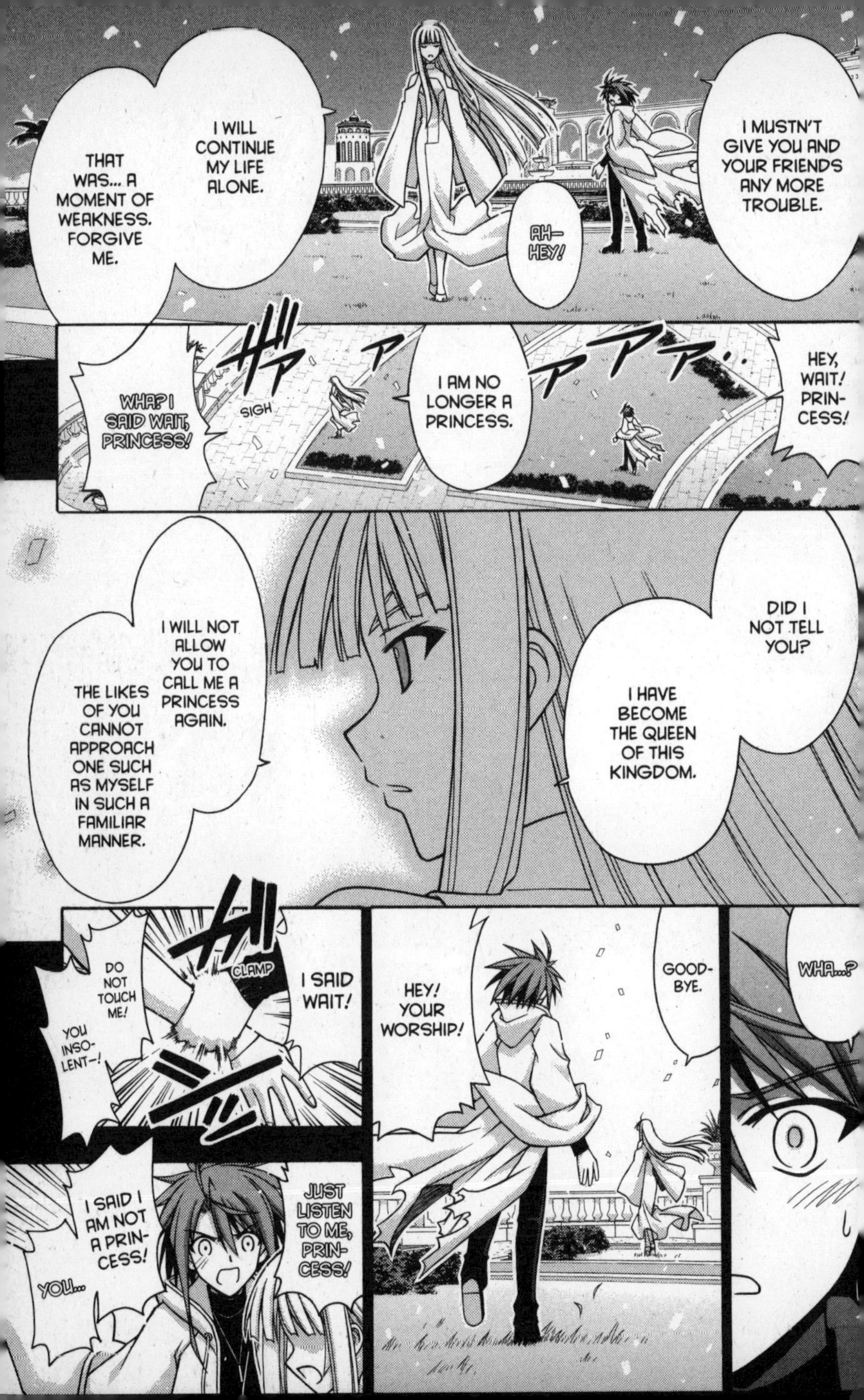
I MUSTN'T GIVE YOU AND YOUR FRIENDS ANY MORE TROUBLE.
AH— HEY!
I WILL CONTINUE MY LIFE ALONE.
THAT WAS... A MOMENT OF WEAKNESS. FORGIVE ME.
HEY, WAIT! PRIN-CESS!
I AM NO LONGER A PRINCESS.
SIGH
WHA? I SAID WAIT, PRINCESS!
DID I NOT TELL YOU?
I HAVE BECOME THE QUEEN OF THIS KINGDOM.
I WILL NOT ALLOW YOU TO CALL ME A PRINCESS AGAIN.
THE LIKES OF YOU CANNOT APPROACH ONE SUCH AS MYSELF IN SUCH A FAMILIAR MANNER.
WHA...?
GOOD-BYE.
HEY! YOUR WORSHIP!
I SAID WAIT!
CLAMP
DO NOT TOUCH ME!
YOU INSO-LENT—!
JUST LISTEN TO ME, PRIN-CESS!
I SAID I AM NOT A PRIN-CESS!
YOU...

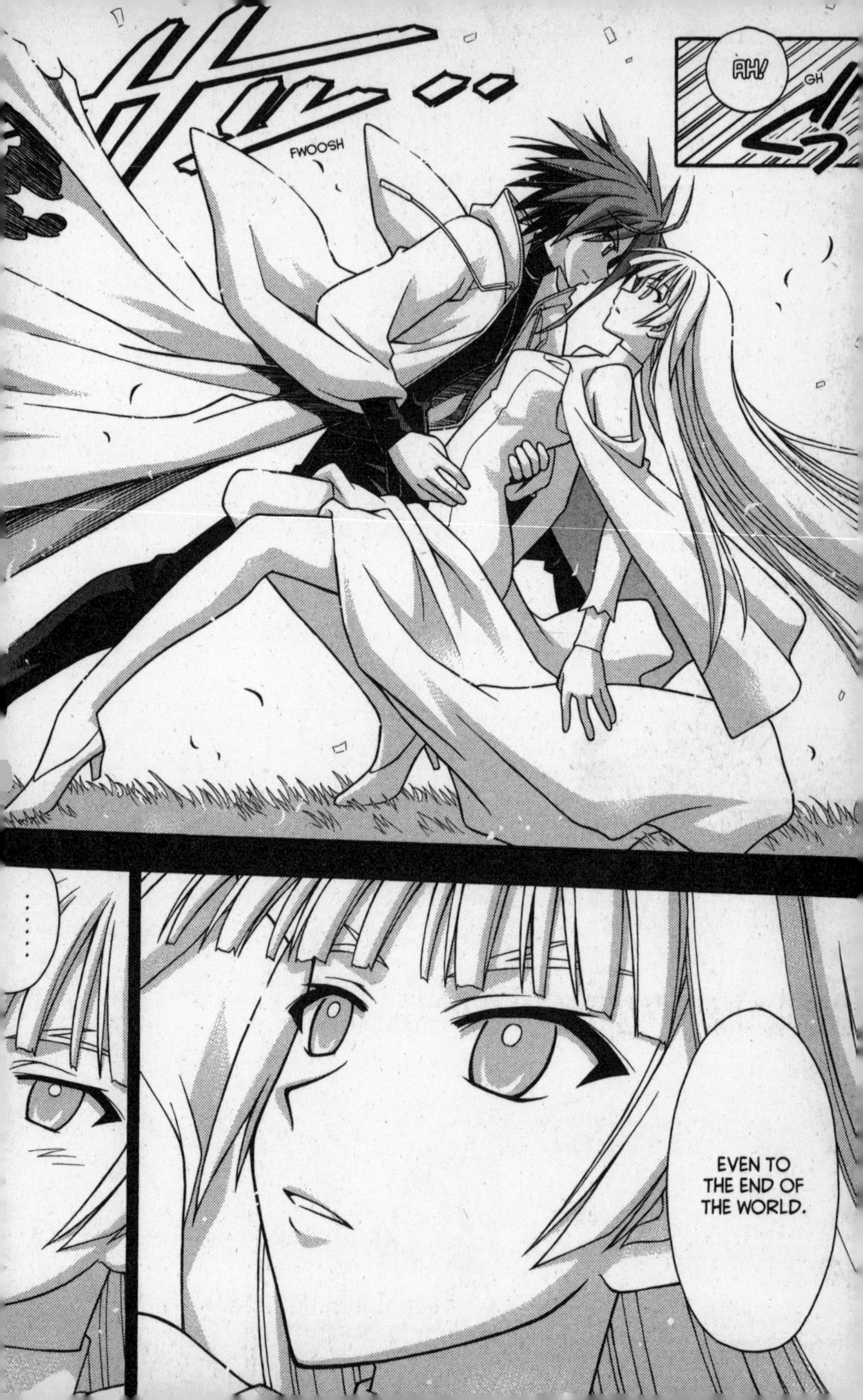
AH!
GH
FWOOSH
EVEN TO THE END OF THE WORLD.
......

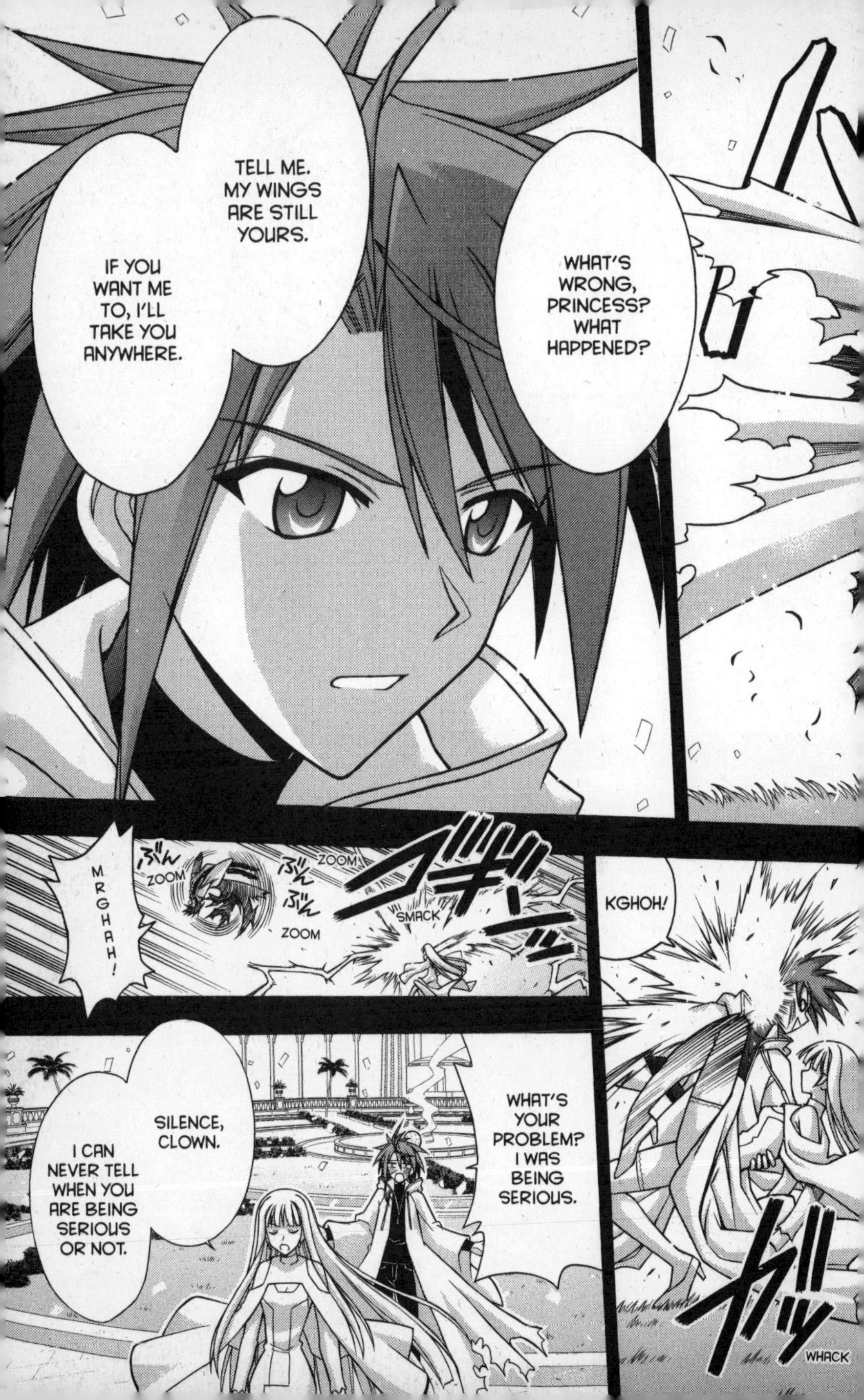
WHAT'S WRONG, PRINCESS? WHAT HAPPENED?
TELL ME. MY WINGS ARE STILL YOURS.
IF YOU WANT ME TO, I'LL TAKE YOU ANYWHERE.
KGHOH!
WHACK
SMACK
ZOOM
ZOOM
ZOOM
MRGHAH!
WHAT'S YOUR PROBLEM? I WAS BEING SERIOUS.
SILENCE, CLOWN.
I CAN NEVER TELL WHEN YOU ARE BEING SERIOUS OR NOT.

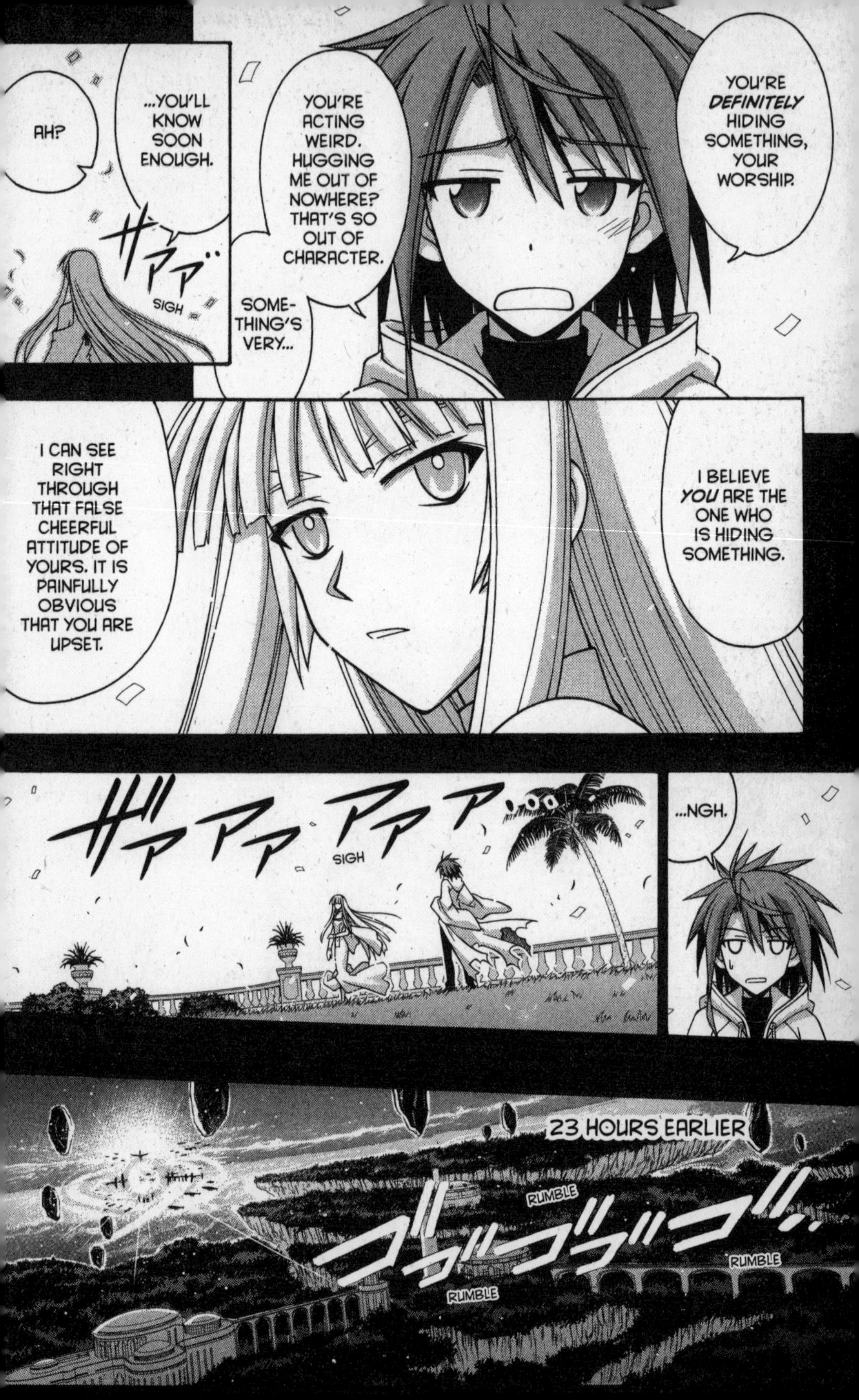

YOU'RE *DEFINITELY* HIDING SOMETHING, YOUR WORSHIP.
YOU'RE ACTING WEIRD. HUGGING ME OUT OF NOWHERE? THAT'S SO OUT OF CHARACTER.
SOMETHING'S VERY...
...YOU'LL KNOW SOON ENOUGH.
AH?
SIGH
I BELIEVE *YOU* ARE THE ONE WHO IS HIDING SOMETHING.
I CAN SEE RIGHT THROUGH THAT FALSE CHEERFUL ATTITUDE OF YOURS. IT IS PAINFULLY OBVIOUS THAT YOU ARE UPSET.
...NGH.
SIGH
23 HOURS EARLIER
RUMBLE
RUMBLE
RUMBLE

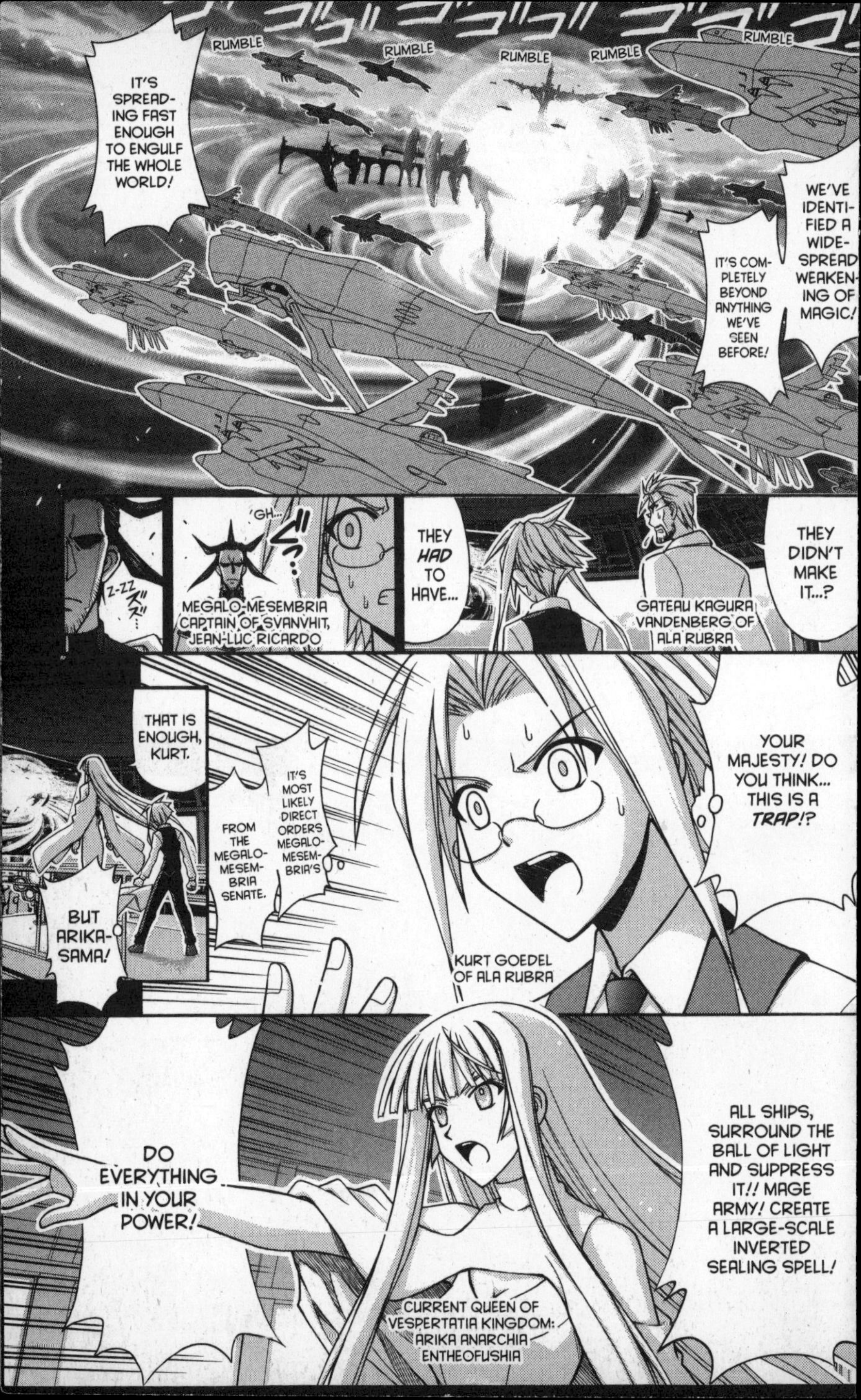
RUMBLE
RUMBLE
RUMBLE
RUMBLE
RUMBLE
WE'VE IDENTIFIED A WIDESPREAD WEAKENING OF MAGIC!
IT'S COMPLETELY BEYOND ANYTHING WE'VE SEEN BEFORE!
IT'S SPREADING FAST ENOUGH TO ENGULF THE WHOLE WORLD!
THEY DIDN'T MAKE IT...?
GATEAU KAGURA VANDENBERG OF ALA RUBRA
THEY *HAD* TO HAVE...
'GH...
MEGALO-MESEMBRIA CAPTAIN OF SVANVHIT, JEAN-LUC RICARDO
Z-ZZ...
YOUR MAJESTY! DO YOU THINK... THIS IS A *TRAP*!?
KURT GOEDEL OF ALA RUBRA
IT'S MOST LIKELY DIRECT ORDERS MEGALO-MESEMBRIA'S
FROM THE MEGALO-MESEMBRIA SENATE.
THAT IS ENOUGH, KURT.
BUT ARIKA-SAMA!
ALL SHIPS, SURROUND THE BALL OF LIGHT AND SUPPRESS IT!! MAGE ARMY! CREATE A LARGE-SCALE INVERTED SEALING SPELL!
CURRENT QUEEN OF VESPERTATIA KINGDOM: ARIKA ANARCHIA ENTHEOFUSHIA
DO EVERYTHING IN YOUR POWER!

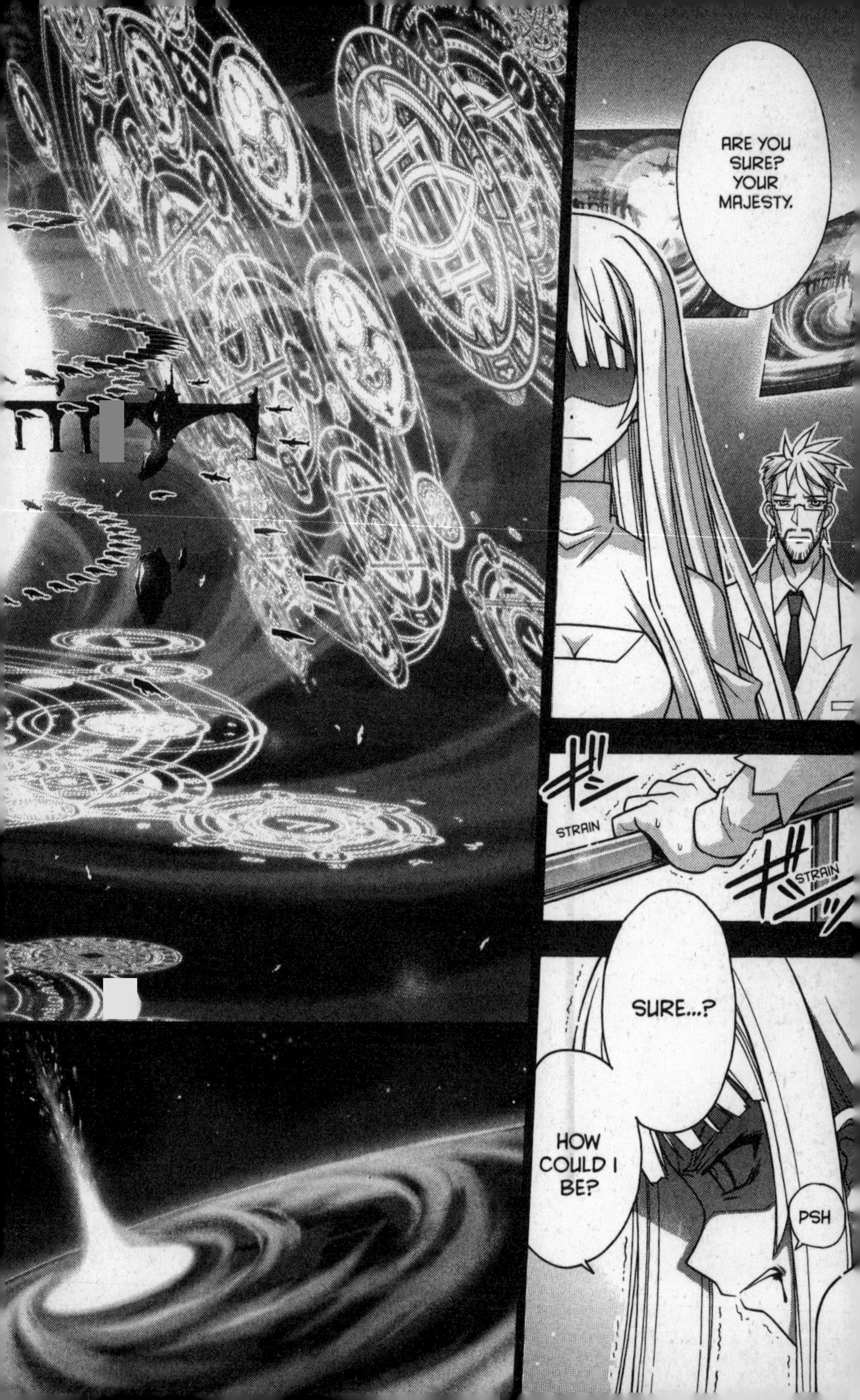
ARE YOU SURE? YOUR MAJESTY.
STRAIN
STRAIN
SURE...?
HOW COULD I BE?
PSH

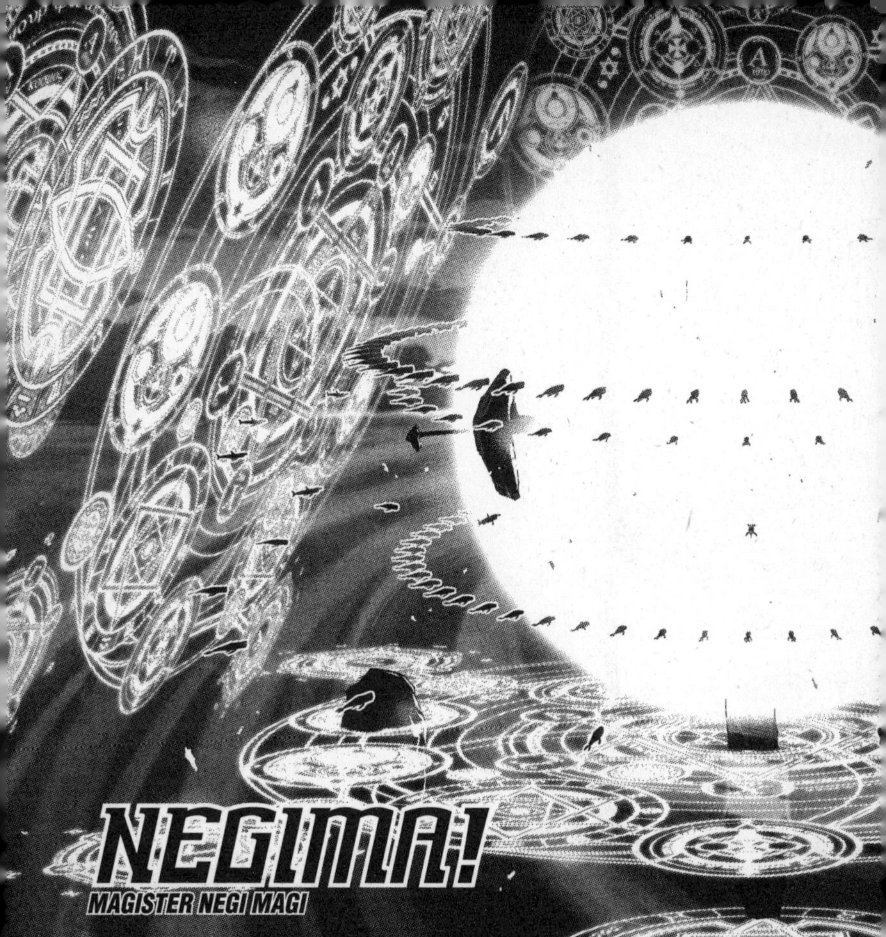
NEGIMA!
MAGISTER NEGI MAGI
267TH PERIOD: FATHER AND MOTHER: THE TALE OF THEIR DESTINY

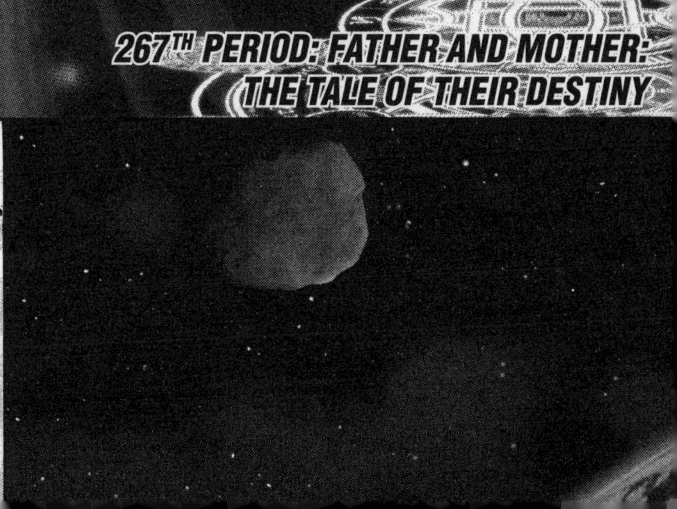

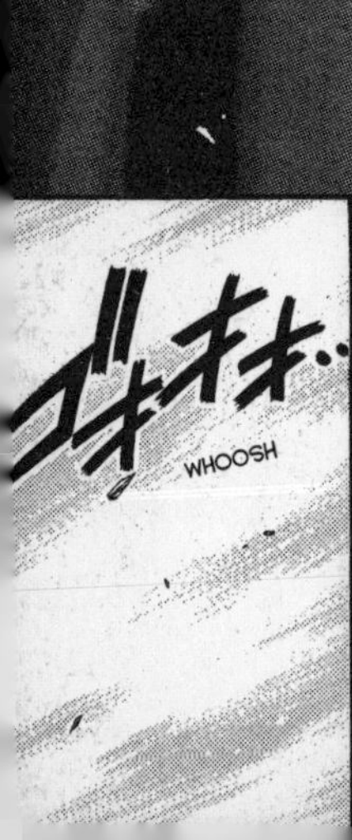
ゴォオオ…
WHOOSH

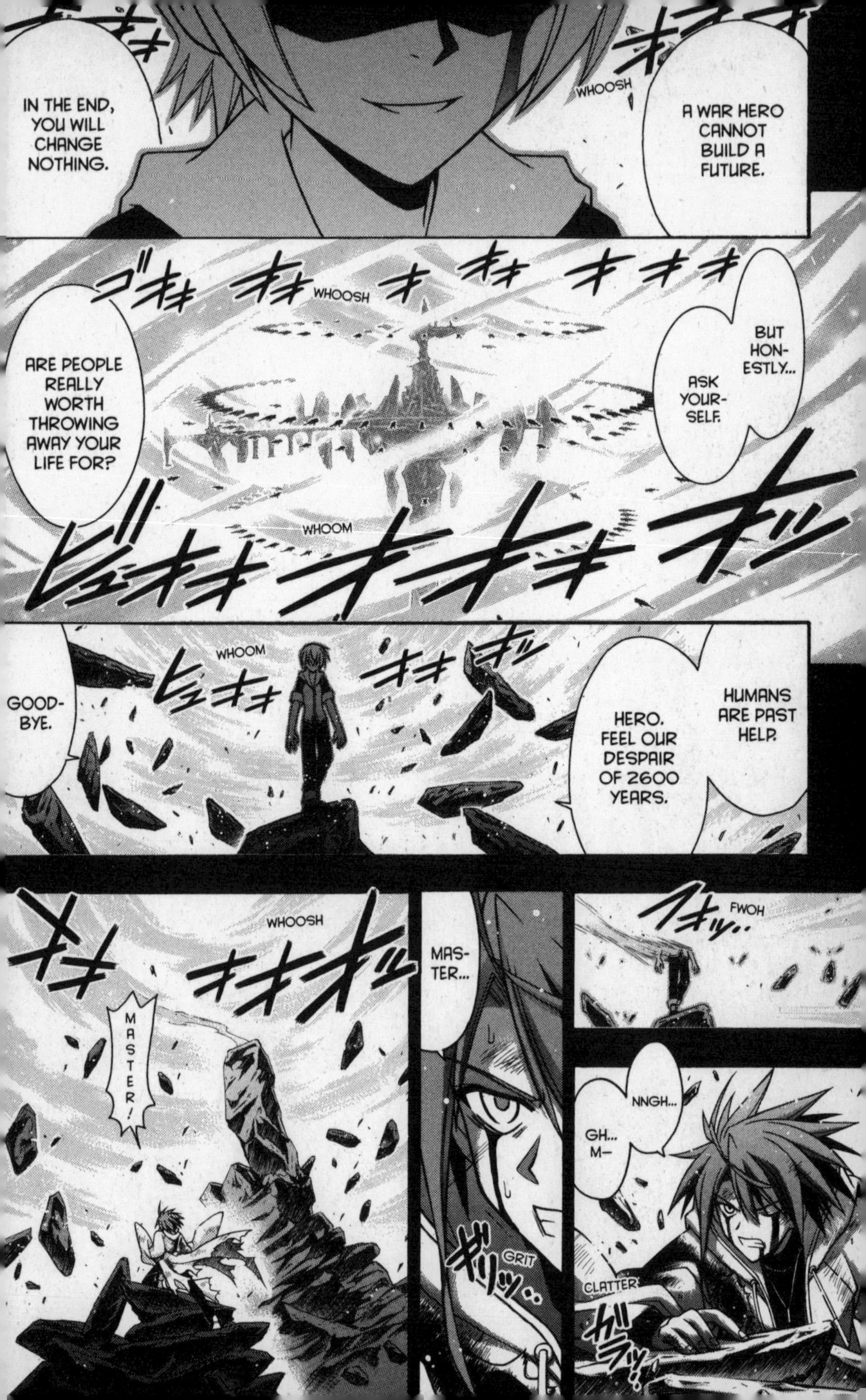

WHOOSH
A WAR HERO CANNOT BUILD A FUTURE.
IN THE END, YOU WILL CHANGE NOTHING.
BUT HONESTLY...
ASK YOURSELF.
WHOOSH
ARE PEOPLE REALLY WORTH THROWING AWAY YOUR LIFE FOR?
WHOOM
HUMANS ARE PAST HELP.
HERO. FEEL OUR DESPAIR OF 2600 YEARS.
WHOOM
GOOD-BYE.
FWOH
NNGH...
GH... M—
CLATTER
MASTER...
GRIT
WHOOSH
MASTER!

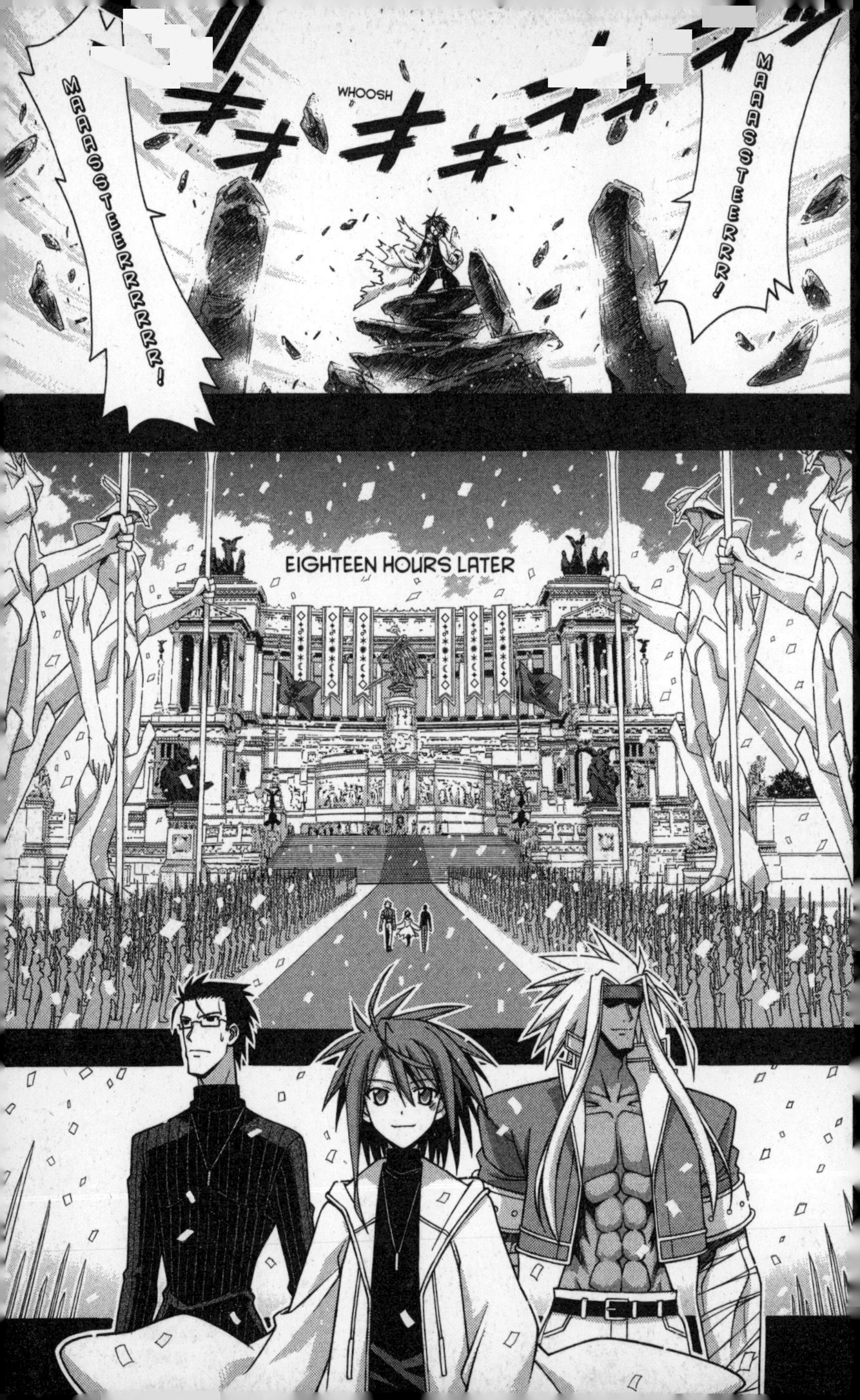
MAAASSTEERRR!
WHOOSH
MAAASSTEERRRRRRR!
EIGHTEEN HOURS LATER

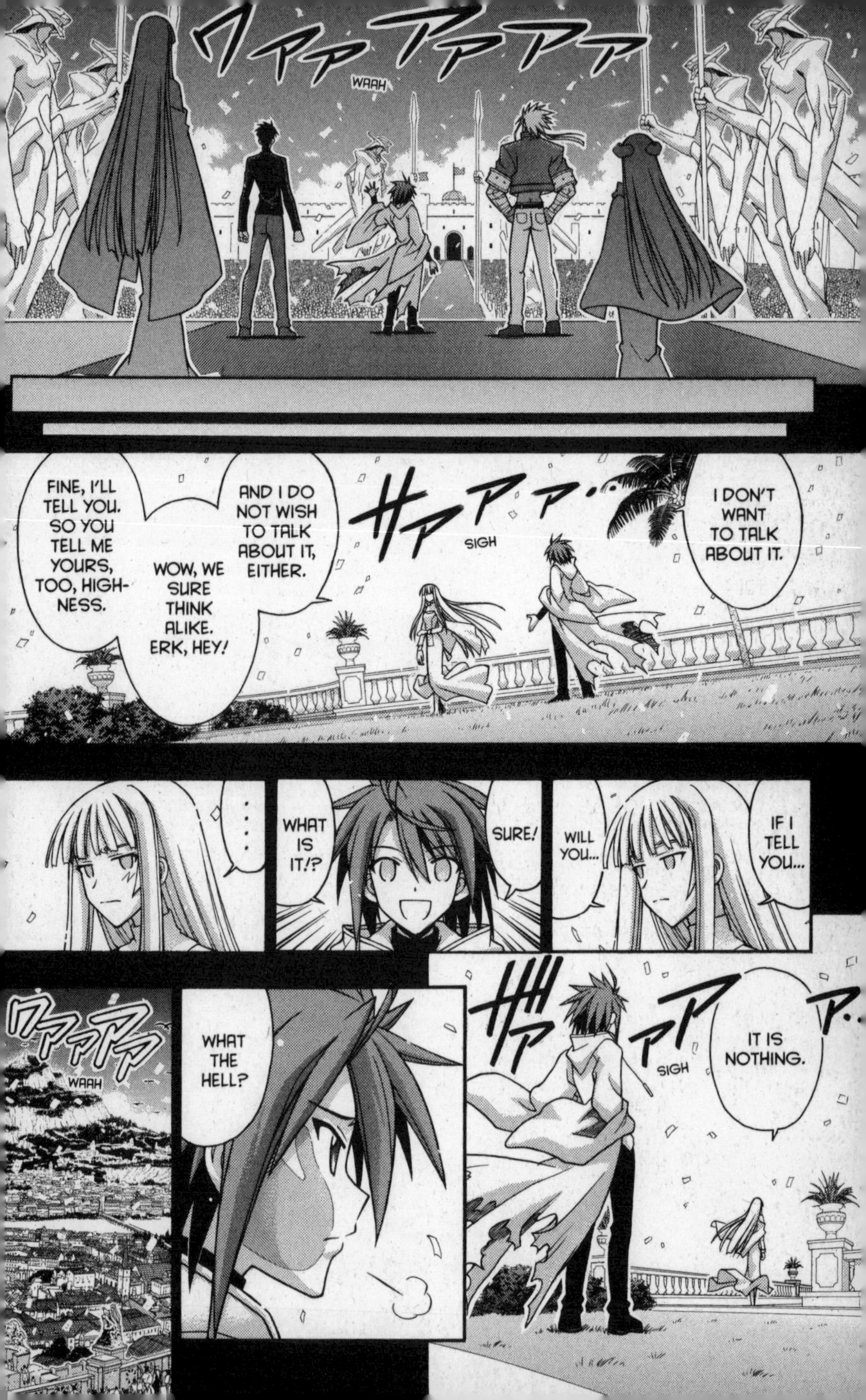
ワァァアァアァ
WAAH
I DON'T WANT TO TALK ABOUT IT.
サァアァ..
SIGH
AND I DO NOT WISH TO TALK ABOUT IT, EITHER.
WOW, WE SURE THINK ALIKE. ERK, HEY!
FINE, I'LL TELL YOU. SO YOU TELL ME YOURS, TOO, HIGHNESS.
IF I TELL YOU...
WILL YOU...
SURE!
WHAT IS IT!?
...
IT IS NOTHING.
ザァァアァ..
SIGH
WHAT THE HELL?
ワァァァア
WAAH

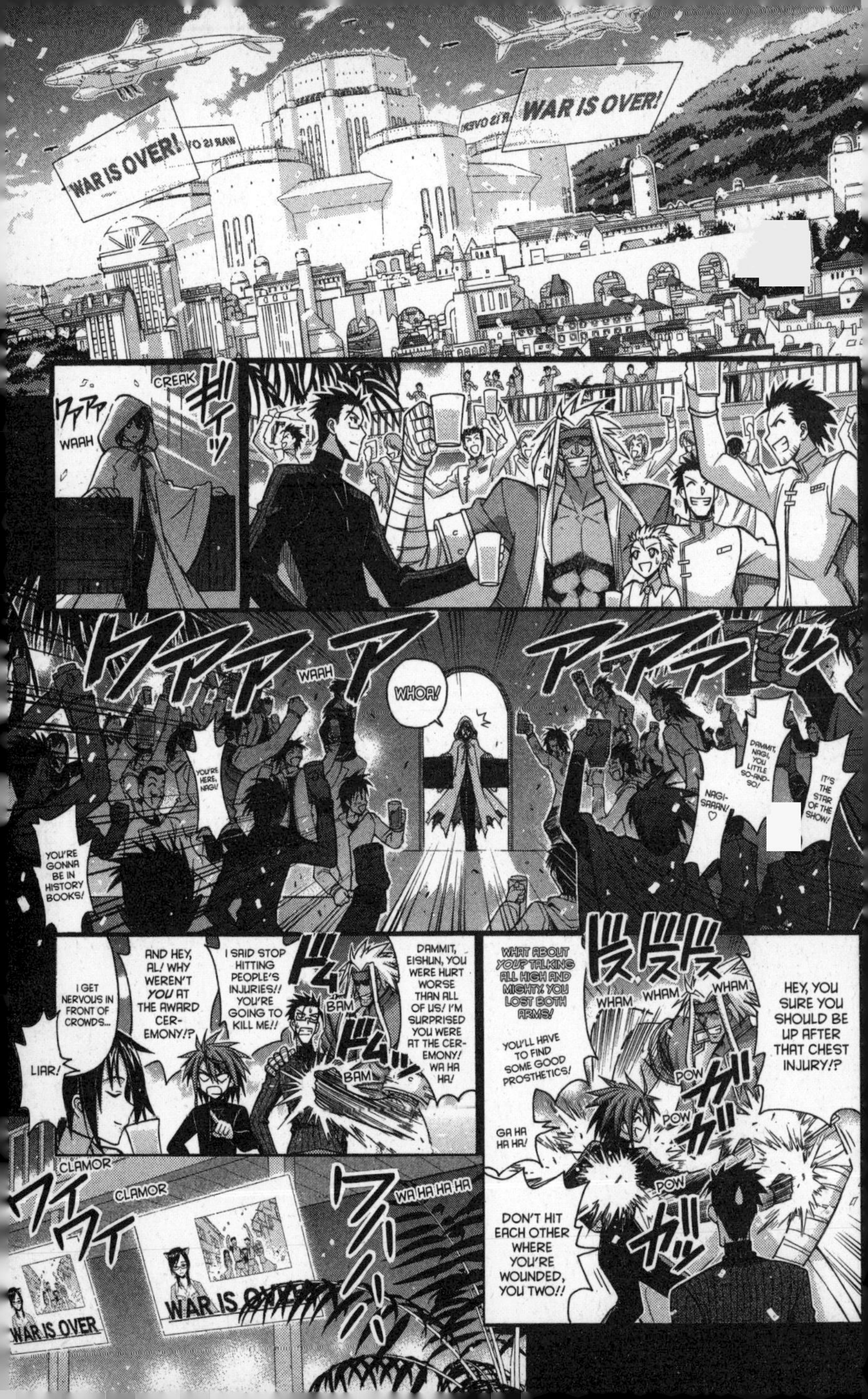

WAR IS OVER!
WAR IS OVER!
CREAK
WAAH
IT'S THE STAR OF THE SHOW!
DAMMIT, NAGI, YOU LITTLE SO-AND-SO!
NAGI-SAAAN! ♡
WHOA!
WAAH
YOU'RE HERE, NAGI!
YOU'RE GONNA BE IN HISTORY BOOKS!
HEY, YOU SURE YOU SHOULD BE UP AFTER THAT CHEST INJURY!?
WHAT ABOUT YOU!? TALKING ALL HIGH AND MIGHTY. YOU LOST BOTH ARMS!
WHAM
WHAM
WHAM
YOU'LL HAVE TO FIND SOME GOOD PROSTHETICS!
GA HA HA HA!
POW
POW
POW
DON'T HIT EACH OTHER WHERE YOU'RE WOUNDED, YOU TWO!!
DAMMIT, EISHUN, YOU WERE HURT WORSE THAN ALL OF US! I'M SURPRISED YOU WERE AT THE CER-EMONY! WA HA HA!
BAM
BAM
I SAID STOP HITTING PEOPLE'S INJURIES!! YOU'RE GOING TO KILL ME!!
AND HEY, AL! WHY WEREN'T YOU AT THE AWARD CER-EMONY!?
I GET NERVOUS IN FRONT OF CROWDS...
LIAR!
WA HA HA HA
CLAMOR
CLAMOR
WAR IS OVER
WAR IS OVER

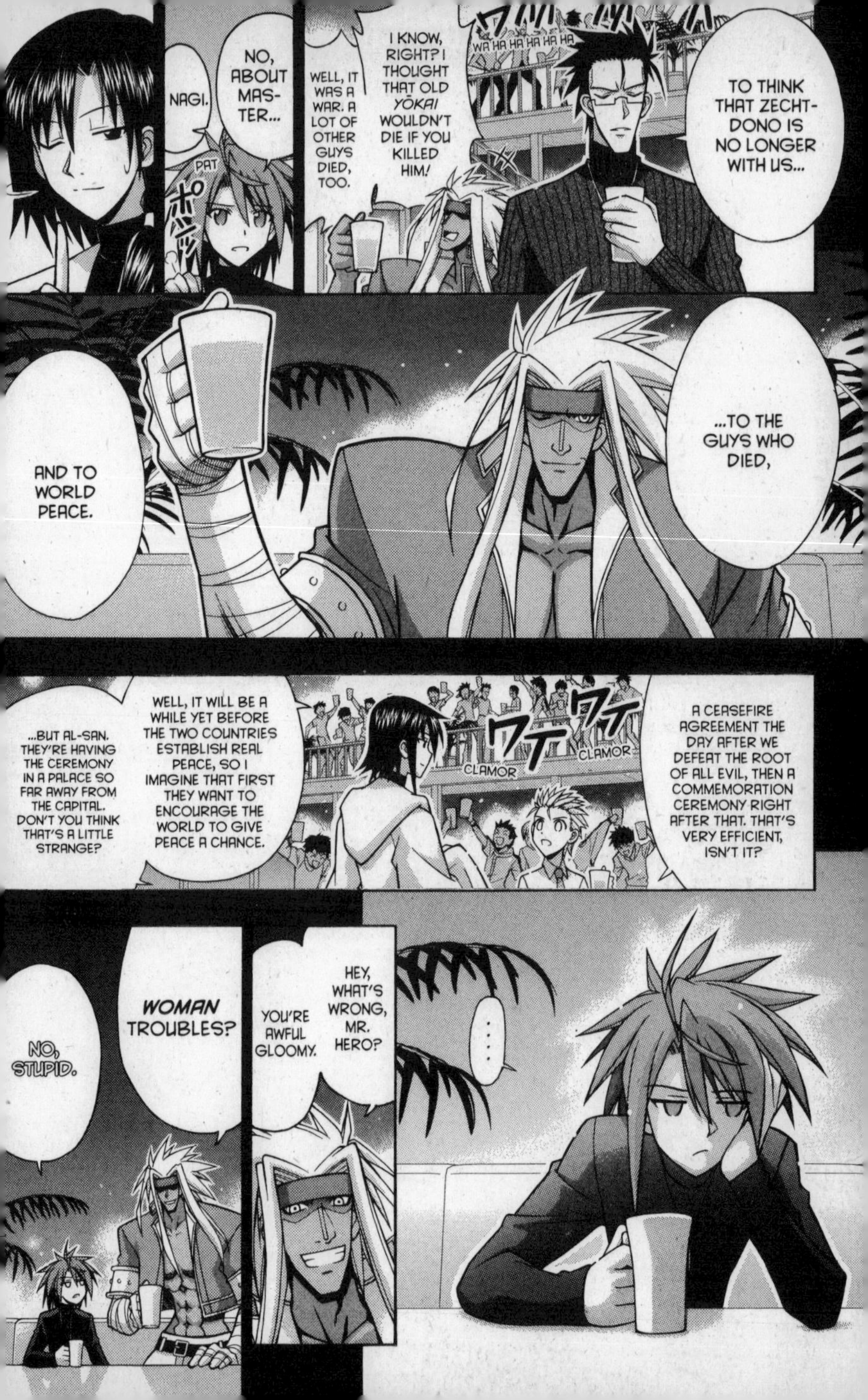
TO THINK THAT ZECHT-DONO IS NO LONGER WITH US...
WA HA HA HA HA HA
I KNOW, RIGHT? I THOUGHT THAT OLD *YŌKAI* WOULDN'T DIE IF YOU KILLED HIM!
WELL, IT WAS A WAR. A LOT OF OTHER GUYS DIED, TOO.
NO, ABOUT MAS-TER...
NAGI.
PAT
...TO THE GUYS WHO DIED,
AND TO WORLD PEACE.
A CEASEFIRE AGREEMENT THE DAY AFTER WE DEFEAT THE ROOT OF ALL EVIL, THEN A COMMEMORATION CEREMONY RIGHT AFTER THAT. THAT'S VERY EFFICIENT, ISN'T IT?
CLAMOR
CLAMOR
WELL, IT WILL BE A WHILE YET BEFORE THE TWO COUNTRIES ESTABLISH REAL PEACE, SO I IMAGINE THAT FIRST THEY WANT TO ENCOURAGE THE WORLD TO GIVE PEACE A CHANCE.
...BUT AL-SAN. THEY'RE HAVING THE CEREMONY IN A PALACE SO FAR AWAY FROM THE CAPITAL. DON'T YOU THINK THAT'S A LITTLE STRANGE?
....
HEY, WHAT'S WRONG, MR. HERO?
YOU'RE AWFUL GLOOMY.
WOMAN TROUBLES?
NO, STUPID.

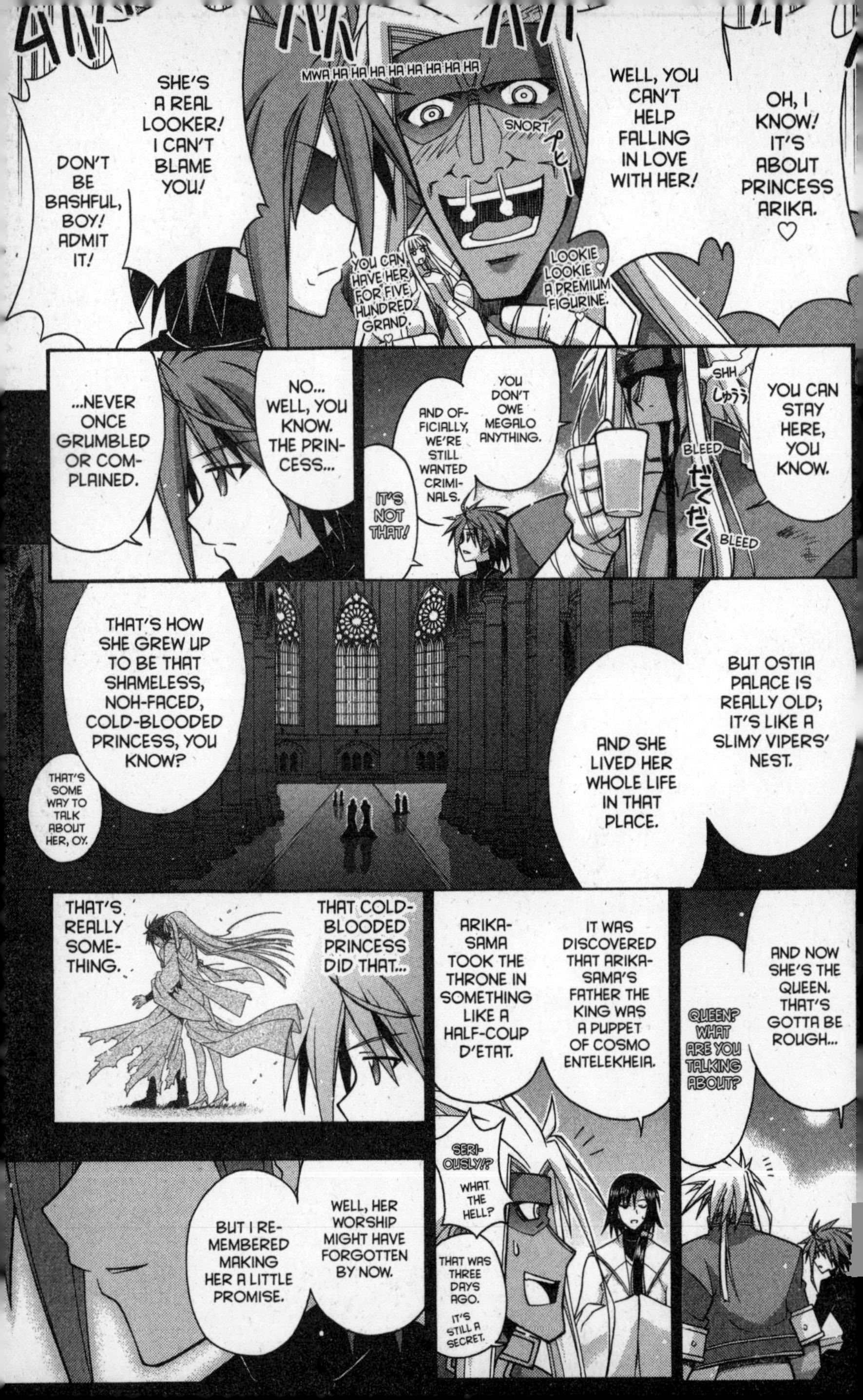
OH, I KNOW! IT'S ABOUT PRINCESS ARIKA. ♡
WELL, YOU CAN'T HELP FALLING IN LOVE WITH HER!
MWA HA HA HA HA HA HA HA HA
SNORT
LOOKIE LOOKIE ♡ A PREMIUM FIGURINE. ♡
YOU CAN HAVE HER FOR FIVE HUNDRED GRAND. ♡
SHE'S A REAL LOOKER! I CAN'T BLAME YOU!
DON'T BE BASHFUL, BOY! ADMIT IT!
SHH
YOU CAN STAY HERE, YOU KNOW.
BLEED
BLEED
YOU DON'T OWE MEGALO ANYTHING.
AND OFFICIALLY, WE'RE STILL WANTED CRIMINALS.
IT'S NOT THAT!
NO... WELL, YOU KNOW. THE PRINCESS...
...NEVER ONCE GRUMBLED OR COMPLAINED.
BUT OSTIA PALACE IS REALLY OLD; IT'S LIKE A SLIMY VIPERS' NEST.
AND SHE LIVED HER WHOLE LIFE IN THAT PLACE.
THAT'S HOW SHE GREW UP TO BE THAT SHAMELESS, NOH-FACED, COLD-BLOODED PRINCESS, YOU KNOW?
THAT'S SOME WAY TO TALK ABOUT HER, OY.
AND NOW SHE'S THE QUEEN. THAT'S GOTTA BE ROUGH...
QUEEN? WHAT ARE YOU TALKING ABOUT?
IT WAS DISCOVERED THAT ARIKA-SAMA'S FATHER THE KING WAS A PUPPET OF COSMO ENTELEKHEIA.
ARIKA-SAMA TOOK THE THRONE IN SOMETHING LIKE A HALF-COUP D'ETAT.
SERIOUSLY!?
WHAT THE HELL?
THAT WAS THREE DAYS AGO.
IT'S STILL A SECRET.
THAT COLD-BLOODED PRINCESS DID THAT...
THAT'S REALLY SOMETHING.
WELL, HER WORSHIP MIGHT HAVE FORGOTTEN BY NOW.
BUT I REMEMBERED MAKING HER A LITTLE PROMISE.

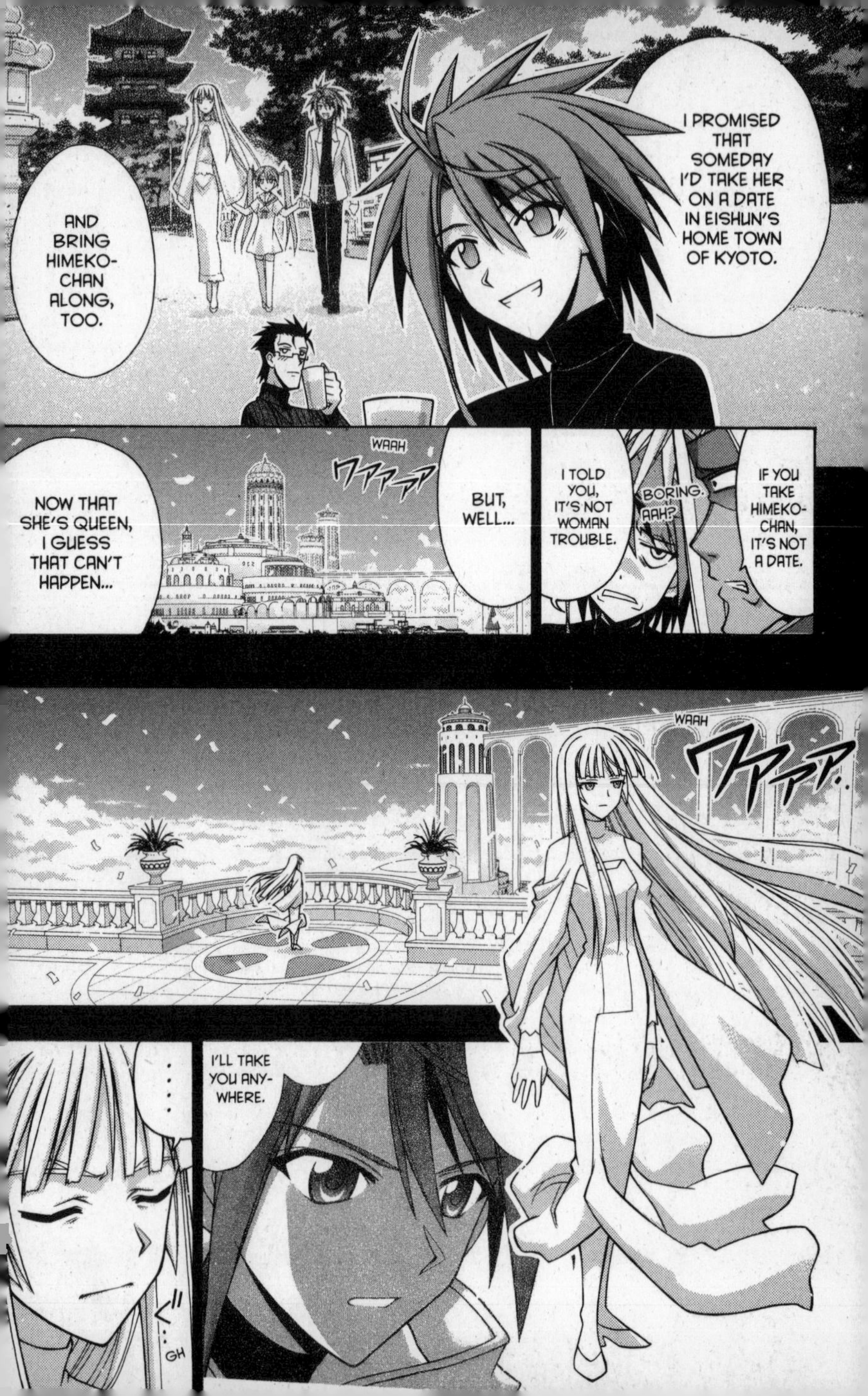
I PROMISED THAT SOMEDAY I'D TAKE HER ON A DATE IN EISHUN'S HOME TOWN OF KYOTO.
AND BRING HIMEKO-CHAN ALONG, TOO.
IF YOU TAKE HIMEKO-CHAN, IT'S NOT A DATE.
BORING.
AAH?
I TOLD YOU, IT'S NOT WOMAN TROUBLE.
WAAH
ワァァァ
BUT, WELL...
NOW THAT SHE'S QUEEN, I GUESS THAT CAN'T HAPPEN...
WAAH
ワァァァ
I'LL TAKE YOU ANYWHERE.
....
GH

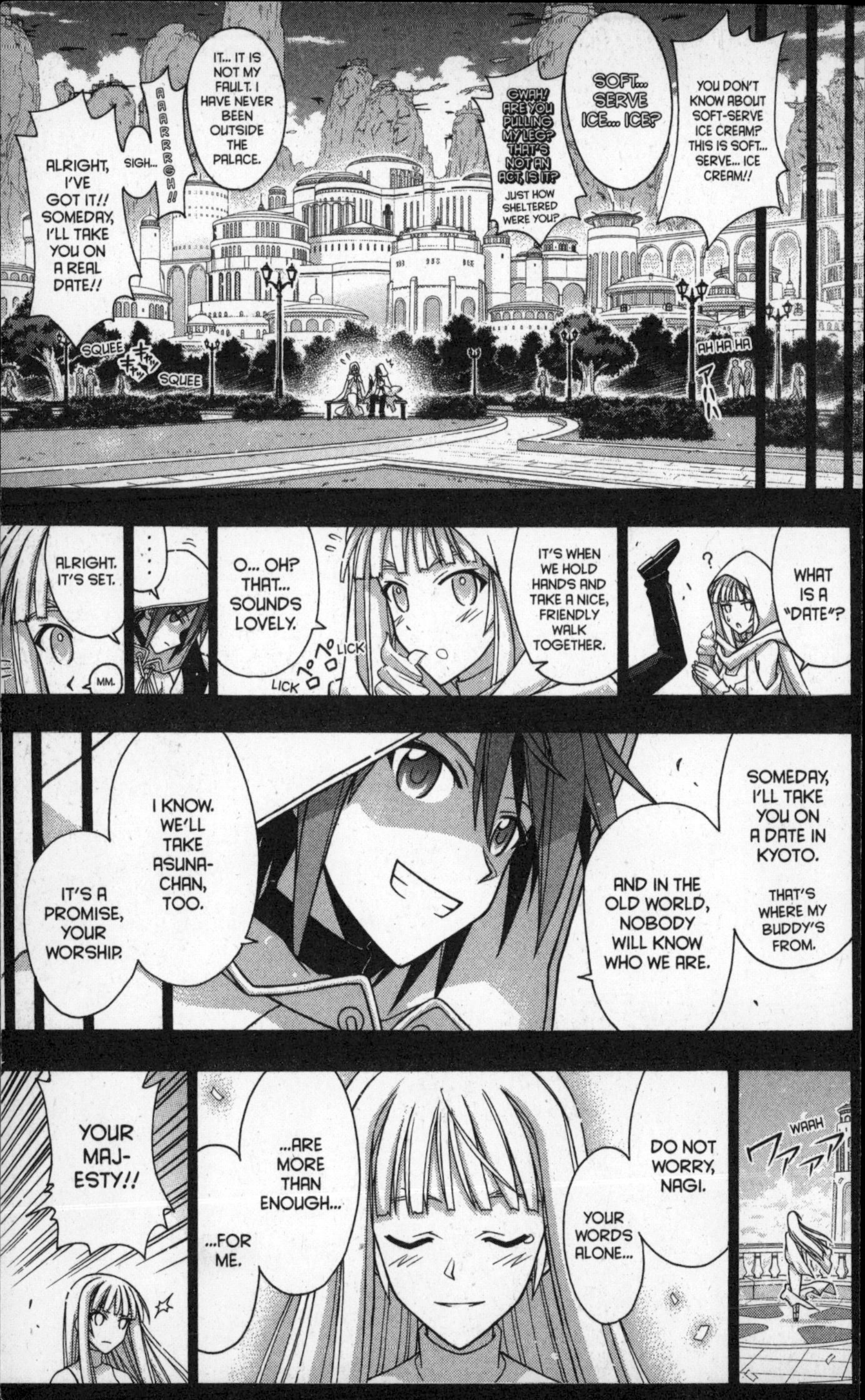
YOU DON'T KNOW ABOUT SOFT-SERVE ICE CREAM? THIS IS SOFT... SERVE... ICE CREAM!!
SOFT... SERVE ICE... ICE?
GWAH! ARE YOU PULLING MY LEG? THAT'S NOT AN ACT, IS IT?
JUST HOW SHELTERED WERE YOU?
IT... IT IS NOT MY FAULT. I HAVE NEVER BEEN OUTSIDE THE PALACE.
AAAARRRGH!!
SIGH...
ALRIGHT, I'VE GOT IT!! SOMEDAY, I'LL TAKE YOU ON A REAL DATE!!
AH HA HA
SQUEE
SQUEE
WHAT IS A "DATE"?
IT'S WHEN WE HOLD HANDS AND TAKE A NICE, FRIENDLY WALK TOGETHER.
O... OH? THAT... SOUNDS LOVELY.
LICK
LICK
...
ALRIGHT. IT'S SET.
MM.
SOMEDAY, I'LL TAKE YOU ON A DATE IN KYOTO.
THAT'S WHERE MY BUDDY'S FROM.
AND IN THE OLD WORLD, NOBODY WILL KNOW WHO WE ARE.
I KNOW. WE'LL TAKE ASUNA-CHAN, TOO.
IT'S A PROMISE, YOUR WORSHIP.
WAAH
DO NOT WORRY, NAGI.
YOUR WORDS ALONE...
...ARE MORE THAN ENOUGH...
...FOR ME.
YOUR MAJESTY!!

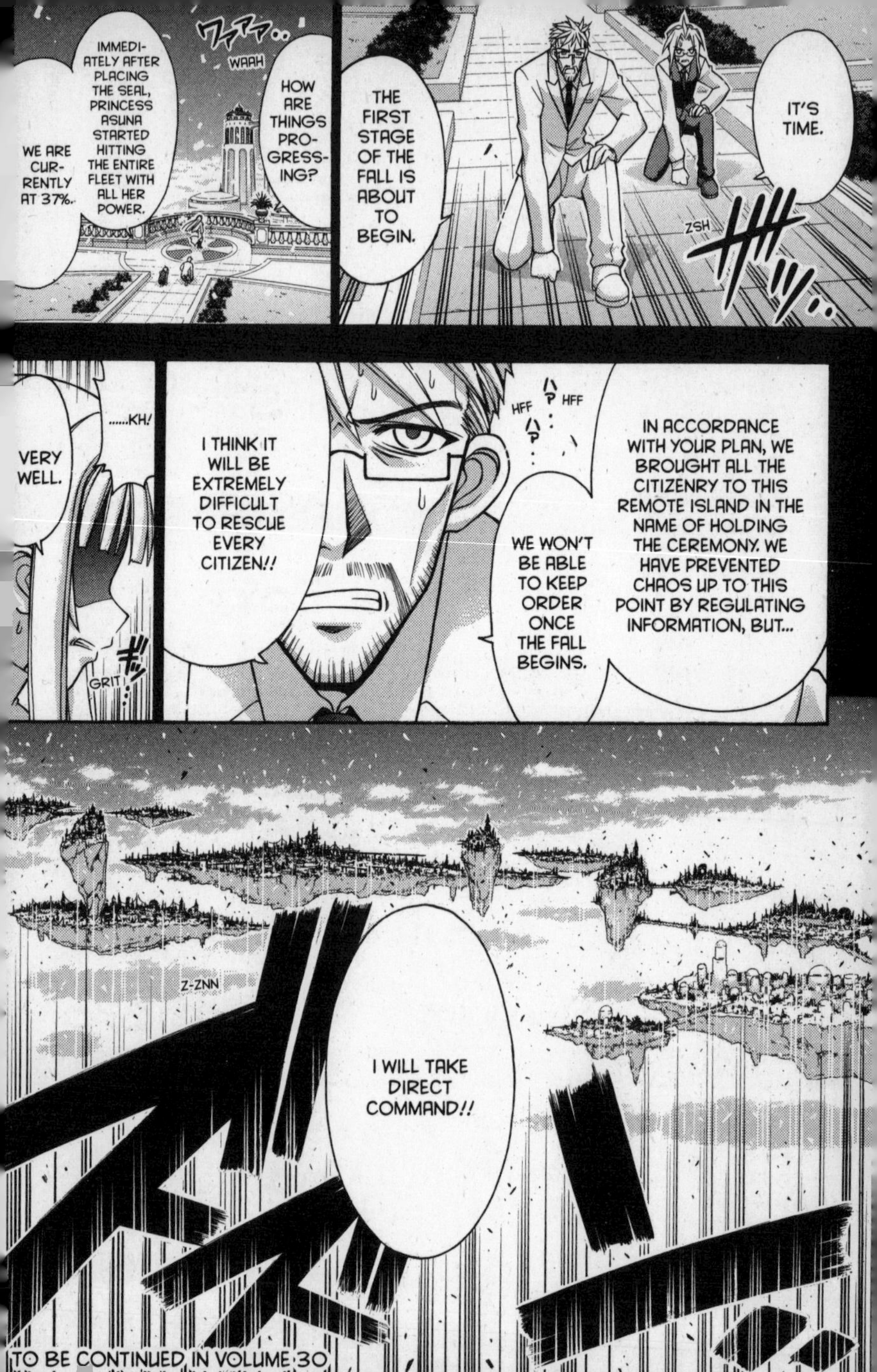
IT'S TIME.
ZSH
THE FIRST STAGE OF THE FALL IS ABOUT TO BEGIN.
HOW ARE THINGS PROGRESSING?
ワァァ..
WAAH
IMMEDIATELY AFTER PLACING THE SEAL, PRINCESS ASUNA STARTED HITTING THE ENTIRE FLEET WITH ALL HER POWER.
WE ARE CURRENTLY AT 37%.
IN ACCORDANCE WITH YOUR PLAN, WE BROUGHT ALL THE CITIZENRY TO THIS REMOTE ISLAND IN THE NAME OF HOLDING THE CEREMONY. WE HAVE PREVENTED CHAOS UP TO THIS POINT BY REGULATING INFORMATION, BUT...
WE WON'T BE ABLE TO KEEP ORDER ONCE THE FALL BEGINS.
HFF
HFF
I THINK IT WILL BE EXTREMELY DIFFICULT TO RESCUE EVERY CITIZEN!!
......KH!
VERY WELL.
GRIT
I WILL TAKE DIRECT COMMAND!!
Z-ZNN

TO BE CONTINUED IN VOLUME 30

-STAFF-

Ken Akamatsu

Takashi Takemoto

Kenichi Nakamura

Keiichi Yamashita

Tohru Mitsuhashi

Yuichi Yoshida

Susumu Kuwabara

Thanks to
Ran Ayanaga

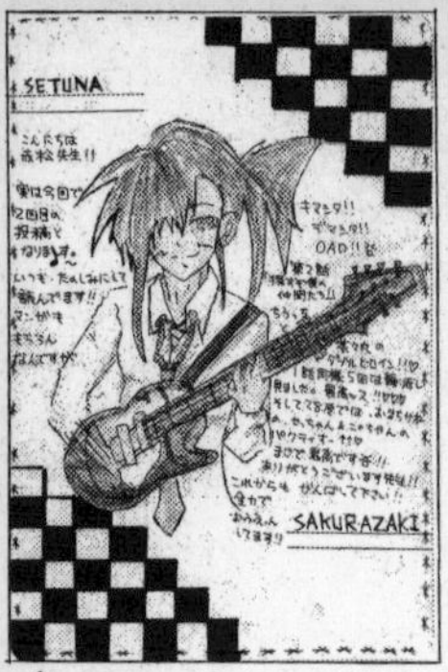
SETUNA
SAKURAZAKI

YOUR LOVE OF THE SERIES REALLY SHINES THROUGH.

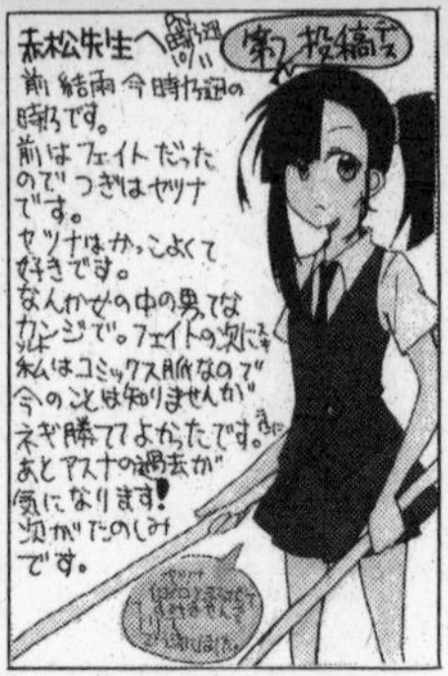
赤松先生へ
第2投稿です
前はフェイトだったのでつぎはセツナです。
セツナはかっこよくて好きです。
なんか女の中の男てなカンジで。
ネギ勝ててよかったです。
あとアスナの過去が気になります!
次がたのしみです。

DOUBLE-SWORD STYLE SETSUNA

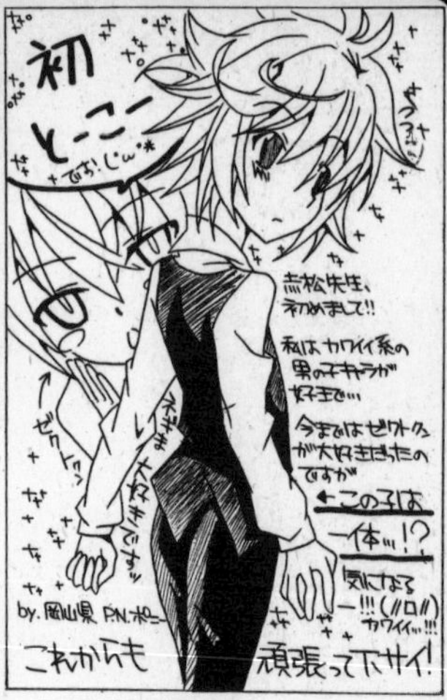
初とーこー
赤松先生、初めまして!!
私はカワイイ系の男の子キャラが好きで…
今まではゼクトくんが大好きだったのですが
←この子は一体…!?
気になるー!!!
カワイイッ!!!
ネギま大好きです
by. 岡山県 P.N. ポニー
これからも頑張って下サイ!

THIS KID SURE IS CUTE, HUH?

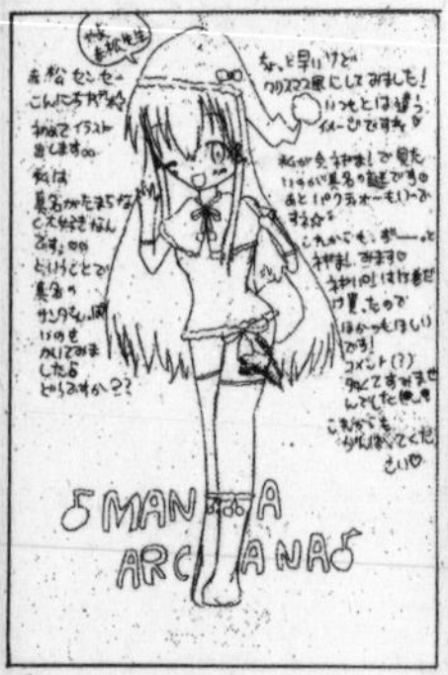

THE COMMANDER CAN BE CUTE, TOO. ★

NEGIMA!
FAN ART CORNER

WE'RE NOT SURPRISED TO BE GETTING A LOT OF SETSUNA SUBMISSIONS THESE DAYS. IT MAKES ME A LITTLE HAPPY TO SEE DRAWINGS OF THE CAPTAIN OF THE IMPERIAL VILLA (LAUGH). OF COURSE, WE LOVE TO SEE SETSUNA, TOO. ♪ I'M VERY SORRY THAT WE LEFT OUT THE COMMENT TO MIYU-SAN FROM GIFU PREFECTURE IN THE LAST VOLUME. THANK YOU FOR THE HIGH-SPIRITED ASUNA. ♪

TEXT BY MAX

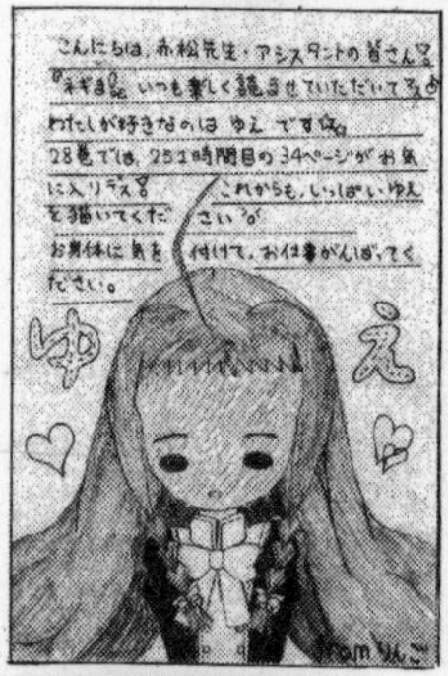
こんにちは、赤松先生・アシスタントの皆さん♡
「ネギま」いつも楽しく読ませていただいてます♪
わたしが好きなのはゆえです。
お身体に気を付けて、お仕事がんばってください。
ゆえ

YUE'S SUPER CUTE!

NEGI MA!

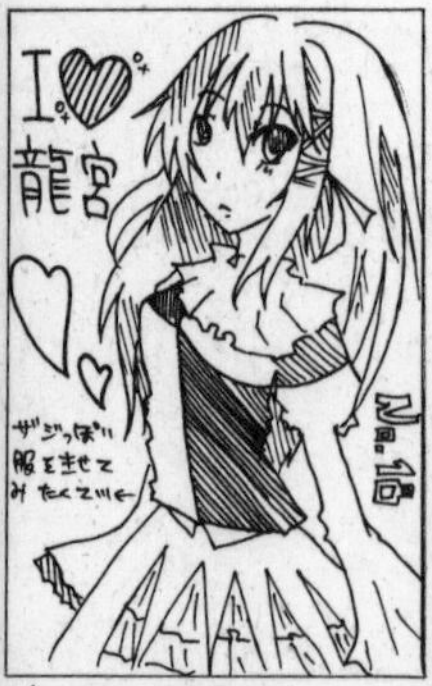
I♡龍宮

THIS IS A GOOD TATSUMIYA!

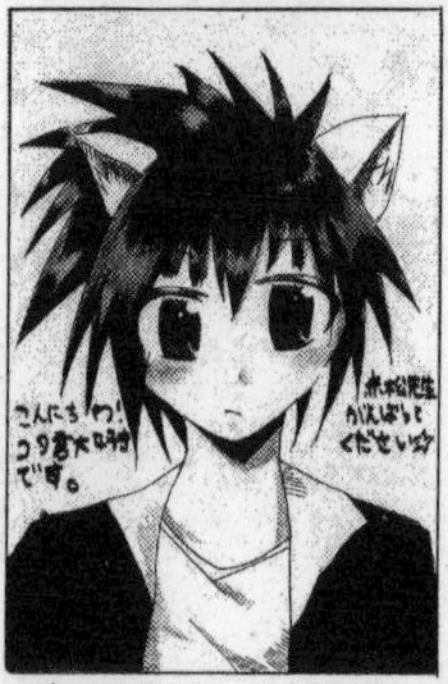

AN INNOCENT KOTA.

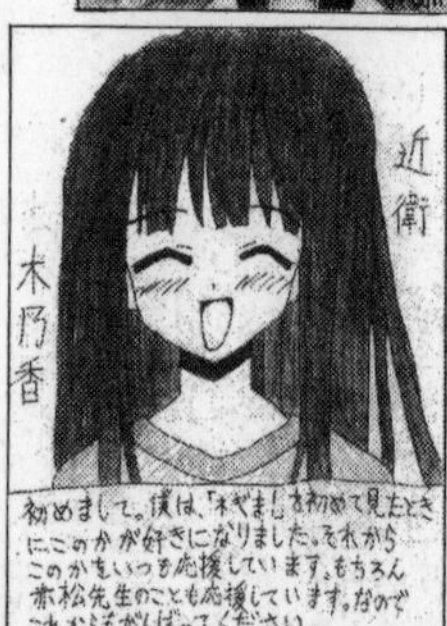
近衛木乃香
初めまして。僕は「ネギま!」を初めて見たときにこのかが好きになりました。それから
このかをいつも応援しています。もちろん赤松先生のことも応援しています。なので
これからもがんばってください。
ぜひ、僕の投稿を載せてください。お願いします。

SHE'S ALL SMILES!

MAGISTER NEGI MAGI

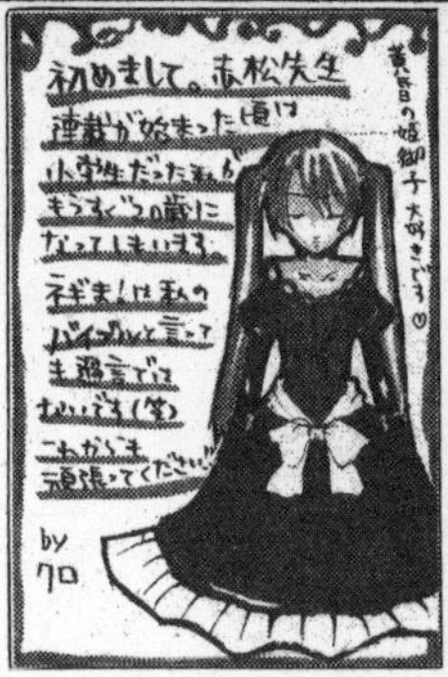
初めまして。赤松先生
by
クロ
▲ A VERY NOBLE IMPERIAL PRINCESS.

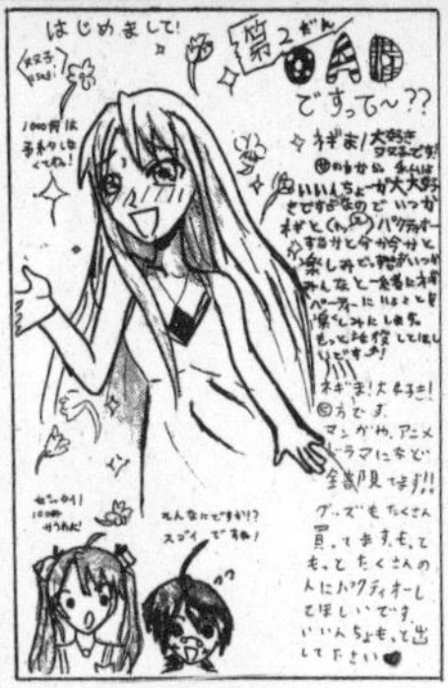
はじめまして!
ですって〜??
▲ YOU WANT TO SEE CLASS REP, I SEE.

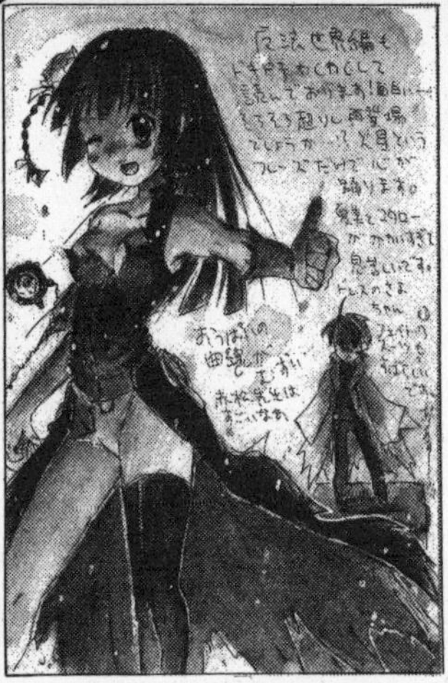
▲ A FANTASY-STYLE USE OF COLOR.

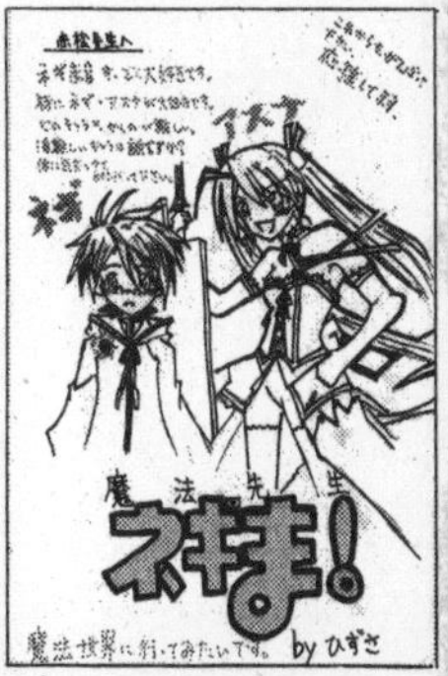
魔法先生
ネギま!
by ひずさ
▲ A RELIABLE ASUNA.

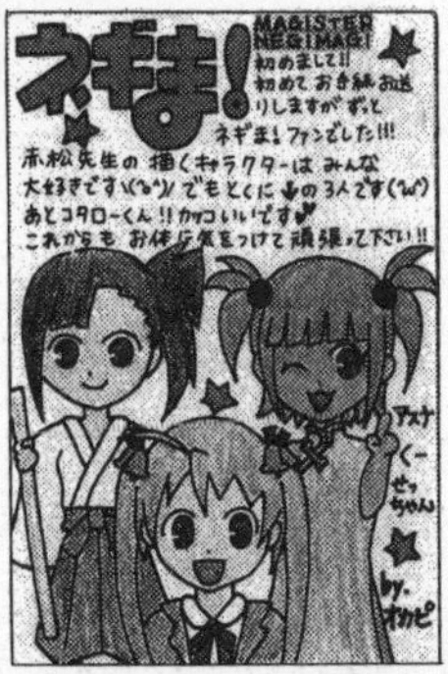
ネギま!
MAGISTER NEGI MAGI
初めまして!!
▲ THEY'RE SO CUTE AND ROUND.

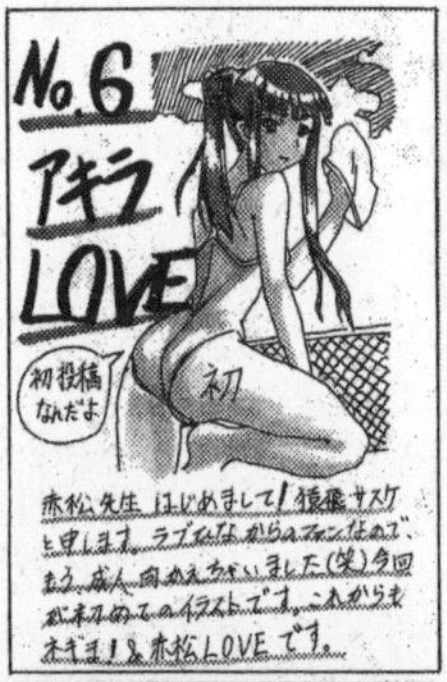
No.6
アキラ
LOVE
初投稿なんだよ
▶ NICE PROPORTIONS.

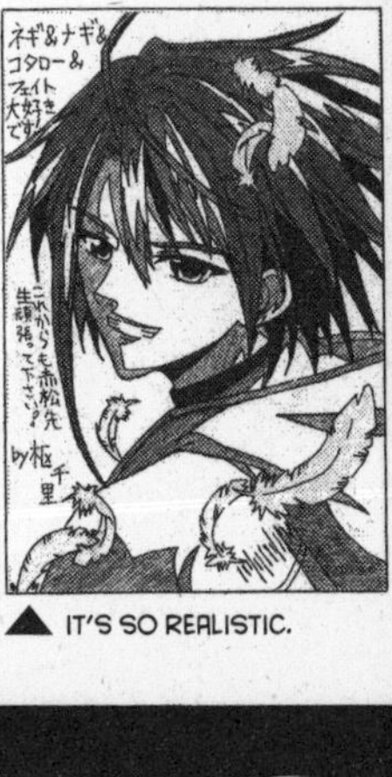
ネギ&ナギ&
コタロー&
フェイト
大好きです!
▲ IT'S SO REALISTIC.

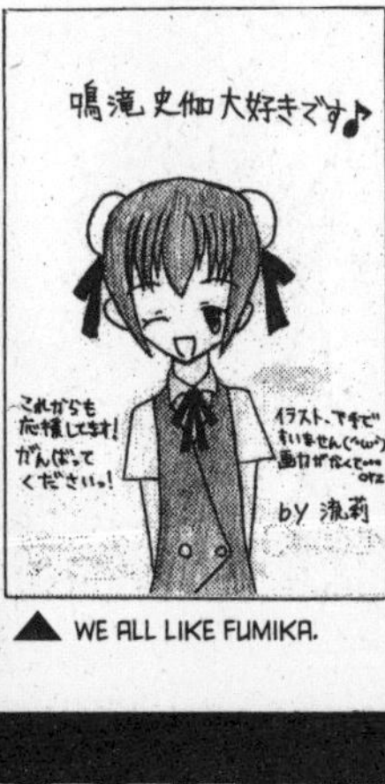
鳴滝史伽大好きです♪
これからも
応援してます!
がんばって
くださいっ!
▲ WE ALL LIKE FUMIKA.

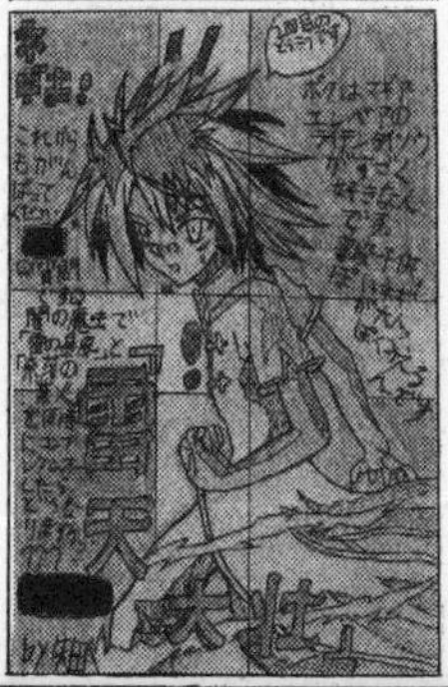
▶ VERY DASHING!

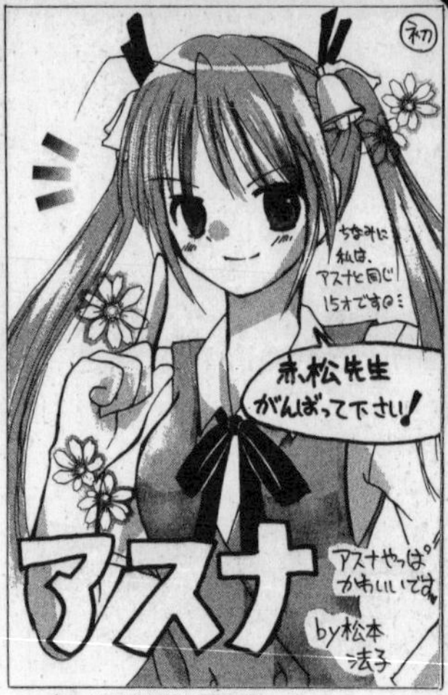
ちなみに
私は、
アスナと同じ
15才です
赤松先生
がんばって下さい!
アスナ
アスナやっぱ
かわいいです。
by松本
法子

▲ VERY WELL DONE.

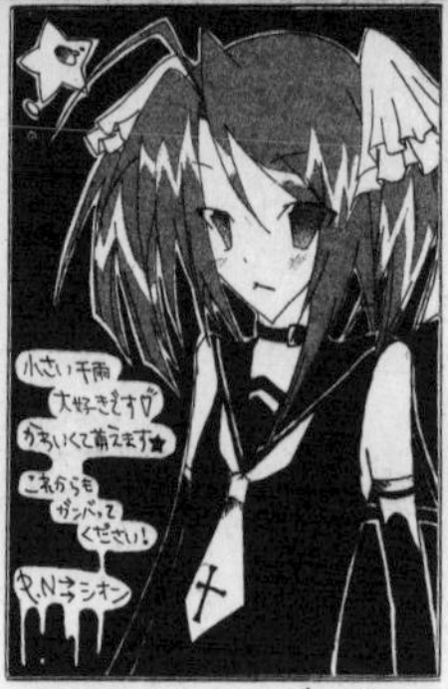
小さい千雨
大好きです♡
かわいくて萌えます★
これからも
ガンバって
ください!

▲ YOU HIT MY MOÉ BUTTON.

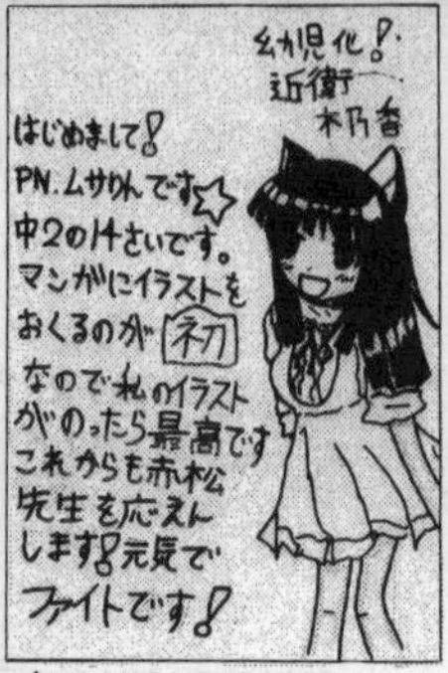
幼児化!
近衛木乃香
はじめまして!
PN.ムサりんです☆
中2の14さいです。
マンガにイラストを
おくるのが初
なので私のイラスト
がのったら最高です
これからも赤松
先生を応えん
します!元気で
ファイトです!

▲ LITTLE KONOKA IS CUTE, TOO. ♪

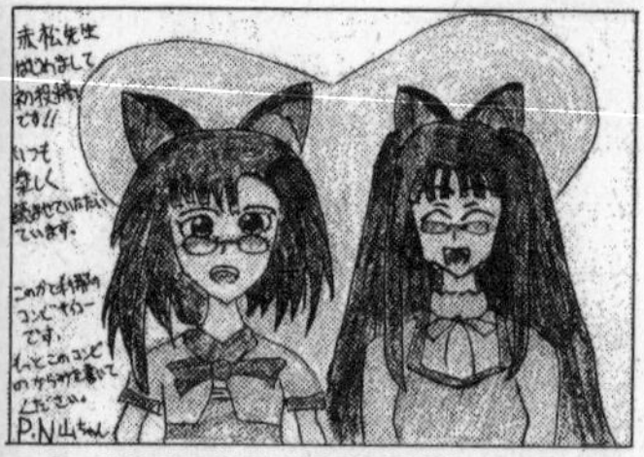
赤松先生
はじめまして
初投稿です!!

▲ THEY'RE SO LOVEY-DOVEY.

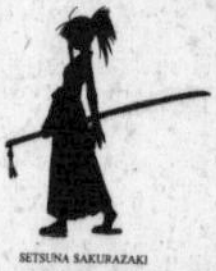
SETSUNA SAKURAZAKI

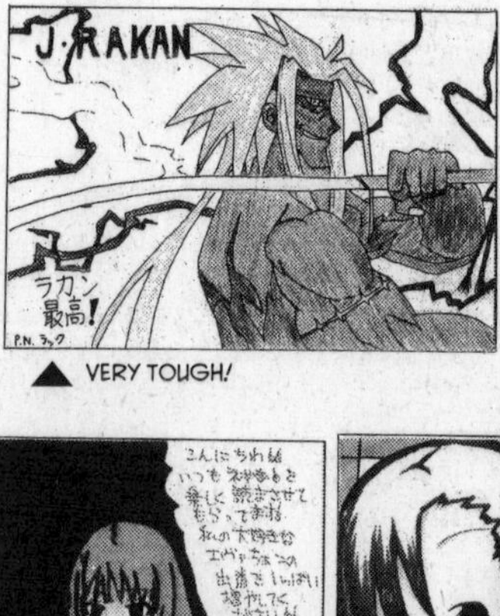
J・RAKAN
ラカン
最高!

▲ VERY TOUGH!

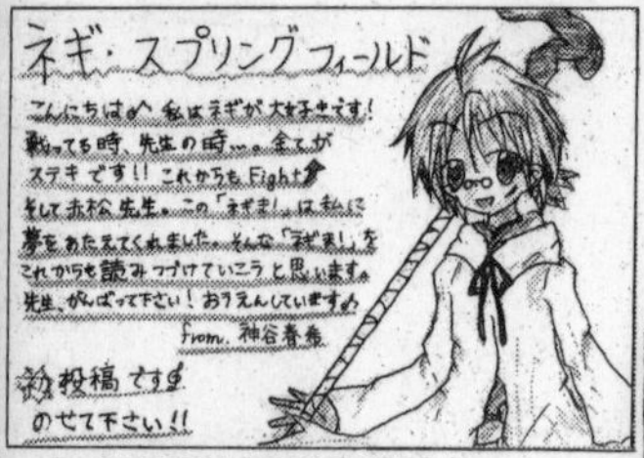
ネギ・スプリングフィールド
こんにちは。私はネギが大好きです!
戦ってる時、先生の時…全てが
ステキです!! これからもFight
そして赤松先生。この「ネギま!」は私に
夢をあたえてくれました。そんな「ネギま!」を
これからも読みつづけていこうと思います。
先生、がんばって下さい! おうえんしています。
from.神谷春香
初投稿です!
のせて下さい!!

▲ A HEART-WARMING NEGI. ♪

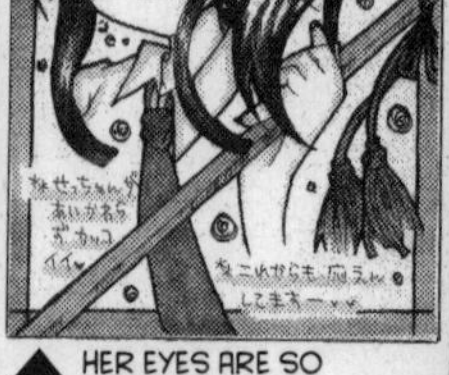
これからも応えんしてます

▲ HER EYES ARE SO EMOTIONAL!

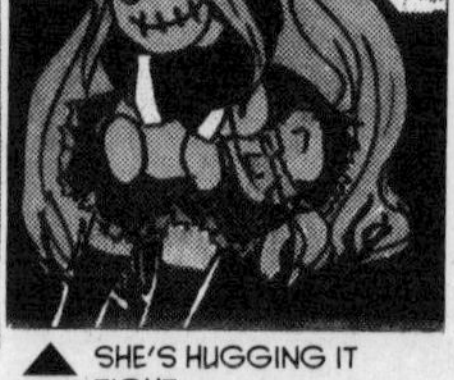

▲ SHE'S HUGGING IT TIGHT.

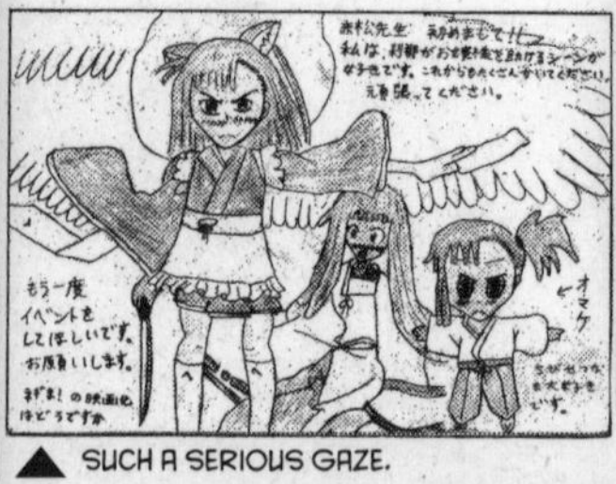
もう一度
イベントを
してほしいです。
お願いします。

▲ SUCH A SERIOUS GAZE.

NEGI MA!

THIS VOLUME'S

MOST DRAWN CHARACTER

AKO IZUMI

RANKING

FIRST PLACE

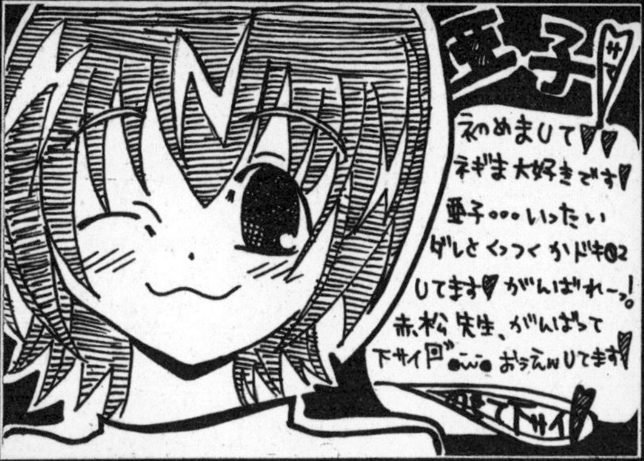
亜子
ネギま大好きです!
赤松先生、がんばって

HER KITTY MOUTH IS SO CUTE. ♡ AKO SEEMS LIKE THE TYPE TO FALL IN LOVE EASILY, SO I'M SURE SHE'LL HAVE ANOTHER GOOD ROMANCE!

(AKAMATSU)

SECOND PLACE

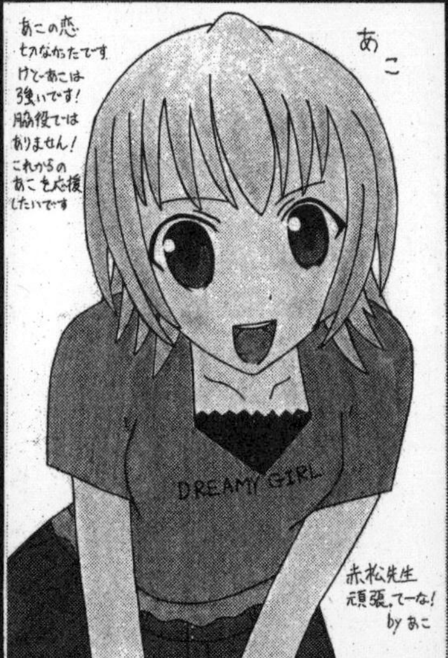
あこ
DREAMY GIRL
赤松先生
頑張ってーな!
by あこ

HEY, HEY!

AKO IS A SIDE CHARACTER, BUT THERE'S NO DOUBT SHE'S A STRONG GIRL. PLEASE CONTINUE TO SUPPORT HER!!

THIRD PLACE

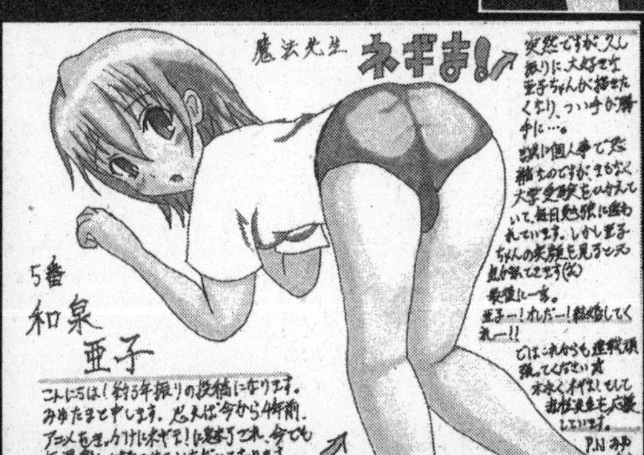
魔法先生
ネギま!
5番
和泉
亜子

OOHH! VERY NICE! ♡ *THEY DON'T USE BLOOMERS LIKE THAT AT MAHORA ACADEMY (LAUGH)

THE WHAT AND WHY OF *NEGIMA!*
CLASSMATE EDITION

NEGIMA!
MAGISTER NEGI MAGI

Sayo Aisaka
■ Is the uniform Sayo wears an old Mahora Academy uniform?
★ Yes, it is. Sayo happened to go to school at the same time that the Headmaster attended Mahora as a student. It would seem that she has no memories of that time period.

Yūna Akashi
■ If Professor Akashi is a wizard, does that mean that Yūna has magic, too?
★ There is a very strong possibility. Or, since her mother was purely a warrior type, it's also possible that she inherited her abilities.

Kazumi Asakura
■ For some time, there have been rumors that Kazumi has a boyfriend. Are they true?
★ It would appear that she does not have a boyfriend. In fact, there seems to be some truth to the idea that her pactio was her first kiss. She may be the type to be in love with her work.

Yue Ayase
■ In 251st Period, in volume 28, when Negi uses the disarming spell and blows all of the girls' clothes off, Yue's boobs seem to have gotten a lot bigger than we've ever seen them before. Why is that?
★ Hey, compared to the panels above that one with Emily and the others, she's still really flat (laugh). But it is certainly plausible that she has grown in both mind and body since coming to the Magical World.

Ako Izumi
■ Why did Ako Izumi want to be the manager of the soccer team? There's nothing in the story about her liking soccer.
★ I understand that she fell in love with an upperclassman on the soccer team. After that, she was dumped spectacularly. She likes to take care of people, but she can't stand blood, so she might not be suited to managing a sports team.

Akira Okōchi
■ Akira is very strong. Is there any connection between her name and Attila the Hun?
★ None whatsoever (laugh). But man, I haven't heard that name in a while. My first-stage exam (now they call them center tests) was for world history.

Misa Kakizaki
■ Kakizaki is the only(?) girl in class with a boyfriend. Is there some special reason for that?
★ The concept I was going for when creating Kakizaki was "modern-day junior high girl," so I designed her looks and her personal life around that.

Asuna Kagurazaka
■ Is Asuna so stupid because she lost a ton of brain cells from having a powerful forgetfulness spell cast on her in her past?
★ I don't think she necessarily lost a ton of brain cells (^^;), but I think that's about the gist of it.

Misora Kasuga
■ Did Misora and Cocone make a pactio by kissing?
★ That is unknown, but my hope is that it was more, like... she gave her her a rosary or something (laugh).

Chachamaru Karakuri
■ Do doll contracts create artifacts?
★ Like vampire contracts, it would appear that there are no artifacts. Also, I have not heard any reports of there being any contract cards, either.

Madoka Kugimiya
■ The flag went up for Madoka and Kotarō at Mahora Fest, but will there be any future developments with them?
★ I can't say that there won't ever be any. In fact, personality-wise, I think they're a perfect match. I think it would be easy to draw the two of them together.

Kū Fei
■ Kū Fei gave Chao the swords that she received from her master; does that mean that her master could use sword techniques as well as kenpō?
★ That's right. Kū Fei is extremely skilled in handling weapons, too. She even got something along those lines for her artifact.

Konoka Konoe
■ I've been wondering this for a long, long time, but what is the connection between Konoka and *Love Hina*'s Motoko?
★ The Konoe family has hired masters of the Shinmei School as bodyguards for generations. In this story, all you see is the one picture where Tsuruko and Motoko visit when Konoka is very young.

Haruna Saotome
■ What kind of manga does Paru always draw?
★ Apparently she draws everything from boys' love manga to sell at Comic Market to manga she can submit to publishers. She's a very skilled artist, and she can match the art style of all kinds of manga and anime.

Setsuna Sakurazaki

■ Setsuna Sakurazaki has two different artifacts. Is it possible to use multiple artifacts at the same time?

★ Yes, it is. When she does, she can receive extra power, such as magic and defense, from both Negi and Konoka. (But the Shinmei School doesn't require magic.)

Makie Sasaki

■ What is the farthest Makie's gymnastics ribbon can reach?

★ According to the rules of rhythmic gymnastics, it has to be at least six meters. But in the story, it does look like it can go about ten meters, doesn't it? (laugh)

Sakurako Shiina

■ In volume two, I think there was a girl that looked like Sakurako who showed up in the elementary school in the chapter about Asuna and Ayaka. Was that Sakurako?

★ Yes, it was. Apparently she was already enrolled in Mahora Academy in elementary school. (Maybe preschool, too?)

Mana Tatsumiya

■ Does Tatsumiya-san have two magic eyes?

★ Only her left one is magic. It helps her to see through monsters' disguises and take aim from long distances. She doesn't usually have it activated.

Chao Lingshen

■ How high is her IQ?

★ For a long time, her IQ had been set at 300 (laugh). But I feel like it might actually be that high.

Kaede Nagase

■ Is it possible to hide in Kaede's artifact forever, and live there?

★ It is possible, but under one condition. It would have to be a permanent contract, as opposed to a probationary one. Just like there are limits when you join a school club on a probationary basis, artifacts that go with probationary contracts do not last eternally.

Chizuru Naba

■ Is the mole on Chizuru's cheek genetic?

★ Can those be genetic? (^^;) When designing her character, I put it there as a symbol of her sexiness and motherliness.

Fūka Narutaki

■ Does she have other sisters?

★ The twins don't seem have any other older or younger sisters. (Looking at the IP address and handle name, did this question come from France? (^^;))

Fumika Narutaki

■ Why did Fumika join the school decor club?

★ According to her character design, she's more of a neat-freak than her sister. But you don't get to see that side of her much in the story...

Satomi Hakase

■ How did Hakase get to be involved in the construction of Chachamaru Karakuri?

★ Hakase was famous as a genius since before she advanced to junior high. And so, Eva, who had lost her powers, made a request to Hakase and Chao for them to make Chachamaru; she injected a temporary soul into her with a doll contract and made her into her partner for the time being.

Chisame Hasegawa

■ Can Chisame use Linux?

★ It is essential knowledge for anything related to hacking these days, so of course she can. Furthermore, if she uses her artifact, she can get a root in a snap.

Evangeline

■ Will there be a pactio between Negi-sensei and Eva!?

★ Eva: "Well, if I'm the master, it might happen. Heh heh heh..."

Nodoka Miyazaki

■ Nodoka's chest size grows and shrinks depending on the picture, but what is it really?

★ It's growing gradually, but basically, she's a flat-chest.

Natsumi Murakami

■ Please tell us Natsumi's real family situation.

★ It really is a very, very normal family. Everything is ordinary for Natsumi; that's why she's always wanting to change.

Ayaka Yukihiro

■ How does Ayaka understand Zazie when she doesn't talk?

★ Apparently understanding all of her classmates' thoughts is one of her natural abilities as Class Rep.

Satsuki Yotsuba

■ What is Satsuki's best dish?

★ It would appear that she's into Chinese cooking lately. But she can basically cook anything.

Zazie Rainyday

■ When will we get to see Zazie in the spotlight?

★ I plan on withholding the explanation of Zazie's true identity until the last arc.

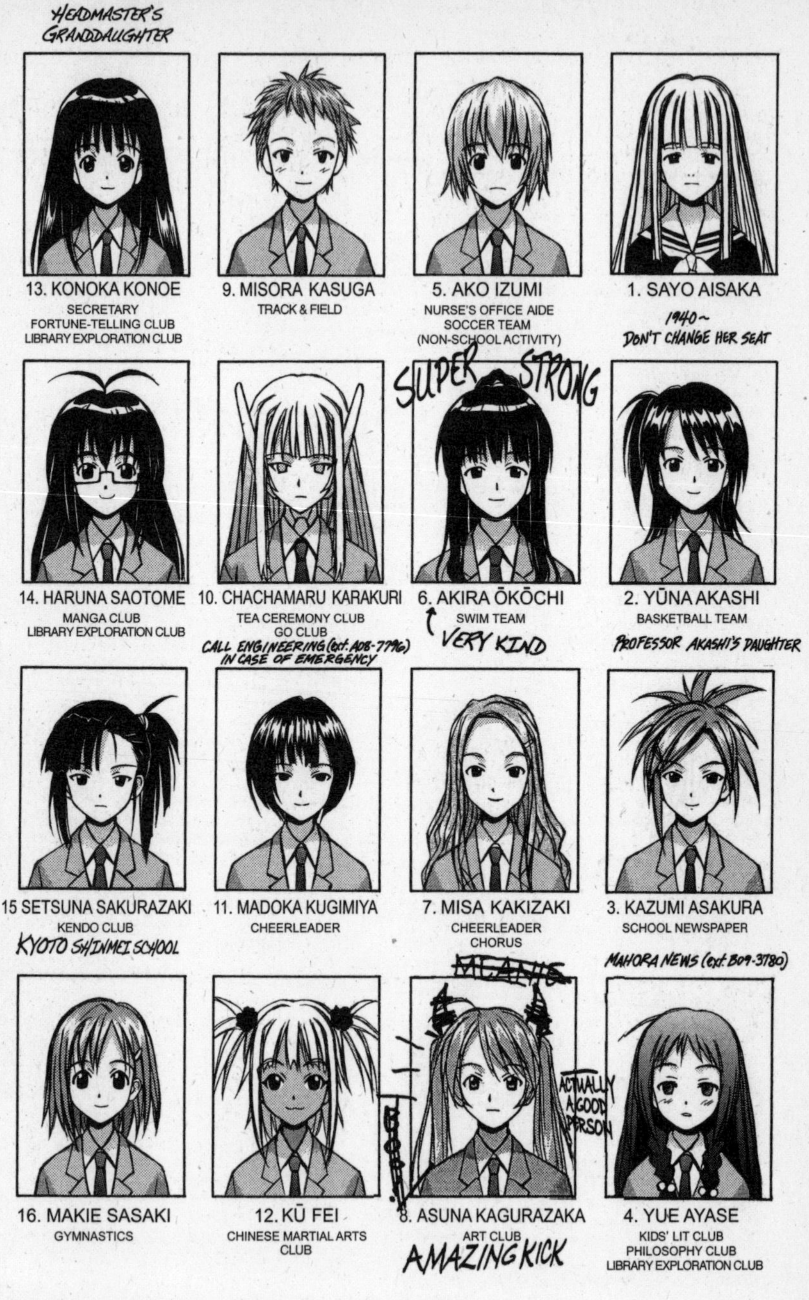

1. SAYO AISAKA
1940~
DON'T CHANGE HER SEAT
5. AKO IZUMI
NURSE'S OFFICE AIDE
SOCCER TEAM
(NON-SCHOOL ACTIVITY)
9. MISORA KASUGA
TRACK & FIELD
HEADMASTER'S GRANDDAUGHTER
13. KONOKA KONOE
SECRETARY
FORTUNE-TELLING CLUB
LIBRARY EXPLORATION CLUB
2. YŪNA AKASHI
BASKETBALL TEAM
PROFESSOR AKASHI'S DAUGHTER
SUPER STRONG
6. AKIRA ŌKŌCHI
SWIM TEAM
VERY KIND
10. CHACHAMARU KARAKURI
TEA CEREMONY CLUB
GO CLUB
CALL ENGINEERING (ext. A08-7796) IN CASE OF EMERGENCY
14. HARUNA SAOTOME
MANGA CLUB
LIBRARY EXPLORATION CLUB
3. KAZUMI ASAKURA
SCHOOL NEWSPAPER
MAHORA NEWS (ext. B09-3780)
7. MISA KAKIZAKI
CHEERLEADER
CHORUS
11. MADOKA KUGIMIYA
CHEERLEADER
15 SETSUNA SAKURAZAKI
KENDO CLUB
KYOTO SHINMEI SCHOOL
4. YUE AYASE
KIDS' LIT CLUB
PHILOSOPHY CLUB
LIBRARY EXPLORATION CLUB
MEANIE
ACTUALLY A GOOD PERSON
8. ASUNA KAGURAZAKA
ART CLUB
AMAZING KICK
12. KŪ FEI
CHINESE MARTIAL ARTS CLUB
16. MAKIE SASAKI
GYMNASTICS

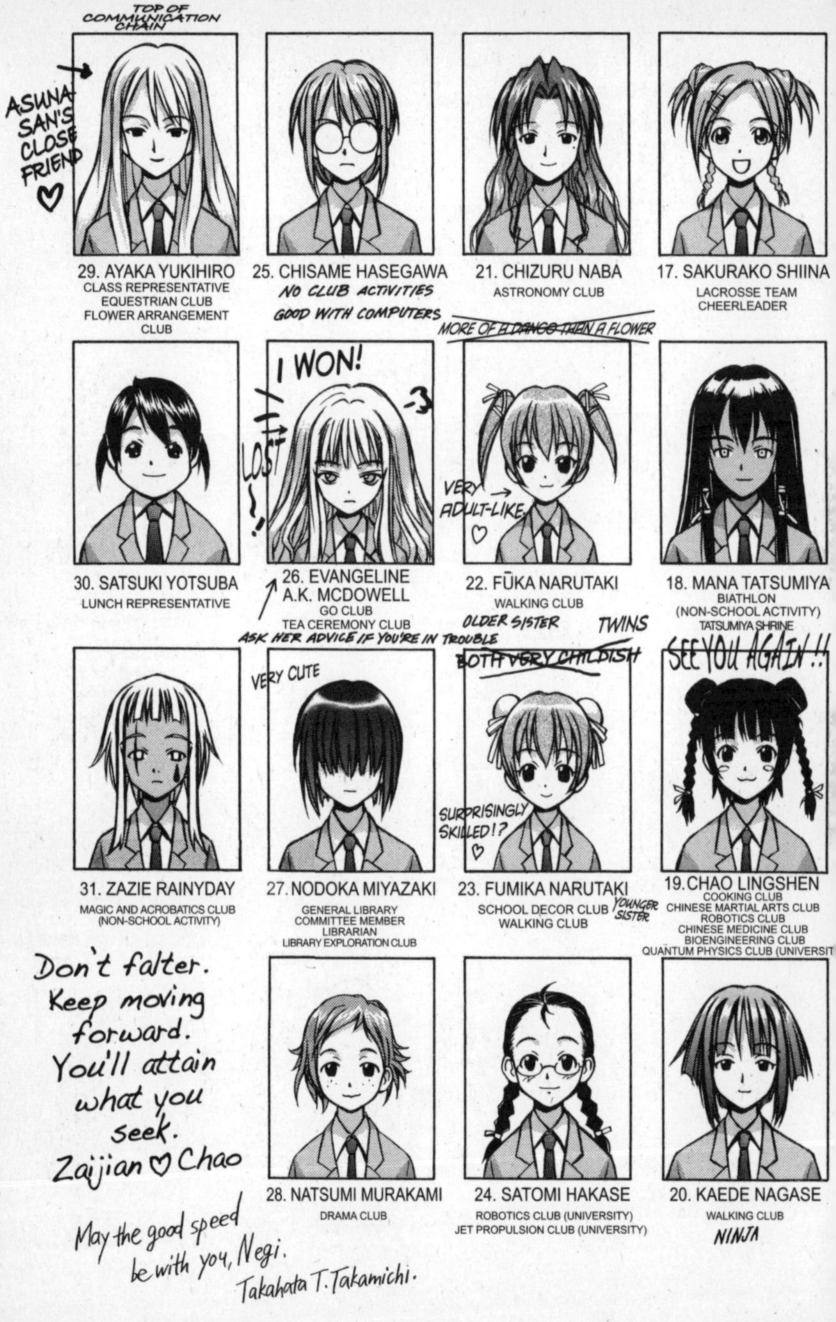

17. SAKURAKO SHIINA
LACROSSE TEAM
CHEERLEADER
21. CHIZURU NABA
ASTRONOMY CLUB
MORE OF A DANGO THAN A FLOWER
25. CHISAME HASEGAWA
NO CLUB ACTIVITIES
GOOD WITH COMPUTERS
TOP OF COMMUNICATION CHAIN
ASUNA-SAN'S CLOSE FRIEND ♡
29. AYAKA YUKIHIRO
CLASS REPRESENTATIVE
EQUESTRIAN CLUB
FLOWER ARRANGEMENT CLUB
18. MANA TATSUMIYA
BIATHLON
(NON-SCHOOL ACTIVITY)
TATSUMIYA SHRINE
VERY ADULT-LIKE ♡
22. FŪKA NARUTAKI
WALKING CLUB
OLDER SISTER
I WON!
-3
LOST
26. EVANGELINE A.K. MCDOWELL
GO CLUB
TEA CEREMONY CLUB
ASK HER ADVICE IF YOU'RE IN TROUBLE
30. SATSUKI YOTSUBA
LUNCH REPRESENTATIVE
SEE YOU AGAIN!!
19. CHAO LINGSHEN
COOKING CLUB
CHINESE MARTIAL ARTS CLUB
ROBOTICS CLUB
CHINESE MEDICINE CLUB
BIOENGINEERING CLUB
QUANTUM PHYSICS CLUB (UNIVERSIT
TWINS
BOTH VERY CHILDISH
SURPRISINGLY SKILLED!? ♡
23. FUMIKA NARUTAKI
SCHOOL DECOR CLUB
WALKING CLUB
YOUNGER SISTER
VERY CUTE
27. NODOKA MIYAZAKI
GENERAL LIBRARY COMMITTEE MEMBER
LIBRARIAN
LIBRARY EXPLORATION CLUB
31. ZAZIE RAINYDAY
MAGIC AND ACROBATICS CLUB
(NON-SCHOOL ACTIVITY)
20. KAEDE NAGASE
WALKING CLUB
NINJA
24. SATOMI HAKASE
ROBOTICS CLUB (UNIVERSITY)
JET PROPULSION CLUB (UNIVERSITY)
28. NATSUMI MURAKAMI
DRAMA CLUB
Don't falter. Keep moving forward. You'll attain what you seek. Zaijian ♡ Chao
May the good speed be with you, Negi. Takahata T. Takamichi.

NEGIMA!

MAGISTER NEGI MAGI

Ken Akamatsu

THE WHAT AND WHY OF NEGIMA!

Q. IS NEGIMA! GOING TO END SOON?

A. IT'S GOING TO GO ON JUST A LITTLE LONGER! (LAUGH)

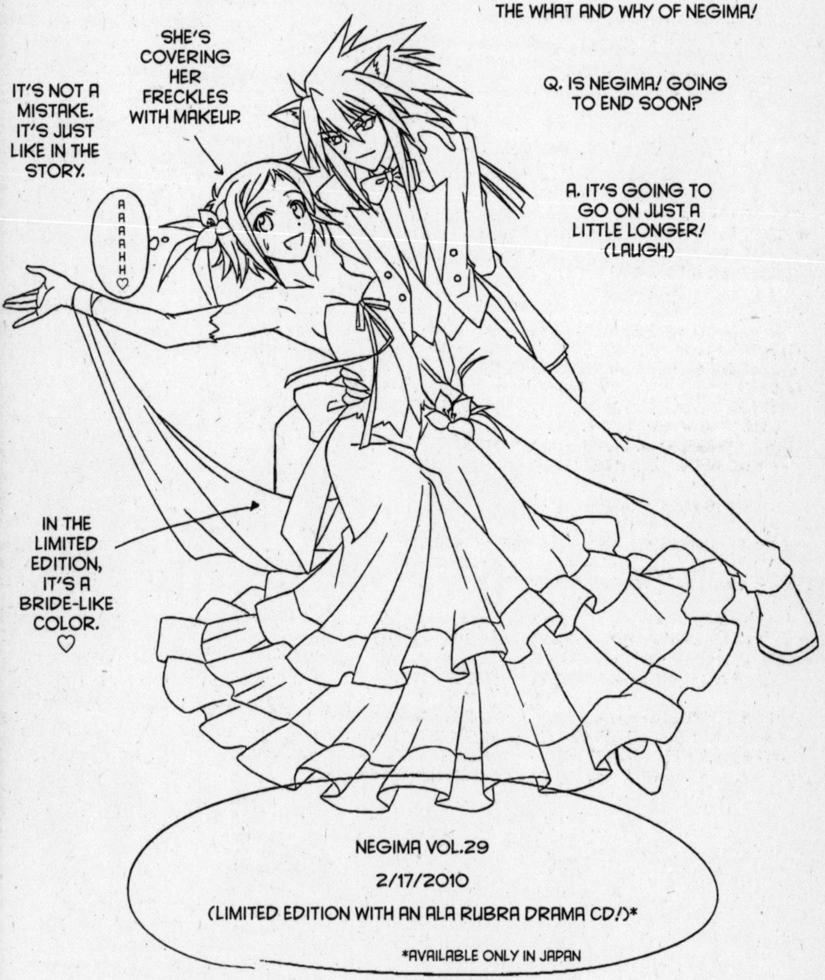
IT'S NOT A MISTAKE. IT'S JUST LIKE IN THE STORY.
SHE'S COVERING HER FRECKLES WITH MAKEUP.
AAAAAH♡
IN THE LIMITED EDITION, IT'S A BRIDE-LIKE COLOR. ♡
NEGIMA VOL.29
2/17/2010
(LIMITED EDITION WITH AN ALA RUBRA DRAMA CD!)*
*AVAILABLE ONLY IN JAPAN

CHARACTER PROFILE

(THE TEACHER) NEGI SPRINGFIELD

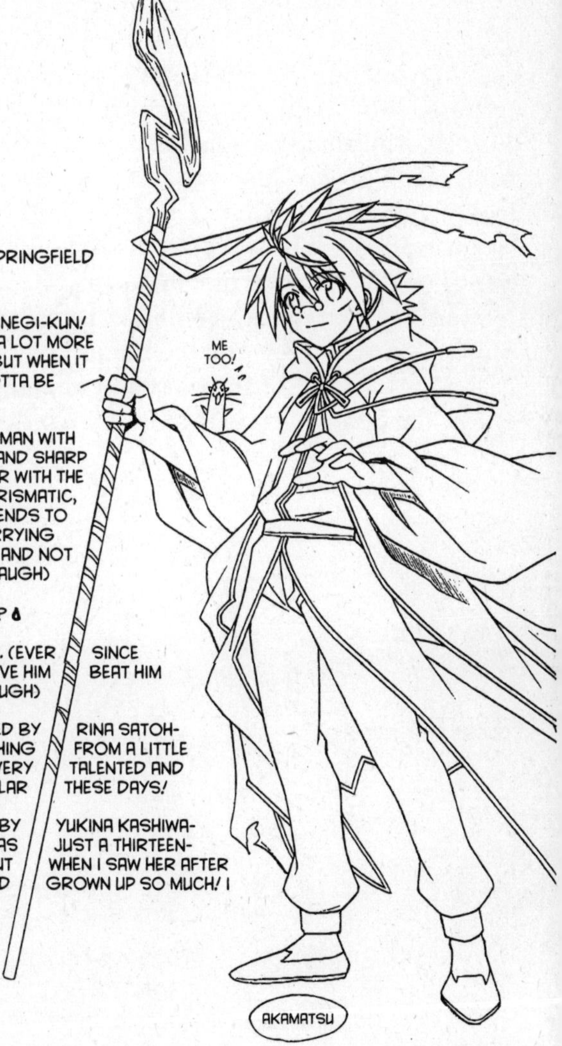
ME TOO!
AKAMATSU

IT'S THE HERO OF OUR STORY, NEGI-KUN! RECENTLY, WE'VE BEEN SEEING A LOT MORE OF HIM IN GROWN-UP FORM, BUT WHEN IT COMES DOWN TO IT, HE'S GOTTA BE LIKE THIS.

HE'S AN INCREDIBLE YOUNG MAN WITH ENORMOUS MAGICAL POWER AND SHARP INTELLIGENCE, WHO IS POPULAR WITH THE OPPOSITE SEX AND VERY CHARISMATIC, BUT FOR SOME REASON HE TENDS TO ALWAYS MOPE AROUND WORRYING ABOUT THINGS; HE'S GLOOMY AND NOT HEROIC IN THE SLIGHTEST. (LAUGH)

WHAT IS WRONG WITH HIM? 💧

HIS ARCH-NEMESIS IS FATE-KUN. (EVER SINCE VOLUME SIX...) I WANT TO HAVE HIM BEAT HIM ONCE AND FOR ALL SOON. (LAUGH)

IN THE ANIME, NEGI IS VOICED BY RINA SATOH-SAN. ♡ SHE CAN DO ANYTHING FROM A LITTLE BOY TO A SEXY LADY. SHE IS VERY TALENTED AND GUTSY. SHE'S SUPER POPULAR THESE DAYS!

IN THE DRAMA, HE IS PLAYED BY YUKINA KASHIWA-CHAN ♡ AT THE TIME, SHE WAS JUST A THIRTEEN-YEAR-OLD LITTLE BEAUTY, BUT WHEN I SAW HER AFTER THE SHOW HAD ENDED, SHE HAD GROWN UP SO MUCH! I WAS SHOCKED.

About the Creator

Negima! is only Ken Akamatsu's third manga, although he started working in the field in 1994 with *AI Ga Tomaranai* (released in the United States with the title *A.I. Love You*). Like all of Akamatsu's work to date, it was published in Kodansha's *Shonen Magazine*. *AI Ga Tomaranai* ran for five years before concluding in 1999. In 1998, however, Akamatsu began the work that would make him one of the most popular manga artists in Japan: *Love Hina*. *Love Hina* ran for four years, and before its conclusion in 2002, it would cause Akamatsu to be granted the prestigious Manga of the Year Award from Kodansha, as well as going on to become one of the best-selling manga in the United States.

Translation Notes

Japanese is a tricky language for most Westerners, and translation is often more art than science. For your edification and reading pleasure, here are notes on some of the places where we could have gone in a different direction with our translation of the work, or where a Japanese cultural reference is used.

Where is he!?, page 14

In the Japanese version, Emily does not repeat herself, but merely adds a "desu" to the end of her question to make it more polite. She must have temporarily forgotten her manners in her excitement.

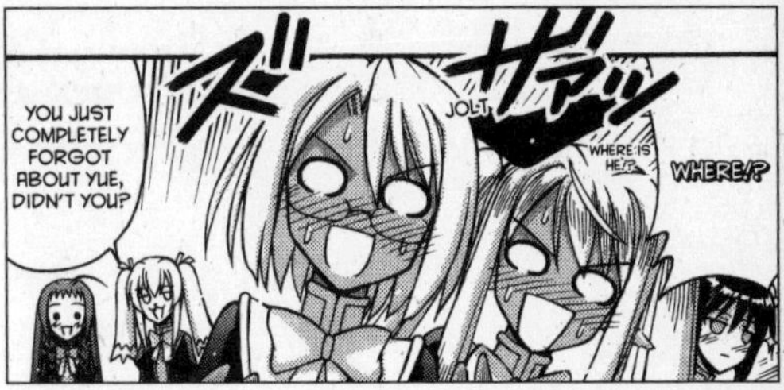
WHERE!?
WHERE IS HE!?
JOLT
YOU JUST COMPLETELY FORGOT ABOUT YUE, DIDN'T YOU?

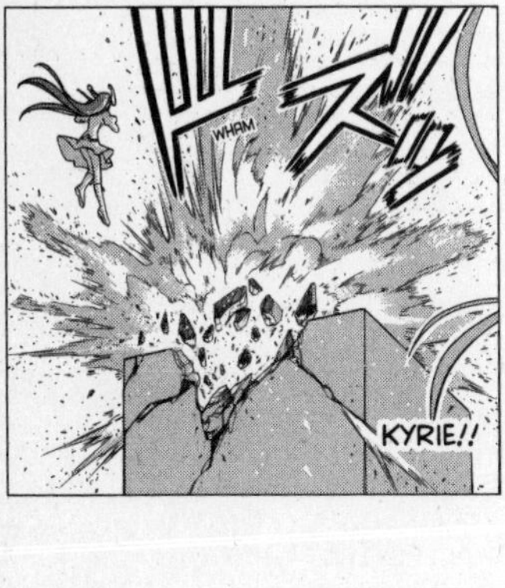
WHAM
KYRIE!!

Kyrie, page 18

As a musician, Shirabe's spells are related to music. In musical terms, a Kyrie, or Kyrie eleison (meaning "Lord, have mercy"), is the musical accompaniment for a prayer of the same name.

Yojimbo, page 51

A *yojimbo*, or *yōjinbō*, is a bodyguard for hire.

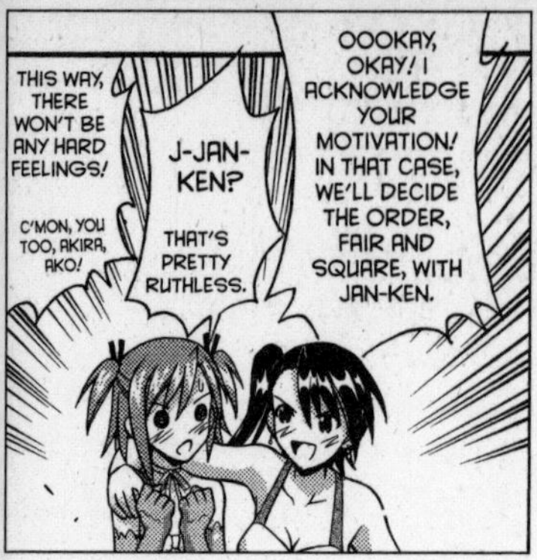
OOOKAY, OKAY! I ACKNOWLEDGE YOUR MOTIVATION! IN THAT CASE, WE'LL DECIDE THE ORDER, FAIR AND SQUARE, WITH JAN-KEN.
J-JAN-KEN?
THAT'S PRETTY RUTHLESS.
THIS WAY, THERE WON'T BE ANY HARD FEELINGS!
C'MON, YOU TOO, AKIRA, AKO!

Jan-ken, page 78

Jan-ken, short for *jan-ken-pon*, is the Japanese term for rock-paper-scissors, the ultimate fair way to decide anything.

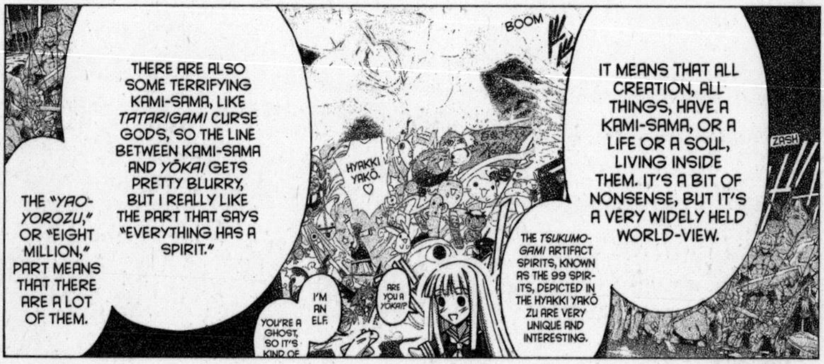
IT MEANS THAT ALL CREATION, ALL THINGS, HAVE A KAMI-SAMA, OR A LIFE OR A SOUL, LIVING INSIDE THEM. IT'S A BIT OF NONSENSE, BUT IT'S A VERY WIDELY HELD WORLD-VIEW.
ZASH
BOOM
THE TSUKUMOGAMI ARTIFACT SPIRITS, KNOWN AS THE 99 SPIRITS, DEPICTED IN THE HYAKKI YAKŌ ZU ARE VERY UNIQUE AND INTERESTING.
HYAKKI YAKŌ. ♡
ARE YOU A YOKAI?
I'M AN ELF.
THERE ARE ALSO SOME TERRIFYING KAMI-SAMA, LIKE TATARIGAMI CURSE GODS, SO THE LINE BETWEEN KAMI-SAMA AND YŌKAI GETS PRETTY BLURRY, BUT I REALLY LIKE THE PART THAT SAYS "EVERYTHING HAS A SPIRIT."
THE "YAO-YOROZU," OR "EIGHT MILLION," PART MEANS THAT THERE ARE A LOT OF THEM.

Yaoyorozu no Kami-sama, *tsukumogami*, Hyakki Yakō Zu, *tatarigami*, and *yōkai*, page 82

As Negi explains, the term means eight-million spirits, or myriad spirits (eight-million being a general number chosen to represent countlessness). While the term *kami* is the Japanese word for god or deity, the Shinto concept of *kami* is more closely related to spirits dwelling within trees, rivers, mountains, forces of nature, etc. The Hyakki Yakō Zu is a famous picture scroll depicting a *hyakki yakō*, or parade of one hundred demons. Among the demons are the *tsukumogami*, or artifact spirits. These spirits were originally inanimate objects but became *kami* when they reached their one-hundredth birthday. *Tatarigami*, or curse gods, are spirits that bring curses on their enemies, but when worshipped they can be powerful guardian deities. *Yōkai* is a general term for supernatural creatures and phenomena, but usually *yōkai* don't get along with humans.

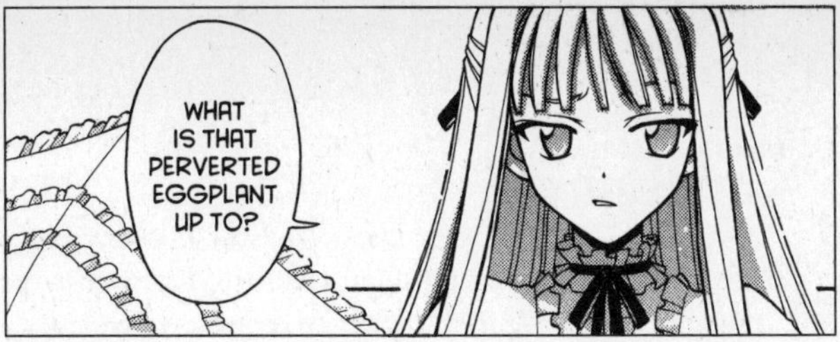
WHAT IS THAT PERVERTED EGGPLANT UP TO?

That perverted eggplant, page 94

In Japan, it's not uncommon to tease people with long faces by calling them "*nasu*," or "eggplant." This would be the Japanese equivalent of calling Al "horse-face."

Princess Noh-Mask, page 145

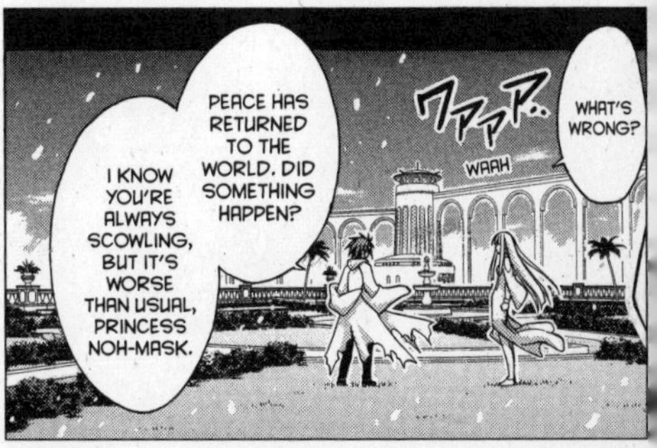
WHAT'S WRONG?
WAAH
PEACE HAS RETURNED TO THE WORLD. DID SOMETHING HAPPEN?
I KNOW YOU'RE ALWAYS SCOWLING, BUT IT'S WORSE THAN USUAL, PRINCESS NOH-MASK.

Noh is a form of Japanese theatre in which the actors wear masks. While the masks are designed to show slightly different emotion based on how the actor holds his head, the facial features don't change at all, just like how Arika's face generally only shows slight variations of the same expression.

First-stage exam and center tests, page 170

Both of these are names for standardized tests for Japanese kids looking to get into college. They're something like the SATs and ACTs, and are taken at testing centers (hence the name "center test").

Preview of *Negima!* Volume 30

We're pleased to present you a preview from volume 30. Please check our website, www.delreymanga.com, to see when this volume will be available in English. For now you'll have to make do with Japanese!

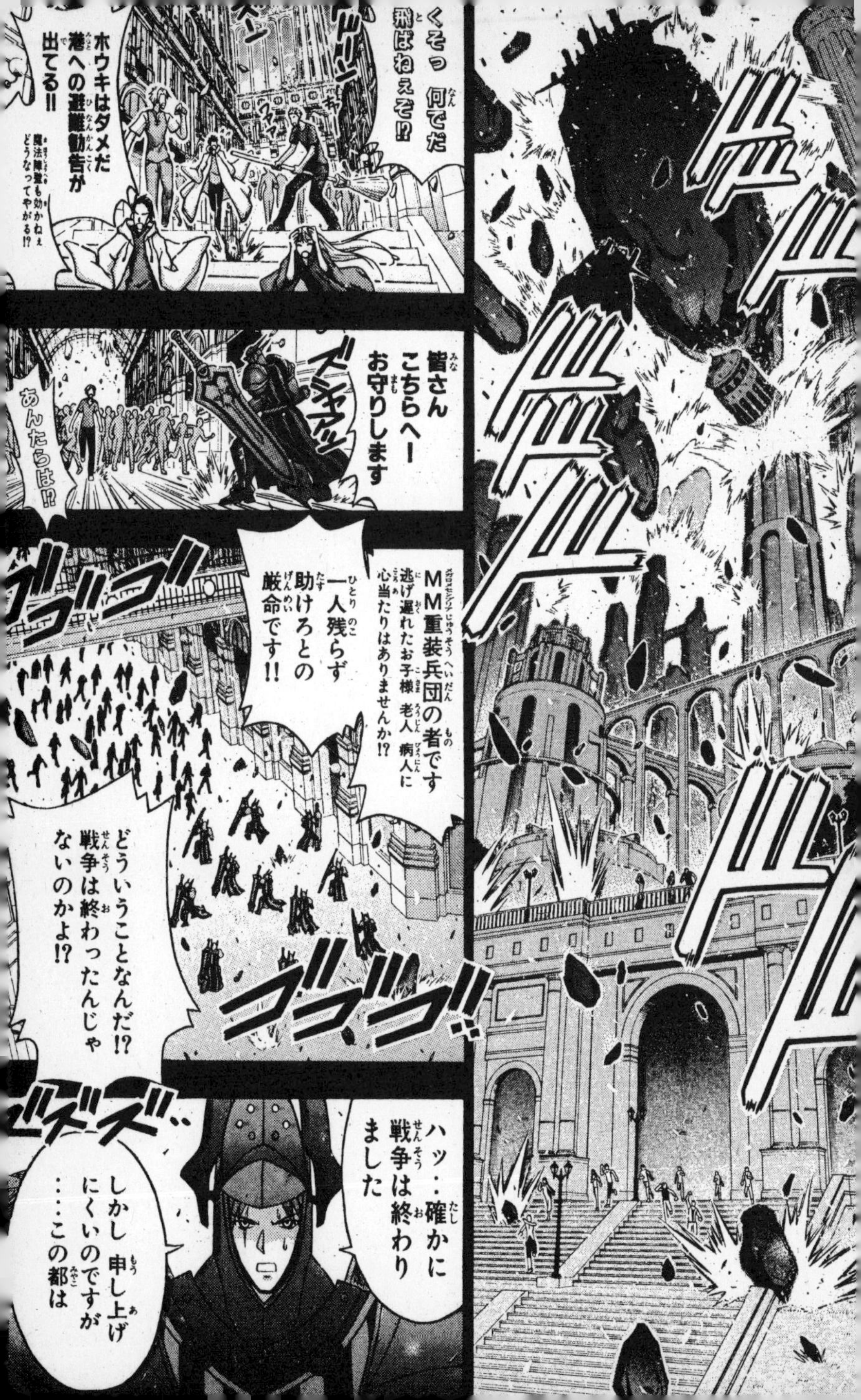
くそっ 何でだ 飛ばねえぞ!?
ホウキはダメだ 港への避難勧告が出てる!!
魔法障壁も効かねぇ どうなってやがる!?
皆さん こちらへー お守りします
あんたらは!?
MM重装兵団の者です 逃げ遅れたお子様 老人 病人に 心当たりはありませんか!?
一人残らず 助けろとの 厳命です!!
ゴゴゴ
どういうことなんだ!? 戦争は終わったんじゃないのかよ!?
ゴゴゴ!!
ハッ…確かに 戦争は終わりました
しかし 申し上げにくいのですが ……この都は
ズズズ…

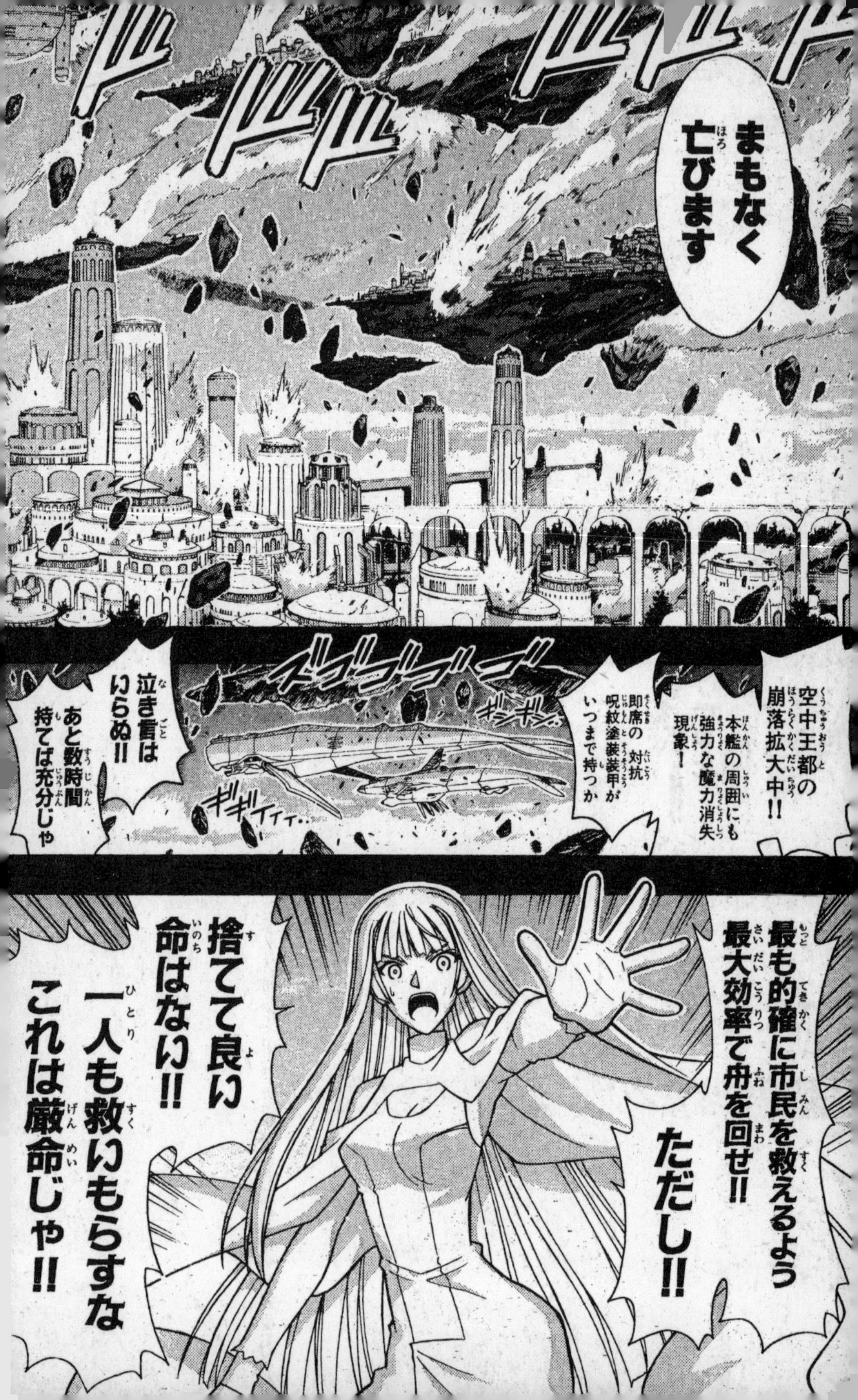

ドドドドドド
まもなく亡びます
空中王都の崩落拡大中!!
本艦の周囲にも強力な魔力消失現象!
即席の対抗呪紋塗装装甲がいつまで持つか
ズゴゴゴゴ
ギシギシ
ギギィィィ…
泣き言はいらぬ!!
あと数時間持てば充分じゃ
最も的確に市民を救えるよう最大効率で舟を回せ!!
ただし!!
捨てて良い命はない!!
一人も救いもらすな
これは厳命じゃ!!

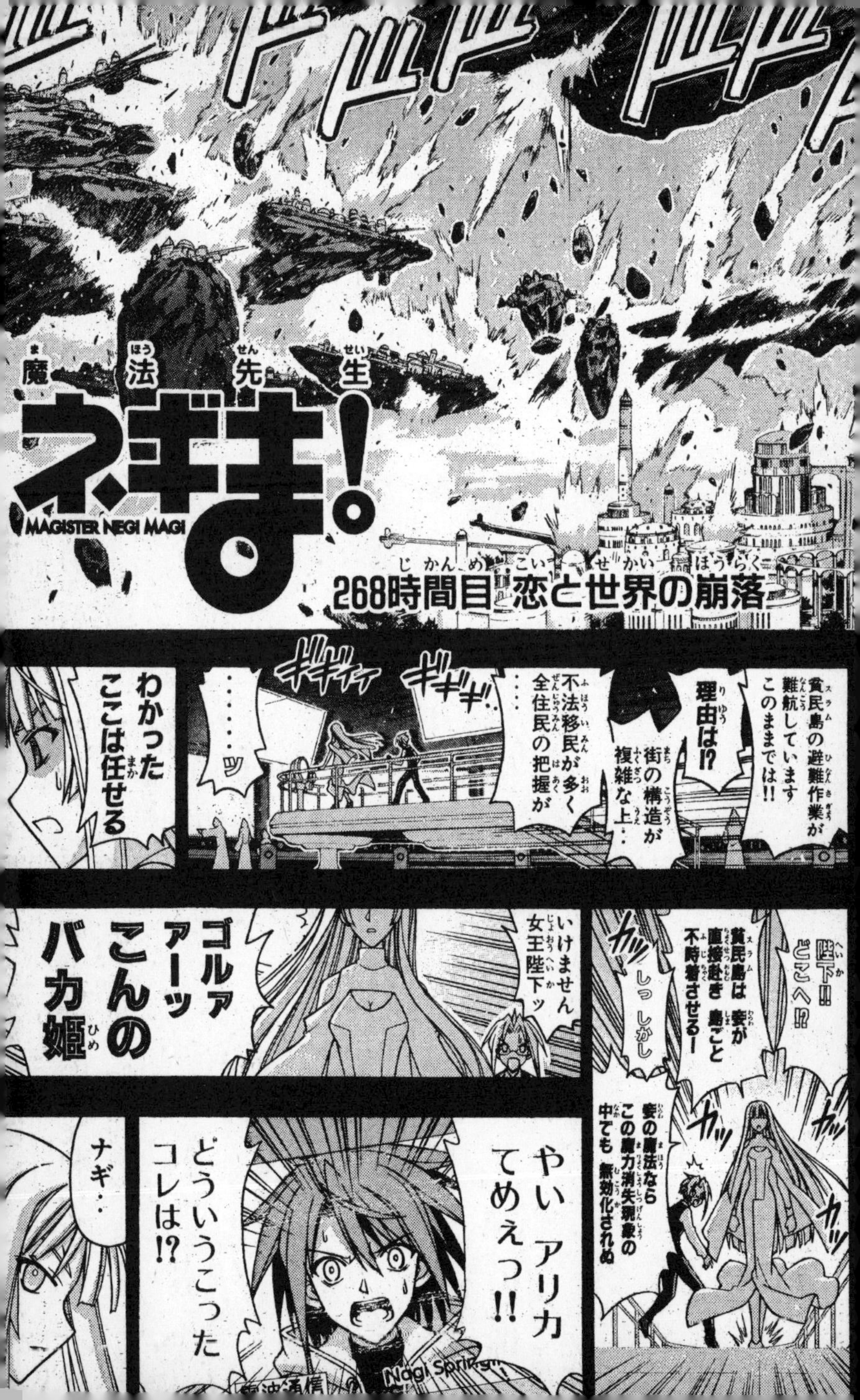

魔法先生ネギま!
MAGISTER NEGI MAGI
268時間目 恋と世界の崩落
貧民島の避難作業が難航しています このままでは!!
理由は!?
街の構造が複雑な上・・
不法移民が多く全住民の把握が・・・
ギギィ ギギギ
・・・・・ッ
わかった ここは任せる
陛下!! どこへ!?
貧民島は妾が直接赴き島ごと不時着させる!
しっ しかし
妾の魔法ならこの魔力消失現象の中でも無効化されぬ
いけません女王陛下ッ
ゴルァアーーッ こんのバカ姫
やい アリカ てめえっ!!
どういうこった コレは!?
ナギ・・

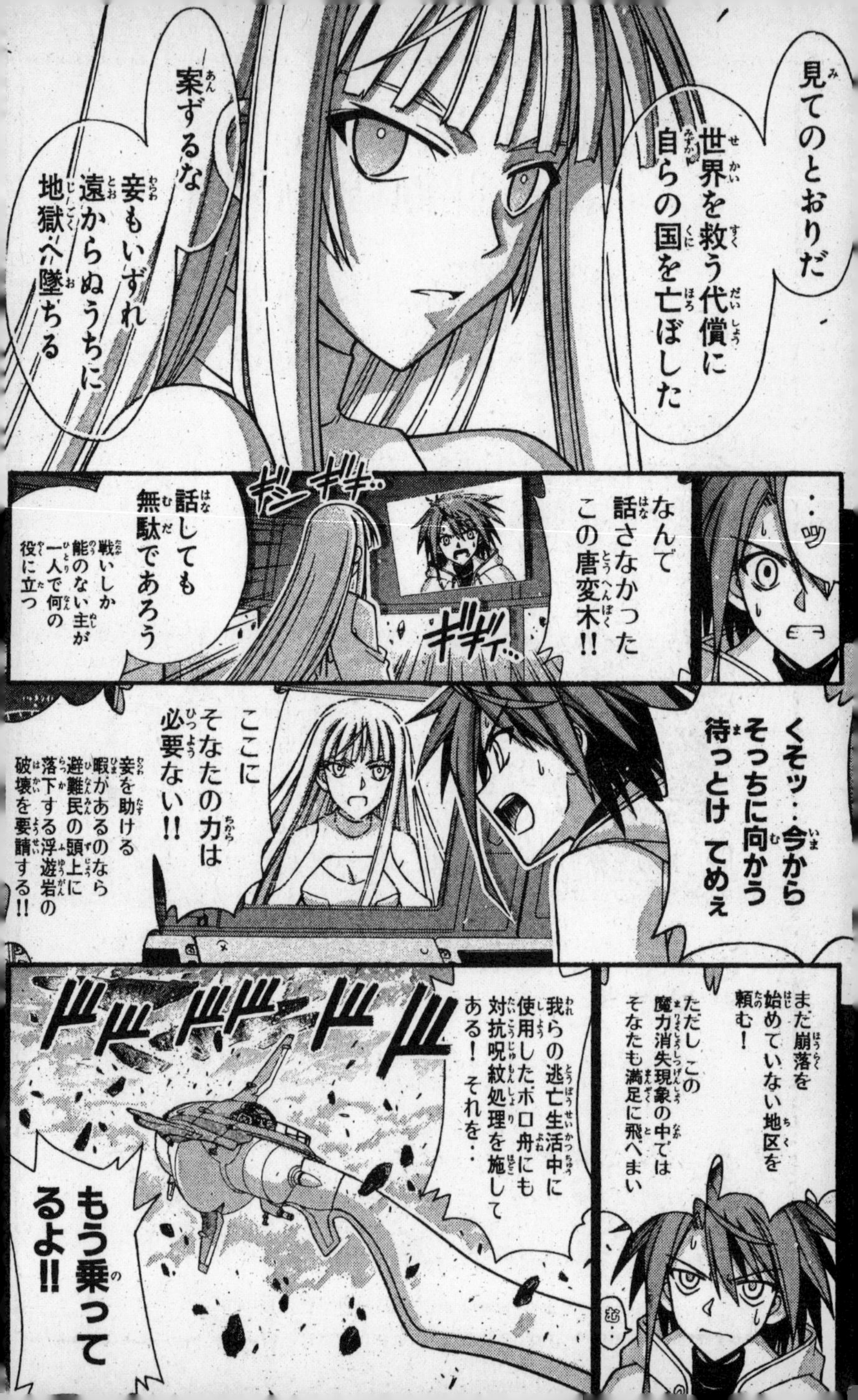
見てのとおりだ 世界を救う代償に 自らの国を亡ぼした
案ずるな 妾もいずれ 遠からぬうちに 地獄へ墜ちる
…ッ
なんで 話さなかった この唐変木!!
ギシ ギシ…
ギシ…
話しても 無駄であろう 戦いしか 能のない主が 一人で何の 役に立つ
くそッ…今から そっちに向かう 待っとけ てめぇ
ここに そなたの力は 必要ない!!
妾を助ける 暇があるのなら 避難民の頭上に 落下する浮遊岩の 破壊を要請する!!
まだ崩落を 始めていない地区を 頼む!
ただし この 魔力消失現象の中では そなたも満足に飛べまい
む…
我らの逃亡生活中に 使用したボロ舟にも 対抗呪紋処理を施して ある! それを・・
ドドドドドドド
もう乗って るよ!!

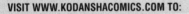

TOMARE!

[STOP!]

You're going the wrong way!

Manga is a completely different type of reading experience.

To start at the *beginning*, go to the *end*!

That's right! Authentic manga is read the traditional Japanese way—from right to left, exactly the *opposite* of how American books are read. It's easy to follow: Just go to the other end of the book, and read each page—and each panel—from right side to left side, starting at the top right. Now you're experiencing manga as it was meant to be.